Complete Book of
Outdoor Survival

Complete Book of Outdoor Survival

J. Wayne Fears

Photos by the author unless otherwise credited
Drawings by Lloyd P. Birmingham

C1

Published by
Outdoor Life Books
New York

Published by

Outdoor Life Books
Times Mirror Magazines, Inc.
380 Madison Avenue
New York, NY 10017

Distributed to the trade by

Stackpole Books
Cameron and Kelker Streets
P.O. Box 1831
Harrisburg, PA 17105

Produced by Soderstrom Publishing Group Inc.
Designed by Jeff Fitschen

Library of Congress Cataloging-in-Publication Data
Fears, J. Wayne, 1938–
    Complete book of outdoor survival.

    Bibliography: p.
    Includes index.
    1. Wilderness survival.   2. Outdoor life.
    I. Title.
    GV200.5.F45   1986   613'.9   85–62164
    ISBN 0-943822-64-5

Manufactured in the United States of America

This book is dedicated to my father George N. Fears—a survival expert, schooled by necessity, who has proven that a positive mental attitude is the key ingredient in all survival situations as well as in life.

GEORGE N. FEARS

CONTENTS

Complete Book of
Outdoor Survival

PREFACE

Anyone who travels into backcountry areas—near home or deep in the wilderness—needs a good working knowledge of survival skills. But one of the first questions I'm asked when conducting a survival seminar, especially when participants are required to attend by their company or other sponsor, is this: "Why should anyone learn survival skills?" Then they challenge: "This is the 20th century. Survival training is no longer necessary."

Few people go into backcountry expecting to become lost, stranded, or injured. That "it-will-never-happen-to-me" attitude gets scores of people into serious trouble each year. All too often they are found dead near snowbound cars, in desert sands, in mountain passes, near aircraft, and in woods near their homes. They are struck by lightning, killed by heat, and drowned by flash floods. Sometimes they even die simply because they lack the will to live.

For an example of the will to live, let's look at the experience of Lance Corporal Karl Bell. In June 1983, this young marine was on leave from Camp Pendleton, near San Diego. Without telling anyone where he was going, he drove to Bear River Reservoir. While hiking along the edge of the steep-sided river canyon about a mile below the dam, he slipped and fell more than 300 feet to the bottom. The canyon was about 4 miles long and a quarter mile wide, with the Bear River raging through it. In his fall, Bell fractured his right ankle and cut his hand. Time after time he tried unsuccessfully to climb out of his canyon prison. Daytime temperatures approached 90 degrees, and he was forced to eat grass, moss, and black ants to survive. And survive he did, for 40 long days before managing to get someone's attention. The story of Corporal Bell's 40 days is one of astounding determination and the will to live.

People are often better prepared for hazards in rough backcountry as here, where treacherous footing, rapids, rain, and ropes could bring havoc fast. Yet many survival ordeals occur in far tamer settings, close to home where people start out ill-equipped and otherwise unprepared for mishaps. (Erwin A. Bauer photo)

A vast majority of people in our technological society think they will never find themselves suddenly cut off from the rest of the world. But newspapers often carry stories about people who suffer and die because they don't have even the basic survival skills to keep themselves alive in an emergency. The truth is that a survival crisis can confront anyone—suddenly.

I have spent most of my life in the outdoors studying the problems of survival. Because of the nature of my career, I've seen both sides of the coin. I have been caught in severe survival situations and have been on many search-and-rescue missions. As a result, I am constantly trying to learn how to improve my skills and how to help others learn to survive.

For many years, I have seen a need for a book on backcountry survival skills that would approach the problem from a realistic viewpoint. So this book teaches survival as a matter of preparedness, rather than a collection of neat tricks that don't work when you really need them. Yes, in this book I do tell you about the solar still, but I also point out that you'll need to practice with it to make it work, and even then a solar still produces little water. I tell about figure-4 deadfalls and snares, but advise that this is an unreliable way of getting food if you lack trapping savvy that includes knowledge of your quarry. I strive to give you the commonsense approach to edible wild plants, rather than listing page after page of flowering plants that won't do you any good in a survival emergency, perhaps because you don't have a copy of the book, or worse, because it's winter!

I have watched dozens of survival students try to start a fire by using flint and steel under ideal conditions. Most of them never got a fire going. What would happen to them if they were scared, cold, wet, and tired, and needed a fire to ward off hypothermia?

So this book takes a realistic approach to

A planned pleasant afternoon of running the rapids of Georgia's Chattooga River turned into a contest with the elements when these men lost control of their canoe in the raging water. Survival training and quick thinking prevented injury to these men, who could have faced harm from the tremendous force of the water, rocks, hypothermia, or drowning. All their gear was lost and the canoe was demolished as it rammed into rock after spilling its contents.

the subject of survival. Throughout, I stress preparing for the unexpected. My aim is to prepare you, both physically and mentally, to survive. The keys are to appreciate that an emergency can befall you and then know what to do. I hope you will encourage other members of your family to learn these skills as well.

My Army survival training emphasized eight basic points of survival skills that have helped get me through many survival situations. As a memory jog, the acrostic below, using the word **SURVIVAL**, helps in recalling these points, which pop up over and over again in this book.

> **S** ize up the situation.
> **U** ndue haste makes waste.
> **R** emember where you are.
> **V** anquish fear and panic.
> **I** mprovise.
> **V** alue living.
> **A** ct like the natives.
> **L** earn basic survival skills.

As well, in order to help illustrate the need for survival training, I have woven true-life survival stories throughout the book. These stories are about people just like you and me, who suddenly found themselves in emergency situations.

Since I've based much of this book on my own testing and experience, I sometimes mention commercial products that I know work. These mentions could help you find proven equipment for your survival kit. Appendix 3 in the back of the book provides addresses for more information. (I have no business connections with these companies.)

A lot of my research material comes from government agencies, private companies, and groups recognized as authorities on survival and rescue. Many of their addresses are listed in Appendix 1, should you wish to write for more detailed information.

Early American explorers depended upon survival skills as a routine part of their everyday life. Today, members of the American Mountain Men keep alive the ways of their forefathers by practicing primitive skills, using primitive weapons, gear, and clothing, and teaching survival skills to others.

As you've noticed, this is not one of those survival manuals that fit in your hip pocket or backpack. This book is a home reference. I hope you will study it as you plan your wilderness adventures, so that you will know how to prevent emergencies. Still, the concepts and techniques you retain should help in the event you do find yourself in an emergency. Also, I hope my book convinces you to take a survival course and learn a goodly range of survival skills.

Once you have studied this book, you may begin giving as much attention and thought to survival training as you do your diet or general health, for it too could help you live longer. As I'll often note in the book, your best survival kit is your mind. Feed it survival knowledge, and it will be ready when that knowledge is needed.

J. Wayne Fears

1
PLAN FOR THE UNEXPECTED

The main reason people get into trouble in backcountry areas is their belief that unexpected emergencies—survival situations such as getting lost or stranded—always happen to someone else. So they aren't prepared and, more likely than not, don't even know about basic survival skills. But a pleasant hike or a leisurely afternoon of hunting can turn into an emergency situation in a matter of minutes, and that can happen to *anyone*—even in familiar terrain. An accidental fall, a capsized canoe, a sudden violent storm, or even losing your bearings can leave you stuck miles from help or shelter. Naturally, these situations don't happen often. But knowing how to take care of yourself until help arrives or until you can get back to civilization is every bit as important as your knowledge of hunting, marksmanship,

or hiking. And sometimes your life may depend on it.

Getting Lost

The most frequent cause of survival situations is getting lost. This happens at one time or other to most people who are active in the

Hunters may face strandings after accidents such as a fall from a tree stand. Or they may simply become lost. Taking a few simple precautions such as wearing a safety belt while in a tree stand, following manufacturer's instructions on all equipment, and keeping survival gear and compass at hand at all times, especially when trailing wounded game, can prevent many survival crises.

outdoors. For most, it is merely a sobering two- or three-hour adventure. In fact, with today's methods of search and rescue, the majority of people are found within 72 hours after they have been reported missing. But for some it ends in tragedy.

People usually get lost when they least expect it. Take the case of Elton Harris, a resident of northern Alabama. One afternoon he decided to go for a rabbit hunt. Taking along his three beagles, he walked from his home into a nearby backcountry area. He didn't give any thought to the possibility of getting lost. So he had no survival gear with him—not even a pack of matches.

For the next few hours Harris became completely involved in the hunt and forgot, as hunters sometimes do, about time and keeping his bearings. Then, suddenly, the sun set and Harris realized he was lost. On an ordinary night in Alabama, he would have only spent a few uncomfortable hours alone in the woods. Then at first light he would have found his way back home.

But an unusually severe cold spell had set in, and as the night wore on, temperatures dropped down to 10°F. Harris suddenly found himself in a really serious survival situation, but he stayed calm and took the necessary steps to keep himself alive.

Because Harris had no matches with him, his most immediate problem was keeping warm through the night. He knew if he could do that he would probably be around to tell friends this hunting story. Seeking shelter, he crawled into a small cave and brought his three dogs in as well. Harris covered himself with leaves and positioned the dogs around him to take advantage of their warmth. This simple idea probably saved his life.

Even so, Harris spent a long, icy cold night. Next morning when he tried to get up, he found that his wet boots and pants had frozen. Unable to move his legs at first, he

worked feverishly to get the circulation going in them. Finally up and walking again, he made his way back home. And did he have a story to tell!

Probably the main reason people get lost is that that they fail to carry a compass and a map of the area in which they travel. This is especially true for areas these people visit regularly. Map and compass, the skill to use

Having a map and compass with you does not keep you "found." You, like the canoeist pictured, must know how to use them properly. (Robert Lindholm/Outward Bound USA photo)

In most wilderness areas, the calm weather in which a canoe is launched is no promise of continued calm. A sudden storm can convert a peaceful scene such as this into a life-threatening nightmare. (Outward Bound USA/Robert Lindholm photo)

them, and the respect for the unknown that encourages you to use them can keep you "found" all your days afield. But remember, having a map and compass with you solves only part of the problem; you must know how to use them properly as well. So a good course in Orienteering® is recommended for anyone who wants to spend time in backcountry.

Another reason many people get lost is that they don't pay attention to their surroundings. No one is born with a sense of direction. Keeping your bearings in the backcountry is a skill that is learned, and the most important part is keeping your eyes open—simple observation. For example, watch for distinctive features in the terrain, such as ridge-lines, streams, and major rock outcroppings.

These will serve as landmarks should you need them.

Being Stranded

Getting lost is not the only cause of survival predicaments. When an accident occurs, it sometimes leaves people stranded miles from the nearest road or telephone. Such strandings are not uncommon and are usually nothing more than a few hours inconvenience. But the more ambitious your trip into backcountry, the more likely a chance accident could leave you stranded for a day or more.

This is what happened to Bob and Ann Martin on a 20-mile, weekend canoe trip down Lake Keowee in South Carolina. The

Martins carried plenty of gear for an overnight stop and had arranged for friends to pick them up at the lower end of the lake on Sunday. Needless to say, the thought of a survival situation was far from their minds.

The trip was uneventful enough at first. The Martins set out in a light, drizzling rain and paddled for about an hour with a gentle breeze blowing at their backs. Then, turning into a creek, they stopped to do some fishing. By about 4:30 P.M. the wind began increasing and the Martins decided to head for their campsite at a county park farther down the lake.

"When we reached the mouth of the creek," Martin said later, "high winds were blowing straight down the main body of the lake. I'd never seen the lake that way before. Whitecapped waves were running before the wind."

The Martins decided to risk the rough water and run with the wind down to the county park. But, shortly after they left the sheltered area of the creek, their canoe suddenly turned broadside toward the waves. A 5-foot wave hit the canoe and capsized it, throwing the Martins into the cold dark water. Thanks to their life jackets, they were able to stay afloat despite the waves and high winds. But they could do nothing to stop their canoe and camping gear from disappearing in the storm-tossed waters.

The Martins had a hard swim but stayed together and eventually reached a pine-covered spit of land jutting out from the shoreline. Cold, wet, and tired from their ordeal, they nevertheless set about improvising shelter. Mr. Martin found a piece of rope lying near the water's edge and, tying it between two trees, used it as the main support for a makeshift lean-to made of pine branches. Meanwhile Mrs. Martin gathered wood for a

These canoeists are obviously experienced in wilderness travel. Their equipment is properly lashed to the canoe, they are wearing life jackets, and their headgear is designed for protection from sun and rain. (Mad River Canoe photo)

fire. They even made sleeping mats by scooping up loose pine needles and spreading them on the ground inside the lean-to.

Martin said that although they had reached land a couple of hours before dark, they didn't see any passing boats that night or Sunday morning. And because they hadn't told county park officials about their plans, they weren't missed, even though they had reservations.

"The night was long and cold," Martin said. "We kept a fire going, but only a small one—we were afraid of a big fire because of the wind." He went on to say that he knew they weren't lost. They could have reached help by following the shoreline. In fact, Sunday morning they did just that. But it was a rugged 4-mile hike before they got out.

"I learned a lesson during that outing," Martin said. "One I'll never forget! Never panic, no matter what, and keep thinking. That's all that saved us."

It's just that simple. One minute you may be enjoying a fishing, hiking, hunting, or canoeing trip, while the next you could have a real survival situation on your hands. People who venture into the woods or other backcountry areas these days need basic survival skills just as much as the mountain men of the 1880s did.

What puts us modern-day Daniel Boones in a survival situation? The Martins weren't lost, they were stranded. That can happen anywhere—out in the Gulf of Mexico because of a stalled engine, on a whitewater stream because of a split canoe bottom, or in a swamp because a truck is hopelessly stuck. A stranding can occur on a main highway or remote road during a snow or ice storm. I was once forced to spend two days deep in the Blue Ridge Mountains because a steep, one-lane mountain road had washed away, cutting off the only way to get my four-wheel-drive vehicle out of an isolated gorge.

Canoe swamping drills, in which canoes are deliberately swamped and overturned, then righted and bailed out, teaches students that their canoes do not sink and that they can handle water emergencies with a degree of confidence. (Outward Bound USA photo)

Strandings are often difficult to avoid. However, the first rule is to let someone know where you are going and when you plan to return. Next, keep your equipment in good repair. Have a backup system, or at least a repair kit, and know how to make repairs. Third, avoid weather that could get you into trouble. And, fourth, avoid going into areas where coming out may be impossible. In other words, use some common sense.

Injury

Yet another way people get themselves into survival situations is by an accidental injury. This kind of trouble can easily become very serious, especially if you suffer an injury that makes it very difficult or impossible to walk. For example, I once went on a hunting trip to the coastal swamps of Virginia with a portly fellow by the name of Dick. Deciding to venture out on his own, Dick walked about three miles from our camp. He was standing on a slippery log when a deer broke cover behind him. As Dick turned, he lost his balance and took such a hard fall that he broke his leg. Unable to move, he had to make a shelter under the log where he fell. We found Dick the next morning and carried him out.

I know of several cases where falls from steep trails have immobilized hikers and made the survival camp a must. A broken leg in the backcountry can put you in a survival situation when you least expect it.

Anyone going into the backcountry should take a few simple steps to prepare for the worst, should it happen. Granted, most of the time these precautions will not be necessary. But if a survival situation does occur, they will be good insurance.

Common Sense Precautions for Backcountry Trips

1. Know the area in which you plan to travel. When planning any trip, be sure to take the time to study maps of the area in detail. It never ceases to amaze me how many people go into the backcountry without knowing the lay of the land, the steepness, where the streams are located, where drinking water may be found, the directions roads run, and other essential information. If you get to know the entire area—a much larger area than the specific location you are going into —beforehand, you will be able to plan an alternate route or quick route out in an emergency.

Time spent studying maps can also alert you to hidden dangers, such as streams that may be prone to flash floods in unusually heavy rainfall, slopes that are much steeper than you had anticipated, areas subject to avalanche, and so on. Get advice from someone who is reliable and knows the area first hand. In parks and forests run by government agencies, this information is available from local administrators. Industrial forests, such as those owned by pulp and paper companies and timber companies, have foresters who can help prepare you for the territory. The more you know about an area before going into it, the safer your trip will be.

2. Know the area weather extremes. If an area is subject to midsummer snowstorms, hail, lightning, flash floods, or other such weather extremes, you should know of them in advance. Be sure to take clothing and equipment needed for protection in the worst weather situation. You never know. You could be caught on the side of a mountain in a sudden snowstorm in July, wearing only shorts and a short-sleeved shirt. Here extra clothing could save your life.

3. Pack a weather radio and use it. Most severe weather situations, such as thunderstorms, floods, tornadoes, blizzards, heat waves, and hurricanes, can, to some degree, be spotted by weather experts before your location is affected. The tough part of early warning, however, is getting the word out to the public. Many people are still unaware of it, but the United States and Canadian weather service agencies have set up special radio stations which can give you up-to-date weather information and warnings, if necessary, at any time of the day or night.

One of the first rules of trip planning for back-country is to know the weather extremes of the area. By packing an inexpensive, portable NOAA weather radio like this one, you will be fore-warned of severe weather and be able to avoid many potential hazards.

The NOAA (National Oceanic and Atmospheric Administration) Weather Radio System (NWR) broadcasts timely weather information for local areas across the country on a 24-hour-a-day basis. The network is capable of reaching 90 percent of all Americans and has a total of 350 transmitters.

Each transmitter has a broadcast range of about 40 miles, depending on local terrain (mountains may hamper reception) and type of receiver used. To minimize interference between any two stations in adjacent regions, transmitters broadcast on three VHF/FM frequencies—162.40, 162.475, and 162.55 MHz (megahertz). These frequencies are much higher than those designated for commercial FM radio stations.

A number of radios on the market today receive these high frequency "weather-band" stations. Some receive both standard AM/FM and weather-band stations. There are also lightweight, battery-operated weather-band radios that are excellent for backpacking trips. But put in fresh batteries before you start out! Some weather-band radios are equipped with an alarm feature. When turned on the "alarm only" feature, these receivers silently monitor the continuous weather broadcasts. The volume increases automatically when the local weather office transmits a special signal before issuing a storm warning. Other alarm-equipped radios sound a loud signal alarm to announce the NWR warnings.

Weather radio broadcasts are specially tailored to the weather information needs of people living within a particular receiving area. Stations along the seacoasts and Great Lakes, for example, provide weather information for boaters, fishermen, and others engaged in marine activities. Inland stations may offer weather information geared to hunters, farmers, and others.

Weatheradio Canada is very similar to the U.S. NWR network and broadcasts up-to-the-minute weather reports 24 hours a day, seven days a week. All Weatheradio Canada stations use one of three frequencies in the very-high-frequency FM band: 162.440, 162.475, and 162.550 MHz. Broadcast range for each transmitter is about 60 kilometers. A special radio receiver, available commercially, is required. That receiver will silently monitor the Weatheradio Canada broadcast and will automatically sound an alarm or come up to audible volume when warnings of severe weather conditions are transmitted.

4. Pack a survival kit. Equipment for any trip into the backcountry, even a day hike or a drive, should include a survival kit. Later you'll find an entire chapter devoted to survival kits.

5. File a trip plan. Before any trip into the backcountry, or anywhere else for that matter, you should file a trip plan with some responsible person who will know what to do if you do not return when expected.

The trip plan should include the following information:

Where you will be going. Give an exact location, on a topo map if possible. It is difficult to begin a search for someone who says he is going into Jasper County, when Jasper County contains 600 square miles of forestlands. Mark the route you plan to take. If you are going on a canoe trip and putting into the river at one point and taking out miles downstream, be sure to indicate these points on your map. The same applies to a snowmobile or backpacking trip. If you plan to return to the starting point, also indicate that.

Purpose of the trip. Always let someone know the purpose of your trip. Is it for photographing wildflowers, climbing the rock face of a mountain, canoeing, or backpacking? If you do not return, this will give rescue

When radio weight is a factor, such as here on day outings or when trekking for many days in wilderness, consider carrying a radio of credit-card size for local weather reports. This radio from Casio is available in either AM or FM. With earphone, it weighs just 1 ounce. (Radio photo by Neil Soderstrom)

teams valuable information for planning their search, as well as some idea of what could have happened.

Mode of transportation. If you plan to drive to a trailhead in your vehicle and then hike from that point into the backcountry, include that in your trip plan. Be sure to indicate where you will leave your vehicle. It is a good idea to record your vehicle license number in your trip plan. That way, if you don't return on time, searchers will know when they have found the right vehicle. This gives them the starting point for their search.

Departure date and time.

Planned return date and time. Try to be as accurate as possible in estimating your return, and if there is any change in the return date, notify the person who has the trip plan. If notification is impossible, do everything possible to stay with the trip plan. This could prevent an unnecessary full-scale search.

Names and addresses of everyone going on the trip. Include the ages of the people on the trip. Many times this information is helpful to search-and-rescue officials.

Name and phone number of someone in the area of your destination who could be called if you do not return as planned. For instance, if you are going to backpack into a national forest, list the name and phone number of the district forest ranger on the trip plan.

There are many factors that could prevent your returning as planned, and filing a trip plan could be a lifesaver. Two brothers from Alabama found that out in 1983, when bad weather put them two weeks behind schedule on a 600-mile kayak trip in the Canadian Arctic.

The pair began their trip after filing a wilderness travel plan at Fort Reliance, Northwest Territories. They fell behind schedule when strong winds made the river too rough for paddling and limited their progress to only a few miles a day. To add to their troubles, the kayak was damaged in rapids, and they had trouble repairing a hole in it. Then a blizzard struck, and they were forced to stay in their tent for three days. By then, the men knew they were in trouble. But fortunately they had filed a trip plan. And when they didn't show up at their destination, the Royal Canadian Mounted Police began a search. Meanwhile, the brothers started rationing their food, which for the last week of their ordeal amounted to a spoonful of lard and a spoonful of oatmeal a day.

Hoping to be spotted by a rescue plane, the men prepared a reflecting mirror and kept bright items handy. But when the first search plane did fly overhead, a mist obscured them from the plane's view. The plane made a second pass as one brother waved an orange gear bag, but then flew off. They tried to believe they'd been spotted and that help would arrive, but as the next day dragged by without rescue they began to have doubts.

Then late that next day, after nine weeks in the Arctic, they heard a helicopter and raced from the tent, desperately waving sleeping bags. This time they were spotted and their long, cold ordeal ended.

As these two men will surely tell you, filing a proper trip plan could save your life. But always remember to terminate the trip plan as soon as you return. I have been involved in several search-and-rescue operations in which the person we were looking for suddenly turned up safe and sound—down the road at a motel; at a friend's house; or, in the case of one extensive search, at a bar buying drinks for everyone to celebrate a successful whitewater kayak run. It is irresponsible to have a trip plan on file with someone and then fail to notify him when the trip is complete. Search-and-rescue operations are expensive, time-consuming, potentially dangerous to searchers, and emotionally wrenching to family members, who often fear the worst.

6. Take emergency rations with you. Always take extra food and water into the backcountry. Take water for vehicles as well as people. I've learned the hard way that extra water for the vehicle can often make the difference between an emergency and a nuisance.

In an emergency, you are much better off with three or four days' food rations than trying to live off edible wild plants and animals. Emergency rations are easy to carry in aircraft, boats, vehicles, and when traveling on horseback. Take along extra rations on a day hike as well. It is a wise safety measure.

7. Take other necessary items. When traveling in, over, or through wilderness country, take other items necessary for your own special needs. If you take medication and are going on a one-day trip, take enough for several days. In a wilderness area, I once had to bring out a diabetic camper who had forgotten his insulin and gone into shock. If you wear glasses or contact lenses, always carry a spare pair and keep them with you.

8. Whenever you park a vehicle and go into the backcountry, leave a note on the windshield. State your name, the area you are going into, and the date you expect to return. This is an extra safety precaution. If you must depart from your filed trip plan, rangers and law enforcement officials who check vehicles will have some idea what your new plans are. Then, if you are overdue, they will know to start a search-and-rescue operation.

9. Understand the need for navigational aids. Anyone who plans to go into a backcountry area shoud have a compass and map of the locale, *and* the skills to use them. For anyone

going on an extended wilderness trip, a good training course in navigation is a must. Many canoeists think they don't need a compass, but an island-dotted wilderness lake or a difficult cross-country portage can change their minds in a hurry. Anyone going into the wilderness by any means—vehicle, aircraft, skis, snowshoes, horse, whatever—should have and know how to use a topo map and a compass.

10. When in the backcountry, let companions know your immediate plans. Anytime you are leaving the vehicle or camp, be sure to tell the others where you are going and when you plan to return. It's as important to file a trip plan on location as it is before you leave home.

What to Do When Someone Is Missing

A growing number of people are taking survival training and know what to do if they become lost or stranded. But very few have any idea of what to do if a member of their group fails to return to camp.

A friend of mine was hunting deer with a group in a large swamp in the Florida panhandle. One night another hunter in the group failed to show up for supper. No one knew where he had hunted that day; so two men took flashlights and set out into the swamp in different directions. Three others got into their trucks and started driving up and down logging roads blowing their horns. Finally, around 2:00 A.M., someone went into town and got the local rescue squad, and by sunrise the group had found the lost hunter.

Though the hunter was glad his friends had done so much to help him, he had a legitimate complaint. Every time he started toward the sound of a truck horn, it moved. He spent the night unafraid, but his chasing the ever-moving horns wore him out.

Understanding the need for navigational aids, such as topo maps and compasses, is essential to safe backcountry travel. (Outward Bound USA photo)

As these same hunters and their rescued companion sat around camp eating breakfast, they suddenly realized that one of the two searchers who had walked into the swamp still had not returned. Another search was underway! By late afternoon the second man had been found, but he was in a state of total panic. Rather than continue to hunt, the group spent the next two days in camp resting up for the trip home.

Those hunters didn't expect to get into so much trouble, and when they did, they were unprepared. They acted out of panic, endangering the lost hunter and themselves. So before you go on any wilderness trip, recognize that the backcountry is one of the easiest places in which to get lost or hurt. Point out that fact to the other members of your group, and set up a system for keeping track of one another. Also, decide what you will do if someone gets lost. Make sure everyone understands the plan.

It's a good rule for every wilderness traveler to carry a police whistle. The sound of a whistle carries a long way and it makes locating someone who is lost much faster. Stress the importance of a lost person staying put until contact is made. Have a prearranged set of signals. Don't do as the Florida group did and blow vehicle horns while driving around. If you blow the horn, keep the vehicle in one place.

Medical problems of any member of the group must be made known to everyone. If someone has a heart problem, fainting spells, or the like, make sure he has a "buddy" to accompany him. There is nothing more discouraging for rescuers than to find out from companions that a lost hunter or fisherman was left on his own, even though he had a medical problem. Too many times the story has a sad ending, which a little forethought could have prevented.

By being prepared for the unexpected, you can avoid most life-and-death ordeals. And if you do encounter one, planning ahead can greatly increase your chances of being rescued fairly quickly.

2
SURVIVAL AND THE MIND

It started out as a typical afternoon squirrel hunt. The three of us were students at Auburn University in Alabama and we had taken the afternoon off to bag a few squirrels in the nearby Tuskegee National Forest. By the end of the day, two of us sat on the fender of the car, reliving the hunt, squirrel by squirrel. Suddenly it occurred to us that it was a long time after shooting light and Mike, the third member of our party, had not yet returned to the car. But we didn't worry because Mike was a highly trained and experienced hunter. He was working on his master's degree in forest management and had just recently returned from four years in the Alaskan backcountry.

A half hour passed, it was dark, and still no Mike. I blew the car horn three times. No response. For the next few minutes we blew the horn and shouted, stopping occasionally to listen. We were sure now that Mike was in trouble and began to ask ourselves questions: Had he shot himself accidentally? Could he have had a heart attack? Mike was a believer in hunter safety and was in excellent physical condition; so these possibilities seemed slight. As the reality that Mike was lost sank in, we began an organized search.

It was after midnight when we found him. A wild-looking man broke through a thicket and into the light cast by the searchers' spotlights. It was Mike, and he was scared and

Like this cross-country skier, those who go into the backcountry with proper planning and equipment will most likely never have the need for search and rescue, even in a harsh mountain environment like this. (Outward Bound USA photo)

confused. His clothing was torn to shreds from the waist down, and his legs and arms were bloody from the scratches he had received. The .22 rifle, hunting coat, and cap he had taken into the woods with him were gone—where, he did not know. We learned later that his hunting coat contained matches, extra ammunition, a pocketknife, and three squirrels, enough survival gear and food to live comfortably for many days.

Mike needed two weeks to recover fully from his brief but brutal ordeal. He recalled the panic that had struck him at dark when he realized he was lost. He remembered running for long periods of time. He also remembered feeling afraid of the strange people shouting and flashing lights in the woods. Embarrassment, guilt, confusion, and exhaustion only added to his sense of panic and helped cripple his ability to exercise proper judgment. Mike, an above-average hunter and

outdoorsman, had come face to face with a survival situation and had not used his skills.

One of the first reactions to being lost or stranded in the backcountry is fear. It is fear that causes many people to panic soon after realizing they are in a survival situation. It was fear that made Mike run blindly and foolishly discard his equipment.

List of common fears. Research has shown us that most people fear the following when in a survival situation:

1. Ridicule or embarrassment. Those I have interviewed soon after rescue said this was the first fear they experienced. It is especially true of experienced outdoorsmen who want to maintain their "Daniel Boone" image.

2. Punishment. It is this fear that causes many lost children and elderly people to hide soon after they realize they are lost. Coupled with this is the fear of being late. Most of us

COMMON FEARS OF LOST AND STRANDED PEOPLE

DISCOMFORT   BEING ALONE

RIDICULE   EXHAUSTION

EMBARRASSMENT   DARKNESS

GUILT   DEATH

THE UNKNOWN   DANGEROUS ANIMALS

CONFUSION   PUNISHMENT

If this man were stranded alone in a harsh environment, he'd have several factors in his favor to ward off the panic that causes many people to make bad decisions: a fire with a supply of wood, a source of water, backpack with supplies, shelter, and adequate clothing. (Outward Bound USA photo)

live as slaves to a clock, and when we aren't where we are supposed to be, when we are supposed to be, we tend to anticipate some form of punishment.

3. Being alone. Many people, including outdoorsmen, have never been truly alone. To them this is a strange and suddenly frightening experience. I once led a small search team for an experienced outdoorsman who had hunted in places around the world. Though he was only lost for a few hours, being lost had put this man into shock. It turned out he had never been alone before except in a room or other such civilized circumstance. On previous hunting trips, he had always been with a guide or group. The few hours he spent lost and alone caused him to give up hunting altogether.

4. Animals. Many people have hidden fears of wild animals and sounds in the woods. In my military career, I saw some of the best-trained fighters in the world become so frightened of wild animals they lost their effectiveness. The fear of wild animals is mentioned by many of those who were lost and stranded, especially children. Most people forget under the stress of survival that wild animals prefer to avoid people and that with the exception of an occasional bear, wild animals in North America don't generally attack people.

5. Darkness. Darkness brings on yet other fears for many people under survival stress. In the dark there are sounds that seem menacing, and this brings on fear. I have heard a beetle crawling in dry leaves that sounded like a a 100-pound animal. The night brings out the worst in our imaginations and scares some people out of their wits. I was once stranded in a remote wilderness with a hunter

While most adults do not acknowledge a fear of darkness, it is one of the most common fears associated with survival situations. A fire can be a welcome friend illuminating the night, as well as providing warmth, companionship, a means of cooking, and many other benefits. (Outward Bound USA/Robert Godfrey photo)

for me? What's that strange noise? Research also shows that people tend to magnify hazards of the unknown. The less the mind has to occupy it, the more it will be plagued by fear.

7. *Death.* Death is something very few people think about or have to face very often. But in a survival situation the thought of death is suddenly unavoidable. During an extreme survival situation in the military, I saw a man cry and repeat over and over, "I will never see my wife and children again." This kind of thinking can overpower the will to live. The fear of death can even paralyze someone who is not in a life-threatening situation.

8. *Discomfort.* This is one of the most common fears. Survival means eating bugs, sleeping on the ground, drinking muddy water, sleeping little, and suffering from insect bites, cold, heat, and many other unpleasant things. While such discomforts are not usually serious, many people in our modern world cannot cope with them and panic instead. Often, with a little calm thinking, most of these discomforts can be avoided.

9. *Ignorance.* This is one of the fears that can be easily avoided with proper training. When frightened by the realization of being lost, people often say, "I don't know the first thing to do. I'm in big trouble!" Their first reaction is to run away from the problem. This only gets them into more trouble.

The fear experienced by people who are lost varies widely in intensity, duration, and frequency of occurrence. Its effects on you may range from mild discomfort to complete disorganization and panic. Fear can take control of your behavior, causing you to react to irrational thoughts, rather than to the problem that caused them. In reality, the survival situations you may face are manageable, with proper training and some self-control.

who was dreadfully afraid of the dark. Each night at dark, he would go into a deep sleep and stay this way until daylight. There was nothing I could do to wake him.

6. *The unknown.* Coupled with fear of darkness is fear of the unknown. Questions fill the mind of a person under survival stress—What should I do? Will anyone look

Signs of fear. The physical symptoms of fear include:
● Quickening of pulse, trembling, feeling of faintness
● Dilation of pupils
● Increased muscular tension and fatigue
● Increased sweating from palms of hands, soles of feet, and armpits
● Dryness of mouth and throat, higher pitch of voice, stammering
● Feeling of "butterflies," emptiness of the stomach, nausea

Accompanying these physical signs of fear are the following common psychological symptoms:
● Irritability, increased hostility
● Talkativeness in early stages, leading finally to silence
● Confusion, forgetfulness, and inability to concentrate
● Feelings of unreality, flight, panic, or stupor

Controlling your own fears. Many of us have come to consider comfort to be our greatest need. Comfort is not essential, but people often value it much too highly in survival situations. You must value your life more than your comfort and be willing to tolerate heat, hunger, dirt, itching, pain—almost any discomfort. If you expose yourself to a bitter cold wind because you have a swollen ankle and think you can't walk to a nearby shelter, you have your priorities out of order. Reason is the key to changing your attitude—reason that identifies the pain of walking as a temporary problem compared to freezing to death.

Knowing how much you can take and understanding your demands for comfort will help you endure discomforts, particularly when they are temporary. Recognition of them as discomforts and as temporary will help you concentrate on effective action.

Here are some other suggestions to help you control your fears:

● Survival training, including knowledge and experience gained in simulated emergency situations, will reduce your fear of the unknown and help you control fear.
● Don't run away from fear; recognize it, understand it, admit it, and accept it. Learn what your reactions are likely to be.
● Learn how to think, plan, and act logically even when you are afraid. Doing this is an effective, positive action to control fear.
● Develop confidence in yourself. Increase your capabilities by keeping physically and mentally fit. Know your equipment and how to use it. Learn as much as you can about all aspects of survival and how much stress you can stand. You will find that you can stand much more than you thought.
● Be prepared. Accept the possibility that "it can happen to me." Be properly equipped and clothed at all times; have a plan ready that you have studied. Hope for the best, but be prepared to cope with the worst.
● Keep informed. Read books on survival. Learn to recognize potentially dangerous situations, and be prepared to take effective action should they be unavoidable. Increase your knowledge of what to do in emergencies and thereby reduce fear of the unknown.
● Keep busy at all times. Do everything you can to prevent hunger, thirst, fatigue, idleness, as well as ignorance about the situation, since these increase fear.
● Know how other members of your group react to stress. Learn to work together in emergencies, to live, work, plan, and help one another as a team.
● Practice your religion. If you have spiritual faith it can help you.
● Cultivate good survival attitudes. Keep your mind on your main goal and keep everything else in perspective. Learn to tolerate discomfort. Don't exert yourself to satisfy minor desires that may conflict with your overall goal, which is to survive.

Controlling fear in others. Survival situations such as strandings sometimes involve one or more persons besides yourself. They could be family members, close friends, or just acquaintances who joined the group for a weekend of hunting, fishing, or hiking. In one way, having someone else along makes an emergency situation much easier—it lessens or eliminates the fear of being completely alone. And you have someone to talk

Laughter is contagious. Finding ways of keeping your spirits up not only makes being lost or stranded less traumatic for you, but it also helps keep the fears of other members of your party in check. One way of keeping spirits up is to attend to personal comfort and health, as this man has done by applying sunscreen cream to prevent burning. (Outward Bound USA photo)

to about emergency plans and to help provide such basic needs as shelter and food.

But there are problems with group survival situations as well. If family members are involved, you may feel responsible for getting loved ones into trouble. Or with acquaintances, you may not know what they can tolerate or how well they handle fear. While you may be able to keep your own fears in check, someone else may not. That person could easily spread a sense of panic among the others and get everyone into still deeper trouble.

The following are some steps to take when in a group survival situation:
• Cultivate mutual support. The greatest support under severe stress may come from a tightly knit group. Teamwork reduces fear while making the efforts of everyone more effective.
• Use leadership. The most important test of leadership and perhaps its greatest value lies in the stress situation.
• Practice discipline. A disciplined group has a better chance of survival than an undisciplined group.
• Use contagion to your advantage. Your own calm behavior and demonstration of control will be contagious, and will reduce fear and inspire courage.

Fear can kill, and it can save lives. It is a normal reaction to danger. But fear can be overcome by understanding and controlling it through training, knowledge, and effective group action.

Other Survival Stresses

Although fear is a major survival stress and the one that must be dealt with first, there are others.

Emotional states associated with survival must be confronted in much the same way you size up survival conditions and available equipment. In the survival situation, the most important element in success or failure is you and anyone else with you. Important concerns to you are: (1) how you and others react to various situations; (2) what various signs, feelings, expressions, and reactions in yourself and others mean; (3) what the tolerance limits of the individuals are; (4) how to use your abilities to control yourself and solve survival problems; and (5) how to be helpful to your companions. In order to size up the emotional aspects of a survival situation, you should be aware of stresses other than fear that are commonly encountered. The most important of them—guilt, pain, thirst, hunger, fatigue, and boredom—are discussed below:

Guilt. Guilt feelings cause many people to lose confidence and composure and may prevent their doing the right thing in an emergency. Guilt can quickly bring on an attitude of helplessness and, later, hopelessness. Here the concern for loved ones and friends, and what they are experiencing, may overpower good judgment. A question often asked is "Why have I done this to my family?"

Pain. The benefit of pain is that it forces you to protect an injured part by resting it or avoiding using it. Pain is upsetting, like fear, but is not in itself harmful or dangerous. Pain can usually be tolerated, and if the survival situation is sufficiently grave, pain should be subordinated to efforts to move, hold out, or perform some other necessary action.

Men have been known to complete a fight with a fractured hand, to run on a fractured or sprained leg, and to land an aircraft despite severely burned hands. Often, they do not feel much pain during the emergency itself. This is because concentration and intense effort can actually stop or reduce the sensation of pain for a time—sometimes this may be all that is needed to survive.

In a survival situation you must know that if you have to move in order to survive, you can move—despite pain. The determination must come from within you, but you can actually get control of pain by taking these steps:
- Understand the source and nature of pain.
- Recognize pain as a discomfort that can be tolerated.
- Concentrate on things you need to do, such as thinking, planning, and keeping busy.
- Work on developing your confidence and self-respect, that is, take pride in your ability to keep going.

You have much greater reserves of strength and endurance than you realize. When your goals are safety and staying alive, and you value these goals highly enough, you will be able to tolerate even severe pain.

Thirst. Thirst and dehydration are among the most important problems of survival. Thirst, like fear and pain, can be almost forgotten if the determination to carry on, supported by calm, purposeful activity, is strong.

In summer desert heat, thirst alone is not a reliable way to tell how much water you need. If you drink only enough to satisfy your thirst, you can still dehydrate slowly. The best plan is to drink plenty of water whenever it is available, and particularly when eating. And your water intake comes from foods and beverages, as well as from your canteen. Only when you get water in some form or other can you prevent dehydration and keep the body at normal efficiency.

When you do not have enough water, you begin to feel thirsty and uncomfortable. Your need for water may increase if:
1. You have a fever.
2. Your fear causes in you a greatly exaggerated consciousness of thirst.

3. You sweat more than necessary because you don't use available shelter to best advantage.

4. You remove clothing or keep your mouth open.

5. You ration water.

6. You overwork or overexercise in the heat.

If your water supply is low, cut down your food intake, particularly foods containing protein. The body must use extra water to carry off wastes from the utilization of protein. This causes the body to become dehydrated more quickly.

At almost any stage, you can reverse dehydration by simply drinking enough water. The important thing is to avoid allowing dehydration to go too far. Once you become weak and sleepy from dehydration, you lose your will and self-control and thereby lessen your ability to function effectively. Knowing where and how to find water, how to purify it, and what to use as a water substitute is an important part of survival training. I devote a whole chapter, later, to water.

Hunger. Many people mistakenly assume that hunger and starvation are the prime haz-

Many survival necessities are overlooked by boaters in salt water. These sailors would have realized the value of a supply of fresh water if they had become lost in this fog. (Outward Bound USA photo)

ards in a survival situation. In fact, they even feel they are on the brink of starvation if they get one of their daily meals later than usual. But few of us would succumb to starvation if deprived of food for several days or even a week or two. Most of us carry around extra pounds that could keep us going, without those three meals, for many days. What we would feel during that time would be discomfort, not starvation.

When you consider that most people are rescued within three days, it's apparent that starvation is an unlikely prospect. Fear of starvation should not be a stress at all, and survival courses should downplay the threat that starvation poses.

A few people each year are caught in a long-term survival situation. But if they do not have emergency food or do not make use of edible wild plants or animals, they will certainly feel the effects of hunger. These are the most important physical effects of undernutrition and starvation: (1) hunger and hunger pains; (2) loss of weight; (3) weakness, characterized by decreased muscular endurance and strength, deterioration of coordination, and slowing down of movements; (4) dizziness and blackouts upon standing up suddenly; (5) slowed heart rate; (6) increased sensitivity to cold; and (7) increased thirst, accompanied by a craving for salt.

Some of these physical reactions arise from the body's effort to adapt and protect itself. The decreased heart rate, for example, indicates the body is functioning at a lower energy level, thus conserving energy. Tests have shown that vision resists deterioration, and that hearing actually becomes more acute.

Hunger pangs, coldness, weakness, and loss of endurance over an extended period will have a negative effect on the mind. The most frequently observed psychological effects are personality and behavior changes, including depression, irritability, nervousness, and general emotional instability; social withdrawal and decrease of communication and social interchange; narrowing of interests with an emphasis on thoughts of food; difficulty in concentration; and slow speech.

Both the physical and psychological effects described are reversed when food and a protective environment are restored. Return to normal is slow, and the time necessary for the return increases with the severity of starvation.

If food deprivation is complete and only water is ingested, the pangs of hunger abate in a few days, but depression and irritability remain. The normal tendency is to continue to forage for food to prevent starvation, and such efforts continue as long as strength and self-control permit.

But because these effects do not appear until many days have been passed without food, hunger is one of the easier problems to deal with in most survival cases. The survivor must be able to adjust to discomfort, adapt to primitive conditions, and apply techniques of the survival routine.

Fatigue. Survival is a constant strain on energy levels that must be watched carefully. Since people in a survival situation get less food and sleep, fatigue can set in and become a major problem. Fatigue makes people more susceptible to hypothermia, judgment errors, and many other physical and mental problems. They become less productive, less effective and more likely to panic.

It is very important in a backcountry emergency to avoid physical exertion as much as possible. Save energy to perform vital tasks such as shelter construction and wood gathering. Just how much energy can be expended on less necessary activities depends greatly on how much food and water are available. Even those things that must be done can be done in as energy-saving a way as possible. If food, water, and therefore energy are at a minimum during an arctic survival situation, for example, a simple hole-in-the-snow shelter would probably be a wiser choice than an entire snow cave, which takes a great deal of time and energy to make.

You, as a survivor, should always be aware of the dangers of overexertion. You may already be experiencing strain and reduction of efficiency as a result of other stresses. So you must judge accurately your capacity to walk, carry, lift, or do any necessary work. Plan and act accordingly.

You may find it necessary to exert yourself to an unusual degree to cope with an extreme emergency. If you understand how fatigue works and the mental states generated by various kinds of effort, you should be able to call on available reserves of energy when they are needed.

Boredom. While preparing this book, I reread notes I made while in true survival situations. One of the most common problems was boredom. Boredom creeps up on you while you await help. It is accompanied by feelings of depression and lack of interest. Boredom can be overcome or at least controlled by staying busy, using patience, thinking positively, and adapting as best you can to your situation.

Will to Live

In an emergency, your survival kit and the surrounding environment furnish the tools and resources you may need to survive for days or weeks. Your survival skills come from this and other books, any formal training you have received, and your own ingenuity. But tools and training are not enough. You must have the will to live.

It is no secret that the human body has considerable reserves of strength and endur-

Once a victim realizes that he is lost, continuing along an unknown route is dangerous and can prolong rescue, often for days. This skier has the basic elements of survival with him and could use them to prepare a survival camp if he were to become lost. (Outward Bound USA photo)

ance that can be called up in an emergency. That does not mean you will be able to run a 50-yard dash with a broken leg or leap high obstructions in a single bound. But if you can keep the right frame of mind, the will to live can help you survive incredible hardships— far more than you ever thought possible. In fact, willpower alone has been the deciding factor in many extreme survival situations. While the following incident is not a good example of survival techniques, it does show that sheer willpower alone can conquer many obstacles.

Some time ago a man was stranded on a vast stretch of Arizona desert without food or water for eight days. During his ordeal, he walked 150 miles in daytime temperatures as high as 120 degrees and crawled the last 8 miles completely naked.

Because of dehydration, he lost 25 percent of his body weight (a 10 percent loss is often fatal). Doctors found his blood was so thick that cuts on his body did not bleed until he had drunk a large quantity of water. The man had had no survival training and broke all the rules for surviving in desert heat. But he wanted to survive and he did, through willpower alone.

Just how much punishment can the body take and still continue to function when the will to live is strong? You would be amazed at some case histories in which people have survived, despite serious injury, lack of food and water, and a hostile environment. The following story is true. Granted, it is unusually brutal and not even typical of emergency survival situations, but it shows man can survive far more than most of us would expect—if he is determined to live.

During the week before Christmas, Timothy Moore, 26, was staying at his cabin in a remote section of San Gorgonio Mountain, north of Palm Springs. One afternoon, he was jumped from behind by two men who beat and kicked him mercilessly and then robbed him of $150. Next they handcuffed Moore's arms behind his back, blindfolded him, and took him to a lonely spot in some kind of vehicle.

The thieves stood Moore on the edge of a cliff and then shot him in the head at point-blank range. Knocked over the cliff by the force of the gunshot, he tumbled 50 yards down to the canyon floor. As if all this were not enough, the thieves fired still more shots. Moore managed to crawl under a rock overhang, but not before being wounded in the arm. Finally, he heard an engine start and then fade off into the distance; the thieves had left Moore for dead.

Badly wounded, battered, bruised, and stranded far from help, Moore might well have been dead by the end of the day, if he had not been so determined to survive. He was in desert country and still handcuffed, but got to his feet and wandered until he found a dry creek bed. That led him to an old dirt road.

"I just started walking," he said. "I slept under rocks and trees."

Despite the pain of his injuries, thirst, and hunger, Moore continued to walk for three days until at last he wandered up to a man who was out in his yard cutting wood. By sheer force of will, Moore had managed to cover 40 miles through the desert to safety.

Moore was treated for gunshot wounds, multiple bruises, dehydration, and exposure. An official thought it was attitude that brought Moore through, pointing out that he even joked with investigators after his incredible ordeal. But Moore himself summed it up best.

"I was given the best Christmas present a man could have—my life."

Most people in survival situations will never confront the hardships that Moore did. But to one degree or another they will have to muster some of the same determination to carry on, despite fear and discomfort. The will to live may be the key factor for survival in these situations, and can unlock the body's tremendous reserves of strength and endurance, should they be needed.

We are all capable of summoning up the will to live, but it is far from automatic. It can be swept aside by fear and panic, because it demands a purposeful, determined frame of mind. But most of all, the will to live can be submerged in what amounts to its opposite—the sense of hopelessness or complete despair. After fear and panic, hopelessness may be the most difficult emotion to deal with in an emergency. And coupled with the shock of being lost or injured far from help, hopelessness can be overpowering. But the important thing to remember is that hopelessness only blunts your sense of purpose and determination to live—the very things you need most to continue your fight for survival.

Hopelessness must be watched for in any survival emergency. While hopelessness may not be easily recognized in oneself, others in a group will notice it. There is a loss of interest in what's going on, along with a loss of appetite and withdrawal from the group. A person who is not treated for hopelessness may soon totally give up the will to live.

Treatment usually means relieving some of the stress. Increased comfort, rest, and morale building from others often work in a short while. The goal is to improve the victim's self-image and make him feel he's an important part of the group.

Stay Calm and Think

The first survival skill is your ability to admit that you are lost or stranded. Once you do this, stop, sit down, and think. Persuade yourself to avoid panic and to stay calm.

Mentally you must accept the challenge posed by the survival situation and prepare to make the best of your adventure. If you told family or friends about your trip before you left, chances are that someone will begin looking for you soon. In fact, most people are found within a few hours after being reported missing. Even in remote areas of North America, 99 percent are found within 72 hours.

Avoiding panic is difficult when dealing with yourself or, if you are part of a group, with the people around you. Most people who are lost probably panic to some degree. But in extreme cases those who panic may forget who they are or where they are. Here is an incident that occurred in 1978.

One weekend, a fisherman I'll call John Adams camped on the bank of the Tallapoosa River in Alabama's Horseshoe Bend National Historical Park. Well before dawn on Saturday morning, he waded into the river to do some fishing. But at some point Adams slipped and apparently went under long enough to really make him panic. He remembers nothing from the time of his accident Saturday to the following Wednesday, one day before he made it to safety.

What apparently happened during that time was that Adams finally managed to crawl up onto land after being washed far downstream. In his panicky stupor, he must have wandered for four days. Eventually, when Adams came to his senses on Wednesday, he was several miles upstream.

This erratic behavior made it difficult for searchers to find Adams. Notified by Adams's fishing buddy, they began looking for him Sunday morning. They found what could have been his tracks well downstream, but they couldn't be sure. They dragged the river, and after a couple of days, Adams's relatives and friends became convinced he had drowned.

When Adams came to his senses Wednesday, he was hungry and exhausted. He ate some wild muscadines and drank water from a creek. That gave him the strength to continue finding his way out of the woods.

"The first thing I remember about it was I had no earthly idea where I was. At that point I figured it was probably Monday or Tuesday. It wasn't until later I found out I had lost three days somewhere."

"When I came out, I was up in a man's yard. He saw me and I was half passed out. He wanted to know what I was doing there. I wasn't too concerned about that. I was just glad to see somebody. I think the first thing I asked him was what day it was. He said Thursday. I just sort of looked at him like I was shocked."

STOP!

Survival instructors teach that the first thing to do once you realize you are lost is to **STOP**. This means:

> **SIT**
> **THINK**
> **OBSERVE**
> **PLAN**

Once the route of travel becomes confused or lost, the first rule is to stop, avoid panic, and determine if travel is warranted. In most cases, staying put at this stage is vital to rescue. Since these hikers have reached a road and only have to figure which way to follow it, it would be safe for them to continue travel on the road.

By following this simple outline you can control the urge to panic.

Sit. By sitting down you can prevent getting into deeper trouble. This one act alone can also start the thinking process, and it suppresses the urge to run or to make hasty decisions. You may need this time to get over the initial shock that you are lost.

Think. First remember that survival is the challenge to stay alive. In order to do this, you must set up priorities. The priorities of survival are known as the Rules of Three:

- You may be doomed in three seconds if you let panic rule.
- You cannot live much more than three minutes without oxygen.
- You cannot live much more than three hours in temperature extremes without body shelter.
- You cannot live much more than three days without water.
- You will need food in three weeks.

These priorities dictate that you think of the real and immediate dangers, not those conjured up by your fears. For example, you may be stranded by severe weather or caught in extreme temperatures. If so, shelter is important. But more than likely, the most immediate danger is your own mind. Don't let fear take control and cloud clear, resourceful thinking.

In a survival emergency, man is at the mercy of his mind. That is the reason many survival experts refer to the mind as the best survival kit. In order to survive, one must keep control of the mind by thinking back to past training, by determination, and by maintaining a positive mental attitude. For most this takes a great deal of effort in a survival situation.

Observe. Observe your surroundings to discover what problems must be solved and what resources you have to solve them. You will need such things as water, shelter, signals, proper campsite, and food. What tools and equipment do you have to meet these needs? What is the physical condition of those involved? What is the environment? This procedure should lead to the three Steps of Organization: (1) identifying problems; (2) setting priorities, and (3) finding solutions to meet needs. If you are in a group, make job assignments. Get everyone involved. Keep them busy.

Plan. Now that you are organized, set plans. This course of action should be built around the following:

1. Select a survival campsite near an open area or at your stalled vehicle.

2. Set up a system of signals, with backups, and keep it ready for instant use.

3. Construct shelter, if you have strength and natural materials are available, and make it reasonably comfortable without wasting energy.

4. Gather firewood, food, and water.

5. Maintain a good survival spirit.

6. Dispel fears.

7. Boost the will to live.

Take Care of Yourself and Your Equipment

People who have been lost or stranded are frequently in sad physical and mental states when they are found. They are cut, bruised, and dirty. Their clothing is badly torn or lost altogether.

Just because you are out in the wilderness is no reason to become careless about your body. In fact, the absence of nurses and doctors out there makes it even more important to take care of yourself and try to stay clean. A cut or sore that would be considered trivial in the city could be a life-threatening wound in certain survival situations.

Regardless of the severity of a survival situation, take the time to practice good first aid. A simple foot blister can become a serious injury in the wilderness if untended. (Outward Bound USA/ Robert Godfrey photo)

Also take care of your clothing, because it is a vital part of your survival gear. Your clothes help protect and maintain your body. Try to keep your clothing clean and dry. Clean clothing is warmer. Do not lose your clothing. Make repairs in clothing as needed.

The Movement of Lost People

Because of fear and other stresses, people in survival situations tend to disregard the basic rule of staying put. They feel they must move on their own to safety. During recent years, much has been learned about how people think when they are lost. Not surprisingly, there are patterns—even when it comes to choices they make when trying to head back to safety.

As a result, search-and-rescue teams are now much better equipped to determine areas of high probability when conducting a rescue operation. The following are ways people tend to behave when lost:

Hunters. Hunters often become lost because they concentrate more on the game they are pursuing than on keeping their bearings. Often in pursuit of game, hunters will go into swamps, heavily timbered areas, thick underbrush, clearcuts, and areas of deep snow with little regard for where they are or whether they are exerting themselves beyond their physical abilities. They will even go into areas long before daylight and stay until long after dark. Many times in the excitement after a kill, hunters will overexert themselves by trying to bring out game that is too large for them to handle. In addition, hunters are frequently unprepared for extremely bad weather, such as heavy rainstorms or snowstorms.

Once hunters realize they are lost or stranded, they tend to travel downhill. Most prefer to use trails, paths, streams, and other routes of least resistance while avoiding swamps, cliffs, and other obstacles. Records show that approximately 20 percent of lost hunters are found within a mile of where they were last seen or where they realized they were lost. Another 50 percent are found between 1 and 2 miles of that same point. Knowledge of these travel patterns and the fact that hunters today often wear bright orange clothing increase their chances of being found by trained search-party managers.

Fishermen. Because fishermen travel along streams or on well-used paths to lakes, navigation is seldom a problem. What most often gets fishermen into trouble and eventually leads to survival situations is an accident, such as falling into deep water, being swept down rapids, or falling on rocks while trying to climb to a better pool. When a report of a missing fisherman comes in, the mission is generally for recovering someone who has been injured or killed, rather than for locating someone who has gotten lost.

Mountain climbers. As a rule, mountain climbers are well equipped and are fairly well trained in their sport. They usually remain on or near their designated routes, and so they are seldom lost. However, they may be stranded because of weather, accidents, or climbing into situations that are beyond their capabilities.

Other outdoors enthusiasts. Outdoor photographers, picnickers, and others who take part in occasional outdoor activities commonly have no survival gear whatsoever with them. These people are often stranded because of sudden bad weather, such as a storm. Generally, they venture out in good weather and do not carry clothing for unexpected bad weather. Because their attention is focused on their special interest, they may pay little attention to landmarks going in and out and are often misled by changes in the terrain. These people will try to walk out rather than stay put. The majority of them are found within 1 and 2 miles of the point where they were last seen or realized they were lost.

Children 1 to 3 years old. Children in this age group have no navigational skills. Usually they are totally unaware of the concept of being lost. Once they wander away, they move aimlessly with no specific direction in mind. It is interesting to note that when they become tired and sleepy, they will seek out a safe spot to lie down and sleep. Often they pick locations that make it difficult for searchers to find them, such as inside a hollow log or tree, under a large rock, or even in the tangled foliage at the top end of a fallen tree. (For more on children, refer to Chapter 22 in this book on keeping track of children in backcountry.)

Children 3 to 6 years old. Children in this age group are capable of walking greater distances. They are very much aware of the concept of being lost and attempt to go back to the point where they left their parents or camp. When tired, children in this age group seek a spot to sleep, like the younger children. Since children from three to six have usually been instructed to stay away from strangers, they may be afraid to respond when searchers call their name. These children usually follow the path of least resistance. But searchers have to keep in mind that the path of least resistance for a child this age often leads underneath vegetation and into brush too tangled for an adult. Usually these children are found between 1 and 2 miles from the point they were last seen, and most of these are found within 1 mile of that point. However, some have traveled as much as 5 miles before being found.

Children 6 to 12 years old. Children in this age group have definite navigational skills but are easily confused in any strange environment. Their psychology is different from that of younger children; they have been known to become lost because they have intentionally run away to avoid punishment, or to get attention from adults. Like children aged three to six, children aged six to 12 often will not answer searchers calling their name, at least during daylight hours. Once darkness sets in, they seem to be willing to return searchers' calls and to seek help. Since children of this age group suffer from many of the same fears that adults do, as discussed earlier in this chapter, feelings of helplessness and hopelessness set in quickly.

Many search-and-rescue officials say that a child in this age group may be one of the most difficult to find in backcountry.

The Problem of Hiding

One of the major problems faced by search-and-rescue workers is that many lost people will hide from them. This has been noted especially in cases involving children and elderly people. Apparently a major reason for hiding is that these youngsters and elderly people suffer a deep-seated fear of punishment for getting themselves into this situation and creating a lot of work for the people responsible for them. However, other groups of people also hide from searchers, and there has been little research on this phenomenon.

I was once involved in a search for a hunter who had been lost for one day. I found him 2 miles from the point where he had been last seen. It was only by chance that I spotted him at all, because he was crouched down, hiding under a bridge on a well-used road. During the ride back to the hunting lodge where his companions were waiting, I asked him why he had been hiding. He didn't have an answer. I never did find out what made him so scared of everything and everybody.

3

HELP IS ON THE WAY

With modern means of communication and transportation, few emergencies go unnoticed for long. Even in remote areas, search crews usually arrive on the scene within a few hours.

Individual situations such as plane crashes, automobile breakdowns, snakebites, stranded boats, or missing persons are usually brief if the simple precautions I give in this book are taken. I have stressed the fact that you should let someone know where you are going, when you plan to get there, and when you will return. If this one rule were followed, fewer people would die each year.

Let's look at a few of today's rescue programs that help keep people alive.

Land Search and Rescue

One of the things people who have been rescued usually say is that while they were lost or stranded, they figured that no one would bother to look for them. How wrong they are.

This is usually false because often there are scores of people using aircraft, vehicles, and other resources looking for one person who is lost. Searches have involved as many as 1,500 to 2,000 people, and it is safe to say that nearly all were complete strangers to the person being sought. Contrary to what many of us believe, when someone is lost or

Provided you've notified a responsible person or agency of your trip plans, you can usually count on being searched for when you've not reported home or to authorities on schedule. No matter the terrain or weather, skilled search-and-rescue teams can usually be mobilized quickly. (Outward Bound USA photo)

stranded in the backcountry, there is no shortage of concerned volunteers willing to give up time and personal comforts to help find him.

It surprises most people how much money search-and-rescue (SAR) operations cost. In the early 1980s, annual search-and-rescue costs in the national parks of the United States were in the neighborhood of $1.5 million. Of this, nearly $1 million was paid by the National Park Service, while the rest was paid by military and volunteers. One search alone in the Great Smoky Mountains National Park cost more than $250,000. And this does not include thousands of hours of time put in by volunteers, or the cost of operating equipment and vehicles they use.

The National Park Service has reported that the average cost of a search-and-rescue mission is about $4,000. Such missions are generally caused by negligence, such as not taking along appropriate equipment, lacking necessary experience or physical conditioning, setting out despite hazardous weather conditions, underestimating time needed to make trips, or failing to notify authorities when the party returned.

While search-and-rescue operations involve lots of people and tremendous amounts of time, energy and money, no one who is

The danger warning sign in this photo was not heeded, resulting in the need for the rescue team with climbing gear to bring out a park visitor. A rescue operation is an expensive and often dangerous undertaking, requiring large amounts of manpower, gear, and skill. (National Park Service photo)

lost should feel that a search won't be mounted. On the other hand, everyone going into the backcountry should take the steps to prevent these expenditures.

Search techniques have improved dramatically in a relatively short period of time. Formerly, search-and-rescue missions in the backcountry usually involved large numbers of people walking abreast through the woods, shouting the lost person's name. Often the search was disorganized, and many times searchers spent days looking in the wrong location.

One such operation involved a search for a lost hunter. Various independent parties were spread out in the woodlands, with searchers walking abreast. The loosely organized base camp for this search was at a public campground. Sometime during the third day, the lost hunter walked in from a direction not covered by search parties. He spent almost three hours in the camp, drinking coffee and talking with would-be rescuers, before realizing he was the object of the search.

Today's search-and-rescue operations are highly organized in most locales. Thanks to research conducted in recent years, vastly improved equipment, and new search-and-rescue techniques, we have eliminated the mass confusion that used to be called a search-and-rescue operation. Instead rescue officials can quickly put together a sophisticated rescue operation that is efficient at locating people in trouble.

Setting up the search organization. A search starts with the local authorities who have been notified that someone is missing. In most cases this is the county sheriff, district forest ranger, park ranger, or conservation officer. Many of these officials have had formal training in search-and-rescue organization and know how to respond very quickly and

Cave and mine-shaft rescue requires specialists and, often, heavy equipment. Yet teams are often assembled for such rescues in short order. (National Park Service photo)

Unexpected bad weather is frequently the major cause of people finding themselves in survival situations. The National Park Service, the US Forest Service, and other government agencies have trained personnel and specialized equipment for conducting search-and-rescue missions under extreme weather conditions. (National Park Service photo)

effectively to emergencies of this type.

Once a person has been reported missing, someone with experience is designated the "search boss." It is the responsibility of the search boss to get the search organization set up and in action as quickly as possible. The search boss must coordinate the efforts of all who are involved. He quickly establishes priorities. At the same time, he must protect the site where the person was last seen. A base camp, set up near the location where the person was last seen, serves as headquarters for the search.

Interview. Another important early step is to interview those people who were last with the missing person, as well as members of his family. This interview process is quite important because it gives the search boss a tremendous amount of data to use in planning. The interview questions are designed to get the following information:

- Name and address of the missing person(s)
- Description
- Purpose for being in the backcountry. Is he a hiker, hunter, etc.?
- Age—a child or an elderly person?
- Equipment he has with him. Is he a hiker who has a backpack filled with equipment necessary for an extended stay in the backcountry, or is he a picnicker who has little more than the clothes he is wearing?
- Exact place last seen. His starting point is an important piece of data, because all search operations center around this point during the early phases of the search.
- Names, addresses, and phone numbers of all the people who were in the immediate area.
- Circumstances of the disappearance. Exactly when and where was the person discovered missing? Was he en route somewhere? If so, where? Exactly how long has he been overdue?
- Type of footwear he is wearing. If possible,

This is a scene from a typical search-and-rescue operation in which a ground team works in conjunction with an aerial search party.

this includes a description of the sole pattern, which is useful for tracking.
● Color of clothing and equipment he has with him
● Brand names of clothing and equipment. This is helpful during a search, because items of clothing and equipment searchers find can be vital clues.
● Brands of such items as cigarettes, candy, and gum he has with him
● Signal capabilities. Did he carry a whistle, flashlight, firearm, or any other method of signaling?
● Experience in the outdoors. Has he had survival training?
● Has he been lost in the past?
● Physical condition. At the time he was lost, was he fatigued, depressed, cold, hungry, ill? What medical problems, if any, does he have?
● Personality traits of the subject. Is he smart, realistic, confident, aggressive, moody, optimistic, or pessimistic? Does he have a good, positive mental attitude, or is he immature, unsure, negative, shy, or depressed?

The search boss looks for answers to these and many other questions during the interview process. They provide information that is valuable as the search gets underway.

Other factors the search boss considers in planning the search include:
● Present weather conditions
● Weather conditions when person was first reported missing
● Type of terrain in which the person is missing
● Type of terrain throughout the probable search area

Based on all this information, the search boss can estimate where the subject is likely to be. This process is known as establishing the "area of probability."

Hasty team. Once an area of probability has been determined by the search boss, several teams of highly specialized people may be asked to conduct searches. A "hasty team" is usually the first team to start searching. It is a group of three or four well-trained search volunteers who go into the most likely areas. Their job is primarily to look for clues—discarded equipment, a footprint, a cigarette pack, broken mushrooms, or any other clue indicating the direction that the person may have taken.

Lookouts and road-check teams. Lookouts are posted at observation points overlooking the area of probability. These individuals are positioned so that they can spot the flash of a signal mirror or catch sight of a campfire or a person walking along a trail or road. If there are roads in the area, road-checks are assigned to watch for someone walking along

Man-trackers depend upon a stick to mark the stride length of the person being searched for. This man-tracker technique is being used more and more by search bosses.

In recent years, search dogs have proven highly effective at finding missing or lost people. The German shepherd shown here is on a search mission in the mountains of California. Dogs of this type have been responsible for finding scores of people and their use will be increased as more dogs are trained for this valuable work. (Judy Graham/National Association for Search and Rescue photo)

the road or to find out if the subject has caught a ride with a passing motorist. Early in the search, planes may be used. A formal request may be made for nearby military aircraft or for the Civil Air Patrol to join the search.

Man-tracking teams. Other highly specialized units sometimes brought into a search are known as "man-tracking" teams. In many areas of the United States these teams are made up of U.S. Border Patrol agents who are trained in tracking illegal aliens. These trackers are highly skilled and can even follow the trail of a person who is trying not to leave any signs at all.

Today many search-and-rescue units other than the Border Patrol have learned man-tracking skills, and as man-tracking becomes more widely accepted by search-and-rescue

authorities it will play a much larger role in finding lost people.

Search dog teams. Dog teams have proven to be one of the most valuable tools in search and rescue. This may conjure up a picture of bloodhounds chasing an escaped convict, but today's tracking operations are much more sophisticated than those of years ago. Not only bloodhounds but German shepherds and other breeds have been trained to locate people both dead and alive. These dogs have often detected a person a quarter of a mile away, even though the individual was hidden or in the dark.

Search-and-rescue dog teams have become so effective that they are beginning to play a major role in almost every mission. In their publication, *SAR Dog Alert*, the SAR Dog

Division of the National Association for Search and Rescue gives examples showing the value of dog teams in a search. The following is adapted from this publication.

Some years ago in early October, an 18-year-old hiker became lost in Virginia's Shenandoah National Park. He had decided to try to beat his friends to the bottom of the mountain by going down the north face, instead of following the trail. When he didn't show up, his companions notified park rangers.

The resulting search-and-rescue operation involved park rangers, two volunteer SAR dogs units, a U.S. Customs Service dog team, two mountain rescue groups, and a volunteer rescue squad. This SAR operation was described by rescue workers as one of the most difficult in Virginia/Maryland history.

After learning that the young man was missing, park rangers hasty-searched roads and trails that evening and began gearing up for a major search effort. The next day, rangers with two dog teams from the Virginia Search and Rescue Dog Association and one from U.S. Customs began working upslope in the areas of highest probability, as determined by the park overhead team. One of the dogs gave an alert at the 2,600-foot level of the mountain's north face.

That evening, members of the Washington, DC, and Charlottesville, Virginia, chapters of the Appalachian Search and Rescue Conference (ASRC) joined the search. They ran night foot patrols on trails above and below the high-probability area and camped at strategic spots to ensure that the subject didn't leave the primary search area.

DOGS-East was called for the next day to augment the dog teams already there. (DOGS-East is an association of search-and-rescue dog owners and trainers that has a high success rate in finding lost people.) At daybreak, dogs and handlers were deployed in four high-

This is the north face of Old Rag Mountain in Shenandoah National Park, where a dramatic three-day search was conducted for a fallen climber. Details are given in the accompanying text. (Bob Panko photo)

probability sectors radiating down from the mountain's summit at 3,268 feet; four of the teams were to work from the top and four from the bottom. *DOGS-East News* described the upper third of the mountain as "very difficult—large, wet lichen-covered rocks, ledges, laurel thickets, downed trees and sheer dropoffs (also sleeping bears in caves)." Weather, with temperatures in the hypothermia range, was made worse by more than 5 inches of rain that fell steadily during the next 18 hours.

By midday, after dogs again gave alerts at elevations of 2,600 to 2,700 feet, climbers were sent to the north face between the summit and the base of the cliffs. *DOGS-East News* reported: "At (4:35 P.M.), one of the ASRC searchers was at the end of a rope, 200 feet below the summit and 40 feet above the next ledge when, through the fog, she noticed a hole in the laurel bushes below—and [the missing youth] on the ledge beneath."

She then directed other nearby searchers to the spot. It took an hour and a half for them to reach the victim. He was suffering from extreme hypothermia, and had apparently sustained head and leg injuries as well. He could only respond weakly and incoherently to his rescuers.

In rainy, overcast situations, the scent plume that dogs can smell often fans out at a constant elevation. The alerts noted on a ridge at 2,600 to 2,700 feet were clues that led to a concerted effort in the cliffs in that area. The victim was found at 3,000 feet, on the ridge immediately west of where the dogs alerted.

Shenandoah National Park's state-of-the-art search management techniques, teamwork among various SAR units with different areas of expertise, and rescuers' determination to overcome technical problems and unfavorable conditions all helped save the young man's life.

Sign cutting. The hasty team may employ a technique known as "sign cutting" (locating sign and hard-to-find clues). Team members search from the point of the last sighting in an ever-widening circle. As they spiral outward, they look for any clues. In many searches the hasty team quickly finds the trail by this method and locates the missing person before a major search effort has been organized. The sign-cutting technique also has the advantage of not obliterating the clues in an area. The large number of people involved in the old grid method often meant clues were destroyed.

Three-men teams. In a search of this type, three highly trained searchers start at a baseline and work in the direction that the search boss thinks is most likely. The middle man is a compass bearer. His objective is to keep the other two people on course. The searchers to his left and right make a zigzag pattern working off the compass bearer. This technique can be used with a number of independent teams, each an equal distance apart.

Wide grid search. The wide grid search method is a spin-off of the old grid method, in which, for instance, 15 searchers would be lined up 20 feet apart and would walk across a given area in a predetermined time. Under the newer wide grid method, the same area is divided vertically into three equal tracts, with a line of five searchers spread out horizontally across each tract. The searchers are spaced 60 feet apart, and each line of five searchers is given a third of the total area. This way, the entire tract of land is searched in one-third the amount of time.

Size of search area. The size of the search area is determined by the distance that the missing person may have traveled. Studying this aspect of rescue work helps you fully

SEARCH METHODS

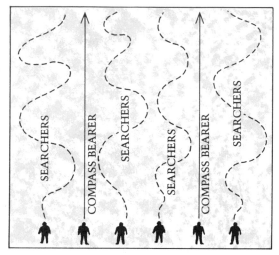
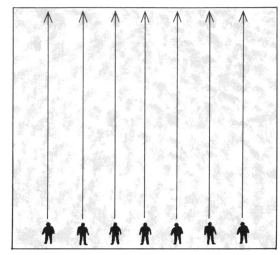

BASE LINE

Left: The three-man team search has proven to be a quick way to search a relatively large area. Here, two teams work side by side off a baseline. Compass bearers walk in a straight line to keep the team on course, while flanking searchers walk a zigzag pattern. ***Right-hand drawing:*** *This illustrates the older method of search, which involved large numbers of people walking abreast.*

15 SEARCHERS

3 HOURS

1 HOUR

This compares the old traditional grid method with the new wide-grid search method. Notice that the same area can be covered in one-third the time with the newer method.

appreciate the value of staying put when you are lost. When you consider that a person who decides to move can go in any direction and that the distance he has traveled from the last point seen becomes the radius of a circle, you can see how not "staying put" quickly enlarges the search area. The accompanying table shows how large a search area has to be and how long the search takes when a person has traveled from 1 to 10 miles. (This assumes the victim is in the last square mile searched, and that the search is conducted one square mile after the other.)

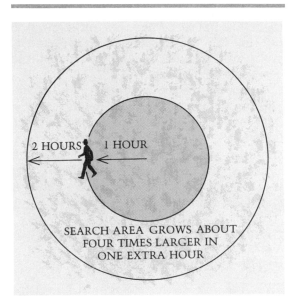

The longer a lost person travels, the greater the necessary search area becomes.

WHEN LOST PEOPLE TRAVEL

DISTANCE TRAVELED (MILES)	APPROX. SEARCH AREA (IN SQ. MI.)	ESTIMATED DAYS TO REACH LOST PERSON
1	3¹/₇	⁹/₁₀
2	12½	3½
3	28¼	8¼
4	50¼	14⅔
5	78½	23
6	113¹/₁₀	33
7	153⁹/₁₀	45
8	201¹/₁₀	59
9	254½	74
10	314¹/₆	92

For an example of just how much demand a traveling lost person could put on the searchers, let's look at a person who has covered 3 miles. This creates a maximum search area of up to 28 square miles. To cover an area this size thoroughly would take some 264 searchers searching for 12 days. Since time is of the essence in many rescue operations, you can see clearly that every step away from the point where you realized you were lost, only gets you into more trouble.

When a search is stopped. Many who are lost or stranded fear that searchers will look for only a day or two, and then give the victim up for dead. The rule that most search bosses use when looking for someone is to estimate how long he can be expected to survive, taking into account the terrain, weather, clothing, and other factors. They then multiply that period by three. For example, a hiker lost on a given mountain range during the winter might be expected to survive four days if he is very warmly dressed and has some outdoor experience. The search boss, on determining that, would keep searching for at least 12 days before seriously considering calling it off. So you can see that search efforts go far beyond even reasonable expectations.

This chapter is not designed to teach search-and-rescue techniques to the reader. There are courses available for those who are interested in acquiring these much-needed skills. The purpose here is simply to point out that should you become lost or stranded, you can be assured that positive, organized action is being taken.

Search-and-rescue operations are expensive, and many times the searchers are the ones who wind up with the serious injuries. So when going into the out-of-doors you should prepare for the unexpected and try to avoid getting into a survival situation. And if you do become lost or stranded, stay put and wait to be found.

Water Search and Rescue in the United States

Today, search-and-rescue activities account for almost 25 percent of the U.S. Coast Guard's operating hours. Distress calls come in at the rate of about 70,000 each year. Of these, 35 percent involve situations where lives and property are in moderate to severe jeopardy. Almost 85 percent of the total distress calls stem from recreational boaters.

The grizzled surfmen who manned the first lifeboat stations could not possibly have foreseen the extent of today's search-and-rescue operations. Instead of setting out in an open wooden-hulled pulling boat, the Coast Guard now uses powerful diesel-engined boats adapted for their rugged mission. These coastal SAR boats handle an average of 77 percent of the emergency calls each year.

Offshore ocean search and rescue is handled by larger cutters, which become involved in 8 percent of all SAR incidents. Additionally, buoy tenders and icebreakers are always ready to divert from their primary missions to perform search-and-rescue duties as they arise. Ship/helicopter cooperation on any mission adds a valuable dimension to overall mission effectiveness.

Aircraft are involved in about 15 percent

This is a typical Coast Guard cutter on patrol. It is capable of responding to distress calls in all weather. (U.S. Coast Guard photo)

of all responses to distress calls. Coast Guard aircraft contribute over 25,000 flight hours annually to search-and-rescue missions. These include prop planes, as well as jets and helicopters.

These diverse resources are connected by a sophisticated communications network. Landline telephone and teletype, radio telephone and teletype, and CW (Morse code) capabilities link all Coast Guard facilities. Coast Guard units also monitor all distress frequencies continuously.

A Rescue Coordination Center (RCC), located in each Coast Guard District Office, performs command and control functions for all SAR activities. They match the SAR resources with requirements for a specific distress call and monitor progress of on-scene units. The RCC also maintains liaison with other agencies, such as the National Weather Service, Federal Aviation Administration, and Department of Defense organizations, whose assistance may be useful in a search-and-rescue incident.

This search-and-rescue system handles a wide array of emergency situations. A mariner may simply be lost, or he may have a sick or injured person aboard. He may have run out of fuel or experienced a mechanical failure. He may be overdue at his destination or be aground on a shoal. His boat may even have collided with another, or it may be on fire.

The Coast Guard responds with an "Un-certainty Phase" when doubt exists as to the safety of a vessel. An "Alert Phase" is implemented when there is definite information that trouble is present, or if the doubt and lack of information persists from the previous phase. A "Distress Phase" begins when immediate assistance is required or if the Alert Phase problems have not been cleared up. Response at these phases may include communications checks, searches of marinas and airports for the boats or aircraft concerned, and/or the dispatch of search units.

The searches themselves are planned using methods based on experience and statistics. The search area center (datum) is fixed by considering factors such as wind, cur-

This boating accident at sea resulted in a rescue operation by one of the Coast Guard's highly trained aerial rescue teams. The victims in this photo have been using their overturned boat as a lifesaving device while awaiting rescue. Note that none of the victims is wearing a life jacket. They are lucky to be alive. (U.S. Coast Guard photo)

rents, tides, and accuracy of the reported incident position. The actual search method takes into account visibility, wave height, time of day, the object being searched for, resources available, and the type of incident and position information.

For example, if a vessel has disappeared somewhere en route to its destination, a "trackline search" along its intended path or a "creeping line search" across and along its path would be appropriate. If an incident position is reasonably well fixed, then an "expanding square search," based on that position, is used. A "sector search" that traces the shape of the blades of a windmill with "datum" as the hub would be an alternative to an "expanding square." These various patterns may also be adapted when more than one unit or type of unit is available to search at the same time.

Besides Coast Guard searches, SAR services include a cooperative international distress response system for open-ocean incidents. This system is the Automated Mutual Assistance Vessel Rescue System (AMVER), which is a computer-based system which annually tracks over 130,000 voyages for more 6,000 ocean-going ships.

The intricacies of AMVER and search planning are part of the curriculum at the National Search and Rescue School maintained jointly by the Coast Guard and the Air Force on Governors Island in New York Harbor. This school has trained thousands of students from over 35 nations.

The SAR School has also trained many members of the Coast Guard Auxiliary. Made up of 46,000 volunteers, the Auxiliary does participate in SAR missions, in addition to conducting various boating safety programs. About 1,000 lives are saved each year by Auxiliary SAR units, whose members volunteer their time, boats, and communications equipment to aid boaters in distress.

The Civil Air Patrol

The Civil Air Patrol Emergency Services Program cooperates with local civil officials and rescue organizations in search-and-rescue operations. It has a mutual support relationship with the American National Red Cross, the Salvation Army, and other humanitarian organizations in conducting disaster relief operations. During a recent year, CAP participated in 1,175 search missions, flew 14,424 hours, and was credited with locating 649 search objectives and actually saving 115 lives.

The CAP also assists search planners in locating lost aircraft by recalling computer-generated records of radar signals. The retrieval of stored radar data at the Air Route Traffic Control Centers (ARTCC) makes it possible, in many cases, to pinpoint or estimate the aircraft's last location and possible condition prior to dropping off radar. The CAP mission coordinator routinely requests and uses this important data in his search planning.

Of course the CAP does get directly involved in rescue operations. The following story is a good example of just how important CAP air search-and-rescue activities can be in backcountry areas.

In this incident, an air taxi pilot arrived for a scheduled pickup at a hunting camp in a remote area of Alaska. But he couldn't find the hunter and the campsite appeared to have been uninhabited for several days. He then reported the hunter as missing and an air search, using two Alaska CAP aircraft, began. But when they finally spotted the lost hunter, the rough terrain made it impossible for them to land. So they radioed the 71st Aerospace Rescue and Recovery Service. A helicopter was sent out and finally picked up the hunter, who had spent five days without food or shelter.

Search and Rescue in Canada

In a country as large and sparsely populated as Canada, locating and rescuing people in remote areas is not easy. Canada's National Search and Rescue (SAR) Organization handles more than 9,000 incidents a year. Headquarters for searches are four Rescue Coordination Centres located across Canada. RCCs coordinate movements of search aircraft of the Canadian Armed Forces, vessels from Transport Canada's Coast Guard, federal fisheries patrol ships, and others (including private aircraft and boats).

Rescue coordination centres (Canada). RCCs are strategically located at Halifax, Nova Scotia; Trenton, Ontario; Edmonton, Alberta; and Victoria, British Columbia. These centers are staffed around the clock by Canadian Armed Forces and Coast Guard Rescue Controllers, who initiate and coordinate search-and-rescue operations.

The Canadian Coast Guard also operates two Search and Rescue Emergency Centres (SARECs), which function like RCCs. Located at Quebec City and at St. John's, Newfoundland, these centers operate in close cooperation with the RCCs and provide a fast response to local emergency situations.

Canada has specially equipped SAR air squadrons, composed of helicopters and fixed-wing search aircraft, which are on call 24 hours a day. These aircraft provide a rapid response to incidents and can search a large area if the location of the distress call is not known immediately. They can also drop emergency supplies and trained rescuers in response to an SOS from an aircraft or ship.

While searches for missing aircraft traditionally have been conducted by Canadian military aircraft and crews, in recent years civilian fliers have demonstrated a greater willingness to help the military carry out this responsibility. Volunteer units in various locales already have made a significant contribution to SAR. Transport Canada's telecommunications and air-traffic-control units also help in the search for lost aircraft. All flight plans are monitored, and whenever a plane is reported overdue the RCC is notified. In addition, airports and aircraft along the flight path are alerted to watch for overdue aircraft.

On the marine side, Transport Canada's Coast Guard fleet provides full-time SAR marine craft of different sizes and types at numerous locations in Canada. Many of these vessels, including offshore and inshore cutters, launches, lifeboats, and even hovercraft, are assigned solely to search-and-rescue work. All other Coast Guard vessels have a secondary search-and-rescue role. A Canadian Marine Rescue Auxiliary of volunteers has also been organized by the Canadian Coast Guard.

In addition to the SAR resources mentioned above, any of the more than 500 Canadian government vessels and approximately 350 government-owned aircraft may be directed to take part in search-and-rescue operations should the need arise.

Search-and-rescue services are also provided through provincial emergency programs, volunteer organizations, municipal and other local programs, and police forces.

Many emergency search-and-rescue missions in Canada are carried out by the Royal Canadian Mounted Police. Their role in ground rescue is vital, especially in some of the more remote parts of Canada. Anyone venturing into the Canadian wilderness would do well to notify the local RCMP office.

As you can see, both the United States and Canadian agencies are ready for most emergencies. I hope this book will help to make all of you readers ready too.

4

SURVIVAL KITS AND ACCESSORIES

A survival kit offers excellent insurance for anyone who travels, regardless of whether the mode of transportation is skis, snowshoes, aircraft, boat, canoe, snowmobile, four-wheel-drive vehicle, automobile, horseback, or foot.

Having a survival kit is only part of the solution, however. One must know how to use the items in the survival kit in order to survive. I know of an avid canoeist who carried a little survival kit with him on every trip for years. Then on a wilderness trip he lost his canoe and gear in a set of rapids, and he almost died because he panicked and didn't know how to use the contents of his survival kit. Learn how to use your survival kit!

Regardless of what type of survival kit you decide you need and whether you buy a commercial kit or put together your own, the kit must provide the basics, which are medical aid, shelter, warmth, signals, water, and food.

If you are short any of the items to meet these needs, then you don't have an adequate survival kit.

The items in your survival kit should enable you to do the following things:
- Carry out basic first aid
- Build a fire using two different techniques
- Construct a shelter
- Signal for help both visually and by sound
- Gather food and purify water for drinking

In some cases you may want to add navigation aids, such as a compass, to your kit. Also, if you take medication or wear glasses,

---

Though most survival kits carry some of the same basic ingredients, even the best ones may need to be altered or supplemented to anticipate special requirements of terrain and season.

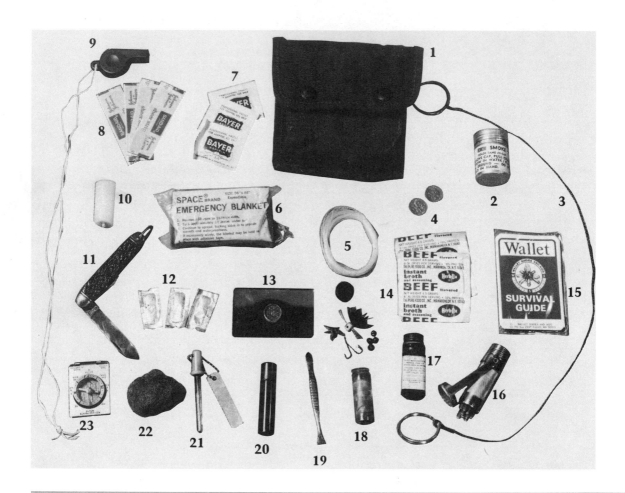

you may want to take extras in your kit.

It is always a good idea to check your survival kit often to make sure your items are all there and in good shape. Some items, such as matches and bandages, must be replaced periodically. Also make sure the kit has a pocket survival manual.

Be sure to keep your survival kit compact and easy to pack or carry. Large survival kits have a way of being left behind. A small, compact kit is easy to carry with you.

The following pages contain some sugges-tions for survival kits for various means of travel. Study the kits carefully, then tailor your kit for your specific needs and the re-gions in which you travel. Use your imagi-nation when you put your survival kit together, remembering you want to be pre-pared for the worst.

Individual Survival Kit

Almost all seasoned backcountry travelers carry a small survival kit with them at all

My individual survival kit is lightweight and takes up little room on the belt. It is homemade and includes the following:

1. A kit bag. This is an Army surplus individual first aid pouch. It is sturdy, fits the belt easily, and when full weighs only about 2 pounds. Its small size also allows you to fit it into a daypack, backpack, vehicle glove box, or tackle box.

2. A blaze-orange smoke signal from Sigma Scientific, Inc. This is an excellent daytime signal device to use in conjunction with ground-to-air signals.

3. A wire saw, which coils up to store easily. It can be used to cut poles for shelter and wood for fires, or for helping quarter large game.

4. Coins. Many survival stories are told of hunters who made it to a parkway or a closed lodge with a pay phone and had no change for a call. Carry enough change for a call or two.

5. A coil of 20-pound-test fishing line. This can be used for shelter-making, mending clothes, and making snares, as well as for fishing.

6. Space emergency blanket. It is the size of a pack of cigarettes, but can be made into a lean-to or used as a blanket reflecting up to 90 percent of your body heat.

7. Aspirin to ease pain and reduce inflammation (Note: Many doctors recommend other pain-killers as safer for youngsters.)

8. Adhesive bandages.

9. Police whistle for signaling.

10. A candle stub for fire starting.

11. A Scout-type pocketknife.

12. Antiseptic for scratches and wounds.

13. A signal mirror. It can be spotted for miles by search planes and forest fire towers.

14. Beef broth. This has some food value and makes wild-food dishes taste much better.

15. The Wallet Survival Guide, to serve as a survival manual.

16. Waterproof matches.

17. Water purification tablets.

18. A small tackle bottle. One can be made from a plastic bottle with several feet of 6-pound-test fishing line wound around it. Hold in place with tape. Place in the bottle several small Tru-Turn fishhooks, split shot, a small bluegill popping bug, and a small dry fly. Think small, as it is usually easier to catch small fish. (The food requirement during survival situations is less than most people think.)

19. Tweezers for removing splinters, etc.

20. Lip balm for protection from wind or sun.

21. Magnesium fire starter which can be used as a backup fire starter.

22. Size 000 steel wool. This is good to use with the magnesium fire starter to get tinder started. One spark in the loose steel wool produces a hot glow that will start dry tinder. Steel wool works even when wet.

23. A backup compass. You should carry another compass on your person.

24. Aluminum foil (not shown) for melting snow for water and cooking.

times. Since the early 1970s, I have been carrying one shown in the accompanying photo. I have used it often. This small kit is easy to carry when hunting, fishing, hiking, skiing, etc. Not only is it my survival kit, but it also serves as a readily available first-aid kit. In it are the items necessary for signaling, shelter, fire-making, navigation, and first aid.

Instead of assembling a kit, you can buy one. In addition to the commmercial kits shown on page 56, others are available from sources listed in Appendix 3. There is a wide assortment of individual survival kits from Brigade Quartermasters, Ltd.

Snowmobile Survival Kit

One of the more experienced snowmobile survival authorities is Jim Elder of Jackson, Wyoming. According to Jim, early snowmobiles offered great winter travel range, but were not exactly reliable. Adventurers often

COMMERCIAL SURVIVAL KITS

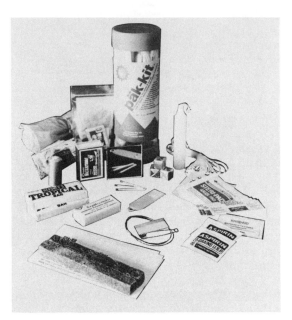

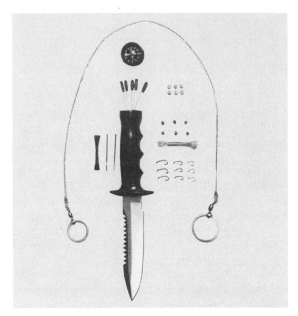

Above left: *The Pak-Kit contains 24 essentials for shelter, signaling, fire, first aid, and food.* **Above right:** *The Lifeknife has a survival kit in the handle. The handle cap is a compass. In the handle are fishhooks, a wire saw, nylon line, snare wire, needles, and matches. The sheath, not shown, has a sharpening stone.* **Right:** *Known as the Lifekit, the aluminum container has stainless-steel closing fasteners, making the kit airtight and watertight. It even floats. The container can be used to cook in and carry water, and as a signal mirror. The kit contains a compass, a wire saw, British Lifeboat matches, a fishing kit with cam-action survival hooks, camouflage snare/utility wire, needles, water purification tablets, bouillon, an energy bar, tea, tape, suture, condom/tourniquet, Band-Aids, aspirin, and a razorlike blade. It can be sealed and resealed as you desire, so you can add other items. (From Lifeknife, Inc.)*

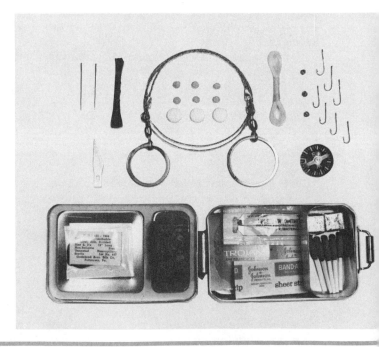

HOW TO USE A WIRE SAW

The wire saw is excellent for cutting fuel wood and butchering. While it may be used with the fingers through the saw rings, it is much easier to saw with either handles or a bow saw rig. The bow saw is made by cutting a green stick approximately 1½ times the length of the saw, notching each end of the stick, and attaching the saw rings to the notches. This causes the stick to bow and so tensions the wire.

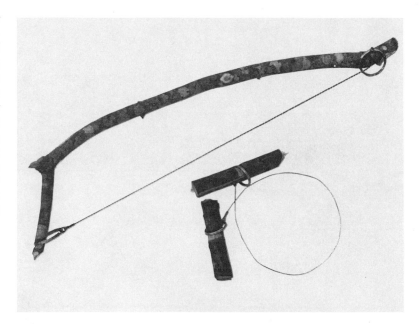

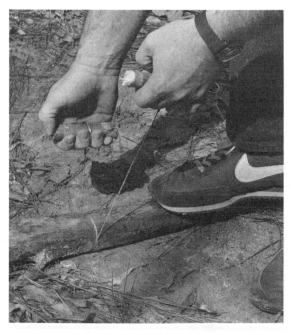

The snowmobile survival kit should include snowshoes, rope, shovel, extra fuel, first aid kit, emergency food, space blanket, cup, fire starter kit, signal kit, wire saw, extra gloves, facemask, wool socks, goggles, spare parts and tool kit, map and compass, and backpack stove. (Jim Elder photo)

carried half a parts department for extended winter travel. The North Pole Expedition in 1968 proved that snowmobile design had matured—that with proper maintenance, the machines were capable of long-distance running in the most hostile conditions.

Since 1968, snowmobile technology has continued to become more sophisticated. If we compared the first snowmobiles to automobiles of the 1920s, the North Pole Ski-Doos would rate with vehicles of the late '40s, and current models with state-of-the-art high-tech cars, motorcycles, and airplanes. Drive belts and spark plugs last at least a season, tracks and skis a decade. Liquid cooling and oil injection, along with CD ignition, have made the modern snowmobile as reliable as any new automobile. Therefore,

the snowmobile is more often found as rescuer than rescuee.

Search-and-rescue groups, Nordic Ski Patrols, state and federal conservation personnel, snowmobile clubs—many organizations and individuals participate in winter survival operations using snowmobiles.

Suggested equipment for "snowmobile survival" therefore must be considered from two angles: first, the items any prudent snowmobiler would carry at all times (even Rolls-Royce owners still carry spare tires and a jack), and second, the extra equipment a snowmobile rescue party might pack.

Most manufacturers supply a tool kit including the basic wrenches, an emergency starter rope, and a screwdriver. Owners should add a spare drive belt and extra spark

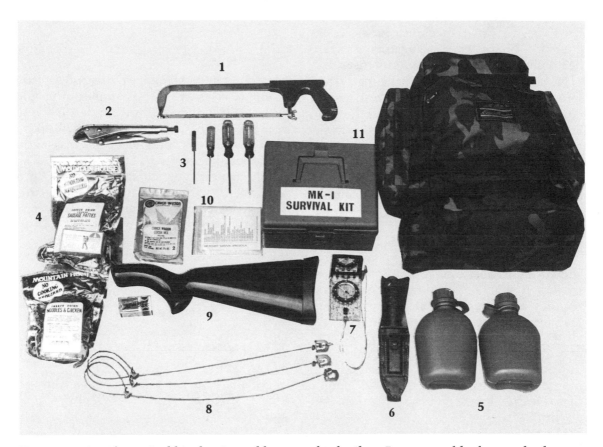

Here is an aircraft survival kit that is used by many bush pilots. Extra space blankets and tube tents should be taken to assure each person has one of each. (Chris Fears photo)

1. *Hacksaw with metal blade and wood blade.* **2.** *Plier, vise-grip.* **3.** *Screwdriver set.* **4.** *Survival food.* **5.** *Canteens of water, two per person.* **6.** *U.S. Air Force fixed-blade survival knife.* **7.** *Compass.* **8.** *Thompson snares.* **9.** *Charter Arms Explorer rifle with box of ammunition.* **10.** Hip Pocket Survival Handbook *by the American Outdoor Safety League.* **11.** *Sigma Scientific MK-1 survival kit, which contains: 12¾-inch plastic bandage strips, 1 roll (2½ yards) ½-inch adhesive tape, 6 antiseptic swabs, 2 tubes burn ointment, 12 aspirin (2 to a package), 2 2 × 2-inch gauze pads, 2 3 × 3-inch gauze pads, 1 roll (6 yards) 1-inch gauze bandage, 1 single-edge razor blade, 6 safety pins, 4 food sticks, 4 coffee packets, 4 soup packets, 1 candy, 4 sugar packets, 2 salt packets, 1 spoon, 1 can water, 1 flashlight, 1 sunscreen cream, 1 whistle, 2 Fusee Signals/fire starters, 3 Skyblazer Aerial Flares 20R, 1 emergency blanket, 1 package tissues, 1 first aid cream, 1 Sting-eze, 1 DM-1 dye marker, 50 water purification tablets, 1 GS-1 ground smoke signal, 1 KFS-1 fire starter kit, 1 MS-23 signal mirror, 1 pair sunglasses, 1 tent, 1 SW-1 Super Saw, 1 PM-48 panel marker.*

plugs. A small pair of locking pliers and a combination-tip screwdriver add to the ability to repair other machines in the backcountry. Night travel suggests a spare headlight bulb and any necessary fuses.

Next are personal items, including a flashlight with extra batteries and bulb, maps and compass, lighter or waterproof matches, and spare sunglasses, prescription if necessary. A good knife, of course, should also be included.

If longer trips are planned, a few clothing and protection items could ensure comfort even if a face shield should be broken, felt liners get wet, a glove lost. Add a face mask, goggles, warm mittens, and wool socks.

Rescue operations require more gear—shovel, snowshoes, tow rope, most likely extra fuel, first aid kit, emergency food, a space blanket, cup, fire starter and more matches, perhaps a signal mirror and flare gun or a strobe flasher, a whistle, an avalanche cord and an avalanche transceiver that can transmit and receive signals, a wire saw, rivets, monofilament line with fishhooks and/or flies, electrical wire and crimp fittings, and a "flint" kit.

Most of the newer machines are so streamlined that cargo capacity is limited. Tools and personal items will fit in the underhood toolbox, but extra gear requires a rack, saddlebags, or one of the cycle-type tank bags. The exception to this trend is the new Skandic Ski-Doo, already becoming a favorite of ski patrol and rescue groups. With its extended track for soft-snow performance, integral cargo rack, and strong hitch system, it combines the handling of sport machines, the comfort of trail sleds, and cargo/tow capabilities approaching the traditional double-track workhorse Alpine.

Suitable snowmobiles (extended track, good snow flotation, strong hitches) can be used to tow rescue toboggans and cargo sleds.

A good commercial snowmobile survival kit is the KS-1 Snow Survival Kit sold by Sigma Scientific, Inc. (See Appendix 3.)

Aircraft Survival Kit

Every aircraft should have a survival kit that is capable of serving the number of people who will be on board. If the aircraft is flying over arid regions, extra water should be taken, and if it is flying over wilderness areas, extra food should be packed.

All survival gear should be stowed in a pack such as the Eddie Bauer Guide Pack. This keeps all survival gear together, it is easy to remove quickly from the aircraft in the event of fire, and if travel is necessary the pack makes carrying the gear much easier.

Truck or Auto Survival Kit

Due to a greater carrying capacity in trucks and autos, the following is recommended to be carried in them as a survival kit:

  1. MK-1 Survival Kit (available through Sigma Scientific, Inc. and camping supply stores)
  2. GE "HELP" model CB radio
  3. Coleman Inflate-All 150 Portable Air Compressor
  4. 1 gallon of water (more if traveling in the desert)
  5. Small tools and replacement parts, i.e., fan belts
  6. Small shovel
  7. Tow cable
  8. Tire chains
  9. Come-along
  10. Jumper cables
  11. Rainsuit
  12. Blankets or sleeping bags for cold weather
  13. Extra food
  14. Hatchet or ax
  15. Boy Scout type pocketknife

Auto survival kits might include: MK-1 Survival Kit, air compressor, water, jumper cables, ax, portable CB radio, emergency food, folding survival knife, survival handbook, shovel, come-along, tool kit, tow rope, rainsuit, space blankets, and tire chains (in ammo box).

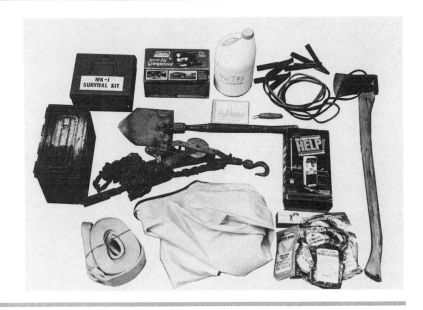

16. Hip Pocket Survival Handbook by American Outdoor Safety League.

Boat Survival Kit

For a large boat, the MK-1 Survival Kit may be used. For a smaller boat, the Pak-Kit Survival Kit is a good selection. It contains:

1. Tube tent (8-foot)
2. Signal mirror
3. High-pitched whistle
4. Basic first aid kit, including adhesive bandages
5. Gauze pads, butterflies, and aspirin
6. Emergency notes on first aid, fire building, weather, shelter, travel, windchill, and hypothermia
7. Candle flaresticks (2)
8. Waterproof matches (50)
9. Nylon cord (20 feet)
10. Safety pin, razor blade
11. Aluminum foil, wire (2 feet)
12. Duct tape (3 feet)

13. High-impact waterproof container of dextrose cubes
14. Energy bars (2)
15. Bouillon cubes
16. Celestial Seasonings herb tea bags (3).

There are many other types of survival kits you can make for your use. The commercial survival kits are worth consideration because, for what's in them, they are economical. Also, they usually come in a better container than what I use for my homemade survival kits. Survival kits are an individual choice, so take the time to design one to fit your needs and test it.

A daypack containing survival items is good to carry hunting, cross-country skiing, snowshoeing, or hiking.

While there are many different types of survival kits that can be bought or constructed, remember that survival kits alone won't save your life—knowing how to use them will. Start now getting ready to get lost or stranded. Learn the skills to live with your

In addition to a compact survival kit, a big-water survival kit should also contain the following: **1.** *1 gallon water per person.* **2.** *Extra food.* **3.** *U. S. Air Force folding survival knife.* **4.** *Signal kit as required by Coast Guard.* **5.** *Life jacket or other flotation device for each person.* **6.** *Rain gear.* **7.** *Tools and spare parts.* **8.** *Bailing bucket.* **9.** *Spare motor or paddles* **10.** *Change of clothing in waterproof bag.* **11.** *Blankets or sleeping bags.* **12.** *Fishing hooks, line, artificial bait, sinkers, pack rod and reel.*

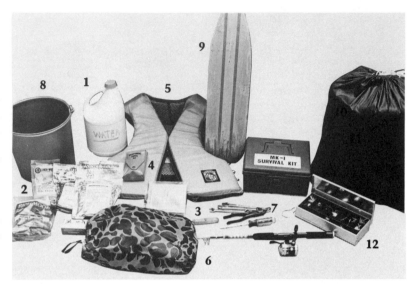

own survival kit. Try living in the woods a few days with it. Then you will know if it has in it what you personally need.

Survival Guns

A common question asked of survival instructors is what the best gun or knife is for use in a survival situation. "The one you have at the time" is probably the best answer to that, as any gun or knife can be used for survival purposes, but some do work better than others.

The purpose of a survival gun, contrary to some people's thinking, is primarily to collect food, not to kill your neighbor because he is after your food. Occasionally there are exceptions, such as defense against a bear that's mad with the world or against looters who think that a natural disaster is another government giveaway program. But these cases are not the most practical reasons for your having a survival gun.

Provided wild animals inhabit the area you are in, the procurement of food in a survival situation is much easier if you have a gun and have been trained in firearms safety for hunting. To have a gun and not be trained is both ineffective and dangerous, so make training a high priority when you get your survival gun.

When selecting a survival gun, keep these facts in mind:

1. Shotguns firing shotshells are most effective on small animals up to the size of a fox. With buckshot or slugs, deer-sized animals may be taken.

2. Centerfire rifles are generally better for big animals, as they destroy much of a small animal.

3. Centerfire pistols firing shotshells can take small game at close range. Firing bullets, they can take larger animals if the shooter is skillful.

4. Rifles and pistols in .22 caliber can take small animals if you place your shots well.

Here are some factors to consider in selecting a survival gun: Will it break down small enough to fit into your daypack, plane, snowmobile, or car? If used on a boat, is it available in stainless steel? Is the ammunition easy to obtain and does it take up much space? Remember, gun laws vary and you should get a gun you can carry with you. For instance, you can't carry a handgun into Canada. Think through your potential uses carefully before you buy a survival gun. Take your time in making the decision, and once you make it, learn to use the gun properly and safely.

Here are some examples of survival guns which have been used by survival experts. There are many more choices, but this will give you a few to consider.

Charter Arms AR-7 Explorer. This 2½-pound version of the famous U.S. Air Force survival rifle features a new carefree anticorrosion finish. It was designed for the serious outdoorsman who wants the security of an accurate semiautomatic .22 LR without the weight and bulk of a full-size rifle. For backpackers, boaters, campers, or bush pilots, it's a cinch to carry or store. It breaks down

For situations that call for inclusion of a survival gun in your outdoor equipment, this lightweight Charter Arms AR–7 Explorer is a good one. It even floats if dropped overboard. And it breaks down into four parts (as shown), with the barrel, action, and clip fitting inside the hollow plastic stock for transport.

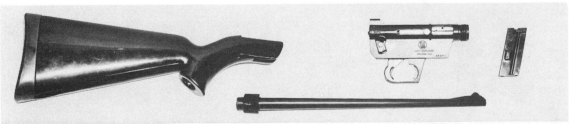

quickly and easily into five separate elements. The barrel, action, and magazine stow away neatly into a waterproof stock.

Disassembled, the AR-7 is only 16½ inches long. Overall assembled length is 34½ inches. Assembly is just as easy as breakdown—simply attach the barrel and action to the stock, feed the clip, and fire. It uses standard or high-velocity .22 LR rounds.

Not only is it waterproof, but it also floats, either stowed or assembled. With the new anticorrosion finish, the AR-7 is especially ideal for boaters. Regular black textured enamel finish is available on the standard model AR-7 Explorer.

Savage Model 24-V. I use this over-and-under gun in a .30/30 caliber rifle barrel over a 20-gauge shotgun barrel. It will take big or small animals. The gun is lightweight and is reasonably short, making it easy to put into an auto trunk or the storage compartment of a plane. It is a high-quality gun and with care should last a lifetime. This same gun is available in several calibers and gauges, depending upon your needs.

Charter Arms Undercover. The stainless-steel .38 undercover with 2-inch barrel is not a survival gun for everyone, but if you are a well-trained pistol shot, it makes an excel-

The Savage Model 24–V over-under is a combination rifle and shotgun. It is capable of taking a variety of big and small game by firing either a .30/30 rifle cartridge or 20-gauge shotshell.

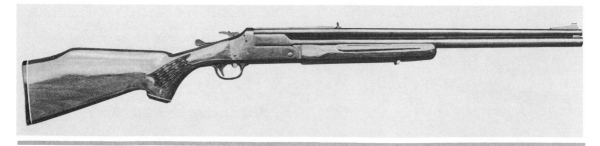

For better grip in all weather, I added Pachmayr rubber grips to this .38 Charter Arms Undercover. For small game, this gun also shoots shotshells.

lent gun to go into the backpack, tackle box, toolbox, or daypack. I have used one for several years in all types of weather and found it to be an excellent handgun. I took off the wooden grips that came on the gun and replaced them with Pachmayr rubber grips for greater holding ability in all types of weather. This little pistol is lightweight at 16 ounces. When shotshells or regular bullets are used it can take small animals at close range. Since it is a short-barreled handgun, you'll need to practice in order to use it effectively.

An excellent all-weather Cordura holster for this handgun is available from Michaels of Oregon. (See Appendix 3.)

Thompson/Center Contender. This is a single-shot survival handgun that I have used extensively for the past few years and found

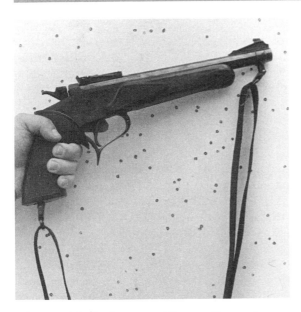

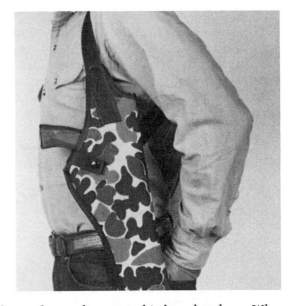

This modified Thompson/Center Contender may be used as a shotgun or big-bore handgun. When used as a shotgun, the Contender is excellent for taking small game. The shoulder holster for the Contender is by Michaels of Oregon.

to be excellent for both small and large animals, provided you have some experience shooting handguns. In order to come up with my survival version of this handgun, I took a Thompson/Center Contender with a 10-inch barrel with choke, in a .45 Colt caliber, and did the following:

1. I replaced the wooden grip with a Pachmayr rubber grip. This improved accuracy and helped make the gun an all-weather gun that could stand some abuse.

2. I replaced the wooden forend with a Pachmayr rubber forend for protection against elements and getting banged around.

3. I had the chamber extended, by a gunsmith, to accept the 3-inch .410 shotgun shell. The pistol will still fire .45 Colt regular ammunition *with the choke out*. This is very important. If the choke is left in place when regular ammunition is fired, it could do damage to the gun and shooter. It will also shoot .45 Colt shotshells or .410 shotgun shotshells with the choke in.

4. I then added a Michaels of Oregon Super 14 swivel sling set on the pistol for easy carrying. Because of the large size of the .45 Colt bull barrel, I had to use a front barrel band from the QD11 SGW-20 swivel set. A shoulder holster is also available from Michaels of Oregon.

With these changes, I now have a long-barreled pistol that is easy to carry slung over my shoulder, will take any kind of weather, and can kill big or small animals including birds on the wing. It is also still small enough to fit into a pack easily. This is one of the most versatile survival guns I've used to date.

Survival Knives

When I studied at the U.S. Air Force Survival School in preparation for this book, I asked a number of survival instructors what they considered the single most important survival tool, and without exception, they all chose the knife. I somewhat agree, but it never ceases to amaze me how little most outdoorsmen know about selecting a knife for survival purposes. Over the years I have seen survival students trying to clean a squirrel with a 10-inch Army surplus combat knife, cut firewood with a small pocketknife, or clean a fish with a commando dagger made from such cheap metal that it would never hold an edge.

Selecting the right survival knife is an easy task if you will just stick to a few basics.

First, we want a knife that's made from a high-carbon or stainless steel that's been hardened and tempered for a long-lasting edge. Since most of us aren't metallurgists, we have to take the manufacturer's word or get advice from a friend who has been using a like knife. Thus the reason for buying from well-known, reputable manufacturers whose advertising you can believe and who will guarantee their knives. Names like Benchmark, Schrade, Kershaw, Western, Camillus, Gutmann, Buck, Victorinox, Crosman, Precise, Gerber, and Chicago Cutlery, to name a few, won't let you down.

The second thing we look for in a survival knife is quality construction. Nobody wants a knife whose handles fall off the first time he cuts a tent peg. Again, this can be eliminated by staying with the well-known brand names.

The third factor to consider is size. At one time a lot of outdoorsmen who had seen too many western movies carried 3-pound, 12-inch Bowie knives. If you are going to defend the Alamo, that's all right, but for survival, forget it. Many deer have been field-dressed with a 3-inch blade. For survival purposes, don't go over a 5-inch blade, and in many cases, a much shorter blade will do. Most animal cleaning work is done with the 2 inches of the blade nearest the point. The

BLADE DESIGNS

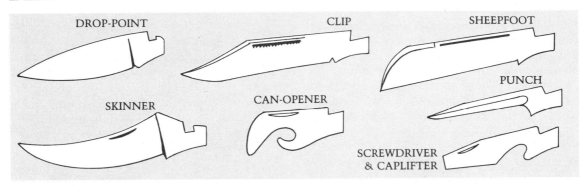

rest of the blade is used only for camp chores, etc. Therefore, a long blade is unnecessary.

The fourth factor to consider is one that causes knife buffs to call one another nasty names: What blade design is best for survival? I think this is a matter of personal preference. The so-called survival knife with a dagger blade is for military use, not simple survival. Many hunters prefer the drop-point blade, while others prefer the clip blade. Some trappers prefer the skinning blade and others prefer the sheepfoot. Whatever blade design you choose, take your time and think about what you want the knife to do. Experience will be your best guide to blade design.

The last factor is which type knife you want to carry—a fixed-blade knife, commonly called a belt knife, or a folding knife. There are arguments for each. The fixed-blade knife is stronger because it has no moving parts. However, the folding knife takes up less room and is easier to wear on the belt when getting in and out of vehicles. Also, wearing a fixed-blade knife on your belt in public may attract attention.

Both designs are good, and again, it is more your preference than anything else. If you do choose a folding knife for survival, you should

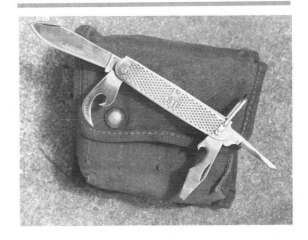

The U.S. Military Folding Survival Knife is made by Camillus. It is the standard Boy Scout pocketknife blade configuration: a cutting blade, screwdriver/bottle opener blade, leather-punch blade, and a can opener. The entire knife, including the handle, is made from stainless steel. This knife is favored by many of the Air Force survival instructors.

get one with a lock blade. I carry a scar from a nonlocking folder that folded when I had my hands inside a deer, cutting.

MORE SURVIVAL KNIVES

The **U.S. Air Force fixed-blade survival knife** (top) is available from Atlanta Cutlery Co. or Camillus. It is made from carbon steel with a 5-inch clip-style blade, with sharp sawtooth top edge. The grooved leather handle is large enough for hard work. The leather sheath includes a sharpening stone. The **SOS Knife** (middle) made by Benchmark Knives, is compact and stainless steel. The blade cover flips back to become part of the handle. The SOS has four common-size hex holes in the handle. This lightweight knife can serve for all-around camping, hunting, and survival use. **Swiss Army Knives** (bottom): These well-known knives, made by Precise and Victorinox, come with a variety of blades, depending upon your anticipated needs. Be sure not to get too many blades, as such a knife will be too large for practical survival purposes or packing. And beware of cheap imitations. The **Argonaut** (top of page 69) made by BenchMark Knives, is an excellent all-around knife with a 4-inch stainless-steel blade. This knife is built for rugged service be-

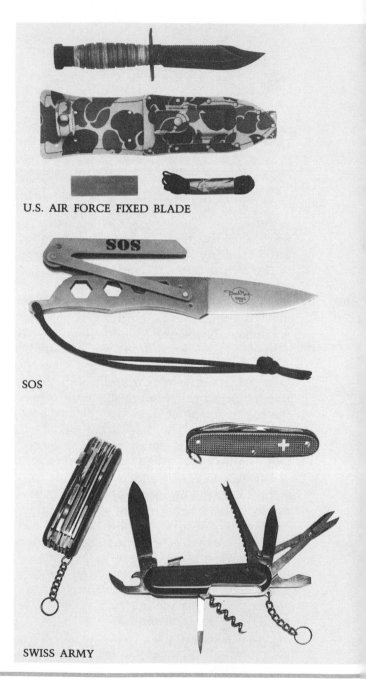

U.S. AIR FORCE FIXED BLADE

SOS

SWISS ARMY

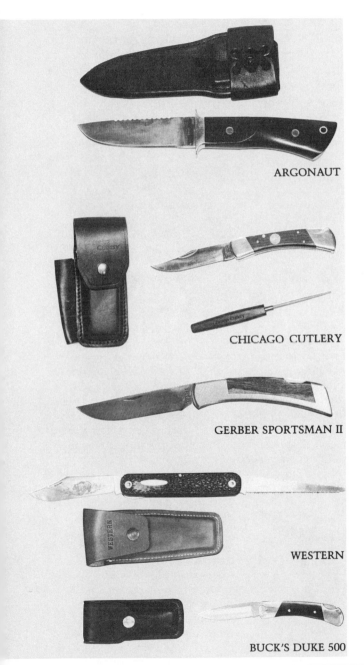

ARGONAUT

CHICAGO CUTLERY

GERBER SPORTSMAN II

WESTERN

BUCK'S DUKE 500

neath the sea as well as above. The experienced skin-diver will appreciate Argonaut's diver's sheath. Argonaut's unique serrated blade makes it equally useful to climbers, backpackers, or any wilderness trekker. The **Chicago Cutlery 5-inch Lock-Back** (second from top) is a high-quality folding knife with a 5-inch locking blade with a break-through point tip and walnut handles. It does most survival chores well and comes with a leather sheath with attached sharpening steel. The **Gerber Folding Sportsman II** (third from top) is an all-purpose survival knife of excellent quality. Its 3½-inch stainless-steel blade locks open. The **Western Knife Saw** is a favorite of many experienced survival instructors. One blade is a 5-inch spring-temper sawblade and the other is a tough 4½-inch knife blade. The knife blade locks open, and the knife comes with the leather sheath as shown. **Buck's Duke 500** (bottom) has a high-quality 3½-inch folding blade of high-carbon steel. It has a drop point for skinning and fits compactly into the survival kit.

There are dozens of knives that could be discussed as survival knives, and quite frankly, there will be situations when one knife cannot do all the chores it is needed to do. What you have to do is to select the knife that best suits your needs in the backcountry setting you go into and learn to use it for as many chores as possible. If you face a chore that it doesn't quite measure up to, keep your cool and improvise.

Sharpening device. No one should go into the backcountry with a dull knife, and if possible, everyone should take along something to sharpen the knife as needed.

After several years of searching for the perfect sharpening device, I have settled on one I like very well—a diamond whetstone. Made by Diamond Machining Technology, Inc., 85 Hayes Memorial Drive, Marlborough, MA 01752, the DMT diamond whetstone will

While not a knife, this Skachet cutting tool has been a favorite of survival experts for many years. Made by Charter Arms Corporation, the Skachet's ingenious design combines all essential elements of a hunting knife, skinning knife, hatchet, and hammer for honest versatility. Compact, lightweight, and balanced, the Skachet is threaded so it screw-mounts onto a green-stick handle. Forged of high-carbon steel, the Skachet edge is so tough you can cut through a quarter-inch metal bolt. And it's an edge that stays sharp. The gutting notch is perfect for cutting through the hide and no deeper. At the end opposite the blade is a polished hammer with a 1-inch-diameter face. For wood splitting, it's safer to use the Skatchet like a wedge, rapping it with a stout log, rather than swinging like a hatchet.

The machete has long been the knife choice in jungles and swamps. It is excellent for clearing trails, cutting and splitting wood, and clearing campsites. However, you'll have trouble cleaning a squirrel or doing other small jobs with the big knife. In a swamp environment, a small knife and a machete make an excellent pair.

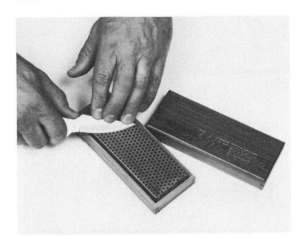 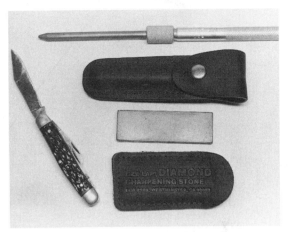

The Diamond Machining Technology whetstone, at left, yields excellent results. Another company making excellent sharpening stones is the Eze-Lap Company, which makes both high-quality diamond whetstones and sharpening steels, shown right. These are small enough to pack in the survival kit.

sharpen any survival knife with a sprinkle of tapwater and a few easy strokes. I have found that constant use will not impair these whetstones' ability to sharpen. The company states that their whetstones remain perfectly flat throughout many years of hard use.

The secret of the DMT whetstone's ability is in its unique construction. A thin layer of perforated steel is molded onto a plastic base. The metal is then covered with diamond particles that are imbedded in nickel. The flat pattern of the plastic islands on a sea of diamonds speeds the sharpening and helps to clean away the filings.

While these whetstones are more expensive than most, their quick sharpening ability and extra long lives make them a sound investment. I have a pocket-size model that I keep in my daypack for sharpening my survival knife in the field and a large bench model that I use for sharpening knives when I am at home.

5
SIGNALING TECHNIQUES

The first step toward being rescued from the backcountry or almost any other survival situation is to make rescuers see you. Assuming you have let someone know where you were going and when you expected to return, soon someone will be looking for you in the area in which you are located. Your first concern should be to let the rescue party know where you are.

Many survival books and manuals devote little space to teaching the many methods of signaling but spend numerous pages on vague information about edible plants. Signaling is a survival skill that no one should take lightly, especially since we now have excellent search aircraft that can be in the air over your area soon after you are reported missing.

To prove that signaling pays off, let's look at a few real situations where signals brought about the rescues.

In 1979 a 13-year-old skier who spent the night in a mountain snowstorm was found unharmed after a ski resort employee saw a giant SOS the youngster had stamped in the snow.

Douglas Grismore became lost skiing down the back side of a mountain. He said he panicked briefly when darkness fell Sunday, but regained his composure and spent the night walking and stamping out an SOS.

In November 1978, a lost backpacker who discovered a chapter on survival in his first aid handbook was rescued after four days in the wilderness when a search-and-rescue

The signal mirror can greatly improve your chances of being spotted.

team spotted the huge SOS he stamped out in the snow.

Arthur Reschke, 47, was airlifted by helicopter from Piute Lake in the Stanislaus National Forest. He said he was passing the time reading his handbook when he came upon the survival chapter and the SOS suggestion.

Walter Yates of Cedar Park, Texas, was flying home from Alaska in 1979 when his helicopter crashed in a thick spruce forest in British Columbia. For 14 days he survived at the crash. He was found because he used a piece of shiny metal as a signal mirror to get the attention of a search-and-rescue plane as it flew over.

In 1963, Helen Klaben and pilot Ralph Flores set a survival endurance record of 49 days when the small plane they were in crashed in the Yukon. The signals they tramped out in a snow-covered clearing finally resulted in their being found by rescuers.

Charles Sassara and a friend were flying a small plane from Anchorage to Bethel, Alaska, when they went down. It took rescuers six days to spot the two men. They were spotted because at the time of their rescue, the men had cut loose the plane's battery and lights to flash signals. Also, they had made a smudge fire of tire chips and motor oil. In addition to these two signals, they were standing in the open on a frozen lake waving. They were determined to be found.

People are found by the scores in and around North America each year, thanks to their knowing how to use signals properly. We don't know how many people perish each year because they don't know how to use signals. Knowing how to signal means knowing how to continue to live.

The most important factors about signals are that you know how to use them properly and that you have them ready for use on short

notice. It is also important that you choose an open area to do your signaling in. Many of the signals we will discuss won't be seen from the air if you sit under a canopy of tall trees to await rescue. Select an open area, if possible, to wait for your rescuers, and have your signals ready. Areas such as an old road, a field, the site of an old forest fire, a seashore, a sandbar in a river, or any other type of an opening will help you be seen early in the search. Remember to stay where you are and don't give in to the urge to travel.

Morse Code. The acronym SOS in International Morse Code means Save Our Ship, but is recognized as a distress signal on land or sea, whether transmitted audibly, as by radio or whistle, or visually, as by flashlight or signal mirror. The SOS code is . . . — — — . . . That is three shorts, three longs, and then three more shorts.

Signal Mirror

Many survival experts and search-and-rescue officials consider survival mirrors to be among the best signal devices available. They are small, many being only 2 × 3 inches, and pack easily in a survival kit or flight bag.

Survival mirrors are found in most outdoor supply stores or can be ordered from outdoor catalogs. Today, most survival mirrors are made from a tough plastic and have the instructions for use on the back of the mirror. While the instructions are easy to follow, no one should wait until he is in a survival situation before learning how to use a signal mirror or any other signal device. The signal mirror has a sight hole in its center that is used for aiming. If you haven't practiced using it and aren't ready at the time the rescue aircraft appears, the rescuers will be gone without ever seeing your signal.

Any shiny surface can make an excellent signal mirror. Left to right are a mirror from a makeup compact, a commercial signal mirror, and a tin can lid with hole punched for sighting.

To use a signal mirror follow these steps: (1) Aim the shiny side toward the sun, moon, or searchlight. (2) Locate the reflected spot by bouncing it onto a nearby object or onto your hand held out in front of you. (3) While watching through the aiming hole, slowly turn the mirror in order to swing the reflected spot toward the target. Here, if you first bounce the spot onto your hand, you can swing your hand toward the target, tracking your hand with the reflected spot until the spot hits the target.

To send a distress signal to ground observers who may be somewhere along the horizon or on a slope, sweep the horizon or slope slowly. If someone does see your signal you may see a mirror signal in return. In this case, signal back, helping rescuers home in on your location as they approach. A single mirror allows you to sweep the reflective spot throughout most of the area around you and above you but not into the blind area as shown, when the sun is at a low angle.

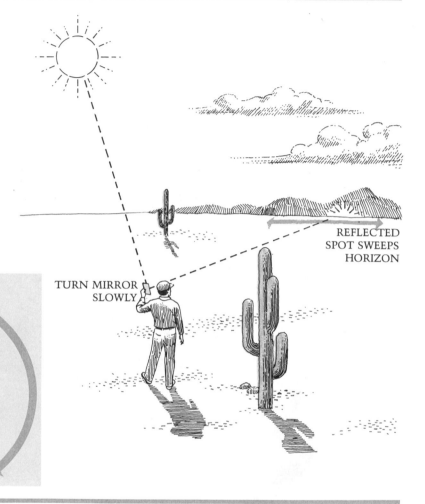

REFLECTED
SPOT SWEEPS
HORIZON

TURN MIRROR
SLOWLY

LOW SUN

ONE MIRROR

BLIND AREA

If you don't have a signal mirror, you can make one from any available shiny material, such as the top of a tin can, a car mirror, a compact mirror, a piece of aluminum foil, or a piece of aircraft. If you are using a mirror, try to scratch a peephole in its center by scraping on its back. If you are using foil or metal, punch a hole in the middle as an aiming hole.

Signal mirrors work best on bright sunny days, but they also work on hazy days, on bright moonlit nights, and when searchlights are used on boats or planes.

It amazes many people to learn that the reflection of the sun from a signal mirror can be seen for many miles. Many sources state that it can be seen from 30 to 40 miles away. Once a signal mirror was seen by aircraft over 100 miles away in the Nevada desert. Lost people have used signal mirrors to attract the attention of people in fire towers many miles away.

To send signals in a general direction away from the sun, you may need two mirrors. The right-hand drawing shows how a second mirror allows you to double-bounce the reflective spot into what would have been the blind area of a single mirror.

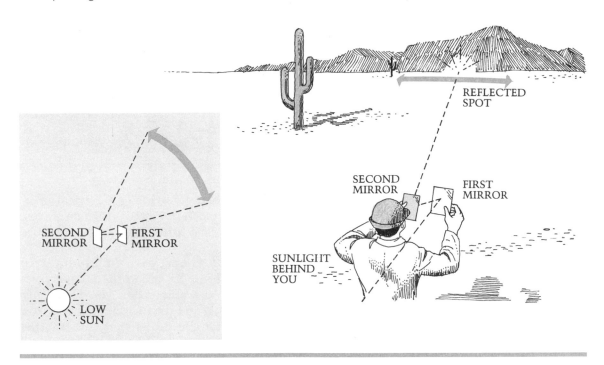

REFLECTED SPOT

SECOND MIRROR

FIRST MIRROR

SUNLIGHT BEHIND YOU

SECOND MIRROR

FIRST MIRROR

LOW SUN

Fire

One of the best-known signals, both day and night, is a fire. At night, a bright campfire in an opening can be seen for miles from the air and a fair distance on the ground, especially in mountains. During the day, the same fire can be made to smoke when wet or green vegetation is piled on it. This smoke can be seen from the air as well as from the fire towers that watch over many of North America's forest lands. Not only does a fire serve as a good signal, but it also keeps you warm, gives you a somewhat reassured feeling, and can be used for cooking if you happen to have food available.

The secret is to have the skill to build a fire successfully. Be sure to read the next chapter in this book, on fire building, and practice building fires with matches and other fire starters until you can build them right the first time even in wet conditions.

An example of a properly executed ground-to-air signal in the snow: The survivors tromped out an "x" in the snow and outlined it with burned sticks so that it was readily visible from the air. Their campfire also produced a significant amount of smoke that initially served to attract the pilot's eye.

If you have left word with someone and you know a search party is looking for you, then one fire will usually be enough. If, however, you didn't leave word and no one is looking for you and you are trying to signal for help, there should be three fires evenly spaced apart. These three fires or columns of smoke serve as an international distress signal.

Smoke signals are effective only on comparatively clear and calm days. High winds, rain, and snow tend to disperse the smoke and lessen its chance of being seen. Smoke signals are not dependable when used in heavily wooded areas; they should be used in open terrain, if possible.

Try to create a smoke that contrasts with its background. Against snow, dark smoke is most effective; against dark turf, white smoke is best. To make a column of smoke visible to a land rescue party, use dark smoke against overcast skies and light smoke against clear skies. To your fire add rags soaked in oil or pieces of rubber (matting or electrical insulation) to make dark smoke, or green leaves, moss, ferns, or a little water to make white smoke.

In order to be effective, the fire must be prepared but not lit before the recovery vehicle enters the area. Then you need only light it quickly and the fire does the rest. You should supplement the fire with other forms of signaling.

Remember to be extremely careful when making and using a signal fire. You are in enough trouble already without getting caught in a forest fire you set. When in a survival situation, most people are upset and excited and mistakes come easy, so be careful with your fire.

Whistle

One of the easiest signal devices to carry and use is a whistle like those that policemen, coaches, and dog trainers use. A whistle is easy to pack in a survival kit or to wear around your neck. It requires very little energy to use, can be heard much farther than the human voice, and can be blown indefinitely; a shouting person soon becomes hoarse. The whistle makes an excellent signal when a ground party is conducting the search. The whistle is easily heard, and if tracking dogs are being used, they can hear a whistle from great distances.

To use a whistle effectively, you should remain calm and not blow the whistle until you think there is someone within hearing distance. To blow a whistle continuously for hours when no one is around only wastes vital energy and brings on frustration. Try giving a few blows on your whistle every 30 minutes just in case someone is nearing your location. Blow in bursts of three. Remain alert, and at the first sign that someone is out there, whistle him in. Remember to stay put and let your rescuers come to you.

A good whistle is one sold by P. S. Olt Co., well-known manufacturer of gamebird calls. The Olt whistle is made from a durable plastic and can take abuse and still work. Since it is made from plastic and not metal, it is a lot easier on the lips in subfreezing temperatures. It is bright orange in color, making it easy to keep track of. Perhaps what is best about this economical signal whistle is that it is easy to blow, giving a high, long-range whistle with little effort. It also comes with a lanyard.

Ground-to-Air Signals

All pilots are familiar with a signaling technique commonly known as "ground-to-air signals" or "pattern signals." These are signals that can be made in an opening on the ground to tell search pilots what the people in distress on the ground need. A copy of these signals should be in your survival kit, since they are somewhat difficult to remem-

Military survival students here learn that ground-to-air signals do work. An "X" was made from parachute material and signal mirrors were used. On the left is a wind sock made from parachute material to aid the rescue helicopter in landing.

GROUND-TO-AIR SIGNALS

X	UNABLE TO TRAVEL
↑	AM TRAVELING IN THIS DIRECTION
I	NEED DOCTOR—EMERGENCY
II	NEED MEDICAL SUPPLIES
F	NEED FOOD AND WATER
K	WHICH DIRECTION SHOULD I GO?
□	NEED MAP AND COMPASS
\/\/	NEED GUN AND AMMO
Y	YES
N	NO
JL	DO NOT UNDERSTAND MESSAGE
LL	ALL WELL

Left: All pilots know these ground-to-air signals.
Above: Ground-to-air signals should be no less than 3 feet in width and 18 feet in length.

ber. The one you should remember is the X. All pilots know that this is a signal for help.

Ground-to-air signals can be made from many things. Rocks, logs, cloth, or anything that will contrast with the ground cover will work. Make your signals large enough to be seen. A good rule of thumb is to use a 6-to-1 ratio. An effective signal must have "lines" that are no less than 3 feet in width and no single "line" of a letter or symbol should be less than 18 feet in length. If the base line of an L is 18 feet long, then the vertical line of the L must be longer to keep the letter in proper proportion.

If you make signals in the snow, use dark brush or rocks to make them stand out.

Make sure your ground-to-air signals are out in the open where aircraft can have a chance of seeing them. Use them in conjunction with smoke or a signal mirror.

Shadow signals. In the Arctic or snow-covered plains, it is often difficult to find materials to make a ground-to-air signal or SOS. If this is the case, build your signal out of mounds of snow so that they cast a shadow. Because of the lack of contrast it is the shadow that the aircraft will see. To be effective, these shadow signals must be oriented to the sun to produce the best shadow possible. In this case, other signal devices should be used in earnest.

Using SOS. If you don't have a copy of or remember ground-to-air signals, using the same techniques and materials, make an SOS on the ground or in the snow. As I illustrated in the beginning of this chapter, the SOS works effectively.

OUR RECEIVER IS OPERATING

DROP MESSAGE TO US

ALL OK, DO NOT WAIT

PICK US UP: AIRCRAFT ABANDONED

DO NOT ATTEMPT TO LAND HERE

CAN PROCEED SHORTLY. WAIT IF PRACTICABLE

AFFIRMATIVE (YES)

NEGATIVE (NO)

NEED MECHANICAL HELP OR PARTS— LONG DELAY

NEED MEDICAL ASSISTANCE URGENTLY

LAND HERE (POINT IN DIRECTION OF LANDING)

The U.S. Air Force suggests using these hand signals when communicating with an aircraft.

Dye marker. Many survival kits contain a water dye marker such as the one made by Sigma Scientific, Inc. This dye comes in a small container which fits easily into a survival kit or daypack. You can throw it in the water to make an orange slick or sprinkle it in the snow in the form of ground-to-air signals or SOS. When used in water it leaves a signal that is visible from the air for up to 8,000 feet.

Miscellaneous Signaling Techniques

Rescue balloon. A relatively new signal device is the lighter-than-air balloon. A popular model is the RES-Q Locating Balloon sold by the Lawrence Co. The balloon comes in a compact kit that is only 6 × 4 × 2 inches in size and weighs only 12½ ounces. It consists of a bright international-orange balloon that, when inflated, is 16 inches in diameter with 200 square inches of surface area; a small bottle of liquid; a dry chemical; a radar-sensitive streamer; and a 600-foot roll of monofilament line.

When the lost or stranded person needs to signal, all he has to do is insert the dry chemical into the bottle of liquid and in approximately 8 minutes, the balloon can be inflated and ready to send aloft. The balloon is made of tough surgical-grade rubber, which allows it to be used through tree branches. The only problem I had with my field test was that the balloon's flight was influenced by winds and the danger of the line being tangled in branches was increased. This can be overcome by using the balloon in an open area, and, if possible, on a hill. The balloon will stay aloft for 12 to 16 hours.

The RES-Q Locating Balloon is being used by several government agencies and is a good addition to a survival kit.

Flashlight. A flashlight or lantern can help rescuers find you at night. This is especially true if the flashlight has an on-off switch that allows you to signal SOS in Morse code. Three short flashes, then three long flashes, then three short flashes is the SOS signal that is known to all rescuers. Even a small light out

A rescue balloon is inflated simply by mixing two substances. Then allow it to drift up well above the vegetation where it may be seen from the air.

in the open can be seen a long way at night by aircraft.

Flares and smoke signals. Several companies such as Sigma Scientific, Inc., and Olin Signal Products manufacture aerial flares and bright orange smoke signals that can be included in a survival kit, tackle box, daypack, or backpack. These signal devices work well when the instructions are followed, but they operate for only a short period of time. Always have other signals ready to back up flares and smoke signals. Smoke can be seen for about 7 miles, and a flare at night for up to 30 miles.

Be sure to get flares that are dependable. I have seen some flares on the market that are in the category of cheap fireworks. They do not work half the time. They are not durable enough to be carried for long periods of time, and they seldom reach the height of a tall tree. Get your flares from a company with a good reputation for producing rescue items. Flares have a shelf life. Replace your flares before the expiration date. Practice using commercial smoke signals and flares so that you know how to use them properly.

Bright clothing, equipment, or panels. If aircraft are used in the search, items such as

HOW TO USE FLARES

Right: *Air Force survival students are being taught the proper use of smoke signals. Note that they are turned so that the wind blows the smoke away from them. As a precaution against burns, the students are wearing gloves.* **Below:** *These are examples of flares, smoke signals, and signal mirrors that are available in many outdoor shops.*

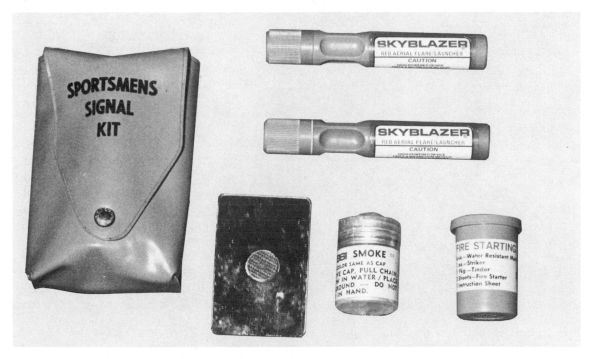

This victim demonstrates how to be more visible during signaling by contrasting his light clothing and skin against the forest floor.

bright clothing (hunter-orange vest, white T-shirt, or yellow rainsuit) or bright equipment (red tent or orange backpack, or bright parachute panels or signal panels) work well to attract attention.

Make a large flag from brightly colored clothing and wave it as search aircraft pass overhead. Moving flags are easier to see than stationary bright cloth.

I was once stranded for a number of days in the wilderness on the border of British Columbia and the Yukon, and due to poor communications with an outfitter, I was hopelessly stranded with no one launching a search for me. Luckily, a mining supply plane far off its usual course flew over. I tied a red shirt to a long pole, waded out into the large lake, and began waving the improvised flag. While the pilot was not searching for me, he recognized my distress signal and I was rescued.

Remember, contrast is the key to effective signals. Without contrast you may be overlooked.

In dark vegetation, white skin has been known to attract rescuers. Again, it is important to be out in the open for these signals to work. Sigma Scientific, Inc., sells a bright orange 4 × 8-foot panel marker that is ideal for survival kits. It also makes a good temporary shelter. The Pak-Kit survival kit has a tube tent in it that is bright orange in color and is good for signaling.

Three shots works only sometimes. Many survival books suggest firing three shots evenly spaced as a help signal. It doesn't work very often. During hunting season, three spaced shots are heard all the time. I was once hunting in near-zero temperature with the editor of a major outdoor magazine when he got his four-wheel-drive vehicle stuck far back in a swamp. Several times he fired three shots, and none of our hunting party paid any attention to his signals. After a long, cold walk, he told us in person of his problem. Save your ammunition and use the three-shot signal only when you feel sure a search party is searching for you, or possibly use it if the hunting season is closed. Three shots are usually meaningless to hunters unaware of your problem.

6
THE ART OF FIRE MAKING

One of the most important skills in survival is the skill of building a fire. Unfortunately, today, few among us can successfully build a fire on the first try, and it's perhaps a growing percentage of people who can't build a fire at all. Anyone who is going to spend time in the wilderness or even flying over it should take the time necessary to master the art of fire making.

The Importance of Fire

Most people in a wilderness crisis are scared, embarrassed, lonely, hungry, often cold, bored, and generally in poor spirits. They need something to help overcome these hardships—fire. Indians said fire had three powers: warmth, companionship, and the power to ward off the bad spirits. They had a point.

What can fire do for you in a survival sit-uation? It provides warmth, gives light, dries clothing, lifts morale, drives away pests, purifies water, cooks food, serves as a signaling device, and aids in the crafting of many useful items. A fire can be used to harden the tip of an improvised arrow. The black charcoal from a fire can be eaten to cure diarrhea, and the white ashes can be eaten to overcome constipation. Since boredom can be a major problem in a survival situation, a fire can help by creating work.

One of the best all-purpose campfires is the keyhole fire, named for the keyhole shape of its rock border. The fire itself is located in the large end of the keyhole, but most cooking is done with hot embers scraped into the small end. There's more on the keyhole fire on page 218.

In short, fire is one of the most valuable aids to your survival. When used properly, it can solve many problems and lead to rescue.

Where to Build a Fire

A survival fire should be built in an opening, if possible, so that it can be seen by search-and-rescue officials. It should be placed away from other flammable materials, overhang-ing branches, or ice and snow. It should be free from wind gusts. If necessary, build a fire in a trench dug into the ground in order to protect it from wind gusts. Also, windbreaks may be made from rocks and logs.

The fire itself should be on bare soil, free of grass, duff, or roots that could ignite.

You should never build a fire on or near rocks that are porous or that have been in water because they can explode when heated.

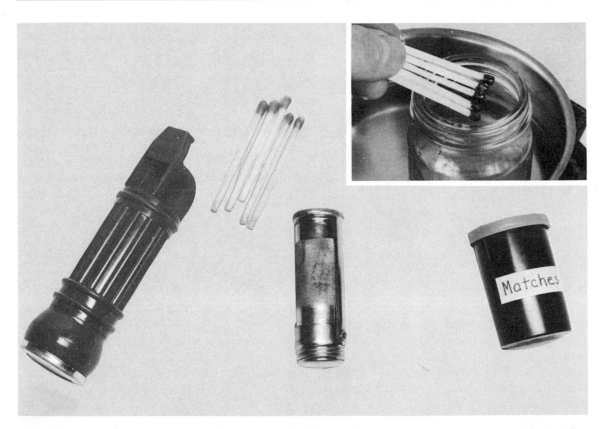

Carry your matches in a waterproof container. At left is a plastic, bright orange case from L. L. Bean with a compass on one end and whistle on the other. Center is a metal case by Marble. At right is a plastic 35mm film canister. As shown in the photo inset, matches should be dipped in melted paraffin to waterproof them and to make them burn better.

Avoid building a fire under a snow-laden tree or directly on snow or ice. If you must build a fire on snow or ice, lay an insulating green-stick platform first.

Requirements for a Fire

The first ingredient for a fire is oxygen, since burning is nothing more than rapid oxidation. Second, you must have a source of heat. This can be anything that can create a spark or flame. Third, you must have tinder, that is, a material that catches the spark or flame easily and starts burning rapidly. Fourth, you must have fuel that will burn readily and for an extended period. Without these four ingredients, you don't have a fire.

Fire Sources

There are many sources of heat and ignition but few people can start a fire with anything other than a match or cigarette lighter, especially under stressful survival conditions. I will cover each source of heat and ignition, but remember that except for the first two below, they require much practice and know-how just to ignite the tinder, much less to ignite kindling and heavier wood.

Matches. In the wilderness, wooden strike-anywhere kitchen matches are the best fire starters and should be the only type of matches carried. Leave book, or paper, matches at home because they will let you down in a damp survival situation. Waterproof your matches by dipping them in melted paraffin wax. Two dippings of the wax used in home canning will give good protection. The whole match must be covered. Save these dipped matches for extreme emergency. However, you should try lighting a few at home after waxing them to make sure they work. If you smoke, you can carry a separate supply of matches for that purpose and for non-emergency campfires.

Your survival matches should be carried in a waterproof match container. There are several good ones on the market, as shown. You can make your own match case from strong plastic pill bottles or plastic 35mm film containers. I don't like the film containers because you have to cut the kitchen matches shorter to make them fit.

There are also some excellent waterproof and windproof matches made by Coghlan's of Canada and available in many sporting goods stores.

Since kitchen matches are packed for long periods of time in match cases and survival kits, check them every six months for their ability to ignite. Matches deteriorate over time.

Cigarette lighter. Some survival instructors prefer throw-away butane cigarette lighters as a fire source. If you use a lighter of this type in your survival kit, get one that has a visible butane supply. Be sure you pack it so that the gas release button cannot be pressed accidentally and result in an empty lighter when you need it. If you are in a survival situation and your lighter runs out of fuel, save the flint as another form of fire source.

Magnesium fire starter. The Doan Machinery and Equipment Company has developed a unique fire-starting tool consisting of a $3/8 \times 1 \times 3$-inch block of solid magnesium with a 3-inch flint inserted along one of its edges. Flame is achieved by scraping the magnesium with a knife until a pile of shavings the diameter of a quarter is accumulated. The sparking insert is then struck with the back of the blade and the shavings will ignite within 15 seconds, flaring up at a temperature of 5,400°F.

It will ignite even damp wood, and if the

MAGNESIUM FIRE STARTERS

Left is the Eddie Bauer magnesium fire starter attached by a chain to a small knife. The two white objects are flammable material capable of catching a spark and burning instantly. At the extreme right is a magnesium fire starter made by Doan Machine and Equipment Co. (Chris Fears photo)

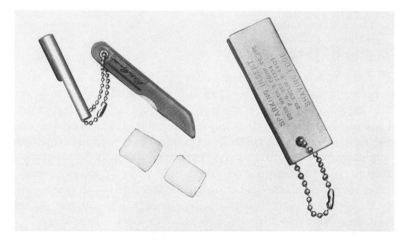

1. *The first step to starting a fire with a magnesium fire starter is to shave off small pieces of magnesium onto flammable material such as the dead leaves in this photo.* **2.** *On the other side of the magnesium fire starter is a strip of flint. Scrape the flint rapidly with a knife blade to create a shower of sparks onto the magnesium shavings. The magnesium shavings will burn hot enough to ignite the flammable material. (Barry Fikes photos)*

tool itself should get wet, you merely dry it off and it's ready to be used. The tool is impervious to weather damage, and it is fireproof in its solid form.

The Eddie Bauer Company has a survival match kit that includes a magnesium and flint stick, knife, and tinder tabs all packed in a small zip-lock bag.

Either of these magnesium fire starters will fit easily into a survival kit. Be sure to practice making a fire with such a kit before you take it into the backcountry.

Lenses. Walter Yates, badly injured when his helicopter crashed in British Columbia, survived 14 days before being found. He was

Anyone who has used a magnifying lens to focus the sun's rays on his own skin remembers the sudden and unbearable hotspot produced. That same magnifier will make paper smoke quite quickly, charring it. But bringing real flames from the focused sun's rays is a challenge of a higher order. The lenses shown in this photo, left to right, include a camera lens, a plastic pocket magnifier, the front lens of a binocular, and a pair of reading glasses. Here the pocket magnifier and the binocular lens focused the ideal tiny beam easily, and in a few seconds brought smoke from toilet paper, newspaper, birchbark, wood shavings, and a candle wick. But no flames could be coaxed from these ideal tinders. Before assuming that a lens will always get you by on a sunny day in a survival crisis, try out a lens at home first. Smoke is not enough. Dipping those tinders in a flammable liquid such as gasoline, kerosene, or lighter fluid might help. (Neil Soderstrom photo)

able to start a fire using his camera lens. Lenses from eyeglasses, magnifying glasses, binoculars, telescopic sights, and many other optics can be used in bright sunlight to concentrate the sun's rays on the tinder. With some practice, these can be good fire starters on sunny days. On overcast days, forget it.

Spark from a battery. Batteries found in planes, boats, automobiles, snowmobiles, and other motors can give you enough spark, assuming they are charged, to get a fire going. Attach wires to each pole on the battery and

scratch the ends together to produce sparks. Direct these sparks into the tinder.

Steel wool and flashlight batteries. If you have two good flashlight batteries and some 00 or 000 steel wool, you can start a fire. Sit one battery on top of the other so that the positive end of the bottom battery is touching the bottom of the upper battery. Make a loose rope from the steel wool about 8 inches long. Set the batteries on one end of the steel wool rope and touch the other end of the rope to the positive tip on the upper battery. Have

HOW TO START A FIRE USING BATTERIES

The battery from your auto, boat, plane, or snowmobile may be used to start a fire when you stretch steel wool from pole to pole or when you attach wires to each pole and scratch them together.

your tinder ready. As the steel wool glows red-hot, place your tinder on it and fire will result. This requires some practice.

Flint and steel. Making a fire by using flint and steel sounds good and is often written about as being an easy way to start a fire, but

Fire starting char-cloth can be made using a tin can, as described in the text on the next page.

If you happen to have steel wool and flashlight batteries, you can start a fire by touching ends of the steel wool to opposite battery poles.

it's tough unless you have had a lot of practice and have the right materials. For several hundred years, if someone wanted fire he simply got out his tinderbox, which contained a flint, steel striker, some charred cloth, and tinder, and matter-of-factly built a fire in a few minutes. Today, with the exception of a few survival instructors, members of mountain men organizations, and a few others, there aren't many among us who could start such a fire in a few hours.

Contrary to popular opinion, it is extremely difficult to pick up a flint rock and bang a file or knife against it and have a fire result. Granted, it can be done with charred cloth as a spark catcher, but this is difficult. If you really want to start a fire by using flint

and steel, order a tinderbox, oval flint striker, and some sharp flint rocks from the Dixie Gun Works (address in Appendix 3). Next, get an old 100 percent cotton T-shirt (cloth containing synthetic fiber won't work). Cut the old T-shirt down into 2-inch squares. Then, find a tin box, such as used for Band-Aids, tea, or shoe polish. Punch a hole in the box lid. Now pack your cloth squares into the tin box. Close the lid and place the box in a fire or on a stove. Watch it. As the cloth inside begins to heat up, it gives off combustible gases which appear as smoke coming from the hole in the can. As soon as the smoke starts to subside, plug the hole, remove the box from the fire, and let it cool down before opening. If you open it while

HOW TO START A FIRE
WITH FLINT AND STEEL

A flint-and-steel kit may be used as a backup for matches, but only when you are proficient in the use of the kit. Items in the kit are the container, steel striker, piece of flint, and charred cotton cloth, or "char-cloth," to catch a spark and set tinder on fire.

1. Nestle the char-cloth in tinder, such as a bird's nest, dry birchbark, or wood shavings.

the cloth is still hot, oxygen in the air will cause it to glow and thus ruin it. Char-cloth has the look of charcoal, but it can be pulled apart into separate layers and will withstand gentle handling only.

You now have char-cloth, the only material I know of that will hold a spark well enough to get your tinder going. Gently place your char-cloth in the Hawken tinderbox.

To start a fire, get some tinder, which I will talk about in detail later in this chapter, and make a loose nest with a piece of char-cloth in the center. Pick out a piece of sharp flint from your tinderbox and hold in one hand. Place the flint striker over two fingers, with the smooth edge to the outside, in the other hand. Strike the flint against the strik-

er. Use the edge of the flint as if it were the edge of an ax and try to chop long slivers of steel from the face of the striker. This usually produces the hottest sparks.

Once the char-cloth has caught the spark and begun to glow, fold your tinder nest firmly against it, hold it above your face, and blow gently and steadily up into it until a flame starts. If you blow down into the nest, you will find yourself breathing smoke. You now have a fire started. With much, much practice you may be able to build a fire with flint and steel almost as quickly as you can with a match.

If you know how to use it, a flint-and-steel kit is a good backup for matches, but it is not a good replacement.

2. *Strike the metal striker with the piece of flint, directing the shower of sparks onto the char-cloth.*

3. *Once the char-cloth begins to smolder, pick up the tinder and blow on it to ignite flames. Place the burning tinder under kindling.*

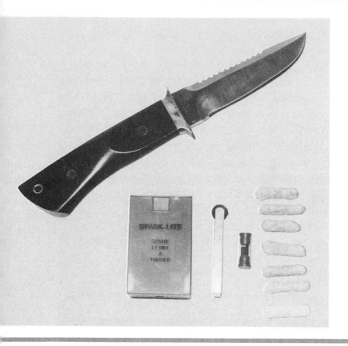

Made by Four Seasons Survival Co., this easy-to-use flint-and-steel kit consists of waterproof plastic container, a cigarette lighter-type striker, called a Spark-Lite, spare flints, and fire starter material called Tinder-Quik. The striker may be used with one hand, and the Tinder-Quik requires only one spark to ignite. When packed in its container, the kit is not much larger than a book of matches. The ingredients may be taken out of the container and placed in the hollow handle of a survival knife. (The knife is nonfunctional in this photo except to provide reference to relative sizes.)

Bow and drill. The bow-and-drill apparatus is composed of four parts—bow, drill, fireboard, and socket.

The bow may be made from any tree branch that is approximately ½ inch in diameter and 20 to 30 inches long. A cord or shoestring is attached loosely to each end of the branch. In effect, you have a bow similar to the archery bow you made as a youngster, but very loosely strung.

The drill should be made from a sturdy branch that is approximately ¾ inch in diameter and about 10 inches long.

The fireboard should be made from a flat piece of wood that is approximately ½ inch thick. A depression should be drilled along the edge with the bow and drill. Next, notch the depression to the outside of the board. This notch is necessary so the hot wood dust and spark will fall into the tinder.

The socket may be made from a flat rock or hardwood. In it a depression must be drilled. The purpose of the socket is to hold the drill straight as the drill spins.

Place the fireboard on a flat surface with tinder adjacent to the notch in the board. Next, place the drill in the bow by looping the bowstring around the drill one time. Place one end of the drill in the depression on the edge of the fireboard and the other end in the socket. Keep the drill perpendicular to the fireboard. By pulling and pushing the bow, spin the drill quickly. This forms a black powdery dust that eventually catches a spark. The spark gets the tinder going.

This is a difficult, energy-consuming method of starting a fire. Rarely will it work for someone who hasn't practiced it a great deal.

Fire plow. A fire plow is another tool for making fire by friction, and like the bow drill,

These are the five major elements of a bow-and-drill system, a tricky one to master.

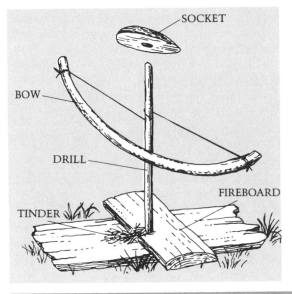

To produce fire with a bow and drill, you must hold the drill perpendicular to the fireboard and spin it quickly.

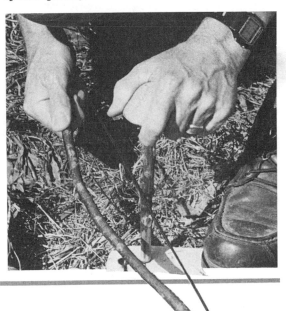

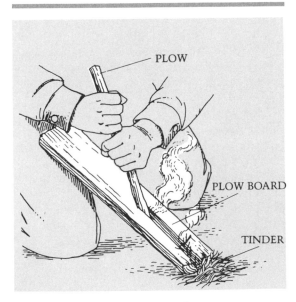

These are the parts of a fire plow.

the fire plow is quite difficult to master.

Cut a groove approximately ½ inch wide, ½ inch deep, and 24 inches long in a flat piece of wood. This is called a plow board. Be sure the groove runs out one end of the board. Next, cut a stick that is ½ inch thick and 18 inches long. This is called a plow. Place one end of the plow board on a rock or log so that it is elevated 8 to 10 inches. Place tinder at the lower end where the groove is cut. Rub the plow back and forth in the groove with a steady but increasing rhythm until smoke in the tinder indicates a spark.

A lot of practice and luck are required to make a fire by this method. This also consumes a lot of energy.

Building a Fire

It is commonly said that you don't just start a fire, you build it. This is true. In order to build a fire, you must prepare everything in order to assure success. The three materials of fire building are tinder, kindling, and fuel.

Tinder. Tinder is anything that will ignite at a very low temperature with a minute flame. Here are some tinders that work well when dry:

• Shredded inner bark from cedar trees
• Birch bark
• Seed down from thistle or milkweed
• Dried pine needles that are several years old
• Dried moss, such as goat's beard lichen
• Steel wool
• Cotton cloth
• Dry straw that is crushed
• Waxed paper
• Dry bird's nest

Kindling. Kindling is readily combustible fuel that is added to tinder as soon as there is sufficient flame to ignite it. Kindling is used to bring the burning temperature up to the point where larger and perhaps less combustible fuel can be added. Here are common materials used for kindling:

• Small twigs
• Wood split to small cross-sectional size
• Heavy cardboard
• Pieces of wood removed from the inside of larger pieces
• Wood that has been soaked in or doused with a highly flammable material such as gasoline, oil, or wax.

Tinder and kindling must be kept dry. Other larger wood can be used even though it is not completely dry as long as sufficient kindling is used to bring the burning tem-perature up to the point where it will ignite. Gasoline or other highly flammable liquids should not be poured on a fire that has al-ready started. Even a smoldering fire doused with flammable liquids can explode and cause serious burns or even cause the fuel con-tainer to explode.

The reason many people cannot build a fire is that they try to add large sticks or logs to the burning tinder without adding kindling first. Good fire building requires a patience for building from small to large.

Fuel. This may be any of the following:
• Dry standing deadwood and dry dead branches. Deadwood is easy to split and re-duce to short sections by pounding it on a rock.
• The inside of fallen tree trunks and large branches. These may be dry even if the out-side is wet. Use the heart of the wood.
• You can find green wood that can be made to burn almost anywhere, especially if it is finely split and you have a hot fire started.
• In treeless areas, you can find other nat-ural fuels, such as dry grass, which you can twist into bunches, peat dry enough to burn (found at the top of undercut banks), dried animal dung, animal fats, and sometimes even coal.

Anytime you are building a fire, prepare a safe fireplace. Pick a site that is at least 15 feet from tents, green trees, dry grass, or any-thing else that could be ignited or damaged by the heat or sparks. Also be sure to check overhead. An unnoticed tree branch can ex-tend directly over the fire area, low enough to be ignited by the rising heat. Be careful not to build a fire over roots or peat moss. Fire can burn and smolder within roots and pop up many hours later as a wildfire around the base of the tree. Peat moss can burn underground for days and start a major fire long after you have moved on. If there are

NATURAL FIRE-BUILDING MATERIALS

Fire-building materials, from left to right: (1) tinder, in this case, a bird's nest; (2) kindling of small sticks and twigs; and (3) fuelwood of larger sticks and logs.

Left: *The dry, peeling bark on birch trees, in this case river birch, makes excellent tinder.* **Right:** *This survival student gathers down from thistles for tinder.*

RATINGS FOR FIREWOOD
Source: U.S. Forest Service

HARDWOOD TREES	Relative heat	Easy to ignite	Easy to split	Heavy smoke?	Throw sparks?	General rating and remarks
Apple, ash, beech, birch, dogwood, hard maple, hickory, locust, mesquite, oaks, Pacific madrone, pecan.	High	No	Medium	Little	Yes, when poked	Excellent
Alder, cherry, soft maple, walnut	Medium	Medium	Yes	Little	Little	Good
Elm, gum, sycamore	Medium	Medium	No	Medium	Little	Fair (wet when green)
Aspen, basswood, cottonwood, yellow-poplar	Low	Yes	Yes	Medium	Little	Fair (good kindling)
SOFTWOOD TREES						
Douglas-fir, southern yellow pine	Medium	Yes	Yes	Yes	Little	Good but smoky
Cypress, redwood	Low	Yes	Yes	Medium	Little	Fair
Eastern redcedar, western redcedar, white cedar.	Low	Yes	Yes	Medium	Yes	Fair (excellent for kindling)
Eastern white pine, ponderosa pine, sugar pine, western white pine, true firs.	Low	Yes	Yes	Medium	Little	Fair—good kindling
Larch, tamarack	Medium	Yes	Yes	Yes	Yes	Fair
Spruce	Low	Yes	Yes	Medium	Yes	Fair (good kindling when dry)

pine needles, leaves, and other combustibles at your fire site, clear them away, exposing the bare earth for 10 to 15 feet. Put this cleared material in a pile nearby so that you can restore your site to its original condition when breaking camp.

After preparing your fireplace, get all your materials together before you start the fire. Make sure your matches, kindling, and fuel are dry. Have enough fuel on hand to keep the fire going. Light it in a place sheltered from the wind.

Arrange a small amount of kindling in a low pyramid, close enough together so that flames can lick from one piece to another. Leave a small opening for lighting and air circulation.

Small pieces of wood or other fuel can be laid gently on kindling before lighting or can be added after kindling begins to burn. Lay on smaller pieces first, adding larger pieces of fuel as the fire begins to burn. Don't smother the fire by crushing down kindling with heavy wood. Don't make the fire too big. Don't waste fuel.

Don't waste your matches trying to light poorly prepared wood. Don't use matches for lighting cigarettes; get a light for tobacco from your fire or use the sun and a lens. Don't build unnecessary fires; save your fuel. Practice primitive methods of making fires before all of your matches are gone.

Carry some dry tinder with you in a waterproof container. Expose it to the sun on dry days. Adding a little powdered charcoal will improve it. Collect good tinder wherever you find it. Cotton cloth is good tinder, especially if scorched or charred; it works well with a lens or with flint and steel.

Collect kindling along the trail before you

A survival stove such as this may be made from an old tin can one-third full with hard pitch that bleeds from the trunks of pine trees. With pitch ignited, an improvised stove like this will burn for about 30 minutes. That's plenty of time to boil a couple of small pots of water.

make camp. Keep firewood dry under shelter. Dry damp wood near the fire so that you can use it later. Save some of your best kindling and fuel for quick fire making each morning.

Split logs burn more easily than round ones. To split logs, whittle hardwood wedges and drive them into cracks in the log with a rock or club.

To make a fire last overnight, place large logs over it so that the fire will burn into the heart of the logs. When a good bed of coals has been formed, cover it lightly, first with ashes and then with dry earth. In the morning, the fire will still be smoldering. Dense hardwoods tend to last longer and provide longer-lasting coals.

If you anticipate search planes, keep plenty of kindling and fuel wood on hand to get the fire going again quickly for signaling. Also, during the day, keep some green or wet leaves

or conifer boughs on hand to create a signal smoke quickly.

Don't waste fire-making materials. Use only what is necessary to start a fire and to keep it going for the purpose needed. When you leave the campsite, put out the fire with water and mineral soil. Mix it until it has cooled enough to allow you to insert your hand.

Pine Pitch Stove

If you are in an area where there are pine trees and you have a tin can, you can make a stove suitable for boiling water and cooking greens or soups. Simply punch a few holes in the side of the can so that air can get to the fire. Obtain hardened pitch from the pine trees and place it in the can. Ignite the pitch and place a cooking vessel on top of the can.

7

SURVIVAL SHELTERS

Faced with protecting yourself from the elements, you must consider using potential places in your immediate area or using available material to improvise a shelter.

When deciding on the type of shelter, you must consider what the shelter is to protect you from—rain, cold, insects, heat. For example, in hot, arid areas, protection from the sun during the day may be the prime consideration. In frigid areas, extreme cold aggravated by high winds or, in some seasons, swarms of insects may be the important factors.

In addition to protection from natural elements and conditions, an adequate shelter also provides that psychological well-being necessary for good rest. Adequate rest is extremely important if you are to make sound decisions, and the need for rest becomes more critical as time passes and rescue is prolonged. Thus, adequate shelter must be placed high on the priority list.

Constructing shelter for your survival camp may or may not be a rush matter. If the weather is mild with no rain, you may postpone constructing a shelter. However, if the weather is bad or likely to be bad, then shelter construction may become very important. One plus for shelter construction, assuming you are in good shape and have

Lean-to shelters with pine-bough roofs offer only marginal protection from wind and rain. They can be made more water repellent by weaving in large leaves or pieces of bark in patterns like those for roof shingles. Better covers for such lean-tos include tarps, plastic sheeting, and the impervious and heat-reflective space blankets.

food and water, is that it helps you keep your mind off your troubles.

I recall fondly one hunter I helped find in Georgia. He had been lost for two days, and when we found him, he had almost established a homestead. In fact, he had built himself such a cozy camp that we used it for an overnight rest before packing out. On the way out, he told us his "ordeal" had been a ball and he planned to get lost again soon.

Most survival camps won't be much fun or cozy. Most will be built under unfavorable conditions.

Many survival students mistakenly make their shelter too large. This effort on behalf of comfort usually wastes time and energy. A survival shelter should usually be small and cramped, but it should protect you from the elements. Don't try to create all the comforts of home in a true survival situation.

As these kids in survival training have done, select your site carefully, avoiding thick brush, standing dead timber, and low swamp areas.

Shelter Site

The location of your shelter will depend on several things. The first priority is that it be where you can be easily seen by search aircraft or ground parties. I was once leading a ground search party looking for two lost hikers. It took us two days longer to find the hikers because of the hidden site they had selected.

If you are with a downed aircraft or a stranded vehicle, boat, snowmobile, or canoe, try either to use the craft as a camp or to set up your shelter nearby, so that you can benefit from the high visibility of the vehicle. Of course, if the vehicle is hidden in thick brush or trees, this isn't a consideration.

If you are walking or skiing, select an open area, if possible. This may require that you cut some brush or small trees.

Avoid constructing your shelter in a low swamp area or in a dry creekbed. Your predicament is bad enough without being overrun with a flash flood or rising groundwater. These areas may also be worse for insects. Also, avoid a site that will receive rain runoff.

Look up before selecting a shelter site. Don't build your shelter under standing dead trees or dead limbs. These could fall on you. Avoid thick overhead vegetation that could conceal you from aircraft as well as block out your distress signals.

Try to construct your shelter so that you can sleep reasonably well. Select a level or near-level site. Remove stones and sticks. Your sleep is vital to conserve energy.

Set up a ground-to-air signal as soon as you have a survival campsite selected. If the weather is not too bad, set your signals up before you construct your shelter. Waiting may cause you to miss a chance for early rescue.

If possible, find an opening and set up your shelter near a source of water. Not only does

Any waterproof material, such as the space blanket shown here, may be used for making a small survival shelter. By keeping the shelter small and simple, construction time and energy may be saved for other necessary survival chores.

this save energy in getting water, but it also is a good place to find animals and plants for food. Many times such an area is visited by man—and thus a rescuer—more frequently than other areas.

SHELTERS FROM TARPS

Tarps may be used to create shelters of widely varied design.

TIE

ROCK

FOLD CORNER
AND TIE

Types of Shelters

The type of shelter you select should be based on several factors:

1. Shelter material you have with you—tent, vehicle, canoe, airplane, tarp, emergency blanket, sheet of plastic, parachute.

2. Equipment you have to aid in shelter construction, such as ax, saw, knife, rope.

3. Natural materials available for shelter construction—rocks, trees, poles, snow.

4. Current and expected weather conditions.

5. Season of the year.

How effective your shelter will be will depend upon these factors, plus your ability to improvise and any previous training you have had in shelter construction.

Automobile or aircraft. Enclosed vehicles usually provide excellent shelter. However, there are two conditions when they should be avoided. In extreme heat, a vehicle can become an oven (see Chapter 15 on survival in desert conditions). In extremely low temperatures, automobiles and aircraft made from metal will be as cold on the inside as the coldest air temperature is on the outside.

Survival shelters are made from whatever is at hand. This lost hiker improvised a shelter from two plastic garbage bags by cutting the bottom from one and attaching it to the mouth of the second with substantial overlap. The resultant tube tent is supported between two trees by a length of cord.

In extreme cold, you may have a better chance of surviving if you erect a better-insulated shelter alongside the vehicle, using it as a windbreak.

Tube tent. If you are traveling through or over a wilderness by vehicle, plane, snowmobile, canoe, boat, horseback, skis, or backpacking, you would be wise to carry a tent. I learned while working in northern Canada and Alaska always to have at least a tube tent with me. I have spent many nights in the wilderness unexpectedly. Always purchase a tube tent that is a bright orange. It makes a good ground-to-air signal.

Lean-to. A tarp, especially one in a bright orange color, is an extremely versatile shelter. It can be stretched over an open boat to make a cozy shelter, or alongside an overturned canoe to form a lean-to, or from a wing of a plane to the ground, or from the side of a jeep to the ground. A tarp makes a good lean-to, especially when you are trying to escape desert heat. Where the tarp is best is in making a lean-to in the woods. With a reflector fire, the lean-to shelter can be comfortable in the worst of weather.

Lean-tos may be made from a raincoat, a sheet of plastic, seat covers, or tree boughs. The tree-bough lean-to offers only marginal protection from rain and wind. But you can tighten such a lean-to by weaving in bark or large leaves.

Parachute shelter. While very few nonmilitary aircraft today carry parachutes, if you happen to be in a place that does contain parachutes, they can be made into lean-tos and tepees. In warm or hot weather, the entire parachute can be tied out to trees, some 6 feet high, with the suspension lines. Then push the center up with a 12-foot pole. The tepee makes a good shelter from rain or the sun. When a fire is built under it at night, the entire parachute glows, making it a great signal.

The rule with parachute cloth is that it

This lean-to is made from native materials including saplings cut for support beams, as well as leaves and brush that provide protection from sun, wind, and rain. If a space blanket, tarp, garbage bag, or other waterproof material is available, it could be used in place of leaves or under the leaves for a much more effective cover. A reflective fire, as shown, can help ensure that a lean-to is relatively warm.

PARACHUTE SHELTERS

When stretched tightly, parachute material is water-repellent and durable, and it can be made into an excellent shelter. Like a tarp, it can be arranged in a variety of configurations, such as the lean-to above or the tepee at right. Since parachutes often have colors easily seen from the air, the shelter may aid in rescue as well.

must be pitched at a steep angle and kept extra-tight in order to shed snow or rain.

Parachute shroud lines may be used for lashing and other chores.

Space blanket. The space blanket, which is sold in many camping supply stores, is a good item to carry in a personal survival kit. This blanket is made from a very thin but strong space-age material that can reflect 90 percent of the heat thrown against it. It is compact,

about the size of a pack of cigarettes. It can be made into a lean-to and, when used with a reflector fire, is very warm. When folded properly, this blanket also becomes a warm sleeping bag.

Plastic shelters. Plastic bags and sheets of plastic can be made into various types of shelters. Two plastic garbage bags may be attached together, with one or both bottoms cut open, to make a tube tent. Here you'll

This survival shelter is covered with a space blanket that also reflects heat back down on the occupant radiated from the reflective fire. Double reflectors!

need to provide sufficient ventilation to carry off condensation of water vapor emitted by your body and breathing.

Tree shelters. Many times freshly blown-down trees can be made into a survival shelter by cutting away the limbs near the ground. If large pieces of bark are around, use them shingle-fashion to tighten the roof.

Hollow logs or trees are often used for shelters. But, you should be careful in warm weather, because these same shelters may be used by wasps, snakes, and spiders. Also, when you're in a tree shelter you're extremely difficult for searchers to spot.

Other natural shelters. A rock overhang or cave can make a good shelter. In fact, during the 1700s the longhunters who were exploring the wilderness west of the Appalachian Mountains spent entire winters in survival-type camps they made under rock overhangs.

During the months when lightning is prevalent, don't select the tallest tree in the area as a lean-to support. The tallest trees attract lightning. A scrap piece of plastic and two long poles make up this simple shelter built under trees of medium height in the area.

If no other shelter is available, a fallen tree can be made into a fair lean-to by cutting away branches on top and directly underneath. Use those branches and foliage to insulate and cushion the floor, improve the roof, and provide windbreak. A reflective fire at the opening can make such a shelter relatively comfortable.

By building up rock walls as windbreakers, one can make these shelters comfortable. However, they are usually difficult for rescuers to spot from the air or from a distance on the ground.

Wickiups. In the arid southwestern United States, windbreak survival shelters called "wickiups" are made from brush. First, build a tripod using three poles 10 to 12 feet long. Spread the legs of the tripod out to 6 feet or so. Next, stack long poles against the tripod until they take the shape of a tepee. Over these poles, place a thatching of sticks, grass, leaves, pine needles, and bark. To make a larger wickiup, simply use longer poles and spread them out farther at the base.

Snow shelters. Cold-weather shelter construction is based on the thermal principle. There are two basic concepts of this princi-

ple: first, the use of the insulation value of dry snow derived from the mass of dry, dead airspace enclosed between individual crystals; and second, the use of heat radiating from the earth when bare ground is exposed inside the shelter. With those principles in mind, you can construct a shelter that will maintain a constant temperature of plus 10° to 20°F inside even though the outside air temperature is below zero.

It is important that your snow shelter be large enough for you and your equipment, yet not so large that it is difficult to heat. The entrance should be closed off from the outside environment. A ventilation hole is necessary if a heat-producing device such as a small stove is used. This is to vent out toxic gases and to dissipate heat enough to prevent a shelter meltdown.

Hole-in-the-snow shelter. Find a conifer tree having limbs extending down to snow

A wickiup is a shelter for arid regions where protection is needed from wind and sun rather than from precipitation. A wickiup is made by building a tepee-type frame of poles and then thatching with brush, leaves, boughs, and reeds.

level; then dig out all the snow around its trunk right down to the ground. Next, trim all the inside branches and use them to line the bottom and finish the top. Since this shelter is hidden, be sure to keep your ground-to-air signals out in a clearing, and be sure to keep them clean of snow.

Snow trench. A snow trench shelter can be made by simply digging a trench down in the snow to the ground or, in deep snow, 4 feet deep, 7 feet long, and 3 feet wide. Cut blocks from packed snow and make a pitched roof. A tarp can be used for a roof also. Never sleep directly on the snow. Provide some type of insulation under your sleeping bag or body—seat cushions, tarp, leaves, or any type plant material.

Snow cave. A snow cave is an excellent cold-weather shelter, but it requires a lot of energy, a shovel or similar tool, and some skill. Begin by finding a packed snowdrift that is about 7 feet high and 12 feet or more wide. Then start digging a low tunnel into the snowbank. After you dig the tunnel into the snowbank 2 feet, hollow out an opening large enough for you to lie down in.

Next, push a pole through the roof at a 45-degree angle to make a vent hole. In the back of the cave, build the bed platform some 18 inches high. To conserve heat, the cave should be built just large enough to sleep, dress, and undress while lying in your sleeping bag. An interior dome shape, rather than a squared shape, will provide better support of the roof. If desired, the sleeping shelf may be walled in to conserve heat. In addition to the ventilation hole through the roof, there should be another at the door.

Take a shovel or digging device in with you at night. You may need to dig yourself out. One storm may deposit a great deal of snow, which may be very hard to remove without a digging tool.

Always check the ventilation holes before lighting a candle in a snow shelter. Carbon monoxide is a great danger.

Since snow shelters cannot be heated many degrees above freezing, life inside is rather chilly. It takes several weeks to accustom yourself to the effects of living in such a cold atmosphere. You will require more food and hot drinks than you would inside a shelter.

KINDS OF SNOW SHELTERS

The hole-in-the-snow shelter is designed to capitalize on the insulating quality of snow and the sheltering effect of the tree. This is a good type of shelter to rig when it's not possible to build a fire.

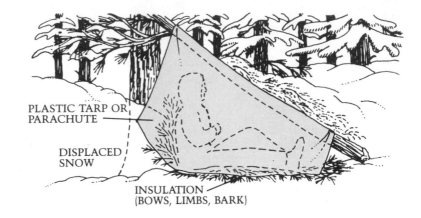

PLASTIC TARP OR PARACHUTE

DISPLACED SNOW

INSULATION (BOWS, LIMBS, BARK)

The snow trench as a shelter is a good option in open regions such as ice packs or where there is hard-packed snow. To build the snow trench, stomp or cut out a trench. Then, using a large knife or saw, cut slabs of ice or packed snow and arrange as shown. Loose snow may be packed over the slabs to provide further insulation.

TRENCH

BLOCK FOR DOOR

A snow cave should be built only when no other shelter is available because a great amount of energy and skill is required for construction. While snow caves can be reasonably warm as a result of the insulating quality of snow, if you increase the inside temperature much above freezing, you increase humidity and cause melting. Even a candle can raise the temperature enough to cause some melting.

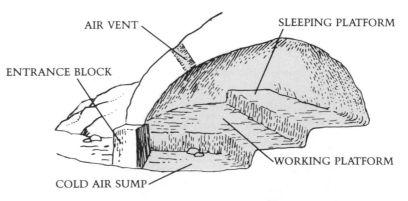

AIR VENT

SLEEPING PLATFORM

ENTRANCE BLOCK

COLD AIR SUMP

WORKING PLATFORM

A snow cave can be a reasonably comfortable shelter. But it is a long way from being comfortably warm. As this young person illustrates, you must stay warmly dressed in a snow cave because the cave interior is only a few degrees above freezing. (Outward Bound USA photo)

An igloo is a valid type of arctic shelter, but it usually is not a good choice for survival conditions because it requires a tremendous amount of energy and skill to build. A snow cave is usually easier to make. (Outward Bound USA photo)

Regardless of how cold it may get outside, the temperature inside a small, well-constructed snow cave probably will not be lower than –10°F, and with a candle it can be heated to a few degrees above freezing.

Snow cave construction requires a lot of work and is not recommended unless you have plenty of food and water and are in good shape. A savvy person with a shovel may need as much as three hours to build a snow cave. During construction, exertion can generate perspiration that will dampen your clothing, which is an added danger.

There are many other crude shelters that can be made. The secret to shelter construction is simple—use what is available to give yourself the protection necessary from the elements. Construct whatever adequate shelter uses the least amount of energy, and, if possible, keep it out where you can be seen.

8

FINDING AND TREATING WATER

Humans are approximately 75 percent water, and the intake and output of liquids are necessary for normal function of the vital organs.

An adult normally needs a minimum of 2 quarts of water daily to maintain proper liquid balance. During cold weather, breathing alone releases a lot of water vapor. Perspiration also releases moisture. Any intake lower than about 2 quarts results in gradual dehydration and the loss of the body's efficiency. Losing water to the extent of 2.5 percent of body weight, or approximately 1.5 quarts of body water, will reduce your efficiency 25 percent. This could be deadly in a survival situation. Although most people can survive only a few days without water, immobile trapped earthquake victims have survived over a week without water.

Water requirements are of prime impor-

tance in trip planning. In the desert your life could depend upon your water supply and how well you conserve your body water. Keep in mind that the minimum daily requirement of 2 quarts of water a day would go up to a gallon or more in hot desert survival predicaments.

When your body runs short of water, dehydration starts to take effect. I have seen men who were almost totally ineffective in a severe military situation because of dehydration. I have guided elk hunters at high elevations where they stopped a ten-day hunt

Portable water filtration and purification units are effective and easy to use as a preliminary to boiling or treating water with chemical purifiers. (Chris Fears photo)

EXPECTED SURVIVAL WITHOUT WATER						
No Walking at All	**Max. daily temp. (°E) in shade**	**Available water per man, U.S. Quarts**				
		0	1 Qt.	2 Qts.	4 Qts.	10 Qts.	20 Qts.
		Expected Days of Survival				
	120°	2	2	2	2.5	3	4.5
	110	3	3	3.5	4	5	7
	100	5	5.5	6	7	9.5	13.5
	90	7	8	9	10.5	15	23
	80	9	10	11	13	19	29
	70	10	11	12	14	20.5	32
	60	10	11	12	14	21	32
	50	10	11	12	14.5	21	32

Source: *U.S. Armed Forces Survival Manual* as reprinted from *Physiology of Man in the Desert.*

after only three days because of dehydration. When I was a student in the Air Force Survival School, I learned that dehydration puts more students out of training than all other causes. If dehydration is this bad, think what it could do to you in a critical survival situation.

Only water in some form will prevent dehydration and keep the body at normal efficiency.

For detailed information on the symptoms, effects, and treatment of dehydration, see Chapter 13, which covers survival medicine.

Where Water Can Be Found

Fortunately, in most parts of North America, we are never far from water. However, in some places at certain times of the year, water may be hard to find. Anyone going into the wilderness should know that there is water when and where they need it or take water with them. If there isn't any water to be had conveniently for whatever reason, follow these suggestions from the Washington State Department of Emergency Services.

Along the seashore. Along the coasts you may find water in the dunes above the beach or even in the beach itself, well back from the high-tide line. Look in the hollows between sand dunes for visible water, or dig if the sand seems moist. Don't ever try to drink seawater or urine. The salt content is too high.

Along the seashore on sandy beaches, dig a hole just over the first sand dune that is directly adjacent to the water. This is where rainwater and drainage from the local water tables collect. Dig until the hole begins to fill with muddy water; a deep hole is not necessary. If you dig deeper into the wet sand, you may strike salt water, which is unfit to drink. Find some wood or brush to shore the sides of the hole to keep the sides from caving in.

When you find a damp area of surface sand, usually in a depression, it marks a good place to scoop out a shallow well. Eventually the impurities and suspended particles will settle and the water will be clear. Clarification can also be accomplished by filtration. Now the water must be made safe for drinking by boiling, if possible.

In desert or arid lands. No one should ever go into a desert or arid area without an ample supply of water and a map with reliable sources of water clearly marked on it. But if you should find yourself in an emergency situation where there is very little water, here are a few general rules for finding it.

All efforts to find water by searching and digging underground will consume energy and water, increasing your water requirements. So if you're caught in this situation you should analyze your emergency situation and water requirements very carefully, weighing all probabilities of being reported overdue or in need of help. If you can expect to be missed and can expect a search to begin within 12 to 24 hours, then it may be wiser to sit and conserve what body water you have. For example, if you plan a two-day trip into the desert and are expected back at a certain time, the chances are you will be found in three days, provided you remain with your easily seen vehicle, expect the worst, and plan accordingly.

In summer desert heat, thirst is not a strong enough sensation to indicate how much water you need. If you drink only enough to satisfy your thirst, it will still be possible for you to dehydrate slowly. The best plan is to drink plenty of water anytime it is available, particularly when you are eating. This necessary water may be taken in as plain water or in some mixture which can serve as a so-called water substitute.

The main way to conserve your water is to control your sweating. Drink water as you need it, but keep heat out of your body by keeping your clothes on. Clothing helps control sweating by not letting perspiration evaporate so fast that you get only part of its cooling effect. You may feel more comfortable in the desert without a shirt or pants, because your sweat evaporates fast and cools you. But the more sweat evaporated, the more

water lost. Furthermore, you risk getting sunburned. Desert sun will burn even if you have a good tan. Therefore, wear a hat, use a neckcloth, and keep your clothes on. Light-colored clothing turns away the heat of the sun and keeps out the hot desert air. During the day, stay in the shade as much as possible.

In general, water is more abundant and easier to find in loose sediment than in rocks. Look for springs along valley floors or down along their sloping sides. The flat benches or terraces of land above river valleys usually yield springs or seepages along their bases even when the stream is dry.

If no encouraging signs of damp sand are found, look in a different spot. (Refer to the discussion of seashore survival sites on the previous page for digging technique.) The bottom of a canyon or the base of a hill is generally the best place to look. Small springs or seeps will support green growth on the shoulder of a mesa, but these springs or seeps often disappear in a short distance. Dry streambeds often have water just below the surface. Try digging at the lowest point on the outside of a bend in the stream channel.

Watch for animals and birds moving in the early morning or late evening. They are probably moving toward water. In addition, if you are fortunate enough to find animal trails in the vicinity, trail forks will probably point toward a water source. As the animals move from their bedding sites, they converge more and more to the same trails as they approach water.

It is a popular belief that the barrel cactus found in some U. S. deserts contains an abundance of fresh, clean water. The fact is that this plant is tough and has thorns that make it hard to deal with. When the top is cut off, there is some moisture inside, but it is a slimy pulp that is difficult to get and bitter to the taste. If you must use the barrel cactus, it is

Although the solar still can be a source of drinking water, it will produce only about 2 pints of water a day.

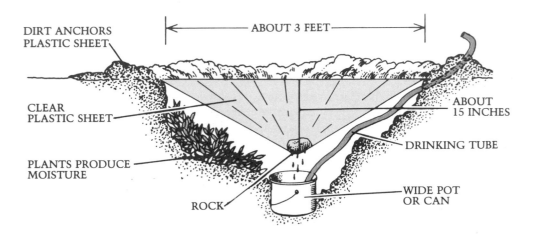

DIRT ANCHORS PLASTIC SHEET

ABOUT 3 FEET

CLEAR PLASTIC SHEET

ABOUT 15 INCHES

DRINKING TUBE

PLANTS PRODUCE MOISTURE

WIDE POT OR CAN

ROCK

best to soak a cloth in the pulp and squeeze the moisture into your mouth.

Desert solar water still. Some plants have capabilities for water storage, but efforts to get sufficient water from these plants is often unsuccessful. One of the best sources of water in hot, arid environments is the solar water still. This ingenious device, when properly set up and lined with vegetation, can produce a pint of water in about three hours.

Solar stills work slowly and require hot sunlight and patience. To make one, dig a pit 3 feet wide and 3 feet deep in the sand at the lowest possible part of your location where water would stand the longest after a rain. Line the bottom of the pit with any green vegetation possible. Install your cup or can in the bottom, at the center. Prop it up with sand and install a water-sucking tube, if you have one.

Place clear plastic across the pit so that it drapes down in the center, making sure that the lowest part of the plastic is directly above the container when you put a small rock on the plastic. Seal the edges with sand and center the rock over the can. Insulate the rock with cloth or paper, because the rock will get hot enough to melt the plastic.

Clear plastic is best. Yellow or semi-transparent color is next best. Dark-colored plastic prevents the sun's rays from reaching the sand and so slows condensation.

Do not open the still unless necessary, because the still needs a long time to resume operation. Since the solar still requires time, try to set it up in the morning so that it can work while you rest in the shade. If you have enough materials, make several stills.

The amount of water that can be obtained from a desert solar still depends upon the amount of moisture in the ground. Most produce only 2 pints of water a day. Also, in order to obtain enough water to sustain life, each person should have four or more stills in operation at once.

A solar still requires patience to set up properly, and anyone going into the desert should learn how to set up and use one before leaving civilization.

Vegetation water still. A recent innovation in solar stills has been introduced that appears to be superior in many ways to the traditional solar still. Tests are now being conducted on the purity or possible contamination of the water if poisonous plants should be used in the process described below. The water produced tastes much like the vegetation you use, but the idea is sound, and when the still is used properly and prudently, that is, when poisonous vegetation is avoided, the still will give you life-sustaining liquids.

To begin, scoop out a crater, size to be determined by whatever plastic bag you may have, on a sloping dune or built-up mound. Place the plastic bag over the crater, the bag opening on the downslope side. Use a stick or something similar to make a tent over the crater. Place clean rocks or weights around the outer crater rim to hold the plastic tent taut. Fill the crater with vegetation. Use care not to have any vegetation outside the hole or touching the plastic. As soon as the vegetation warms up, water will condense on the inside of the plastic and droplets will run down the tent to the outside of the crater.

Form a sand trough downslope from the crater to a catch hole or pool for the condensed water. Close the plastic bag tight and wait in the shade. To get water out of the bag, scoop a deeper hole just below your catch pool. Open the plastic bag just a little bit and pour out the condensed water. Do not drink the water the vegetation sat in in the crater.

Arctic and winter conditions. Dehydration is almost as great a problem in cold conditions as in the desert, because all the water is frozen into snow or ice. Some streams or lakes may provide access to flowing water (but be very careful not to fall into the water). If the sun is shining, you can melt snow on a dark plastic bag or tarp, flat rock, or any surface that will absorb the sun's heat. Arrange the surface so that the melted water will drain into a hollow depression or container.

Anyone traveling under frigid conditions should always carry a small portable gas-type stove and pot for melting ice or snow. Whenever possible, melt ice rather than snow because ice yields more water for the volume with less heat and time. Snow is 17 parts air and 1 part water. If you melt snow by heating, put in a little snow at a time and compress it, or the pot will burn. If water is available, put a little in the bottom of the pot to protect the pot and add snow gradually.

When melted, glacial ice gives roughly twice the water per fuel unit in half the time that snow does. In addition, snow more often contains dirt, soot, and animal and human contaminants.

Don't try to eat ice or snow. A day or two of taking water in this manner will make the mucous membrane of your mouth so swollen and raw as to prevent eating or drinking until the inflammation subsides. Also, your body gives up heat to melt the snow. Dogs eat snow and get away with it; humans can't.

Collecting dew and rain. Dew sometimes forms on metal auto hoods and airplane wings, or on plant leaves that can be sponged with a cloth. Some water can be obtained as dewdrops on the underside of a plastic sheet spread on the ground during the night. Use every possible means of water conservation and supplementing your water supply.

Watch the weather signs and be ready to collect rain water. To waterproof fabric for collecting rainwater, rub the fabric with wax, candles, or butter.

Spread out your waterproofed clothes to catch the rain. Remember that big leaves of trees, holes in tree trunks, and depressions in rocks will collect water for you also. Dig a hole in the ground and line it with cloth, canvas, plastic, oiled paper, or leaves—anything to stop rapid drainage into the earth.

Rainwater can be diverted from leaning trees and branches by a long cloth wick (torn from any cloth) leading into a container.

Making Water Safe to Drink

In the wilderness, finding water is only the first problem. Making it safe to drink is the second problem and is equal to the first in importance.

How often do people outdoors drink water from nearby streams or creeks without first boiling it? The water may look clear, cool, and refreshing, but looks can be deceiving. Water sources that lie downhill from homes, campsites, and industries may be contaminated with pollutants ranging from organic matter to caustic chemicals. A lovely, clear desert spring may contain arsenic. An inviting mountain stream or inland lake may contain animal wastes or parasites that render it unfit for drinking. For example, on Isle Royale in Lake Superior, inland water contains hydatid cysts borne in moose droppings; the cysts eat away at the lungs of moose and can be transmitted to humans if the water is not treated before consumption. Thus, you should never trust any water you

are not absolutely sure of, no matter how crystal-clear it looks. This rule especially applies to lakes and streams.

Once I was trout fishing with a friend in a western state. The stream we were wading looked crystal-clear, and according to our map, flowed from a wilderness area several miles upstream. We stopped for a lunch break near another angler and started to bend down to drink the water. "Hold it!" the stranger shouted. We looked up as he walked over to where we were. "This stream runs through a new ski area and cabin complex about two miles upstream," he told us. "There is raw sewage seeping into this very stream up there." Then he offered us water from his canteen, which we gladly accepted.

Since survival involves vigorous activities, our need for pure drinking water is important.

Our need for water has given rise to many myths about what is safe water. I have been told by many outdoorsmen that water running swiftly over rocks gets purified. In fact, I know one fellow who swears that water is purified as it tumbles over the ninth rock. Don't believe any of these claims! Water running over rocks may be aerated, but not purified.

Another myth claims that if clear water sits in the sun for an hour the germs are killed. Again, this is untrue. Nature produces clean water, but once it becomes unclean, rarely does nature reclean it. Treat any questionable water.

If you drink untreated water you may contract dysentery, cholera, typhoid, or the less-known but greatest threat in wilderness areas, giardiasis. One of the country's leading experts in survival medicine, Dr. Robert Sheppard of Carrollton, Alabama, explained to me what giardiasis is and its threat to humans.

According to Dr. Sheppard, giardiasis is caused by a one-celled parasite called *Giar-*

Even the most remote waters may have the dangerous one-celled parasite called Giardia, *especially if beaver are present, as in this beaver pond. (U.S. Fish and Wildlife Service photo)*

dia lamblia. This small parasite is little larger than a red blood cell and inhabits the small intestine of its host, which is often beaver, cattle, dogs, or other animals, including man. While the parasite is in the host animal, a protective cover is formed around it. Next, this parasite is passed from the host in fecal material and often finds its way into streams and lakes. It can survive for over three months in water about 40°F. It is killed when water is frozen or when it is exposed to temperatures over 120°F.

Dr. Sheppard says that when a person drinks water in which the *Giardia* are found, the results can include nausea, abdominal cramps, and almost always watery diarrhea, which may persist for several weeks. He has treated a growing number of patients with this infection in the South, and it is his opinion that giardiasis is more common than we think. Giardiasis also occurs in wilderness areas of the Rocky Mountains and as far north as the Yukon. Most of the cases are in areas where beaver are found.

Since water treatment tablets are not completely effective against *Giardia* and other water-borne health hazards, Dr. Sheppard tells me that the only sure way to treat water that is questionable is to boil the water 10 minutes before drinking. In the mountains, boil water an additional minute for each 1,000 feet of elevation.

I hunt and fish a great deal with Dr. Sheppard, and I have noticed that the only untreated water he drinks in the field is from flowing springs and artesian wells. These are usually safe.

One filtration device that I have found effective is a small filtration pump, which I carry in my daypack. The two filtration pumps I use which have been proved to filter out *Giardia* and other harmful threats are the First-Need Water Purification Device made by General Ecology, Inc., and the Katadyn Pocket Filter, sold by Katadyn USA, Inc. These little units fit into a daypack easily and require little effort to produce clean, safe drinking water.

What if you can't boil your water for some reason, such as an injury or the lack of fire or a pot, and don't have a device to use? There are some other methods of killing many water

The most reliable method of assuring safe drinking water is to boil it up to 10 minutes.

Underground water sources, such as this artesian well, are usually safe.

germs, though these would be your last choices, sensible only if it is impossible to use either of the previous methods.

There are many commercial tablets available at drugstores for treating water. These tablets contain either chlorine or iodine. Each of these ingredients has its strengths and weaknesses. That is, chlorine is more effective in dealing with some bacteria and viruses, and iodine works better with others. While either of these will usually render the water significantly safer, it is important to remember that no tablet has yet been produced which is effective against *Giardia*. If you do carry water purification tablets, be sure to check the stamped expiration date often because the tablets have a relatively short shelf life.

The iodine you have in your first aid kit can remove some water-borne hazards. Add 5 drops of iodine to 1 quart of clear water and 10 drops to cloudy water. Let it stand for 30 minutes.

Any time you are treating water in a canteen or container, be sure to splash some of the treated water on the cap, spout, and lid. You don't want to miss any germs or other critters that may come in contact with your mouth or water.

9

FOOD FOR SURVIVAL

In the United States, especially, the need for food is greatly overemphasized. The additional fat most of us carry around gives mute testimony that we eat too much and usually too often. In a survival situation, the need for food is not nearly as critical as the need for shelter, water, warmth, and signaling. Hunger strikers throughout the world have demonstrated just how long people can go without eating and still survive. Strikers have gone 50 to 60 days without eating before they either quit their self-imposed ordeal or died. Of course, in cold-weather circumstances the need for heat-generating foods is more critical because food helps prevent hypothermia.

Many survival books and manuals spend page after page telling the reader how to select edible wild plants or how to butcher a deer or how to make various primitive traps. This makes interesting reading when you are in your warm home, sitting in a comfortable chair, waiting to be called to a big pot roast dinner. But how valuable would this information be to you, even if you had the book with you, if you were in your fifth day of being lost, in the dead of winter, in northern Nevada? You are cold, tired, embarrassed, lonely, hungry, confused, and untrained. Where are those berries and flowering plants shown in your survival book? All you see is sagebrush. Where are the deer you are sup-

People who figure they will always be able to live off the land in a survival situation overlook many factors that may stack the odds against them, such as injury, weather, and terrain. It is smarter to carry a modest supply of lightweight and easily prepared survival foods into backcountry.

126

INSTANT QUAKER OATMEAL
Regular Flavor

Directions
1. Empty packet into bowl.
2. Add about 2/3 cup of boiling water and stir. For thicker oatmeal use more water, for thinner oatmeal use less water.
For best results, let stand a minute before eating.

MOUNTAIN HOUSE
FREEZE DRIED
PRESSED

GREEN PEAS

SERVING INSTRUCTIONS:

1. Break one disc into several pieces and add to 1¾ cup (10 oz.) boiling water. Package contains two discs.
2. Cover and simmer 5 to 10 minutes, stirring as needed. More water may be desired. Season as desired.
3. Green Peas are derived from 20 oz. of frozen product. When rehydrated, contents will yield six 1/2 cup servings.

NET WT. 4.5 OZ.

RICH-MOOR

APPLE CHIPS

A GREAT TRAIL
MUNCHING

MOUNTAIN HOUSE

ADD HOT WATER

FREEZE DRIED
Precooked
SCRAMBLED EGGS
FLAVORED WITH REAL BACON
SMOKE FLAVOR ADDED
2 SERVINGS (APPROX. 1 OZ. EACH) ARE
EQUIVALENT TO 3 1/3 EGGS.
INGREDIENTS: WHOLE EGGS, NONFAT DRY
MILK, CRUMBLED BACON, SALT AND SMOKE
FLAVORING. CRUMBLED BACON IS CURED
WITH WATER, SALT, SUGAR, SODIUM PHOS-
PHATES, SODIUM ERYTHORBATE, SODIUM
NITRITE.

SERVING INSTRUCTIONS:
1. Add 1 cup (8 oz.) warm to hot water to eggs.
For firm scramble use boiling water.
2. Wait 3 - 5 minutes.
3. Drain excess water from eggs and serve.
4. Spices may be added if desired.

NET WT. 2.1 OZ.

MOUNTAIN HOUSE
MFG. BY OREGON FREEZE DRY FOODS, INC.
ALBANY, OREGON 97321 U.S.A.

RICH-MOOR
CORNED HAM BAR
WITH RAISINS

INGREDIENTS: Ham, raisins, brown sugar, salt, spices, smoke flavoring, water, sodium ascorbate, sodium nitrite.

MOUNTAIN HOUSE

NO COOKING REQUIRED

Lipton
Recipe Soup Mix
Onion

SOUP DIRECTIONS
Bring 4 cups (32 oz.) water to a boil, then add contents of can.

FOR MICROWAVE
In 2-quart casserole, heat water at HIGH (600 to 700

Carnation
Rich Chocolate
Flavor
HOT COCOA MIX
Just add hot water

NET WT 1 OZ (28

FREEZE DRIED
CHICKEN and RICE
MAKES TWO 7.8 OZ. SERVINGS

INGREDIENTS: Cooked Chicken Meat, Instant Rice,
Carrots, Corn Oil, Modified Corn Starch, Salt, Hydro-
lyzed Vegetable Protein, Monosodium Glutamate,
Sugar, Chicken Fat, Onion Powder, Spices, Dehydrated
Parsley, Turmeric.

SERVING INSTRUCTIONS:
1. Add 1½ cups (12 oz.) boiling water to the inner package. Stir to wet all ingredients.
2. Wait 5 to 10 minutes. No cooking required!
3. Now ready to serve.

NET WT. 3.7 OZ. 105 G

MOUNTAIN HOUSE
MFG. BY OREGON FREEZE DRY FOODS, INC.
ALBANY, OREGON 97321 U.S.A.

Vegetable Soupmix
IMPORTED
Knorr Swiss
Vegetable Soupmix

makes SIX
6 oz servings

NET WT. 1⅝ OZ.

NATURE VALLEY
Granola Bars
Oats 'n Honey

posed to butcher? Even if you had one lying dead at your feet, would you really know how to butcher it? And where should you build your primitive traps? You have seen a few rabbits, but they don't stick to one trail in this flat country. Anyway, to be honest, you don't understand how those traps work or how to build one. They are nice survival techniques to read about, but difficult to construct and set properly.

Before we talk about finding food in the backcountry, let's discuss a few facts. Most people in North America carry enough surplus fat in their bodies to get by in a survival situation for a number of days without having much to eat. I've done it, and while the stomach cramps hurt, the head was dizzy, and I felt sick several times, I came out of the situation in good shape.

A vast majority of the people lost, injured, or stranded in the wilderness are rescued in a matter of a few days. Consider these facts. Air crashes involving planes that file a flight plan and have a working emergency locator transmitter (ELT) on board are located in an average of 13 hours. Lost or stranded people who have told some responsible person their plans are found in an average of 72 hours. With today's modern technology and methods of conducting search and rescue, there is little reason for the person who takes the time to let someone know his plans, sticks to those plans, and follows good survival rules to worry about starving to death during a backcountry crisis.

However, there are exceptions. There are people who don't file a flight plan or trip plan. There is the rare situation in which a plane crashes under foliage and can't be found. There is the situation in which a guide or other person responsible for your well-being puts you in a long-term survival situation. And there is the case where you must wait out bad weather before rescuers can

come to your aid and take you to safety.

A light plane crash occurred in Idaho on May 5, 1979. There were two survivors of the crash. They were not found until they walked out to safety on May 24. In order to survive, they felt they had to turn to cannibalism. It was for people who find themselves in such situations that the next two chapters are written.

Carry Food with You

As I hope to make evident in the next two chapters, the gathering of edible wild food, both plant and animal, is difficult for the untrained. Even those who are trained must

Killing a large animal under emergency conditions requires a combination of luck and skill, but the challenge does not end there. The animal must also be field-dressed properly and butchered. Toward this end, you must remove all internal organs and remove the hide. The carcass should be cooled as quickly as possible to inhibit bacterial and chemical decomposition, and then protected from insects, vermin, and scavengers. There is more on field care of meat in Chapter 11, beginning on page 174.

practice regularly to be effective in a survival situation. Consequently it is a good policy for those going into, over, or through wild country to take extra food with them. Since most people's food requirements are little for up to three weeks, you don't have to take a huge box of food. Today there is a wide assortment of freeze-dried foods that take up little space and, with the addition of water, become tasty food. These foods are packaged to give them a long storage life regardless of the conditions.

There are many other foods and snacks that are easy to take along with you in case you are detained in the wilderness unexpectedly. Here are two examples of what is available:

Chuck Wagon Foods Meal Packs are designed to meet the needs of adults or youngsters for base-camp or trail use. These freeze-dried and dehydrated foods are light in weight, need no refrigeration, and come packed in waterproof plastic. There is no litter problem—everything is either consumable or burnable. There is a choice of 15 different menus for breakfasts, lunches, and suppers in packs for two, four, or six people. They are fast-cooking, there is nothing to spoil, and the portions are big for hearty outdoor appetites.

The Mountain House Security Pak is similar to the U.S. military's Long Range Patrol (LRP) Ration. Each of the seven complete meals available contains a generous serving of a freeze-dried entree—approximately 1 pound (488 grams) reconstituted—plus orangeade or lemonade, tropical bar or fig newton cake, a packet of pilot breads, salt, pepper, a napkin, and a plastic spoon. Entrees include vegetable stew with beef, beef and rice with onions, chili with beans, rice and chicken, potatoes and beef, chicken stew, and beef stew.

There are also many trail foods that are easy to make at home and store easily. Refer

In order to learn to identify edible plants, carry well-illustrated field guides in all seasons. Although identification of the fruit of this staghorn sumac (used to flavor water) is relatively easy, sure identification of many of the more common edibles can be difficult, even with the aid of field guides. (Neil Soderstrom photo)

to Appendix 2, "Recommended Reading," for sources of these recipes.

Foods of this type should be a part of the survival gear in any vehicle, snowmobile, aircraft, boat, canoe, or pack going into the backcountry. Even the hunter or canoeist who employs an outfitter or guide should have a daypack with him at all times with food in it.

An excellent free camping food service has been set up by Dr. William Forgey, a physician with a vast amount of survival and expedition experience. It will help you plan and select your survival foods for the backcountry. Write Indiana Camp Supply, Box 344, Pittsboro, IN 46167. (This is also a unique source of other wilderness survival supplies.)

Remember, it's a lot easier to have survival food with you than it is to try to recall or imagine mountain-man skills while you try to live off the land.

10
EDIBLE WILD PLANTS

If you are caught without a supply of survival foods, then you may be forced to turn to living off the land. Since there are usually more plants in the wild than animals, and since plants are a lot easier to get your hands on, we will look at them first as a food source.

There are a large number of edible wild plants in North America; estimates run as high as 2,000 species. Also, there are a large number of poisonous plants, over 700 species. Explaining how to distinguish one from the other in a book chapter is impossible. This is especially true when you consider that in some plants, such as common elderberry, one part is edible and another part is toxic; and that in other plants, such as pokeweed, one stage of growth is edible, but another stage is dangerously poisonous; or that some edible plants look almost identical to poisonous plants, such as sweetflag (edible) and iris (relatively poisonous).

It is a common misconception that people can eat any parts of wild plants that animals eat. Don't believe that! Deer, squirrels, and birds eat dogwood berries, which are toxic to man. Deer love poison ivy and poison oak, which are highly toxic to man. Birds love mistletoe berries, which can kill man.

In order to learn about edible wild plants, you must first learn to identify plants. This requires a lot of practice under the tutorship of a knowledgeable instructor. Once you

Botanist Dr. James A. (Jim) Duke, eminent authority on wild plants, is here uprooting arrowhead and cattail. For survival fare, Jim considers wetlands generally excellent for foraging. In a single autumn weekend, Jim served as guide in locating and photographing most of the plants shown in this chapter. (Neil Soderstrom photo)

know how to identify plants, you must review your knowledge often in order to remember which is which and what each looks like at each season. Next, you must learn which plants and parts of plants are edible and how to prepare them. Acorns from red oaks, for example, are so bitter they are edible only after being boiled several times in fresh water.

Perhaps the real drawback to learning about edible wild plants is that you can learn to identify the plants native to your area. But you may not get caught in a survival situation there. When a survival situation occurs, you may be in an unfamiliar region where most of the plant life is unknown to you.

You will probably notice that mushrooms are not included in the list of edible wild plants in this book. Mushrooms are low in food value and an expert is required to identify the ones that are edible, so they shouldn't be considered a survival food.

There are many books available on the subject of edible wild plants, and the serious survival student would do well to study the ones listed in Appendix 2 in the back of this book. But remember that after studying these books, you will still need a great deal of practice in the field before you can count much on your skills.

The plants on upcoming pages are but a few of the many edible wild plants that may be available in a survival situation. But I must reemphasize that great care must be used in learning to identify these plants, and if there is any doubt, they should be avoided.

Don't expect wild plants to taste like something from the supermarket. Though some are tasty, others range from tasteless to bitter. You should enter into a diet of edible wild plants slowly and develop a taste for them over a period of time. This gradual approach will also give your digestive system a fair chance to adjust.

It's a mistake to assume you can eat all plants you observe wild animals eating. For example, this poison ivy is a favorite food of deer, but it is dangerous for man to touch—let alone eat.

In order to make wild foods taste better, I always carry some beef or chicken bouillon in my survival kit. A little bouillon makes flat-tasting wild greens seem like a gourmet dish, especially after a week with no food.

Here are some rules for eating wild plants:

1. Do not eat anything you cannot positively identify. There are poisonous plants you must avoid.

2. Be prepared to study. There is no shortcut to learning about edible wild plants. The best way to learn is to have a guide who takes you on field trips. The next best way is to take a course. A third possibility is to buy books and study on your own.

3. Learn scientific names. Too many dissimilar plants have names such as pigweed, chickweed, wild spinach, and so on.

4. Learn to identify the plant in all stages of growth: first shoots of spring, flowering plant, fruit stage, dry winter stage.

5. Start with one or two. You cannot hope to learn all edible plants in one season.

6. Know what part of the plant is edible and when it is edible. For instance, the fruit of the elderberry is edible when ripe, but toxic when green. The green twigs are always toxic.

7. Use recipes. In order to enjoy wild plants, you have to prepare them properly.

8. Eat just a sample the first time. Our 20th-century stomachs are not accustomed to pioneer fare. Also, different people react differently to new foods.

9. Watch out for contamination on and around the plants in the forms of sprays, fertilizers, or animal wastes.

10. Know the common poisonous plants of the area. When learning a new edible plant, a good question to ask is "Is there anything poisonous that looks like this?" Some of the more common poisonous plants are presented at the end of this chapter.

Some Edible Plants

A few wild plants are fairly common throughout North America and have edible parts during some part of the year. Here is but a sample that the survival student should know, here listed alphabetically by their most commonly used *common* name.

- Arrowhead, page 134
- Blackberry, page 135
- Burdock, page 136
- Cattail, page 138
- Chokecherry, page 140
- Chufa, page 141
- Clover, page 142
- Dandelion, page 143
- Dock, page 144
- Evening primrose, page 145
- Greenbrier, page 146
- Groundnut, page 147
- Hickories, page 148
- Jerusalem artichoke, page 149
- Lamb's-quarters, page 150
- Milkweed, page 151
- Oaks, page 152
- Pines, page 154
- Plantain, page 155
- Pokeweed, page 156
- Prickley pear, page 157
- Purslane, page 158
- Roses, page 159
- Sassafras, page 160
- Sheep sorrel, page 161
- Watercress, page 162
- Wild plums, page 163
- Wild onion, page 164
- Wild Strawberry, page 165
- Yellow pond lily, page 164.

ARROWHEAD, WAPATO, DUCK POTATO, KATNISS, SWAMP POTATO

SCIENTIFIC NAME: *Sagittaria latifolia*

RANGE: Throughout most of the U.S. and southern Canada

WHERE GENERALLY FOUND: These aquatic plants grow along the margins of ponds and streams and in ditches. One of the most common places that I have found them is along beaver dams. Also, in many areas, they are found along the edges of marshes and bogs.

DESCRIPTION: A perennial plant growing from 2 to 4 feet high, with fibrous roots de-

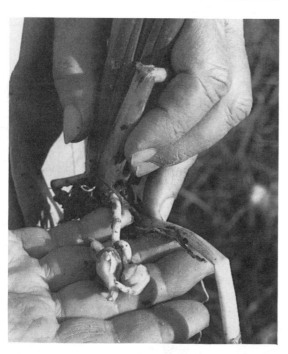

Left: *Arrowhead tubers may extend over 5 feet from the base of the plant.* **Right:** *Here are an arrowhead fruiting stem and leaves. (Neil Soderstrom photos)*

veloping potatolike tubers which may be as large as 2 inches in diameter. The leaves grow from long stems, are somewhat arrowhead-shaped, and are anywhere from 4 to 10 inches long. Throughout most of the summer, the flowers of this plant will be seen growing in clusters of three, with each flower having three white petals. These flowers are from 1 to 1½ inches broad, and the flower stalk is usually taller than the leaf stalk.

EDIBLE PARTS AND SEASONS: Arrowhead is one of our most widely distributed and best survival foods. It is usually considered a fall and early spring plant for food, but many times I have eaten the larger, older tubers throughout the summer and into the fall. The only edible parts of the plant are the tubers which grow along the root system. The pioneers and Indians found the arrowhead to be one of the most valuable native food plants. The Indian women would wade in the water, using their toes to dislodge the hard tubers. In a survival situation, it is easy to take a long stick and stir the mud at the base of the arrowhead plant. Once the tubers are dislodged, they float to the surface and may be easily gathered.

PREPARATION: Starchy tubers are good baked, boiled, roasted, or even french-fried. They are also eaten raw, but they have a bitter taste when raw. They are best baked or boiled for about 30 minutes and served along with meat or fish. Also, the tubers may be dried for future use by boiling them until they are tender, then slicing them ¼ to 1 inch thick. Dry thoroughly in the sun. Be sure they are stored in a warm, dry location. Before serving the dried tubers, soak them for 20 minutes in water and cook them again for an additional 20 minutes.

BLACKBERRY

SCIENTIFIC NAME: *Rubus* species
RANGE: Throughout much of the U.S.
WHERE GENERALLY FOUND: In open areas in woodlands, particularly in areas of rich soil and high moisture. However, these plants have been found in remote mountain valleys as well as high dry plateaus.

DESCRIPTION: The blackberry bush is well known. It is one of the thick-growing, rambling bushes considered by many to be nothing more than a thorny shrub. The leaves are generally in stems off the main branch and in groups of three with a serrated edge. The flowers are white with five petals. Usually the overall blackberry bush will grow some 6 feet high. Flowers are usually found on the plant from April through July. The fruit

SPECIES OCCUR WIDELY

Blackberry (Leonard Lee Rue III photo)

may be found anywhere from June through September, and it appears, true to its name, to be black—a mound of small black bubbles covered with a fine hair. Before the blackberry is ripe, it is red; it is not edible until it reaches its true black color.

EDIBLE PARTS AND SEASONS: Along with the fruit, the dried leaves may be used to make a tea, and tender blackberry shoots may be used to make a salad in early spring. The best time for gathering leaves and fruit is during the summer months.

PREPARATION: The fruit, which is rich in vitamin C, may be eaten when picked, or it may be kept in a cool location for several days and added to a mixture of fat to make pemmican or added to a bannock mixture. Tender young sprouts and twigs gathered in the spring may be eaten raw or mixed with other edible wild greens to make a salad. The leaves gathered during summer may be boiled for a tea.

BURDOCK

SCIENTIFIC NAME: *Arctium minus*

RANGE: Throughout much of the U.S. and southern Canada

WHERE GENERALLY FOUND: This plant is more common where people have lived than in the backcountry. It is often found along paths and roads and near old homesites, farm buildings, and abandoned fields.

DESCRIPTION: This is a biennial plant and

These are burdock fruits of a second year plant, which grows up to 6 feet high and aids in locating nearby first-year plants. (Neil Soderstrom photo)

The low, leafy burdock plant in its first year, left, provides edible roots like that shown at right. (Neil Soderstrom photos)

grows up to 6 feet high. The stems are upright, smooth, and branched. The leaves alternate along the stem and are from 12 to 20 inches long and 8 to 12 inches wide. They are widest near the base. The upper stem limbs are generally smaller. Also, the leaves are slightly woolly. This plant is usually seen flowering from July through

October. The flowers range in color from pink to purple and emerge from a thistlelike burr. EDIBLE PARTS AND SEASONS: During the spring of the year, the leaves and leaf stalks may be used as a salad or boiled in several changes of water to be eaten as greens. The roots of the first-year plants can be boiled for 30 minutes in two changes of water and also served as a vegetable. Early summer is the best time to dig root stock. The flower stalk may be eaten after removing all the green rind. Many people eat it like celery or boil it tender.

CATTAIL

SCIENTIFIC NAME: *Typha latifolia*

RANGE: Throughout most of North America into the midsection of Canada, and all of the U.S.

WHERE GENERALLY FOUND: In ditches, marshes, swamps, shallow water, lakes and ponds, and almost any other habitually wet area

DESCRIPTION: The cattail is a tall, flat-leafed plant with a sausagelike head which grows at the top. It is usually found in groups and grows from 2 to 10 feet tall. The flat, slender leaves are sheathed at the base and are approximately 1 inch wide. The sausagelike head is brown.

EDIBLE PARTS AND SEASONS: The cattail has long been one of our most beneficial edible wild plants. Historians tell us that Indians often selected their village sites near waterways which were abundant with cattails. They ate parts of the plant every day. The roots of the cattail are the most nutritious part of the plant. They contain up to 46 percent starch and 11 percent sugar. They grow just under the mud and can be pulled up easily. The roots are abundant and grow in chainlike fashion about 1 inch in diameter and vary in color from black to reddish brown. The best time for collecting these underground parts is late in the fall and into the winter to early spring. The cattail root is covered by a spongy layer that must be peeled off; this is easy to do with the fingers. The roots can then be eaten raw or boiled. After boiling for approximately 30 minutes, they

Left: Cattail fruiting spikes. Right: Cattail pollen, a flour supplement. (Neil Soderstrom photos)

Right: *Cattail stem.* **Below:** *Cattail roots. (Neil Soderstrom photos)*

taste much like potatoes. Also, the roots may be sliced thin and dried for future cooking or ground into a white flour. During the early spring, young shoots which grow from root stocks can be peeled to a tender white core and eaten raw or cooked like asparagus by boiling for 15 minutes. The shoots remain tender and delicious until they reach about 18 inches in height. After that, they are tough.

The new green spikes at the top of the flower stalk can be gathered and husked as you would corn, dropped into boiling, salted water to simmer until tender, and eaten like corn on the cob. As the bloom spikes ripen and produce pollen, it is easy to gather large quantities of pollen by shaking the heads over a container. This pollen is high in protein and may be eaten raw in a survival situation.

CHOKECHERRY

SCIENTIFIC NAME: *Prunus virginiana*
RANGE: Throughout the northern half of the U.S. and the southern half of Canada
WHERE GENERALLY FOUND: In open areas in woodlands, along fencerows, and other open areas where the soil is moist
DESCRIPTION: The chokecherry is commonly regarded as a shrub or small tree with a reddish-brown bark that is usually smooth. The leaves are egg-shaped with rounded or wide wedge-shaped bases. They are pointed at the tip with numerous sharp teeth along the

margin and are dark green and smooth. The flowers are produced in short, cylindrical clusters from 4 to 6 inches long, each with five white, rounded petals. The fruit is fleshy, rounded, and usually dark red or black.
EDIBLE PARTS AND SEASONS: The fruit is the edible part of this plant, and it is usually found throughout the summer and into early fall. The chokecherry is perhaps best known as a thirst-quencher, as the cherries are very juicy. The juice may be made from the chokecherry by crushing 1 quart of the cherries in 1 cup of water. Simmer for approximately 30 minutes and strain out the juice.

CAUTION: The pits in the middle of the fruit, like those of the domestic peach, are poisonous and should be avoided. Also, the leaves are poisonous.

Blackcherry, with more palatable fruits than chokecherry, can be distinguished from chokecherry by the blackcherry's slightly blunter-edged and longer leaves. (Neil Soderstrom photo)

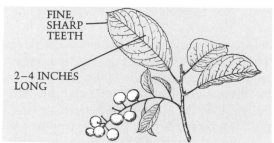

Chokecherry (from Sargent)

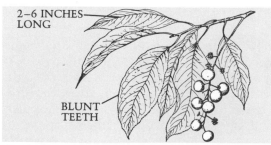

Blackcherry (from Sargent)

CHUFA, NUTGRASS, EARTH ALMOND

SCIENTIFIC NAME: *Cyperus esculentus*
RANGE: Throughout much of the U.S. east of the Rockies and California. Also found in parts of southern Canada.
WHERE GENERALLY FOUND: Abundant in rich, moist soils in open areas, such as abandoned and cultivated fields, along the edges of roads, and ditches
DESCRIPTION: Chufa looks very much like what most people consider a grass. The leaves are narrow and range anywhere from 8 to 24 inches long. All leaves emerge from one central point on the plant. The flowering head grows taller than the leaves emerging from

Shown in autumn, this is one of several Cyperus *species, which many people refer to as chufa. (Neil Soderstrom photo)*

the center, and at the top there is a flowering cluster of cylindrical spikelets.
EDIBLE PARTS AND SEASONS: This well-known weed is one of our most plentiful edible roots and is easy to recognize. The edible parts are the tubers, which grow in the soil immediately under the plant. The tubers appear nutlike and taste sweet and nutty. They are edible throughout the entire year.
PREPARATION: Once the tubers are washed, they may be eaten raw, boiled, dried, ground into flour, or used as a coffee substitute. For use as coffee, they should be roasted, ground, and brewed like coffee. The chufa is an excellent survival plant, since it is easy to gather many of the nutlike tubers and dry them and carry them with you.

Chufa plant with tubers

CLOVER

SCIENTIFIC NAME: *Trifolium* species

RANGE: Throughout most of the U.S. and southern Canada

WHERE GENERALLY FOUND: In fields, along sides of roads, around old homesites, pastures, open woodlands

DESCRIPTION: There are some 75 varieties of clovers found in North America. These plants have leaves branched from a stem, usually in leaflets of three, and depending upon the variety, the leaf will range in size from ⅛ inch to 1 inch. The flowers of the clover are usually on a long, leafless stem and range in color from white to red. The main stems of the clover plants are usually runners. These plants may be seen flowering anywhere from early April through late October.

EDIBLE PARTS AND SEASONS: Young leaves, flower heads, and seeds of clovers are edible and are well known for their richness in protein. The flower heads and tender young leaves are best if soaked for several hours in salty water or boiled for 10 minutes. The dried flower heads make an interesting tea, and the dried flower heads and seeds may be ground into a flour. Tender young leaves have also been added to other edible wild plants to create a salad.

Red Clover (Trifolium pratense), *above right, and a white clover (Neil Soderstrom photos)*

DANDELION

SCIENTIFIC NAME: *Taraxacum officinale*
RANGE: Throughout much of North America
WHERE GENERALLY FOUND: In lawns, yards, homesites, open fields, and open woodlands
DESCRIPTION: The dandelion leaves are basal, ranging from 3 to 14 inches long and from 3 to 5 inches wide. They are widest near the tip and rounded to pointed at the tip. They are irregularly lobed along the margin and taper to a narrow base. The leaves are hairy underneath and have a milky juice. The flowers are produced throughout the spring at the tip of a hollow stalk. The flower

INTRODUCED & GROWS WILD

heads are from 1 to 2 inches across and are composed of numerous small, narrow orange to yellow flowers. It is interesting to note that they remain closed on cloudy days. Once the fruit is formed, a delicate ball of fuzzy seeds is at the tip of the flower stem.

EDIBLE PARTS AND SEASONS: The dandelion is well known for having saved people from starvation. The edible parts are its roots, the crowns of the plants, and the tops from young leaves and flower buds. These plants are edible year-round and are rich in Vitamin A. The leaves may be eaten by boiling them in water, changing the water, and then boiling them a second time for approximately 15 minutes. In order to eat the roots, peel them, slice them thin, and boil them in two changes of water for approximately 20 minutes.

Dandelion with leaves characteristically wider at tips (Neil Soderstrom photo)

DOCK, SOUR DOCK, CURLED DOCK, YELLOW DOCK

SCIENTIFIC NAME: *Rumex crispus*

RANGE: Widespread throughout much of North America

WHERE GENERALLY FOUND: Common at old homesites, old sawmill sites, roadsides, fields, and other open areas

DESCRIPTION: Docks are a bulky plant with stout stems and basal leaves. The leaves vary in size from a few inches to a foot in length and are commonly tapering but sometimes heart-shaped. One of the most noticeable characteristics of the leaves is that the edges are curly. There is a  papery, straw-colored sheath around the stem where the leaves are attached. The flowers are small, usually greenish, stalked, and densely clustered on one to several narrow elongated stalks. The fruit is three-parted, dark red to reddish brown, and each fruit has three nutlets.

EDIBLE PARTS AND SEASONS: This plant is edible year-round. In the spring the young leaves may be cooked for about 10 minutes in a small amount of water. In the summer, the older leaves may be cooked for 20 to 30 minutes with one or two changes of water to make them tender and to remove the bitterness. While this is an edible plant, a large amount can cause stomach upset. The fruits of the plant may be ground into flour. Dock is high in calcium, phosphorous, and potassium, as well as other essential nutrients.

INTRODUCED & GROWS WILD

Left: *Dock plant in early autumn.* **Right:** *Dock pods and seeds. (Neil Soderstrom photos)*

EVENING PRIMROSE

SCIENTIFIC NAME: *Oenothera biennis*
RANGE: Throughout much of the eastern half of the U.S. and southern Canada
WHERE GENERALLY FOUND: Along roads, in prairies, fields, and old homesites
DESCRIPTION: This is a biennial plant and usually grows approximately 5 feet high. The stems are upright and very hairy. Leaves of the first year grow in a rosette on the ground, and the second-year leaves grow on a tall flower stalk. They are alternate, lance-shaped, from 3 to 7 inches long, from 1 to 2 inches wide, and pointed at the tip. Leaves are tubed along the edge. The flowers are bright yellow in color and have four  large petals, approximately 1½ inches long. Flowers open after dusk and are usually closed by the middle of the morning. The fruits are cylinder-shaped capsules from ½ to 2 inches in length, and contain small reddish seeds. The flowers usually are found from June throughout October.

EDIBLE PARTS AND SEASONS: The plant offers edible food during the autumn, winter, and spring. In the autumn and winter, dig the taproots of the first-year growth. Peel the roots and boil in two changes of water for approximately 30 minutes. Also, the taproot may be sliced thinly and fried. In the spring, the young leaves of this plant may be used mixed with other edible wild plants for a salad or they may be boiled for 20 minutes in two changes of water and eaten as a vegetable. When eaten alone, the leaves have a slightly bitter taste.

Left: *Evening primrose, second-year plant.* **Right:** *A root still attached to its first-year rosette and flowers from a second-year plant. (Neil Soderstrom photos)*

GREENBRIER, BULL BRIER, CAT BRIER

SCIENTIFIC NAME: *Smilax bona-nox*

RANGE: Throughout eastern U.S. and southeastern Canada

WHERE GENERALLY FOUND: In open woodlands, along the edges of fields, and also in the open areas of woodlands where the soil is damp

DESCRIPTION: This plant is a perennial climbing vine whose older stems are woody and branch frequently. On the vine are tendrils. Some of the vines contain thorns, while others will be thornless. The leaves  are alternate, approximately 1 to 3 inches long, and triangular. They are broadest near the base and pointed at the tip. The flowers on this vine are found from June through September, and they grow in clusters on a short stem emerging from the vine. The flowers range in color from a dull white to a dull green. The fruit appears as small black berries, which are *not* edible.

EDIBLE PARTS AND SEASONS: The young shoots and leaves of this plant are edible during the spring and summer as long as they are tender and juicy. They may be eaten raw, added to a salad, or boiled in water for 15 minutes. The root stock is also listed as an edible, but its complicated preparation makes it unworthy as a survival food.

Greenbrier young shoot and mature plant (Katy McKinney photo)

GROUNDNUT

SCIENTIFIC NAME: *Apios americana*
RANGE: Throughout much of the eastern half of the U.S. and southeastern Canada
WHERE GENERALLY FOUND: Moist woodlands, bottomland, stream banks, and thickets
DESCRIPTION: The groundnut is a small vine. There are fragrant clusters of brown pealike flowers in the juncture of the leaf and stem. The leaves are light green, smooth, with five to seven egg-shaped, short, pointed leaflets. The flowers generally appear between July and September, and their fragrance resembles

that of violets. The fruits are dry, linear pods from 2 to 5 inches long, containing anywhere from two to six seeds.

EDIBLE PARTS AND SEASONS: The tubers which grow underneath this plant are excellent potato substitutes and have a flavor very similar to a turnip. This edible tuber is available year-round. To prepare the tuber, thoroughly wash and boil for approximately 20 minutes. Also, tubers may be roasted, or sliced and fried. In order to enjoy the full flavor of this plant, eat it while it is still hot. This is one of the best edible wild plants for a person in a survival situation. Each plant will have a long stream of walnut-sized tubers, and they may be dried and carried for long periods of time. The tubers may be eaten raw, but they are much better when cooked.

*Left: Groundnut plant with tubers. **Above:** Groundnut vine entwined on shrub; note groundnut seed pods. (Neil Soderstrom photos)*

HICKORIES

SCIENTIFIC NAME: *Carya* species

RANGE: Throughout most of the eastern half of the U.S.

WHERE GENERALLY FOUND: In a variety of landforms, ranging from deep, rich soils of floodplains and bottomlands to dry, upland slopes

DESCRIPTION: Hickories, by the time they are old enough to produce nuts, are large trees with rounded crowns and a light gray, somewhat shaggy bark. The leaves are alternate, deciduous, with five to seven leaflets that range from 3 to 9 inches long and 2 to 5 inches wide. They are pointed at the tip and toothed along the margins. The fruit produced by a hickory tree may be one nut or pairs of nuts covered by a thick husk. When the husk is removed, a whitish-colored, thick, hard-shelled nut is revealed.

EDIBLE PARTS AND SEASONS: Gather the hickory nuts in autumn as the leaves turn and fall begins. Remove the outer husk and crack the hard shell that surrounds the nut meat. The nut meat may be eaten raw or may be mixed with almost any other type of food. The meat from the nut is very nutritious and mades an excellent autumn survival food. Also, it is interesting to note that during the winter and spring, the trees may be tapped for sap and a hickory syrup, similar to maple syrup, may be made from the boiled sap.

Mockernut hickory (U.S. Forest Service photo)

Big shellbark hickory (from Sargent)

Shagbark hickory (U.S. Forest Service photo)

JERUSALEM ARTICHOKE

SCIENTIFIC NAME: *Helianthus tuberosus*

RANGE: The original range of the Jerusalem artichoke was south-central Canada and eastern and central U.S. to Arkansas. However, this plant is becoming more widely distributed and may be found in other areas.

WHERE GENERALLY FOUND: In almost any open area, such as roadsides, along the edges of fields, and in abandoned fields. It prefers a damp soil. Its wide distribution is attributed to the Indians, who cultivated the plant in many parts of the eastern U.S.

DESCRIPTION: The Jerusalem artichoke is a wild sunflower with a hairy stem growing 6 to 10 feet tall. The leaves are thick and hard, hairy on top, and downy underneath. The bright yellow flowers may be seen from July through October. The leaves are opposite or in whorls of three on the lower part of the stem and alternate above. They are 10 inches long and from 2 to 6 inches wide. The flower heads are rounded with a central disk, approximately 1 inch across. Ten to 20 rays, approximately ½ inch long, make up the flower. Each plant may have several flower heads on slender stems from the leaf bases on the upper part of the stems. Usually if you find one Jerusalem artichoke, you will find a large number of plants, as they prefer to grow in colonies.

EDIBLE PARTS AND SEASONS: The edible part of Jerusalem artichoke is the tubers which grow underneath the plant. These tubers are edible during the winter and spring. They are delicious and are said to be more nutritious than potatoes. To prepare the tubers, scrape and cook them as you would potatoes. They are also good when sliced and eaten raw, and they may be served with other greens.

Left: Jerusalem artichoke flowers. **Right:** Jerusalem artichoke tubers. (Neil Soderstrom photos)

LAMB'S-QUARTERS, PIGWEED

SCIENTIFIC NAME: *Chenopodium album*
RANGE: Widespread throughout much of the U.S. and southern Canada
WHERE GENERALLY FOUND: Common in yards, roadsides, abandoned fields, and occasionally open woodlands
DESCRIPTION: This is an annual plant which grows approximately 2 feet high. Stems are erect, usually branched, with a pale green or whitish cast to the leaves and stems. The leaves are alternate and the

INTRODUCED &
GROWS WILD

lower ones are almost triangular and up to about 4 inches long. They are blunt at the tip and coarsely toothed along the margin. The leaves on the underside are white. This plant flowers in late spring, throughout the summer, with tiny, inconspicuous flowers that are greenish, occasionally turning reddish.

EDIBLE PARTS AND SEASONS: The tender leaves and tips of newly emerging plants are edible in spring and summer and into the autumn. The tender leaves and tips are excellent when steamed or boiled for approximately 15 minutes. On older plants the young leafy stems which grow near the tip are edible. Autumn seeds make good porridge.

Left: Lamb's-quarters, young plant. **Right:** *Leaves and fruits (Neil Soderstrom photos)*

MILKWEED
SCIENTIFIC NAME: *Asclepias syriaca*
RANGE: Throughout much of northeastern U.S. and southeastern Canada
WHERE GENERALLY FOUND: Generally along roadsides, the edge of woodlands and meadows, and fields
DESCRIPTION: This is a perennial plant which grows to be approximately 6 feet tall. The stems are upright and usually unbranched and hairy. Leaves are opposite, broadest near the base, coming to a rounded tip. The leaves range from 4 to 11 inches long and are  wavy along the entire margin. Also, the leaves are thick and leathery, hairy above, and have a milky sap. The flowers grow in dense, rounded heads from 2 to 4 inches across, and each flower in the cluster is a dull purple to greenish white with five petals. The fruit is an elongated pod from 3 to 5 inches long and covered with a soft green projection.

EDIBLE PARTS AND SEASONS: Milkweed is an easy-to-find spring and summer survival food. The young shoots, leaves, unopened flower buds, flowers, and young pods are all edible. Cover the young shoots with 6 inches of boiling water and cook for approximately 15 minutes, changing the water two or three times. The top leaves, flower buds, and young pods may be prepared in a similar manner. Also, the flowers can be dipped into boiling water for approximately a minute and covered with a batter and fried to make a fritter.

CAUTION: This is one of the few edible wild plants that has milky sap. It is a basic rule for edible wild plants to avoid plants with a milky sap, so proper identification is important. It is easy to confuse this plant with young shoots of dogbanes or butterfly weed, which may be toxic.

Milkweed flower and young pod (Marcia Stevens photos)

OAKS

SCIENTIFIC NAME: *Quercus* species

RANGE: Throughout much of the U.S. and southern Canada

WHERE GENERALLY FOUND: There are approximately 55 native oak species in North America which offer important food sources in a survival situation. Oaks may grow in a variety of situations, ranging from damp floodplains to high, dry, mountainous areas.

DESCRIPTION: Space restrictions in this book don't allow descriptions of all 55 oaks. Generally, oaks in North America are broken down into two groups—the white oak group and the red/black oak group. The white oak group has the more palatable and edible acorns, and these trees are distinguished from other oaks by a combination of characteristics. The leaves are toothed or lobed, but never bristle-tipped. Acorns mature at the end of the first growing season on the current year's twig, and the inner surface of the acorn shell lacks hairs. The bark of these trees is usually a light gray, and the edges of the leaves are rounded rather than tipped. The red/black oak group is characterized by leaves that have sharp edges and always with a bristle-like tip extending beyond the margin of the leaf. The acorns mature at the end of the second year on the previous year's twigs, and the inner surface of the acorn shell is hairy. The acorn meat in this group is bitter, and it is not as desirable as that of the white oak group.

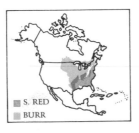

EDIBLE PARTS AND SEASONS: A few white oaks have acorns sweet enough to be eaten raw or roasted. But most acorns have an extremely bitter taste. This bitterness is due to the abundance of tannin, which is readily soluble in water. In order to prepare acorns for eating during the fall and early winter, strip them of their shells and boil in repeated changes of water until the water no longer turns brown. Then the acorn meats may be roasted or eaten as nuts. Acorn meats that have been boiled repeatedly may be dried and ground into meal and used to make bread. Acorns were a major food of the Indians.

White oak (U.S. Forest Service photo)

Southern red oak (U.S. Forest Service photo)

Bur oak (U.S. Forest Service photo)

Blackjack oak (U.S. Forest Service photo)

Chestnut oak (U.S. Forest Service photo)

PINES

SCIENTIFIC NAME: *Pinus* species

RANGE: Throughout much of North America.

WHERE GENERALLY FOUND: Anywhere from low river bottoms to the top of some of our tallest mountains just before reaching the timberline.

DESCRIPTION: Pine trees are evergreen trees with clusters of long, slender needles along the twigs. The needle clusters are bound at the base into bundles, each bundle with from two to five needles. Trees will have the familiar pine cones located on them.

EDIBLE PARTS AND SEASONS: The pine is edible year-round. The parts of the tree that are edible are the inner bark, or cambium layer of the inner bark, young shoots, and young pine needles. The tender new shoots may be stripped of their needles and peeled and eaten. Pine needles, when they are new and starchy, are nutritious to chew upon. The green needles of the pine tree can be made into a tea, which is rich in vitamin C. Place a handful in a pan and cover them with boiling water. Let them steep until the tea tastes strong enough.

The most edible part of the pine tree is the inner bark. This is perhaps one of the best-known wild edibles in the world. It may be eaten either raw or cooked. Many early settlers gathered the inner bark in the springtime, dried it throughout the summer, and then ground it into a flour for the fall and winter. Also, it may be scraped and eaten raw as it comes straight off the tree, or it may be cut into strips and boiled in water like spaghetti. The seeds are also good food.

The inner bark of pines is edible.

White pine, above, and red pine, below (U.S. Forest Service photos)

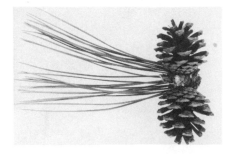

PLANTAIN

SCIENTIFIC NAME: *Plantago major*

RANGE: Widespread throughout much of North America

WHERE GENERALLY FOUND: Common in any open area, along roadsides, in yards, and around old homesites

DESCRIPTION: This low-growing plant has six to eight leaves emerging from one central point. The leaves are from 2 to 8 inches long and from 1 to 4 inches wide. They are rounded to pointed at the tip, toothed, and wavy along the margins. The flowers are tiny and are numerous along the upper part of an erect spike which generally will grow some 8 inches high. Fruits are tiny capsules produced along the flower spike.

EDIBLE PARTS AND SEASONS: This is an excellent plant to eat during the spring, summer, and early fall. Pick the young leaves before the flower stalk appears in order to get the tastiest leaf. Older leaves are stringy and tough to chew and digest. The most tender leaves are good in salads or cooked with other greens to form a vegetable. To eat plantain leaves as a separate vegetable, soak the leaves in salt water for approximately 5 minutes. Boil them in just enough water to cover them until they are tender. Also, this plant may be made into a beverage by steeping a handful of leaves in a pint of boiling water for about 30 minutes.

Plantain with fruiting spike
(Neil Soderstrom photo)

POKEWEED

SCIENTIFIC NAME: *Phytolacca americana*
RANGE: Throughout much of the eastern half of the U.S. and becoming widespread in the western half
WHERE GENERALLY FOUND: Grows profusely along fencerows, roadsides, open areas in woodlands, and along the edges of fields
DESCRIPTION: This is a large perennial plant that grows to 10 feet high. The stems are branched, upright, and smooth, with an unpleasant odor when broken. Leaves are alternate, 3 to 12 inches long, and 2 to 5 inches wide. They are pointed at the tip. The flowers are greenish to white, produced in narrow, elongated clusters. Each flower is only approximately 1/10 inch long and is whitish. The fruits are a purple color in clusters appearing as 5 to 12 berries. This plant can be recognized by the reddish color of the stalks and stems. Occasionally the older stalks will become deep purple.

EDIBLE PARTS AND SEASONS: The first rule in eating pokeweed is to remember that the root and all other parts of the plant except the young shoots are poisonous. However, this is a standard plant that is eaten not only by people in a survival situation but by many rural homeowners who look forward each spring to eating the delicate shoots as they first emerge. The rule to follow is if any shoots show purple coloration, avoid them. During the spring, locate emerging, tender young shoots and boil them 10 minutes with two or three changes of water. Be sure to drain the water before eating, as the water will occasionally make you ill. Once you have boiled the shoots and poured the water off, pour in fresh water and simmer them until they become tender. While this plant has

INTRODUCED IN WEST

toxic parts and if eaten when it matures can be poisonous, it is an excellent survival food during the early spring.

Pokeweed leaves are shown in spring, at the only edible stage. The plants are easily located by the tall, broken, and hollow dry stalks of the previous year, also shown here. (Neil Soderstrom photo)

PRICKLY PEAR, INDIAN FIG

SCIENTIFIC NAME: *Opuntia humifusa*

RANGE: Throughout the eastern and mid-western U.S.

WHERE GENERALLY FOUND: Dry, rocky areas and sandy grasslands

DESCRIPTION: Most people refer to the prickly pear as a cactus. It is cactuslike in appearance, having fleshy segments that are from 2 to 8 inches long, flattened, and from 1 to 5 inches wide. It has spines and barbed hairs.

PRICKLY PEAR

INDIAN FIG

It produces a yellow flower from June to July on the upper segments and a fruit that is long, red to purple, club-shaped, and fleshy.

EDIBLE PARTS AND SEASONS: This plant is edible during the spring, summer, and autumn. When harvesting the young segments, wear heavy leather gloves or be extremely cautious because the spines and barbed hairs easily penetrate the skin. Late summer and the fall is an ideal time to pick the fruits of the plant as they ripen. In order to prepare the fleshy segments of the prickly pear, use a flame from a fire to remove the spines, and then roast the fleshy segments over the fire. Then peel them. While they are edible, many people find the sticky consistency less than desirable. The fruits are edible if you open the fruit up and scoop out the sweet pulp. This pulp may be dried for later use.

Prickly pear (Opuntia humifusa) *of eastern U.S., often lacking large spines (Neil Soderstrom photo)*

Prickly pear (Opuntia phaeacantha) *of southwestern U.S. (U.S. Forest Service photo)*

PURSLANE, PUSLEY

SCIENTIFIC NAME: *Portulaca oleracea*
RANGE: Widespread throughout much of North America
WHERE GENERALLY FOUND: A common garden weed that may be found in any open area
DESCRIPTION: This annual plant grows flat on the ground, forming mats up to a foot square. The stems are smooth and shiny and often red to purple. Leaves are alternate and opposite and are from 1 to 2 inches long and approximately ½ inch wide. The small, delicate flowers grow at the tip of the branches and contain five yellow petals. The fruit appears as capsules, and late in the season the capsules drop away to expose the dark red to black seed.

EDIBLE PARTS AND SEASONS: The purslane is a summer food. The edible parts are the young leafy tips, which may be picked from June to September. This is one of the best wild shoots to cook or to serve raw in a salad. To cook the shoots, you should boil them for approximately 10 minutes.

Purslane has red to purplish stems and green leaves. (Neil Soderstrom photo)

ROSES

SCIENTIFIC NAME: *Rosa* species
RANGE: Throughout North America
WHERE GENERALLY FOUND: There are about 35 species of roses native to North America, and they are found anywhere from along streams, rivers, and moist areas to high, dry fencerows and plateau-type areas. They generally prefer an open area where sunlight may hit them for much of the day.
DESCRIPTION: Roses are shrubs which normally have spiny branches and alternate, featherlike compound leaves. The large, beautiful flowers usually have five petals and their aroma is known to almost everyone.

EDIBLE PARTS AND SEASONS: The rose is an excellent edible wild plant for use during the summer, autumn, and winter. The fruit, which is known as the rose hip, is perhaps one of the best-known sources of vitamin C. Gather the fruits as they ripen in the fall, usually after a frost, or during the winter. Wash and remove the dried flower parts at the top of the hip, then slit the tip open and remove the seeds. Eat the pulpy portion of the rose hip or dry it for later use, which makes it an excellent survival food. A tea may be made from the young fresh or dried leaves of rose plants, simply by steeping in hot water.

Left: Multiflora rose has thorns characteristic of nearly all of the many rose species. Note the winglike appendages on the base of leaf stems, also characteristic of many roses. *Below:* The hip of the wrinkled rose (Rosa rugosa) may be up to 1 inch in diameter. (Neil Soderstrom photos)

SASSAFRAS
SCIENTIFIC NAME: *Sassafras albidum*
RANGE: Throughout much of the eastern half of the U.S.
WHERE GENERALLY FOUND: In moist soil in open woodlands, along fencerows, and in bottomlands.
DESCRIPTION: This plant is a small to medium-size tree with a smooth to irregularly furrowed reddish-brown bark. The leaves on one tree may be found in three shapes. It may be an entire leaf, or it may have two or three lobes. The leaf is generally from 4 to 6 inches long and 2 to 4 inches wide. It is  bright green and when crushed has a spicy odor similar to root beer.

EDIBLE PARTS AND SEASONS: The roots of the sassafras tree may be used year-round to brew a delicious tea. For harvesting, dig down and cut a few of the roots. Wash the roots and boil them in water until the water becomes deep red. Sassafras tea makes an excellent hot or cold drink. The roots may be reused several times. Also, the roots may be dried and pulverized into a powder to make a meat spice. The winter buds and young leaves may be used in a salad.

CAUTION: Reports have it that sassafras may have carcinogenic properties. But such claims are somewhat counteracted by backwoodsmen who use sassafras heavily and still live to a ripe old age without any problems.

Sassafras leaves occur in three shapes on the same tree; left to right: entire, mitten, and lobed. Insert photo shows a sassafras root section. (Neil Soderstrom photo)

SHEEP SORREL

SCIENTIFIC NAME: *Rumex acetosella*

RANGE: Throughout much of the northern half of the U.S. and in Canada

WHERE GENERALLY FOUND: Likes acid soils and may be found in many open areas, such as old fields and along roadsides.

DESCRIPTION: This is a low-growing plant which sometimes reaches a height of 20 inches with upright stems. The basal leaves are shaped like a narrow arrowhead, pointed at the tip with a papery sheath around the stem where the leaves are attached.  The tiny flowers are green, yellow, red, and purple and cluster on a narrow, elongated spike.

EDIBLE PARTS AND SEASONS: Sheep sorrel is an excellent spring, summer, and autumn edible wild plant. Pick or cut leaves from the deep green plants. Avoid the flowering plants because they may be tough. These leaves make an excellent addition to any salad when mixed with other edible greens. For a beverage, boil 1 cup of the packed leaves in 1 quart of water for 2 or 3 minutes. Then cover and steep for at least 15 minutes. Strain and serve hot or cold. In order to use this as a cooked green, boil leaves in two changes of water for 15 to 20 minutes.

CAUTION: Avoid eating large quantities of sheep sorrel, because this generally causes stomach distress.

Sheep sorrel (Neil Soder-strom photo)

WATERCRESS

SCIENTIFIC NAME: *Nasturtium officinale*
RANGE: Throughout the U.S. and southern Canada
WHERE GENERALLY FOUND: In slow-moving, clear water, especially around springs and cool streams
DESCRIPTION: This is a perennial plant which grows in shallow water and occasionally in mud. The stems are weak and easily broken and the plant is usually seen partially floating in water or lying flat on the mud. Its leaves are alternate, from 1 to 6 inches long, and 1 to 2 inches wide. The leaves are dissected into from 3 to 11 lobed, and usually round, dark-green leaflets. The flowers are numerous in narrow, elongated clusters and contain four white petals. The fruit is a narrow, slender capsulelike pod which contains several reddish-brown seeds.

EDIBLE PARTS AND SEASONS: Wild strawberries appear in late spring and throughout summer. They may be eaten raw. The leaves of this plant may be dried and used to make a tea high in vitamin C. Spread the leaves on a clean surface in a warm, dry area, and dry thoroughly. Crumple the leaves and steep 2 handfuls in 1 quart of boiling water for 5 minutes. The tea leaves also may be stored for future use.

Watercress (Neil Soderstrom photo)

WILD PLUM, COMMON AMERICAN PLUM

SCIENTIFIC NAME: *Prunus americana*
RANGE: Throughout much of the eastern and midwestern U.S.
WHERE GENERALLY FOUND: Along streams, fencerows, edges of fields, and in old abandoned fields

AMERICAN PLUM

FLATWOOD PLUM

DESCRIPTION: The wild plum appears as a shrub and sometimes attains enough height and width to be referred to as a small tree. It has spiny branches and leaves which are alternate, 2 to 4 inches long, 1 to 2 inches wide, with a double row of sharp, pointed teeth along the margin of the leaves. The leaves are dark green and smooth. The flowers are produced two to five in a cluster in early spring, often before the leaves fully develop. The flowers are white and look similar to cherry blossoms. The fruit appears during the early summer; it is round and approximately 1 inch in diameter. When the fruit is ripe, it is orange to red and very juicy.

EDIBLE PARTS AND SEASONS. The ripe fruit may be eaten raw or used to make pies and other desserts.

CAUTION: Avoid the highly toxic pits and seeds. Be sure not to swallow them.

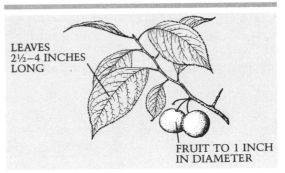

LEAVES 2½–4 INCHES LONG

FRUIT TO 1 INCH IN DIAMETER

Wild plum (from Sargent)

Chicksaw plum fruit may grow to 1 inch in diameter. (U.S. Forest Service photo)

WILD ONION

SCIENTIFIC NAME: *Allium cernuum*

RANGE: Throughout much of the U.S. and southern Canada

WHERE GENERALLY FOUND: Dry woodlands, rocky slopes, prairies, abandoned fields, and other flat areas with rich soil

DESCRIPTION: This plant has several leaves emerging from the base ranging up to 24 inches high. When broken, the stems will have a strong onion odor. They are soft and flexible. Flowers emerge on long stems growing taller than the leaves with several white to pink flowers at the end of the flower stalk.

EDIBLE PARTS AND SEASONS: This plant has a bulb which grows just under the ground at the base of the plant and is edible during the spring, summer, and autumn. These bulbs may be eaten raw or added to salads, or as seasoning in other dishes. Also, the young tops before the flower appears may be gathered and mixed in salads or boiled and eaten with other foods.

CAUTION: Avoid any onionlike plant that does not have an onion odor.

Wild onion flower and dried bulbs (Marcia Stevens photos)

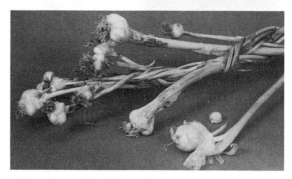

YELLOW POND LILY, SPATTERDOCK

SCIENTIFIC NAME: *Nuphar advena*

RANGE: Throughout much of the eastern half of the U.S.

WHERE GENERALLY FOUND: In ponds, swamps, and slow-moving streams

DESCRIPTION: The egg-shaped, V-notched leaves and their bright yellow globe-shaped flowers float on the surface of water. The leaves are large, ranging from 4 to 16 inches long and from 2 to 6 inches wide. Often the leaves will be raised above the water level. Other times they will appear to be floating.

EDIBLE PARTS AND SEASONS: This is an excellent year-round edible wild plant. The thick, porous, somewhat sweet roots are very rich in starch and are good eaten raw, dried, or boiled. They are also excellent when roasted with meat.

WILD STRAWBERRY

SCIENTIFIC NAME: *Fragaria virginiana*
RANGE: Widespread throughout much of the U.S. and Canada
WHERE GENERALLY FOUND: Open woodlands, yards, margins of woodlands, fields
DESCRIPTION: This is a low-growing plant whose leaves appear at the end of stems that are 6 to 8 inches long. The leaflets are sharply toothed along the margin and hairy underneath. Flowers appear at the end of a flower stem, often in a cluster, each with five white petals. The fruit, when ripe, appears to be red, in a classic strawberry look, and is sweet to the taste.
EDIBLE PARTS AND SEASONS: Wild strawberries appear in late spring and throughout summer. They may be eaten raw. The leaves of this plant may be dried and used to make a tea high in vitamin C. Spread the leaves on a clean surface in a warm, dry area, and dry thoroughly. Crumple leaves and steep 2 handfuls in 1 quart of boiling water for 5 minutes. The leaves also may be stored for future use.

Wild strawberry plants (Animals Animals/Wendy Neefus photo)

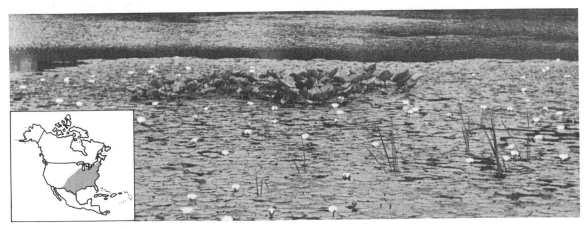

***Above:** Yellow pond lilies in flower (Leonard Lee Rue III photo).* ***Opposite page:** Characteristic split leaves (U.S. Forest Service photo)*

Some Poisonous Plants

Because there are many plants which can cause death or illness, it is essential that people wishing to use edible wild plants understand the dangers involved in eating unfamiliar plants. Here are some plants that poison to varying degrees:

COMMON NAME: **American yew**
SCIENTIFIC NAME: *Taxus canadensis*
TYPE: Shrub
RANGE: Northeastern U.S. and southeastern Canada
TOXIC PART: Leaves and seeds. Foliage more toxic than berries.
EFFECTS: Fatal. Death is usually sudden without warning symptoms.

COMMON NAME: **Buttercup**
SCIENTIFIC NAME: *Ranunculus* species
TYPE: Slender herb
RANGE: Northeastern U.S., southeastern Canada, along the Pacific coast range.

TOXIC PART: Leaves and stems
EFFECTS: Irritant juices may cause severe injury to digestive system.

American yew in fruit (Neil Soderstrom photo)

Buttercup (Neil Soderstrom photo)

COMMON NAME: **Butterfly weed**
SCIENTIFIC NAME: *Asclepias tuberosa*
TYPE: Tall herb
RANGE: Eastern U.S.
TOXIC PART: All parts
EFFECTS: Causes weakness, staggering, seizures.

COMMON NAME: **Death camas**
SCIENTIFIC NAME: *Zigadenus venenosus*
TYPE: Onion-like plant
RANGE: Western U.S. and Canada
TOXIC PART: All parts
EFFECTS: Staggering, collapse, death. *Extremely poisonous!*

COMMON NAME: **Dogbane**
SCIENTIFIC NAME: *Apocynum androsaemifolium*
TYPE: Upright herb
RANGE: Widely distributed throughout U.S. and Canada
TOXIC PARTS: All parts
EFFECTS: Affects the cardiovascular system.

Butterfly weed in fruit (Neil Soderstrom photo)

Death camas, Z. paniculatus (Animals Animals/ Robert C. Fields photo)

Dogbane with fruiting seed pods (Neil Soderstrom photo)

COMMON NAME: **Jimsonweed**
SCIENTIFIC NAME: *Datura stramonium*
TYPE: Herb growing approximately 5 feet high
RANGE: Widespread throughout North America
TOXIC PARTS: All parts
EFFECTS: Impaired vision, thirst, delirium, unpredictable movement, coma, death.

Jimsonweed open brown fruit, left, and fruiting branch (Neil Soderstrom photos)

COMMON NAME: **Mayapple**
SCIENTIFIC NAME: *Podophyllum peltatum*
TYPE: Low-growing herb
RANGE: Eastern U.S.
TOXIC PARTS: Leaves, roots, and seeds
EFFECTS: Causes violent cathartic reactions, gastric upset, and vomiting. Death may occur from large quantities.

Mayapple flower, left, and mayapple "spears and umbrellas" sprouting in spring (Leonard Lee Rue III photos)

COMMON NAME: **Moonseed**
SCIENTIFIC NAME: *Menispermum canadense*
TYPE: Vine
RANGE: Eastern U.S. and Canada
TOXIC PART: Berries; blue-purple colored berries resemble wild grapes
EFFECTS: Fatal if eaten.

COMMON NAME: **Nightshade**
SCIENTIFIC NAME: *Solanum dulcamara*
TYPE: Vine
RANGE: Eastern U.S. and Canada
TOXIC PART: All parts, especially the unripe berries
EFFECTS: Fatal; intense digestive disturbances and nervous symptoms.

COMMON NAME: **Ohio buckeye or horse chestnut**
SCIENTIFIC NAME: *Aesculus glabra*
TYPE: Tree
TOXIC PARTS: All parts. Seeds resemble chestnuts; however, they are poisonous.
EFFECTS: Vomiting, stupor, twitching, paralysis, death.

Nightshade fruiting branch left; flowering branch right (Neil Soderstrom photo)

Moonseed by Lloyd Birmingham

Ohio buckeye (U.S. Forest Service photo)

COMMON NAME: **Poison hemlock**
SCIENTIFIC NAME: *Conium maculatum*
TYPE: Large herb, growing to 10 feet high
RANGE: Eastern U.S.
TOXIC PARTS: All parts. Stems, leaves, fruits, and roots are extremely poisonous.
EFFECTS: Nervousness, trembling, reduced heartbeat, coma, respiratory failure.

COMMON NAME: **Poison ivy**
SCIENTIFIC NAME: *Toxicodendron radicans*
TYPE: Low shrub or vine
RANGE: Widespread in U.S. and soutl Canada
TOXIC PARTS: All parts
EFFECTS: Rash, blisters; if eaten, may blister mouth, throat, nasal passages.

Poison hemlock (Neil Soderstrom photo)

Left: *Poison ivy, with dark-green shiny leaves of spring and summer.* **Right:** *Poison ivy with duller red and then yellow leaves of autumn. (Neil Soderstrom photos)*

COMMON NAME: **Star of Bethlehem**
SCIENTIFIC NAME: *Ornithogalum umbellatum*
TYPE: Low-growing herb
RANGE: Widespread in eastern U.S. and Canada
TOXIC PARTS: All parts, especially bulb
EFFECTS: Intense irritation and burning of the mouth and tongue.

COMMON NAME: **Water hemlock**
SCIENTIFIC NAME: *Cicuta maculata*
TYPE: High-growing herb
RANGE: Throughout North America
TOXIC PARTS: All parts
EFFECTS: Fatal. Abdominal pains, exces salivation, vomiting within minutes of consumption. One of the most deadly poisonous North American plants.

Star of Bethlehem (Marcia Stevens photo)

Water hemlock silhouetted, above, and among cattails, right (Gottscho-Schleisner photo)

Treatment for Ingestion of Poisonous Plants

If possible, get the victim to a doctor as soon as possible. Be able to give the doctor a sample of the plant or the name, if you are certain, or at least a good description of the plant and to indicate how much of it and which parts were eaten and how recently. Also report any known history of medical problems or allergies that the victim may have, and any symptoms that you observed before reaching medical help. If a doctor is unavailable and you cannot get the victim to any type of medical care, and the victim is not unconscious or is not having convulsions, have him drink plenty of water and then try to induce vomiting to clear the stomach. Vomiting may be triggered by pressing the back of the throat with a finger. Have the victim repeat the vomiting process several times until the stomach is thoroughly cleaned out and the vomit is clear. Then have him drink plenty of liquids and keep him calm, warm, and as comfortable as possible. If the victim becomes unconscious or goes into convulsions, do not try to induce vomiting. Keep his mouth and throat free from any obstructions, and if necessary give him mouth-to-mouth resuscitation.

THE TEMPTATION OF MUSHROOMS

There are over 3,000 kinds of mushrooms in North America that range from edible, to disagreeable, to mildly poisonous, to deadly poisonous. Comparatively few are excellent edibles or deadly poisonous, and your physiological reaction to them often depends on your unique body chemistry. Nutritional value of the edible mushrooms is relatively low anyhow, so it's unwise to consume mushrooms unless you have excellent field training.

This is the Amanita muscaria, *a poisonous mushroom. Caution: In its younger stage, the muscaria mushroom's more globular-shaped cap easily can be mistaken for an edible puffball. (Leonard Lee Rue III photo)*

Edibility Test

If you are caught in a situation where there are wild plants but you don't know which ones are edible, the U. S. Air Force Edibility Test may be of help:

1. Take a small mouthful and chew it. Wait five minutes for any effects such as burning, stinging, or numbing.

2. If there are none, swallow and wait eight hours for any effects such as diarrhea, cramps, pains, numbing, vomiting, etc.

3. If there are none, repeat the process, using a handful of the plant, and wait another eight hours for ill effects.

4. If none, the plant is safe to eat.

5. Never use mushrooms or fungi.

6. Poisonous plant life means all parts of plants, including flowers, can be poisonous. Use caution with plants having these characteristics:

- Discolored or milky sap
- Spines or fine hairs (may be irritant)
- Bitter or soapy taste
- Beans or bulbs
- White or red berries, unless there is positive identification

This is the Amanita verna, *better known as Destroying Angel. Its poisons are especially hazardous because symptoms are often delayed up to 24 hours, long after vomiting can be induced with positive effect. Mushroom authority Alexander M. Smith reports that digestion of these plants may cause a higher percentage of deaths than rattlesnake bite. (Leonard Lee Rue III photo)*

11
EDIBLE WILD ANIMALS

Most of North America has been blessed with a population of animals that crawl, walk, fly, or swim. And most of them are edible. However, in some regions, animals are scarce. The Lewis and Clark Expedition almost failed at one point because of the lack of food. Of course, that was before the days of urbanization, pollution, and overdevelopment.

I have been in areas of Alaska that were almost totally devoid of animal life. It was difficult to find a small bird, much less the larger mammals. Contrary to popular opinion, wild animals are not found everywhere. If your survival situation occurs where there are very few of them, you'd better think about something else to eat.

Many survival books make it sound as though all you have to do to eat well in a survival crisis is to build any of a number of elaborate traps and food is on the way. This

is not the case at all. Even with the benefit of a modern firearm, obtaining wild animals for food can often be difficult. As a hunting guide, I know many deer hunters who have modern equipment and hunt in areas of high deer population and still have gone years without taking their first deer.

Traps, such as figure-4s, deadfalls, and snares, set by an experienced trapper, will occasionally take an animal. However, when

There is much more to getting a meal in the woods than setting a trap you have read about. You must know something of the habits and habitat of the animal to be trapped. I snared this rabbit by hanging a Thompson wire snare in the opening at the base of this tree after I spotted a well-used trail leading to the opening. (Chris Fears photo)

a person has no trapping experience and knows little about the animals he is trying to trap, he stands little chance of success.

I've been involved in many survival schools where as many as 90 people were sent out with snare-making materials and given several days to snare food. Rarely did anyone take an animal.

Hunting and trapping even in the most ideal situations require extensive training and knowledge of the animal and its movements, of trap construction, of proper and safe methods of using firearms, and of marksmanship. Without these skills, only good luck would allow meat meals with regularity.

Many survival situations occur during periods of severe weather, and during this type of weather, most animals, like people, prefer to wait it out rather than stir about. This adds to the already challenging task.

On the positive side, if a person has had extensive training, has practiced using snares and deadfalls, and is familiar with the animals he is trying to trap, he can sometimes pick up an animal that will sustain life. Also, if the person is a highly skilled hunter, with some luck, he can take animals too.

What is perhaps overlooked by most people approaching a survival situation is that protein can be obtained from sources other than deer, squirrels, and rabbits. Smaller forms of life are high in protein too. These include reptiles, crustaceans, fish, and insects.

Following are some of the many ways of obtaining animal protein. If you anticipate going into the backcountry on a regular basis, you should take a course in trapping and spend a lot of time developing your fishing, hunting, and trapping skills. Then if the day comes when you must eat off the land, nothing will be more valuable than your training and experience.

Fish and Fishing

I am convinced that fish is the best source of edible wild food in North America for the

Most streams in North American contain enough fish for them to be a dependable food supply. There is little reason for anyone near such a stream to go hungry, even in a survival situation, because fish can be caught in an unlimited number of ways, such as a shirt seine, improvised rod and hooks, fish traps, set lines, trotlines, and spearing.

person in a survival crisis. Freshwater lakes and ponds, streams, creeks, and rivers, are abundant food reservoirs.

In the Army, undergoing extensive escape and evasion training in swamp country, I found that I could use my shirt as a makeshift seine and catch the small minnows that are abundant in pools. I boiled the minnows in an old tin can I found. And while the minnows were not too tasty, I did not suffer the hunger pains that many of my colleagues did.

Throughout much of North America, waterways are fairly close to most people in a survival crisis. Generally speaking, these ponds, lakes, and streams support more animal life in a smaller area than the land does, and often the food they harbor is easier to acquire. You can count on finding not only fish, but also frogs, tadpoles, crustaceans, and many other edible forms of life.

Of the animal life in waterways, fish are probably the most difficult to catch. It may take hours or even days before you have enough fish to feed yourself or your group. However, successful fishing can be done, even with crude fishing equipment, if you are patient and know where, when, and how to fish. Obviously, the when, where, and how to fish questions are asked by fishermen every day. There are many books written on the subject. However, I'll reduce this information down to guidelines for survival.

When to fish. Different species feed at different times, both day and night. As a rule, expect fish to feed just at dawn and just before dusk, just before a storm as the front is moving in, and at night when the moon is full. Watch the actions of the fish. Rising fish and jumping minnows are often signs that fish are feeding.

Where to fish. The place you select depends upon the type of water available and the time of day. In fast-running streams in the heat of the day, try deep pools that lie just below the ripples. Toward evening and in early morning, float your bait over the ripple, trying to run it beside submerged logs, rocks, undercut banks, and overhanging bushes.

On lakes in the heat of the summer, fish deep, because fish seek the cooler, deeper waters. In the evening and early morning in summer, fish the edges of a lake. Fish are more apt to feed in shallow water during these times of day. Lake fishing in the spring and late fall is more productive along the edges where the water is shallow, because fish are either bedding or seeking warmer water.

With practice you can locate the beds of some fish by the strong fishy odor associated with the concentration of fish. Also, observe areas of still waters, such as covers of lakes or areas cut into the banks of rivers. Often this still water contains high populations of small fish.

How to fish. In a survival situation, you should concentrate on catching smaller fish, rather than large fish. Usually, where there are lots of small fish, they are relatively easy to catch, and while it may take you a little more time to catch enough food for you or your group, it is much better than gambling on catching one big fish. Generally, the larger the fish, the more difficult it is to catch.

As a rule, fish bite bait from their native water. Be sure to study the situation before you begin fishing. Look in the water near the shore for minnows, insects, worms. If you catch a fish, inspect its stomach to see what it has been eating, and then try to match this food.

Caught fish also can produce a bait for you. Use intestines, eyes, and other scrap parts for bait. If you use worms, cover the hook completely. Fish are smarter than many people believe, and an exposed hook will often cause fish not to bite. With minnows, pass the hook through the body of the fish, just under its dorsal fin. Be sure you do not sever

When using small fish or minnows for bait, be sure to hook the baitfish so it will remain alive for as long as possible. The best way to do this is to pass the hook through the body of the fish just under the dorsal fin, being careful not to sever the backbone.

the minnow's backbone because it will die instantly and so won't be active and attract a hungry fish.

You can make artificial bait from pieces of brightly colored cloth, feathers, or bits of bright metal fashioned to duplicate insects, worms, or minnows. Strive to make your artificial bait look natural by moving it slowly, or copying the actions of natural fish food.

In many waters throughout North America, a small strip of red flannel attached to a fish hook is all that is necessary to take fish.

Fishing equipment is an essential part of any survival kit, but if you are caught without any, there are many ways that hooks may be improvised. I asked Medrick Northrop, who is one of the survival instructors in my survival schools, to go to his backyard and see how many different types of fishhooks

Fishhooks can be improvised from an almost limitless variety of items. A few examples of materials that might be used are (top, left to right) wood, bird wishbone, hog tusk, paper clip, nail, fossilized shark's tooth, screw-on earring, sewing needle, (bottom, left to right) bird's claw, thorn, pencil clip, nail and wood, horseshoe nail, tip from rifle-cleaning rod, wire. The hooks may be attached with and hung from thread from clothing and equipment, sinew from the leg of a deer, dental floss, or whatever else is available.

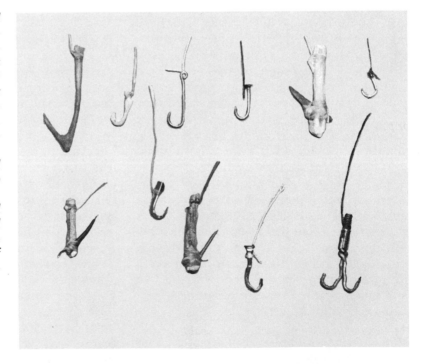

IMPROVISED FISHHOOKS

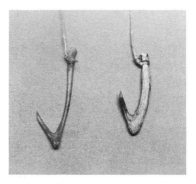 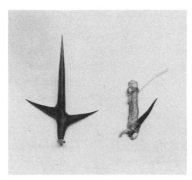 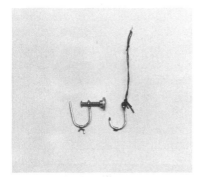

Left: A bird wishbone and wood twig. *Middle:* A thorn (left) can be tied to a twig as shown at right. *Right:* An earring can become a fishhook.

 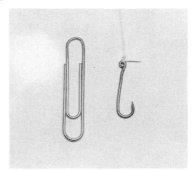 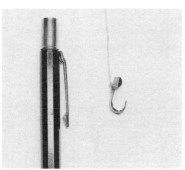

Left: A bird's claw fishhook. *Middle:* A single paper clip could provide several hooks. *Right:* A pen or pencil clip provides a serviceable hook.

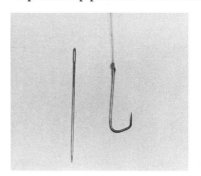 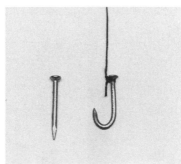 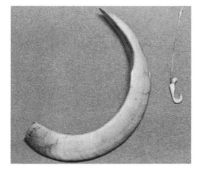

Left: A sewing needle makes an excellent hook. *Middle:* A fishhook made from a nail could withstand the tugging of large fish as well as seabirds, such as gulls. *Right:* With a good tool kit of even Stone Age tools, it's possible to fashion hooks from bone—in this case from a hog's tooth.

he could make from materials he found around the yard. To my surprise, Medrick came up with 20 improvised fishhooks, all of which were capable of catching fish. These hooks were made from pins, pieces of bone, pieces of wood, thorns, discarded metal items that he found in his yard, and other materials. He made much of the line for these hooks by using twisted bark, cloth fibers, and tendons from animals.

Since small fish are generally easier to catch, when improvising fishhooks efforts should be concentrated on making small hooks. The exception to this, of course, is in a large lake or ocean where large fish are predominant. In such circumstances even fishhooks improvised from pocketknives have been known to catch fish consistently. But be wary of risking your only pocketknife in a survival situation. Study the fishhooks

illustrated in this chapter, and spend some time making them. It is amazing what a variety of materials can be used for fishhooks. Everything from the claw of a bird's foot to a thorn off a tree can become a very efficient hook.

There will be times when the most elaborate line and suitable bait will not yield a single fish. However, the rule of thumb is to not become discouraged, because if line and hook do not work, there are still many other methods for catching fish.

Set lines. One of the best ways to catch enough fish is to have a lot of hooks out at one time. Set lines provide a practical method of catching fish while you are awaiting rescue. Simply cut several lines 3 to 4 feet in length. To each of these lines, tie a fishhook. Bait these hooks and fasten each line to a long-hanging branch that will bend when the

Set lines are simply lines tied to branches overhanging a stream or lake with a baited hook dangling in the water.

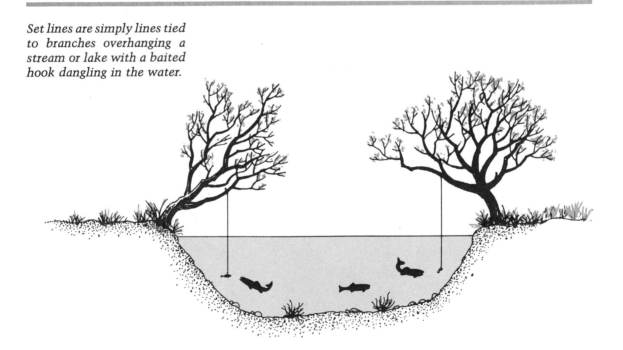

fish is hooked. Go along the edge of the lake or the edge of the stream and tie these lines so that the hooks are hanging down in the water 1 to 2 feet. Check the lines periodically to remove fish and rebait the hooks.

An excellent improvised hook on a set line is one that is known as a "skewer." Sink the skewer into a chunk of bait. After the bait enters the fish's stomach, the skewer swings crosswise and lodges in there, securing the fish to the line.

Trotlines. A second method for catching lots of fish is to make a trotline. A trotline simply is a long cord that can stretch across a bay, inlet, or small stream. To this main line, every 3 feet tie another line 2 to 3 feet long which has a hook on it. When you stretch your main line across the water, each of the shorter baited lines hang in the water. In swift water, you may need to weight the main line to keep the baited lines deep enough.

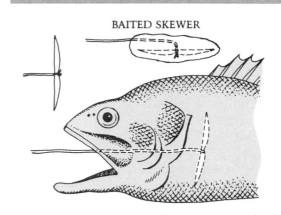

The "skewer" fishhook is an effective device that may be easily improvised from a piece of bone, wood, wire, or other material. The principle is to bait the hook so that the fish swallows it flat, but a struggle by the fish turns the hook perpendicular to the line, lodging it.

A trotline is tied across a stream and weighted.

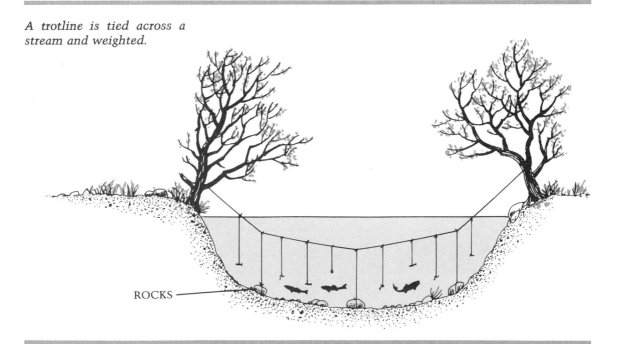

A spear such as this can be effective, especially where larger fish are congregated. Note that the spear point itself is the single point between Y branches which "funnel" the fish toward the spear point. The backward jutting spikes help prevent a fish's slipping back off the point.

For another form of trotline, cut a long sapling, and to this sapling every 2 to 3 feet tie a fishing line with a baited hook. Ease the sapling out into the water and anchor it securely. Periodically pull the entire sapling back to the bank, remove the fish, rebait the hooks, and put the assembly back out again.

Catching fish by hand. You may also use your hands to catch fish. When I was a youngster growing up in Alabama, one of my favorite Saturday sports involved going to the local river and swimming around rocks, hollow logs, and other debris in the river and feeling under these objects for catfish, catching them with my hands. This method is effective in small streams with undercut banks and in shallow ponds left by receding floodwaters. Place your hands in the water and allow them to reach under the banks slowly. Keep your hands close to the bottom, if possible. Move your fingers slightly until you contact a fish. Then work your hands gently along its belly until you reach its gills. Grasp the fish firmly behind the gills, and pull it up quickly.

Spearing. Spearing has been successful in many survival situations. This method is difficult where fish are small. But if fish are large and numerous, such as during spawning season or when fish are congregated in pools, spearing works well. A spear may be made by tying a knife on the end of a pole, or by sharpening a pole, or by creating a forked spear as illustrated. Also, spear points may be made from bone, pieces of scrap metal, and so on.

The best method for spearing fish is to use a light at night and wade along in shallow water. Another method is to position yourself on a rock over a fish run and wait patiently and quietly for the fish to swim by. The advantage of spearing fish is that you can select larger fish. The disadvantage is that it requires a lot of patience, and because of the distortion of the water, it requires practice in aiming slightly under where the fish appears to be.

Shooting. It is possible to shoot fish with a firearm. Bullets will penetrate water effectively for about 2 to 4 feet, depending upon the caliber and the load. The larger the caliber and the heavier the load, the deeper the bullet will penetrate. Be aware though that bullets striking water at an angle can ricochet and be dangerous to anyone standing in the wrong place.

When ammunition is in short supply, however, you must decide whether or not shooting fish is the best way to spend your ammunition. If larger game is available, perhaps the ammo would be better spent there. To shoot a fish, correct the water's visual distortion by aiming slightly under the fish.

Netting. The edges and tributaries of lakes and streams are usually abundant with small fish, and in these locations, nets are often the best way to catch them. A shirt can be made into a good seine by tying a stick to either side of it and wading up into small inlets. With the shirt stretched out along the bottom, you can often catch fish by this method.

Also, with some practice, if you have a great deal of line with you, you can improvise a gill net. However, because of the amount of time and energy needed to build a gill net, other methods of fishing would usually be a wiser survival effort. The best locations for a gill net are up in quiet coves and along eddies. If you are fortunate enough to have a commercially made gill net with you, it can be a very effective way of catching lots of fish.

Trapping. Fish traps, or weirs, as they are commonly called, are very useful for catching both freshwater and saltwater fish, especially those that move in schools. In lakes or large streams, fish tend to approach the

In small bodies of water where minnows, crayfish, and other aquatic life are plentiful, a seine improvised from a shirt and two sticks can be effective. To operate the seine, push it in front of you as you work your way toward a bank or small cove. When you reach the extreme shallows, lift the seine quickly and remove the catch. This can often yield more food than fishhooks can.

banks and shallows in the morning and evening. Saltwater fish traveling in large schools regularly approach the shore with the incoming tide, often moving parallel to the shore and guided by obstructions in the water. A fish trap is basically an enclosure with a blind opening where two fencelike walls extend out like a funnel from the entrance. The time and effort you put into building a fish trap should depend upon the need for food and the length of time you expect to stay.

In salt water, pick your trap location at high tide and build it at low tide. One or two hours of work should do the job. Consider your location and try to adapt natural features to reduce your labors. On rock shores, use natural rock pools. On sandy shores, use sandbars and the ditches they enclose. The best fishing off sandy beaches is in the lee of offshore sandbars. The best type of fish trap to build in this situation is made from sticks, as shown in the accompanying drawings.

In small, shallow streams, make your fish traps with stakes set into the stream bottom, or make smaller cane-basket fish traps with an inverted-cone opening weighted down with stones so that the stream is almost blocked by your fish trap. You may speed up the process of catching fish in the fish trap by wading with the fish trap, herding the fish into your trap. These fish traps work best in muddy streams. In some streams, your wading will muddy the water, blinding the fish so that they don't see either you or the trap.

Fish traps may also be used to store fish. Fish, especially catfish, may be kept alive for days in a fish trap because the incoming water keeps them fed.

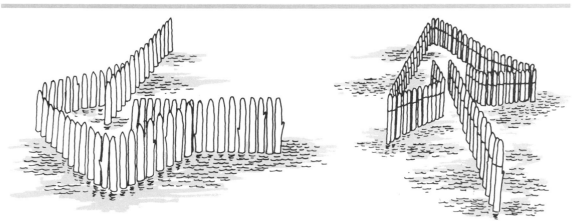

Fish traps for tidal flats and seashores can bring in the bigger fish as well as small ones.

These basket-style fish traps may be open on one or both ends. They can be fashioned from cane, reeds, or straight branches and tied with string or twisted grasses.

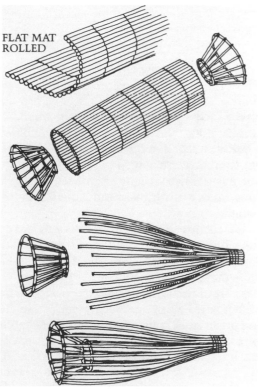

FLAT MAT
ROLLED

In small shallow streams, especially where water is muddy, you can often herd fish into a trap.

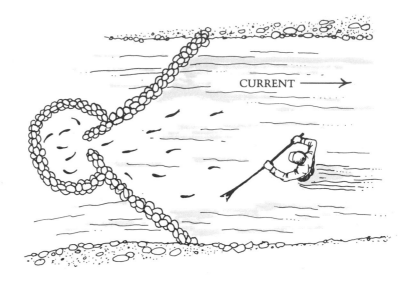

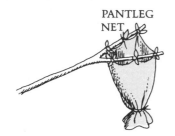

PANTLEG NET

CURRENT

Fish traps may be large or small, depending upon the size of the water in which you are working. Some of the most effective fish traps that I have used were made from small cane found along the edge of a creek. Approximately 3 feet long and 1 foot in diameter, these traps were placed in small eddies along the edge of the stream. It amazed me to find how many minnows and small fish they caught.

Ice fishing. In winter, ice fishing may be your only means of obtaining fish. Since fish tend to gather in deep pools, if the ice is safe to walk on, cut your ice holes over the deepest part of the lake. Brush laced over the hole and heaped with insulating snow can help keep the hole from freezing over. A hatchet or ax will serve best for cutting. Use a tip-up ice-fishing rig, as illustrated. When the rig tips up, you'll have a fish. In order to increase your catch, you can fish with tip-ups in several holes at once.

This ice-fishing tip-up tips up to alert you when a fish is on the line.

Cooking fish. All freshwater fish should be cooked as soon as possible after catching, unless you can keep them alive in water in some type of trap or on a mouth stringer. Eaten raw or even smoked, freshwater fish may be dangerous because many of these fish are contaminated with parasites. Fish may be boiled, roasted, baked, or fried. Often I have seen pictures of people cooking fish on a stick over an open fire, and while I have done this many times, I am always disappointed in that nine times out of ten, as the fish begins to get done, it will begin to fall apart and most of it will fall into the fire. Perhaps the best method of cooking fish is to broil them. Any scrap piece of metal you might have may be used for broiling. Aluminum foil that may be included in survival kits is ideal.

Saltwater fish are excellent when smoked. Smoking not only makes a fish good to eat, but also preserves the meat. Here is a smoker that I learned to make from Indians in Alaska:

1. Obtain three poles, each 8 feet long, and lash them together at one end. Spread the opposite ends outward to form a three-legged tepee frame.

2. Lash a fish-hanging stick between each of the tepee legs approximately 4 feet above the ground. Strong cord tied between the legs will also work.

3. Cover the tepee frame with a tarp, heavy plastic, or rescue blanket. Leave an opening at the tepee top for smoke to exit, and make sure the bottom is left off the ground so that air will be fed into the tepee.

4. Start a small fire in the center of the tepee with small pieces of dry wood, then add green hardwood or water-soaked hardwood chips. Keep the fire small and smoky so that the fish will not cook and you will not burn your tepee cover.

5. Maintain a steady smoke for approximately 12 hours.

In order to prepare fish for the improvised smoker, fillet the fish as you usually would, except leave the fillets attached to the tail. This allows you to hang the two fillets, still

Saltwater fish to be smoked should be filleted with the fillets attached at the tail so that they can be hung in an improvised smoker. Freshwater fish should be cooked rather than smoked.

attached, over a hanging stick or cord in the tepee. Next, dry the fillets with a towel or dry cloth and rub the fish with salt, if available. After salting, hang the fillets to air-cure for four hours. When you are ready to hang the fillets in the smoker, make five or six shallow cuts across the width of the fillets to expose more surfaces to the smoke. Smoke the fillets for 12 hours. Store the smoked fillets in a porous sack, and keep them dry.

A rock broiler may be made for cooking fish by placing a layer of small stones on top of hot hardwood coals and laying the fish on top. Scaling before cooking by this method is not necessary, and small fish need not even be cleaned. Cooked in this manner, fish have a moist and delicious flavor. Crabs, lobsters, and crayfish may also be placed on the stones and broiled.

When fishing in a survival situation, the species of the fish is not too important, and often fish that we commonly refer to as "trash fish," such as bullhead, carp, shad, etc., may be the easiest fish to catch. When you're hungry and starvation is at your front door, don't be picky about the species of fish that you elect to eat.

Insects

Pound for pound, insects probably have as much protein as anything you could catch to eat. But you'll consume a lot of energy gathering enough insects for a meal. Also, there are many among us who find eating insects repulsive. In extensive survival training programs, I have seen even extremely hungry people be finicky about eating grasshoppers, grubs, and ants.

There are some insects to avoid for food. Spiders, particularly if you are unable to distinguish poisonous spiders from nonpoisonous, should be avoided. Centipedes, or "thousand-legs," as they are commonly called, should not be eaten, because they can

While not appetizing to most people, insects are high in protein. This catalpa worm, found in summer months on catalpa trees, mostly in southern states, may be used as a protein supplement for soups and stews.

have a venomous bite. In the southern half of the United States, the beetle-like bug commonly referred to as a "kissing bug" should be avoided. The weird-looking "wheel bug" found in the southern two-thirds of the United States should not be eaten, as its bite may be painful.

While ants are often readily available, fire ants and harvester ants found in the southeastern United States should be avoided because of the severity of their bites. Someone who was not familiar with fire ants and thought he had found an abundance of food in a fire ant mound could find himself thoroughly bitten and in serious trouble as a result. The colorful "velvet ant" (actually a wasp) found in the southern and western parts of the United States should also be avoided because of its bite. In the western half of the United States, blister beetles are found in large numbers. A fluid released by these animals may create painful blisters.

There are three caterpillars which can

Imported to the U.S. in the 1920s, the fire ant is red and measures only about ¼ inch long. It builds earthen nests that may rise 3 feet above ground level. When the nest is disturbed, the females attack, leaving bites that burn for hours and sometimes cause death. Range is the southern U.S. (USDA photo)

caterpillar's body. Many of these spines are attached to poison glands Aside from these insects, most insects, while they may not be delicious, are edible.

When looking for insects, be sure to look under rocks, leaves, and logs, and especially to dig into rotten logs. One method of catching edible insects, such as beetles, mayflies, and other night-flying insects, is to place a vessel of water underneath a lantern or torch light. These insects will be attracted to the light and will blunder into the water, where they may be captured.

While some insects, such as the large black carpenter ant, may be killed and eaten raw, insects are better as a protein mixed in soups

cause pain and should be avoided. The first is the "io moth" caterpillar. This full-grown caterpillar is from 2 to 3 inches long, pale green, with lateral stripes of red or maroon over white running the length of the body. Near the center of each body segment is a partial row of hairlike structures, or spines, which are venomous and cause pain if you touch them. The fuzzy golden caterpillar commonly called the "puss caterpillar" or "flannel moth" also has some venomous hairs which may cause pain on contact. The third caterpillar to avoid is the "saddleback" caterpillar. The saddleback is easy to recognize, since its brown, sluglike body is covered with markings that resemble a brown or purplish saddle sitting on a green-and-white saddle blanket. Upon close examination, stout spines can be observed along the

Though grasshoppers are a good source of protein, they may contain parasites that can be transmitted to man and so should be cooked. (USDA photo)

INSECTS TO BEWARE OF

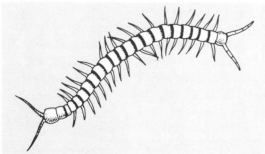

Centipedes give a venomous bite. They measure from 1 to over 10 inches long, with one pair of legs per body segment. Depending on species, there may be from 15 to 100 pairs of legs. Range varies by species. Most occur in the South.

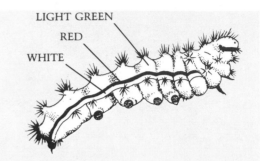

The io moth caterpillar is a larva of the io moth and measures 2 to 3 inches long. Green and black spines connected to poison glands may break off and penetrate skin on contact. Range is east of the Rocky Mountains.

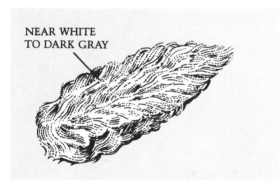

The puss caterpillar is the larva of the flannel moth, and is in some regions called an "asp" because of the venomous sting of body hairs. Length is about 1 inch. Range is primarily in the southeastern U.S.

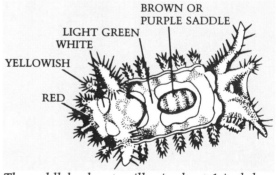

The saddleback caterpillar is about 1 inch long and is distinctively marked. Spine-like hairs are actually connected to poison glands. Range is southeast of a line from Massachusetts through middle Texas.

and stews. (Carpenter ants, or black ants as they are commonly called, are found throughout much of North America in dead or decaying trees. They are shiny black in color and range in length from ¼ to ½ inch.) Also, cook grasshoppers because they often contain parasites you could otherwise pick up.

Grubs are the white larvae of certain insects and are rich in protein. They may be dug from moist, rotten logs or leaf mulch in damp woods. Certain species of snails are

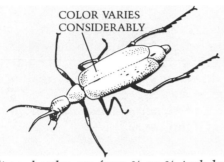

Blister beetles are from 3/8 to 3/4 inch long and vary in coloration. They emit a blister-causing fluid from their legs and body parts when squashed or even brushed against a person's skin. At night, they are attracted to white light and so pose a hazard if you attempt to attract insects for food that way. Blister beetles occur mainly in the western U.S.

The wheel bug is mouse gray in color and measures 1 to 1½ inches long. Hazard is from its beak, designed to inject a salivary fluid that kills insect prey. In humans the "bite" results in immediate and intense pain that usually subsides in three to six hours. Most wheel bugs are found in the southern two-thirds of the U.S.

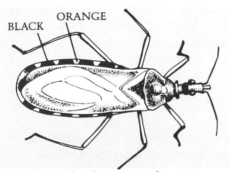

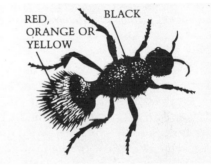

The kissing bug, also known as the cone-nose, is about ½ to 1 inch long, depending on species. It feeds on the blood of mammals, including humans, at night. The bite often causes no immediate sensation, with skin reactions ranging from small lumps to bleeding lesions. Range is mainly the southern half of the U.S.

The velvet ant is a wasp that resembles an ant and measures ½ to 1 inch long. The female has a formidable stinger and roams alone rather than congregating as other wasps do. Most species occur in the southern and western U.S. One species occurs on sandy beaches of Lake Erie.

considered delicacies by many people. However, many of the snails found in North America in fresh water are host to various parasites which can be transferred to man. It's best to avoid snails as a food, or if you must eat them, to cook them thoroughly first.

Mollusks and Crustaceans

Near water, two possible food sources are mollusks (clams, mussels, periwinkles, etc.) and crustaceans (crayfish, lobsters, shrimp, etc.). Most mollusks are edible. But, it is es-

Seashores offer an abundance of edible shore life that can be caught easily. Even the smallest crabs offer some food substance, and their meaty parts may be used as bait to catch larger animal life.

sential that mollusks be fresh and that you boil them. Never eat mollusks raw because they are bottom feeders and absorb potentially dangerous organic life and chemical pollutants.

Mussels, which live in fresh water, may be found in the shallows, especially in water with a sandy or mud bottom. Near the sea you can find creatures such as sea urchins and clams at low tide, especially in tidal pools. In the case of mussels, if there is a chance that a stream is polluted, this form of food should be avoided because they may contain the water's pollutants.

Crustaceans, such as freshwater and salt-water crabs, crayfish, lobster, and shrimp are edible, but they spoil rapidly. None should be eaten raw. Crayfish, which are considered a delicacy in the Deep South, are usually found in still water under rocks or other cover. You have to be quick to catch them by hand. In swamps they can be caught by cutting a

long pole and attaching 8 feet of fish line to one end. No hooks are needed. Tie a piece of spoiled or scrap meat to the end of the line and throw the baited line into the water. Occasionally lift the bait to the surface, but not out of the water, as the crayfish will drop off once it has cleared the water. If a crayfish is attached, slip a net or some other means of catching it underneath it.

Amphibians

Frogs and salamanders are the best of the amphibians as sources of wild food. By day, frogs are often found sunning themselves along the edges of slow-moving streams and around lakes and ponds. By night, frogs may be located by their croaking and spotted with a light. Day or night, they may be taken with a fish spear, clubbed with a stick, or shot with a small-caliber firearm.

While frogs are most noted for their edible hind legs, the entire body contains food value after skinning. Take care not to eat toads. Toads are dry-land animals and are rarely found along the edges of lakes, ponds, and streams. They may be distinguished by their grayish color and warty covering.

Tadpoles, which are found in still pools of water, may also be netted or caught by hand and are edible. They are especially good as a protein supplement to soups.

Salamanders are found under rotten logs, damp leaves, or rocks in wet areas and may be delicious when boiled. They are also a good addition to soups.

Reptiles

Snakes, lizards, alligators, and turtles are all very good to eat. Freshwater snakes, both poisonous and nonpoisonous, are found around lakes and streams where the water is sluggish and the banks are covered with

HOW TO DISTINGUISH FROGS FROM TOADS

The many species of frogs and toads are widely varied in description. It's better to avoid toads for food because the warty skin glands emit a fluid that is caustic to mucous membranes—so caustic that dogs learn after one mouthful to stay away for life. Frog meat resembles that of chicken in taste and appearance. The bullfrog, as shown, is found throughout most of the U.S. It is the largest of frog species, measuring from 3½ to 6 inches in head-body length. Frogs generally have a thin, shiny wet skin, while toads, such as the American toad shown, look dry and warty. Frogs have slimmer bodies and longer legs for leaping, while toads have squatty bodies and shorter legs, and hop just a few inches. Bullfrogs have a ridge near the eardrum; many other frogs have similar ridges, which may extend along each side of the back. Toes on many frogs are webbed all the way to the tips. (Toad photo by Leonard Lee Rue III; bullfrog by Neil Soderstrom)

EARDRUM

GLANDULAR RIDGE NEAR EARDRUM

WET, SMOOTHER SKIN

LARGE PAROTID GLANDS ON EACH SIDE

EARDRUM

DRY, WARTY SKIN

This slimy salamander is one of hundreds of species found in North America. Most are nocturnal and can be found during daylight by lifting logs and large rocks. Salamanders may have head-body lengths from just a few inches to over 20 inches. It's important to distinguish salamanders from their cousins, the newts, because newt skin-gland secretions range from irritating to toxic. Salamanders have slimy skin. Newt skin is rougher and not as slimy, and newts do not exceed 5 inches in head-body length. Also, salamanders, which resemble some reptiles, can be distinguished by their lack of claws and scales. (Leonard Lee Rue III photo)

driftwood or overhanging branches. Dry-land snakes may be found around brushpiles, rock outcroppings, areas with thick vines, and fallen logs. Although snakes are all edible, extreme caution should be used when searching for them, especially where poisonous snakes are found. Also, while water snakes are edible, often they have a very unpleasant taste and odor. If possible, search for land snakes if you are going to depend upon a diet of snakes.

The safest way to kill a poisonous snake is to shoot it with a firearm, from a safe distance. The next safest way is to hit the snake behind the head with a stout stick that is longer than the snake's body. Since the snake's spinal column is weak, it may be broken by a rather light tap. Many people fear that a snake can strike the length of its body; however, it has been my experience that snakes rarely strike more than one-third their body length. Whether you shoot a snake or break its spine with a stick, you are wise to crush the snake's skull with a stick and cut the head off, burying it so that no one will accidentally contact the fangs. Since ammunition is usually at a premium in a survival situation, a stick may be a more economical weapon if the snake is easy to reach, and certainly if the snake is nonpoisonous.

Cleaning snakes is relatively easy. Again, in the case of a poisonous snake, the head should be cut off and discarded in a safe place; if you stick yourself with a fang, venom can be injected even from a dead snake. Once the head is removed, slit the bottom side of the skin the full length, all the way to the vent. Then simply peel the skin down to the vent and cut it off at that point. Scoop out the intestines from the hollow underside of the snake, and it is ready to be fried, broiled on a stick over an open fire, or added as soup stock.

All lizards, with the exception of the Gila monster, are edible. Remove the skin, then boil or fry the meat.

Alligators contain a tremendous amount of meat, especially a large one. While all of the alligator, once skinned, is edible, the tail is the most delicious part. Alligators are dangerous and should only be hunted with a firearm from a position that allows a clean shot between the eyes.

Marine, freshwater, and land turtles are

Snakes are relatively easy to skin and clean, and the meat is delicious. The skin can be peeled back from the neck as shown. If you don't have a firearm, the next best way to kill any snake is to crush its head or break its spinal column behind the head with a large rock or stick. Even after snakes have been killed, nervous reactions cause thrashing about, so keep your distance from venomous snakes until all movement has stopped. (Chris Fears photo)

edible and are widely distributed both on land and in the water. Smaller freshwater turtles may be caught with the hand, clubbed, or caught on a line like a fish. When catching the larger snapping turtle or loggerhead turtle, be careful, as they can inflict a serious bite.

In order to clean a turtle, break the lower half of the shell off, then remove the meat from the inside. It is easy to remove the in-

testines from the turtle, leaving a delicious meat.

Turtle eggs may be found during late spring and summer and are also edible. In order to find turtle eggs, watch for tracks leading up on sandbars. Then you will see a depression where the female turtle has dug a hole, deposited her eggs, and walked back into the stream. If you dig in the sandbar where the tracks stop, you can usually find a clutch of 10 to 12 eggs.

Alligators contain a tremendous amount of meat, but may be dangerous to try to take for food. Since they are very difficult to kill, you should only attempt to take one with a firearm, and then only if you can make a clean shot right between the eyes. (Photo courtesy of Don Pfitzer/U.S. Fish and Wildlife Service)

Left: Large snapping turtles are a source of excellent meat. But they can be formidable quarry if you don't have a firearm for a well-placed head shot. They can "run" surprisingly fast and, when at bay, strike out viciously at anything that moves in range of their extendable neck. Without a firearm, one ploy is to tease the turtle into striking and clamping its jaws onto the end of a stout stick, followed by your lopping its head off with a machete or hatchet. Caution: A big, growling snapper earns well-deserved respect from most people. It is no pushover, like some turtles that become helpless when flipped onto their backs. A snapper can right itself quickly. In this photo, the eggs would offer an easier meal—after mama has departed. *Right:* Turtle eggs are edible, but they are difficult to find. During the summer months they may be found on sandbars along rivers and streams by following tracks of the turtle from the water to its nest site. (Snapping turtle photo by Leonard Lee Rue III)

Birds

Birds can be killed easily if you have a gun, especially a shotgun, but they can be especially hard to kill without one. In late spring or summer, you can occasionally find birds nesting. All bird eggs are edible when fresh, even with embryos in them. Large wading birds, such as cranes and herons, often nest in mangrove swamps or in high trees, such as cypress trees, near water.

Ducks, geese, and swans nest around the lake edges of colder climates. During the molting season, these birds can be clubbed or netted. Seabirds along low coastlines commonly nest on sandbars or low sand islands. Steep rocky coasts are favorite nesting places for gulls, auks, and cormorants. Night is the best time to try catching roosting birds.

One of the least humane, but most effective, methods of catching birds in a survival situation is with the use of fishhooks baited

Seagulls are easily caught on fishhooks or by trapping, as the birds are relatively unafraid of man. If this man were in a survival situation, he could use the bits of fish he is feeding the seagulls as bait attached to a fishhook and line. Snares, deadfalls, and other traps can be baited with fish on the shore to catch seagulls. (Photo above by U.S. Forest Service)

with cut pieces of fish or minnows. This is an especially effective way to catch seashore birds, such as seagulls and some wading birds. Generally these birds are attracted to people fishing, because they think they can get a free handout of fish. Simply take a 3-foot section of fishing line with a hook on the end, bait it with a piece of fish, and tie it to a stake. Back off and the bird will do the rest.

Inland birds, such as wild turkeys, quail, and grouse, may be caught by stringing a line between two trees with several 3-foot sections of line tied to it, each with a hook on the other end. Bait the hooks with some type of seeds, food scraps, or corn. These birds will come along, eat the bait, and swallow the hook. Again, this method is illegal, inhumane, and not recommended except in a situation where starvation is imminent.

The ptarmigan in the far north, and the spruce grouse farther south, act almost tame at times and may be killed with rocks or sticks.

Birds can also be caught in a gill net, if you have constructed one for fishing purposes. At night, set the net vertical to the ground in some natural flyway, such as an opening along dense foliage. During the day, anchor one end of the net to the ground and attach the other end to a tree limb so that you can release it from a distance. Bait the area under the net, wait for the birds to gather, and then pull down the net. Birds can also be trapped with deadfalls, which will be discussed later on in this chapter. However, this method is not highly recommended, as it is rarely effective and requires a tremendous amount of patience and knowledge of trap building in order to get one bird.

Preparation of birds, while involving some work, is relatively easy. Most birds should be plucked and cooked with the skin on to

Nesting birds of all types can lead you to eggs, such as these eggs that were left partially covered by a hen turkey. (Leonard Lee Rue III photo)

This shows the rock ptarmigan of the North Country in winter plummage (left) and summer plummage (right). (Leonard Lee Rue III photos)

retain food value. After the bird is plucked, cut off the neck near the body. Next, make an incision from the anal opening of the bird to the point of the sternum. Then reach up into the bird and remove all the innards. Wash it out with fresh, clean water. The heart, liver, neck, and gizzard should be saved for soup stock.

Scavenger birds, such as buzzards and crows, should be boiled for at least 20 minutes before you cook them because they often contain parasites and would be dangerous to eat otherwise. Be sure when cleaning birds to save all the feathers. You may want to use them to insulate clothes or shoes, or for bedding, or for arrow fletching. Also keep in mind that the small bones from birds may be crafted

into fishhooks. The wishbone is especially good for fishhook making.

Large and Small Mammals

All mammals found in North America are edible. However, some precautions are necessary.

Trichinosis is a disease caused by the presence of *trichinae*, a very small nematode worm whose larvae infest the intestines and voluntary muscles of man, pigs, bears, and other animals. Most arctic game, large and small, may harbor trichinosis. Trichinosis may also be found farther south in bear and wild hogs. By eating infected meat that has not been thoroughly cooked, man may contract the worms and suffer from fever, nausea, diarrhea, and muscular pains. Thoroughly cooking meat will make it safe for human consumption.

Tularemia is commonly known as "rabbit fever." While some rabbits carry tularemia, by no means do all of them. Tularemia is also commonly found in other rodents, especially beaver. Avoid rodents that appear to be sick or weak. Tularemia is most commonly contracted when the infected blood comes into contact with the eyes or cuts and scratches, or from drinking water containing the bacteria. While all water acquired in the field should be boiled or otherwise treated before drinking, the precaution is especially important where there is a high beaver population. Cooking meat thoroughly does alleviate the hazard. Tularemia, which is accompanied by fever in humans, is rarely fatal.

The livers of the polar bear and bearded seal are known to contain a high enough concentration of vitamin A to be toxic and should be avoided. Remember also that most small game, especially rabbits, contains very little fat, and a steady diet of small game without fat being added in some way can be dangerous to one's health. Many old-timers in the far north have starved to death through a long winter of rabbit-only diets. If possible, add available fat when cooking and supplement your diet with fruits and greens.

When subsisting on wild animals, it is wise to eat the eyes, as they are an excellent source of salt.

Hunting for animals. Anyone who intends to hunt, even in a survival situation, should be well trained in hunter safety and marksmanship. As a professional hunting guide and wildlife biologist, I have spent my whole life observing untrained people who fail to succeed as hunters. Also, anyone who anticipates spending much time in the backcountry

should take the time to learn the habits and habitats of both large and small animals. Having a firearm and knowing how to use it safely and accurately will not be enough to put food on the table if you don't know the animal you are hunting. Without this knowledge, you are depending totally upon luck to keep you and your group fed.

Marksmanship is extremely important. Under the stress of a survival predicament, circumstances may not promote marksmanship. It is extremely important to approach as close to game as possible before shooting. It is also extremely important that you make a good enough shot to kill the animal in its tracks. Many survival guns are light and require a good tight shooting position. The stress and exertion of the survival situation, coupled with the excitement of having an animal in your sights, will increase the possibility of trembling, which can affect your shot. If possible, get into the prone position for a steady shot. If this is not possible, consider a sitting or kneeling position because these supported positions will help steady your aim. Or, once you approach within range of your quarry, use a rest, if possible—a log or a tree limb or anything else that will help you steady the firearm. Take your time in aiming. Pick a vital spot. On most animals' side view, the shoulder shot is best. From head-on, a chest shot will probably be the best spot. Do not shoot unless the vital spot is in clear view. Wasting precious ammunition and wounding an animal does nothing to increase your survival chances.

Once your first shot is fired, even though it appears to be accurate and the animal has fallen, reload immediately and ease up on the animal to make sure it is dead. Be prepared to shoot again if necessary. If you wound an animal, sit down immediately and wait for approximately 30 minutes before beginning to follow a blood trail. This will allow the game enough time to move off, determine

SHOOTING BASICS

Since every firearm has individual characteristics, be sure you've had plenty of range practice with any gun you plan to take into the backcountry.

One-shot kills are a must in survival situations where ammunition is extremely limited. One of the steadiest shooting positions is the prone. The elbows provide steady support for accurate shooting. (Michaels of Oregon photo)

This shooter in the sitting position utilizes his left elbow and knee as support, as well as the rifle sling to further tighten the rifle against the shooter's body. (Michaels of Oregon photo)

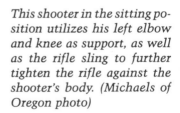

that it is not being followed, lie down, and die without running far. Go to the point where you hit the animal and at that point begin following the blood trail slowly. Blood-trailing a wounded animal is an art in itself, and for one who is untrained in this art, it is extremely difficult. Patience is required, and it is best, if possible, to mark each splotch of blood while trailing the animal so that you can look back when you lose the blood trail and get back on it. This will also prevent you from becoming lost again!

Most game animals are wary and hard to kill. To hunt them requires skill and pa-

tience. The best method for a beginner is what is commonly referred to as stand hunting. In stand hunting, find a place where the animal is most likely to pass, such as a trail, feeding area, or water hole, and then hide nearby. Always stay downwind of where you anticipate the animal will appear. Most animals have a keen sense of smell, allowing them to pick up your scent if even the slightest wind is blowing from you to them. One of the tricks to taking game under these conditions is to remain absolutely motionless. If you find it necessary to move when you have animals in front of you, wait till they

Blood-trailing a wounded animal is an art. Since blood drops are difficult to see in vegetation and usually can only be seen up close, use toilet tissue to mark blood when you find it. Looking back at your toilet paper trail periodically can often help direct you where an animal is headed, especially if blood has stopped flowing. The T.P. trail can also help you find your way back. Before trailing wounded game, unless there is rain, wait 20 to 30 minutes before beginning. This way the animal doesn't feel it's being pursued and so will lie down sooner and die, or greatly weaken, rather than continue running.

Locating good hunting areas requires scouting for sign, such as the track of this good-sized wild turkey.

Some animals, such as the armadillo, are found throughout much of the southern United States. They can be run down and killed with a stick.

are feeding or looking the other way. Then move as cautiously as possible. If they look your way, freeze.

The best times to hunt are usually very early in the morning and late in the afternoon. If hunting becomes a part of your survival routine, you must employ scouting techniques. Be observant for the tracks of animals in your immediate area. Watch for droppings. Keep your eyes open for places where animals may be feeding. Be on the lookout for trails.

It is a surprise to many beginning hunters to find that most game prefers what is known as the "edge effect"—the edges of forests, fields, thickets, etc.

In a survival situation, night hunting is one of most expedient ways of finding and taking game, since many animals prefer to move at night. Using a flashlight or a torch, go into an area where animals are likely to be feeding and watch for the shine of the light

Trapping. In many survival books, there is more space devoted to the trapping of animals for food than to almost any other aspect of survival. A great deal has been written about the use of deadfalls and snares. However, I have found few people who, after reading this material, can trap animals effectively enough to make their effort worthwhile.

Having grown up on a trapline and spent much of my adult life trapping, I know the difficulties of trapping under ideal conditions. Even the seasoned trapper with modern equipment, modern traps, cover scent, attracting scents, and an area that is abundant with game will often have trouble taking animals. So the person in a survival situation who is under stress, cold, lonely, tired, and hungry and who must make traps from primitive materials has an extremely difficult task.

On the other hand, a person who has studied the art of snaring animals and using deadfalls can, under some conditions, take enough food to keep himself alive, and for that reason, I'll cover the basics of snares and deadfalls.

While simply reading this section will not make a trapper out of anyone, it will be a starting point. Anyone who has an interest in going into backcountry and considers trapping as even a remote possibility in a survival predicament should spend time learning how to snare animals and set deadfalls.

The first rule for successful trapping is to know the animals you intend to trap, whether they be small or large. All snares and deadfalls should be simple in construction and should be set out as soon as possible. They should be set on game trails and logs crossing creeks, at den sites of burrowing animals or dens under logs or rocks, and in areas that may be baited up for animals.

Snaring. Wire snares are best for small mammals. You can make snares from light wire that may be part of your vehicle. Two

In a severe survival crisis, night hunting with the aid of a light—jacklighting—can be justified. A bright light tends to spellbind deer.

in the animals' eyes. They will be partly blinded by the light, and this allows you to approach much closer than you can during daylight. If you have a gun, hunting under these conditions is relatively easy. If you have to depend upon a spear or makeshift bow and arrow, the kill becomes much more difficult.

With practice, a slingshot can be very effective on small game. To make one, fasten a shock cord or other similar piece of elastic from a plane, snowmobile, or backpack, to a forked stick. Use round pebbles, such as those found around rivers and creeks.

Beavers are populous in much of North America and can be an abundant food source because there are usually about four beavers to a colony. They may be shot or caught in wire snares. Caution: Beaver meat must be thoroughly cooked because it may carry any of several diseases that can be transmitted to man.

or three twists around the long end of the wire should be sufficient. When using twine or fish line, make a slip knot. But commercially made snares will do a much better job than anything you might make on your own. Thompson Survival Snares, made by the Raymond Thompson Company of Lynnwood, Washington, are excellent for small game. These snares have long been used in U.S. Armed Forces survival kits and come with good instructions. These snares have a locking mechanism that secures the animal more tightly if the animal moves. It is virtually impossible for the animal to get out of the snare by jumping and jerking.

For the untrained person, trying to catch mammals in a snare is betting the next meal pretty much on luck. But if you are forced to use snares, you will want to use as many as possible to increase your chances. Place several snares in the run or trail that is used by small animals. Secure the anchor end of the snare to a stout pole, log, or tree. Open the loop approximately 4 to 6 inches and set it in the runway about 4 inches off the ground. This is commonly known as a "drag snare." The theory is that the animal will run its head into the loop and lunge forward, trying to get free, while the loop tightens around its neck.

Another good place to put snares is at the entrance to small animal dens. Animals such as groundhogs and marmots are easily snared this way. Simply attach the anchor end of the snare to a nearby bush or tree, then open the snare up so that as the animal comes in or out of its den, it will stick its head through the loop. This is commonly referred to as a "den snare."

If you are in an area where you are competing with other carnivores, such as wolves, for the game you snare, attach the anchor end of your snares to green saplings, with a trigger mechanism that allows the sapling to snatch the animal up into the air, keeping it out of reach of your animal competitors. This type of snare is called a "twitch-up snare." The accompanying drawing shows how to rig a twitch-up.

Consider setting a snare under the ice in winter for beavers. There are several methods of ice snaring. One is to cut a hole in the ice near a beaver lodge. Fasten the anchor end of the snare around a stout pole and lay the pole across the top of the ice. Beneath the ice the snare is adjusted to about 1 foot in diameter. Suspended into the snare opening is a bait stick. The goal is to attract the beaver to the bait. Once the beaver takes the bait and attempts to swim, the noose will tighten on its neck.

Bait sticks during winter should be fresh-cut green willow, alder, cottonwood, birch, or any local green wood that you observe beavers eating. If you find a hole a beaver uses to emerge from under the ice, you may

This twitch-up is a good snare to use when you are competing with wild animals, such as wolves, for food. The twitch-up can snatch the trapped animal into the air and beyond the reach of the competition.

BASIC SNARE SET-UPS

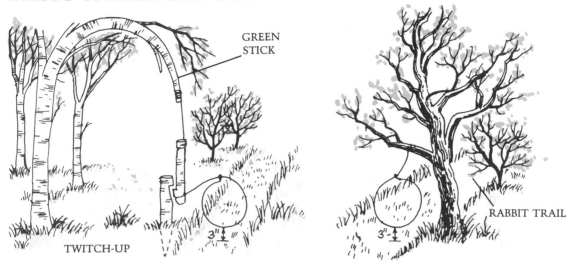

Above left: *This is the twitch-up shown in the photo at left.* **Above right:** *Rabbit snares should be set along well used trails.*

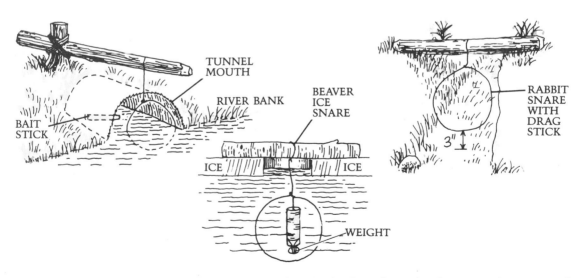

Middle: *The beaver ice snare, baited with a fresh green limb, will catch a beaver under water. The loop should be 6 to 8 inches in diameter. Caution: In a survival predicament, no beaver is worth your falling through thin ice.* **Left:** *The den snare is used for animals such as beaver, which burrow into stream banks.* **Right:** *A drag stick soon hangs up a rabbit.*

MORE SNARES

Hollow-log snares are good ones for a novice to set because the logs are easy to find. Log dens are used by many animals, from little chipmunks to big bobcats.

Animals use log bridges regularly. Snares placed to catch an animal as it starts across often prove effective.

want to attach the anchor end of the snare to a stout pole or log and then put the loop into the hole.

Rabbits often stick to trails, so trail snares are very effective when placed approximately 10 yards apart along a well-used rabbit trail. Simply attach the anchor end of the snare to an overhanging limb or bush, and open the loop up 4 to 6 inches, keeping the bottom of the loop approximately 3 to 4 inches off the ground. The more snares you can have on a trail of this type, the better the odds are that you will take game. I have utilized this snaring method many times and often have taken two or three rabbits quickly.

If you suspect that an animal is using a hollow log as a den, you can anchor one end of your snare there to a solid pole and make your loop end of the snare smaller than the end of the hollow log. Any animal coming in or out of the hollow log is likely to catch its neck in the loop, pulling the loop tighter.

If you find a log crossing a creek, animals such as bobcats and raccoons will cross the creek over the log rather than get into the water. If you put a snare at either end of the log so that the animal will stick its neck into the snare when it starts across, you stand a good chance of catching something.

The largest animal I have snared was a whitetail deer. Deer follow trails on a fairly consistent basis, so if you have a strong piece of cord, such as nylon parachute shroud line, consider trying to snare a deer. You simply find a trail that appears to be used by deer on a regular basis. Then, in a narrowly confined spot, such as among thick brush, between two trees, or in some other type of confinement, position a loop 3 to 4 feet in diameter at about your waist height. Be sure that you have a slip knot that will slip easily. Then anchor the other end of the strong line to a solid tree or heavy log. When a deer realizes it is tied up in a cord of this type,

its tendency is to lunge forward. This will secure the loop around the neck, and you will have an abundance of meat.

I've described but a few of the many ways snares can be used. If you are interested in learning more about snaring you would do well to write the Raymond Thompson Company listed in Appendix 3 for a copy of its publication *Snares and Snaring*. This is an excellent guide covering many more ways of snaring game. Also, I would advise anyone considering assembling a backcountry survival kit to include a few Thompson snares.

Deadfalls. A second method of trapping, known as deadfalls, works fairly well in the backcountry. On the negative side, deadfalls require a great deal of time, energy, and skill to construct. Also, the figure-4 trigger device for deadfalls is very tricky to make.

The theory behind the figure-4 trigger, used with the deadfall, is that an animal will pass underneath a heavy object, such as a rock or log, to eat the bait on the figure-4 trigger. As the animal moves the crossarm of the trigger, the overhead deadfall drops, killing or pinning the animal. Deadfalls work fairly well along animal trails, beside a stream, or in areas where animals are known to feed.

The next trick is to find a deadfall of sufficient weight to kill or pin the animal. Rather than use a deadfall that will kill the animal, many trappers build a cage of green sticks that will fall over the animal, trapping it alive. But many animals will dig their way out of a homemade cage before long. So if you use a cage-type fall, check it often.

Also, since a deadfall leaves an animal on the ground, the trapper must check it often to keep larger animals from stealing the game.

While the figure-4 trigger is difficult to make, the rest of the system is easy to rig. The illustrations on upcoming pages are worth study. As in the case of snares, the more deadfalls you can have out, the better

HOW TO MAKE A FIGURE-4 DEADFALL

The figure-4 deadfall's supporting sticks collapse entirely when the bait is disturbed, allowing the deadfall to pin or kill the quarry. When set up, the weight of the deadfall exerts an outward pressure at the bottom of the diagonal stick where it fits into the notched end of the horizontal. This pulls the horizontal stick directly away from the baited end, thereby holding the notched middle of the horizontal fast against the vertical stick. Note that the vertical stick is balanced on a small platform. A box live trap is shown at bottom.

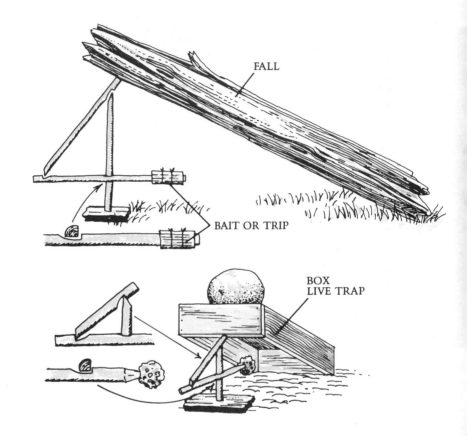

FALL

BAIT OR TRIP

BOX
LIVE TRAP

your chances of taking animals for dinner. Also, like snares, deadfalls are limited only by your imagination. They may be built many different ways, utilizing the same figure-4 trigger. Improving traps and building more traps are good occupations while awaiting rescue, provided you have the energy necessary to build traps and run traplines and provided your efforts bring you meat.

Field-dressing big game. Small game can be brought back into the survival camp and dressed there, but game that is the size of deer or larger must be field-dressed where it was taken by hunting or trapping, and then brought into the camp.

In the survival camp, all animal parts have a value. Skins may be used for clothing and shelter, bones for fishhooks and utensils, antlers for tools or buttons, and eyes as a source of salt.

But even though you are in a survival situation, make every effort to maintain a clean camp, as animal remains can attract unwanted guests, such as bears. In bear country, avoid having meat and animal scraps around

This illustrates the careful balancing effort often necessary to set the figure-4 deadfall properly.

the camp. On the other hand, these remains may be placed away from camp and used as bait for trapping.

It is important when field-dressing an animal to take your time and not get excited. If you cut yourself while trying to field-dress an animal, you add considerably to the dangers you face in survival conditions.

In field-dressing large game, remember that there are three major points where the innards are firmly attached to the carcass: the vent, the diaphragm, and the windpipe/gullet. Field-dressing consists of opening up the skin, cutting the innards free from the hide at these three points, and disposing of the innards. After you complete the field-dressing, you are ready to drag the animal back to your survival camp, if possible, and butcher it. If you don't feel up to dragging the whole animal back to camp, consider quartering it and packing the quarters back.

Skinning and butchering. Under survival conditions, skinning and butchering of any animal must be done carefully so that every edible bite of meat is saved.

HOW TO FIELD-DRESS A BIG ANIMAL

Field-dressing big game is easier if you have the animal on fairly level ground where you can move around it easily, preferably with its head slightly uphill.

1. *Move your deer to a fairly level spot where you have room to walk around the animal. Turn the deer on its back with its underside facing you.*
2. *If your deer is a buck, remove the testicles and the penis by grasping them in one hand and cutting them completely free, taking care not to cut into the organs themselves or the intestinal wall. (If butchering a doe, begin here with Step 3.)*

3. *Cut around the anus, under the base of the tail, being careful not to puncture the anal tube. Core around the tube with your knife, in the same fashion as coring an apple, using the bone around the anal cavity as a guide.*
4. *Place two fingers into the opening you have made and slowly cut the hide toward the chest. Use the fingers to lift the skin away from the intestines while you cut, so as not to puncture any innards.*

5. *When you reach the diaphragm, the strong layer of tissue separating the chest cavity from the abdominal cavity, press on the visceral contents and cut the diaphragm loose from the rib cage.*

6. *Reach inside the neck and cut the gullet and windpipe as near the head as possible, because spoilage occurs quickly here.*

7. *Reach inside the rear of the body cavity and slowly pull the anal tube forward to the inside, carefully using your knife to cut any tissue that prevents it from sliding through. Be careful not to cut the bladder or allow any of its contents to spill. Roll the deer onto its side and pull out the innards. Save the edible heart and liver. Drain as much blood as possible to assist cooling.*

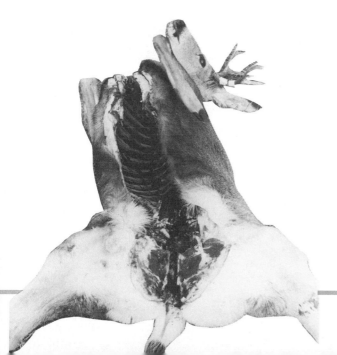

8. *Roll the deer back on its back and prop the body cavity open with sticks to allow maximum cooling through air circulation.*

HOW TO SKIN A SQUIRREL

1. Here's an easy way to skin a squirrel: First, make a crosswise incision just under the tail. Pull the tail forward.

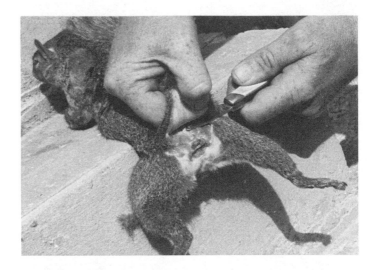

2. Put your foot on the squirrel's tail, hold the squirrel by the hind legs, and pull upward so that the skin pulls off to the head.

3. Loosen any unyielding skin with a knife as you go. Then cut off the head and feet. Remove the insides.

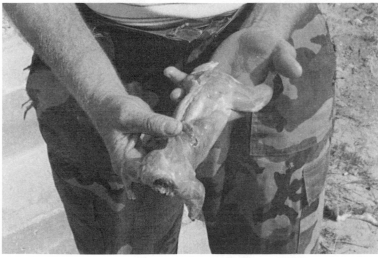

4. Wash the squirrel and it is ready for cooking.

Also consider saving the skin. A square of skin long enough to reach from your head to your knees will not weigh much when dried, and it is one of the best ground cloths to use under your sleeping bag on frozen ground or snow. Snow will not stick to the skin if you lay the hair side up. Also, as the mountain men learned years ago, skins can be used for making many useful objects for the survival camp. You can make clothing, water vessels, and pouches for carrying utensils. In a long-term survival situation, skins could become quite valuable.

The best time to skin and butcher is immediately after an animal is killed. When the carcass is still warm the skin will slide off with a minimum of effort. Also, fresh killed meat is easier to cut up.

When preparing meat under survival conditions, be careful not to discard edible fat. This is especially important when, as is often the case in the Arctic, the diet must consist

Rabbits have very thin skin, making them easy to clean. Simply tear or cut a small opening across the center of the back and pull the skin in opposite directions. Cut off the feet and head, and remove the insides. Then simply wash and cook.

almost entirely of meat. Fat must be eaten in order to provide a complete diet. Under survival conditions, when sugar and vegetable oils are lacking, you must eat fat to remain healthy. As I stated earlier, a diet of rabbits lacks in fat, and the fact that a man will die on a diet consisting of rabbit meat alone attests to the importance of fat in the primitive diet.

The same thing is true of birds, especially birds such as the ptarmigan in the Arctic.

Cooking meat. Assuming you have killed a wild animal, how would you cook it if you didn't have a cook kit or any utensils?

I was once lost for three days on a squirrel hunt and found myself cooking chipmunks over hot coals on a hickory stick. On another occasion, a canoeing mishap left me walking out of strange land for several days. Again, not having any equipment forced me to cook with what I could find.

The primitive man knew more about fires

The simple spit with one support is a good means of cooking small game and birds that can be easily skewered. This hasty broil over flames can result in burnt dinner, unless closely watched.

The keyhole fire is the best fire for cooking purposes. The large area can be used for cooking over flame and to burn down coals to be dragged to the narrow end for slower cooking. The spit with two supports can be used over an open fire as a rotisserie. This is a versatile means of cooking food from very small to very large in size simply by using larger sticks.

than most modern outdoorsmen. These early survivors realized that the best heat for cooking comes from hot coals and not from leaping flames. Probably the best fire for cooking is the "keyhole fire." It is simply rocks laid in an old-fashioned keyhole outline and filled with tinder and firewood. In the round part of the keyhole, a fire is kept going to supply hot coals for the narrow part where the cooking takes place. This type of fire warms as well as cooks. As more coals are needed in the cooking portion, take a stick and pull hot coals from the fire. This also allows you to cook somewhat removed from the searing heat of the main fire.

Another means of building a cooking fire is in a pit no larger than 20 to 30 inches in diameter and approximately 10 inches deep. Line the bottom of the pit with rocks. Allow the fire to burn until you have a hot bed of coals. You are now ready to cook.

A word of caution about using rocks in any type of fire: Porous rocks gathered from stream beds or wet ground may contain enough water to build up steam and explode when heated in the fire. Try to locate dry, dense rocks for your cooking fire.

When cooking in a primitive situation, be sure to use hardwoods, if at all possible. Resinous woods, such as pine, spruce, and fir, will give a turpentine flavor to any food the smoke touches.

A spit offers one of the easiest methods of primitive cooking. One form of spit cooking is to affix the raw food to a stick and hold the stick near the heat—like roasting marshmallows. Another way is to cut two Y-shaped sticks and drive them into the ground on either side of the fire pit. Their Y-branch should be the same height above the ground, some 14 to 16 inches above the coals. Next, impale the meat on a spit and rest the spit horizontally in the forks of the upright sticks. Rotate the spit every 10 to 15 minutes, one-quarter turn, to cook the meat evenly. Be sure the spit is a green hardwood stick so it won't burn.

For cooking a steak or similar cut of meat on a spit, use a spit which is forked at the end. Stick the fork into the meat from the narrow side. This will permit you to turn the meat over without its slipping.

Here a spit becomes a "dingle stick," suspending a cooking pot by means of a whittled pothook.

POTHOOK

HOW TO MAKE WOVEN GRILLS

A grill for cooking small birds, fish, and slabs of meat can be made by weaving green hardwood branches as shown in the photo and in accompanying drawings.

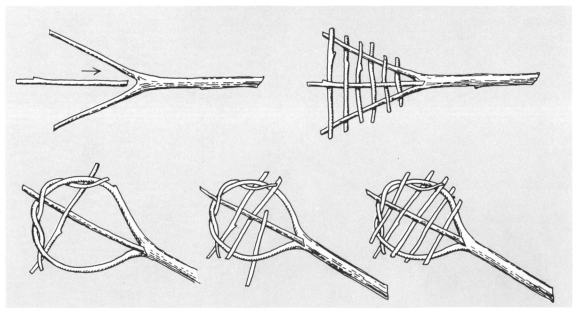

Small animals or strips of meat can be cooked by simply tying them with wire in a coil around the stick or skewering them with the stick and holding it over the fire. Slowly turn the stick, and the meat will cook evenly.

Fish are often difficult to cook on a spit. One way to cook fish is to weave a grill out of green branches of a hardwood tree. Interweave long branches over and under one another at right angles. With some practice you will find this to be an easy chore. The bending branches have tension enough to hold themselves in place. Sometimes it is necessary to tie the corners to hold the grill together. Obviously, the grill will soon dry out, so you'll have to construct a new one periodically. For cooking, the grill should be rested on stones about 10 inches above the coals.

Smoking. In a survival situation, smoking is done primarily to enhance the flavor, since there are no spices available. Yet for the preserving of meat, drying is a better method. Another advantage of smoking is to give a favorable color to the exterior of the meat. It also helps keep insects off the meat.

My brother has developed a method of smoking meat that works well in any outdoors camp. He calls it "smokehole cooking." The smokehole system can make meat taste better than anything you ever put a knife to.

Here's the way it works. Dig a firepit about

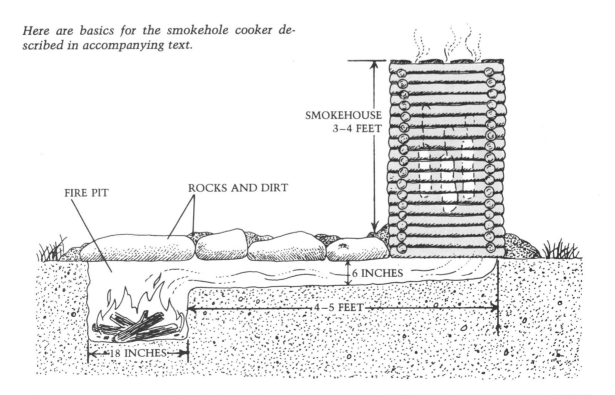

Here are basics for the smokehole cooker described in accompanying text.

SMOKEHOUSE 3–4 FEET

FIRE PIT

ROCKS AND DIRT

6 INCHES

4–5 FEET

18 INCHES

18 inches square and leading from it dig a shallow smoke trench 6 inches square. Cover the trench with flat rocks and bank the rocks with dirt to keep the smoke from escaping.

At the end of the trench, which should be 4 to 5 feet long, build the smokehouse. The smokehouse is constructed by cutting and notching saplings and stacking them log-house fashion until the house is 3 or 4 feet high. Another method is to drive four saplings into the ground to form the vertical corners and cover them with aluminum foil. Bank the bottom of the smokehouse with dirt so that no smoke escapes. Loosely place a few strips of bark over the top of the smokehouse to serve as a damperlike lid.

Hang strips of meat inside.

Get your fire going in the pit with dry hardwood and then add some green hardwood. Hickory or oak will do. After the green wood catches fire, cover the pit with a flat rock and bank it with dirt. Properly built, a good fire will last for hours, because the smokehouse limits the amount of draft and thus the amount of air mixing with flame and wood.

Before you try cooking with smoke, remember that it takes hours for most meat to get done. Jerky can be dried entirely in the smokehouse, but if you are smoking simply to add flavor, the meat can be half-cooked first over the open fire to cut down on smoking time. Big game heart, liver, and tongue will be more tender if they can be boiled for a few minutes before smoking.

With some practice, you can learn to use this method of smoke cooking well enough to satisfy any palate.

Rock oven. A rock oven lets you cook any type of food without utensils. First, dig a hole approximately 2 feet deep and 2 or 3 feet square, depending on the volume of food to be cooked. Then select rocks from a dry area, green limbs approximately 3 inches in diameter, plenty of firewood, and grass or leaves for insulation.

Lay a fire in the hole. Place the green limbs across the hole. Pile the rocks on the green limbs. Light the fire and keep it stoked. When the green limbs burn through and the rocks fall into the hole, the oven is ready to use.

Remove the rocks and ashes. Clean any live fire from the hole. Line the bottom of the hole with hot rocks. Place a thin layer of dirt over the rocks. Place grass, moss, or other insulating material on the dirt. Put in the food to be cooked, more insulating material, a thin layer of dirt, and hot rocks, and cover with remaining earth.

Small pieces of meat (steaks, chops, etc.) cook in 1½ to 2 hours. Large roasts take 5 to 6 hours.

Rock broiler. Vegetables, fish, crustaceans, fruits, and eggs may be cooked on a rock broiler. A rock broiler may be made by placing a layer of small stones on top of hot hardwood coals and laying the item to be cooked on the top. When cooking an egg in this way, pierce the small end and place the egg on the rock with the large end down. Prop it in place and turn it often. It will cook in approximately 10 minutes.

Jerky. One of the best ways to preserve meat without cooking is to make it into jerky. Jerky is simply thin strips of dried meat that will last for months without refrigeration.

Here is how to make it in a survival camp:

1. Build a tripod of three 6-foot-long poles. Tie the poles together at the top and spread each pole out 3 feet. Tie wire, rope, string, or vines to the poles in several locations from which to hang the meat.

2. Cut your meat into 6-inch strips about ½ inch wide and ¼ inch thick. Be sure to cut the strips with the grain running lengthwise.

To make jerky, dry strips of meat on tripod until the meat becomes dark and stiff. Jerky will keep for months as long as it is kept dry.

3. Trim off all fat because fat will turn rancid.

4. Lay strips of meat on the wire, string, or vine on your tripod to dry.

5. Protect the meat from rain.

6. When the meat turns dark and gets stiff, it's ready.

7. Store where it won't get wet.

Pemmican. Once you have made jerky, it is easy to make one of the best-known survival foods in the history of North America—pemmican. Our history is rich in accolades to pemmican. Alexander McKenzie cached pemmican in grass-and-bark-lined holes in the ground for his return trip during the first crossing of North America. America's greatest hunting trip, the Lewis and Clark Expedition, depended upon pemmican for trail food. Admiral Peary's successful journey to the North Pole was accomplished with pemmican as a staple food which Peary and his men ate cold twice a day. The admiral wrote that it was "the most satisfying food I know."

In order to make pemmican, combine equal parts of jerky, wild berries, and boiled fat from animals. Mix the ingredients well. Then roll the pemmican into 1-inch-by-3-inch rolls and wrap in skins or leaves until it cools. This food may be carried on the trail, and people have been known to survive for literally weeks eating nothing but pemmican. Since jerky lacks fat, you cannot live nearly as long on a jerky diet as you can on pemmican. I recommend that anyone in a long-term survival situation make jerky first, then convert as much of the jerky into pemmican as possible.

As I stated at the beginning of this chapter, depending upon edible wild animals to survive usually shouldn't happen to those who take proper precautions. However, to prepare yourself for the worst, attend a field training program to learn how to trap and hunt wild animals for food. In many areas of North America, living off the land is difficult, even for the experts. Not having hunting, trapping, and primitive cooking skills can put you in serious trouble should you find yourself in a long-term survival situation.

12
BACKCOUNTRY NAVIGATION

One of the major reasons survival books are written is that many people venture into the outdoors without any knowledge of navigation. Finding one's way skillfully through backcountry has always been a challenge. Some people find their way far better than others. Research studies indicate that the ability to find your way is not instinctive and a "sense of direction" is not a gift one is born with. Anyone who has hunted in flat country on a gray, overcast day knows that it takes a lot more than a so-called sense of direction to get back where you started from.

The word "navigation" scares many beginners. For them it calls forth images of sextants, chronometers, altimeters, and other complicated instruments. But as any seasoned backpacker, hunter, fisherman, or trapper can testify, good navigation is using

® Orienteering and Silva are registered trademarks.

map and compass skills as well as natural aids such as the sun and landmarks. Sometimes, good navigation is having the sense to know when you need a guide instead.

Before you can learn map and compass navigation you need a good compass to practice with. There are many compasses on the market. However, the best type for learning navigation is the Orienteering® compass,

The so-called "sense of direction" does not exist. Navigation is a skill that must be learned. It is knowing how to use map, compass, and natural aids such as the sun and landmarks, and it involves solving problems beginning with "Where am I?" and "Where do I want to go?" (Outward Bound USA photo)

which combines a rotating compass housing on a protractor plate. I find that the Silva® Ranger best serves my purposes. After you buy a compass, be sure to study the instructions accompanying it.

When you use a compass, it is important to keep it away from metallic objects such as cars, guns, knives, belt buckles, and other compasses, because the iron in them can affect the magnetic needle, causing you to be off course.

In this chapter, I will illustrate techniques

BASIC ORIENTEERING COMPASS

Here are features of a basic Orienteering compass by Silva. (Neil Soderstrom photo)

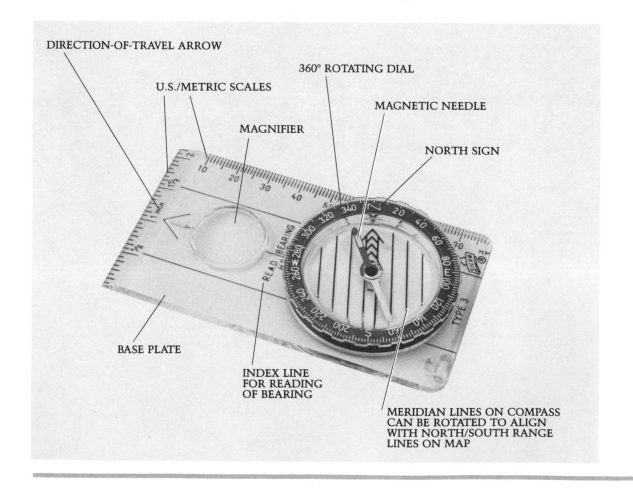

DIRECTION-OF-TRAVEL ARROW

U.S./METRIC SCALES

360° ROTATING DIAL

MAGNIFIER

MAGNETIC NEEDLE

NORTH SIGN

BASE PLATE

INDEX LINE
FOR READING
OF BEARING

MERIDIAN LINES ON COMPASS
CAN BE ROTATED TO ALIGN
WITH NORTH/SOUTH RANGE
LINES ON MAP

using the Silva Orienteering compasses rather than the lensatic compass, because the Orienteering compass is simpler, and the Silva system of land navigation allows you to learn navigation quickly.

The conventional compass is simply a magnetized needle pivoting on a point in a housing marked in 360 degrees around a full circle. On all U.S. compasses, 0 (or 360) degrees marks north. Degree graduations move clockwise around the compass, with 90 degrees for east, 180 degrees for south, and 270

ORIENTEERING RANGER

This is Silva's full-featured Orienteering compass, called the Ranger. One model is available with a clinometer, as well, which allows you to measure the angle of slope of a distant mountain. The two chief advantages of the Ranger over other Silva compasses are (1) the declination adjustment screw, which lets you adjust the degree-reading dial to match the declination (degree difference) between magnetic north and true map north for the region you are in, and (2) a mirror with line of sight etched in, which allows you to take highly precise readings to distant points in a manner similar to that shown next for the lensatic style compass. (Neil Soderstrom photo)

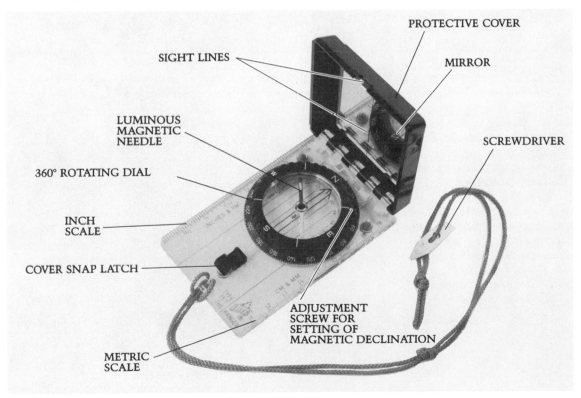

LENSATIC COMPASS

These are the features of the Precise Pathfinder Lensatic Compass. (Barry Fikes photo)

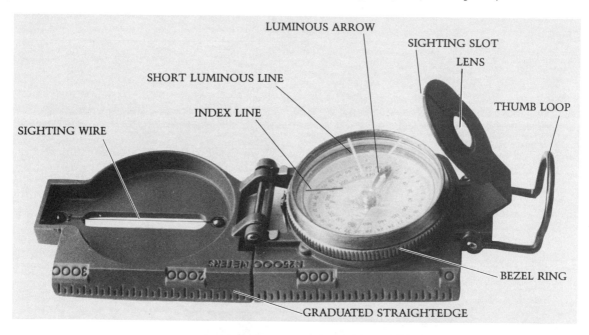

LUMINOUS ARROW

SIGHTING SLOT

LENS

SHORT LUMINOUS LINE

THUMB LOOP

INDEX LINE

SIGHTING WIRE

BEZEL RING

GRADUATED STRAIGHTEDGE

A lensatic compass allows you to take a precise bearing reading to a specific point. To take a bearing reading, use the compass hairline to sight, through the sighting slot, on a prominent landmark or feature. Read the magnetic bearing from the front of the compass dial. The lens under the slot may be used to magnify the bearing numbers. (Barry Fikes photo)

degrees for west. Old compasses and today's cheaper compasses have needles pivoting in air, but the better compasses are liquid filled. The liquid slows down the swinging of the needle and brings the needle quickly to rest.

The basic Orienteering compass has a transparent plastic base plate, which has its edges marked for measuring distances on a map. The magnetic needle, the revolving compass housing, and the base plate are designed to be used together with your map.

The compass needle points to *magnetic* north, not *true* north. The north (red) end of the needle is attracted by the *magnetic* North Pole, which is about 1,400 miles south of the true North Pole. Maps are drawn with lines of longitude converging at true north. This means that you must account for the difference between magnetic north and true north when you are using your compass and map, especially over long distances.

The angle of difference between true north and magnetic north is called *declination*. The angle varies as you move east or west across North America from a line of 0 declination which runs north roughly from Florida through Lake Superior. The angle of declination, in degrees, is noted on most maps.

This angle of declination must be used to orient the map properly with a compass. You can do this by simply extending the magnetic north line found in the declination diagram at the bottom of a topo map as shown in the accompanying photo. To do this, place

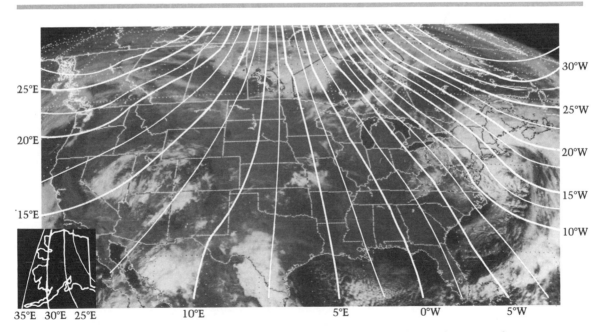

This photo illustrates the increasing difference between magnetic north and true north as you move farther east or west of the agonic line, or line of zero magnetic declination. Failure to compensate for declination can take you far off course, even over relatively short distances. (National Oceanic and Atmospheric Administration photo)

THE DECLINATION DIAGRAM

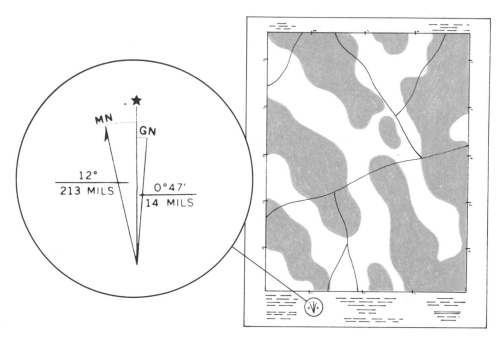

This shows where you'll see the declination diagram on U.S. topo maps. For compass declination, you need to know the difference between magnetic north (MN) and true north (★). This diagram shows a 12° westerly declination found in New York state. Some diagrams, as shown here, also indicate grid north (GN), which is of interest primarily to map makers and can be disregarded in the field.

the rectangular compass base plate edge along this line and draw a magnetic north line across the topo map. By adding parallel lines, you can correct for the declination on any part of the map.

The method I've explained for preparing a topo map for magnetic north is the simplest and quickest method for the novice. In some regions of the extreme West, the difference between magnetic and true north may be as much as 25 degrees. Where the difference is this great, you will be about ¼ mile off course after you have traveled 1 mile if you fail to

correct for declination.

Some compasses have built-in declination adjustment mechanisms, which make using the compass with a number of different maps very easy. After setting the declination compensation on your compass, you have no need of adding or subtracting degrees with each bearing you make in your travels.

I suggest that anyone going into or living in an area with more than a 10 degree declination get a compass which has an adjustment for magnetic declination.

If you find yourself with a compass that

By drawing lines throughout a topo map parallel to the indicated magnetic declination (in this case 12° westerly), you obtain a quick means of orienting map and compass. From this it is simple to press the compass base plate against the map and rotate the dial so its north aligns with magnetic north. This allows easy taking of bearings that (of course) do not compensate for declination. (Neil Soderstrom photo)

cannot be adjusted, here is how you can correct your compass readings for the respective declination. Let's say you are in the far West where the declination is 20 degrees east. When correcting the compass for easterly declination, note the degree reading of your compass, then subtract from that reading the amount of declination and reset your compass housing accordingly. In this example, if your reading is 50 degrees and the easterly declination is 20 degrees, you reset your compass to 30 degrees.

If you were in eastern Canada with a westerly declination, you add the amount to the degree reading of your compass. For example, if your compass reading is 90 degrees and you have a 30-degree westerly declination, you reset your compass to 120 degrees.

When subtracting to get an easterly declination, if you have to subtract a declination larger than your compass dial reading, "borrow" 360 degrees (in a full circle) and add it to the dial reading. For instance, if your compass dial reads 10 degrees and the declination to be subtracted is 20 degrees, figure 10 + 360 = 370. Then 370 − 20 = 350. Your reading should be 350 degrees.

When adding to get a westerly declination, if you get a reading that is larger than the 360 degrees found on the compass dial, you subtract 360. For example, if your compass setting is 350 degrees and the westerly declination is 30 degrees, figure 350 + 30 = 380. Then 380 − 360 = 20. Your reading should be 20 degrees.

As you can see, this can be very confusing. It is a real pain to have to add or subtract degrees every time you take a reading. Should you forget to consider an 18-degree difference on a 3 mile hike, you will miss your objective by 1 mile. For the small additional cost of a compass with a declination adjustment, you can set it before you leave home and forget all this confusing math.

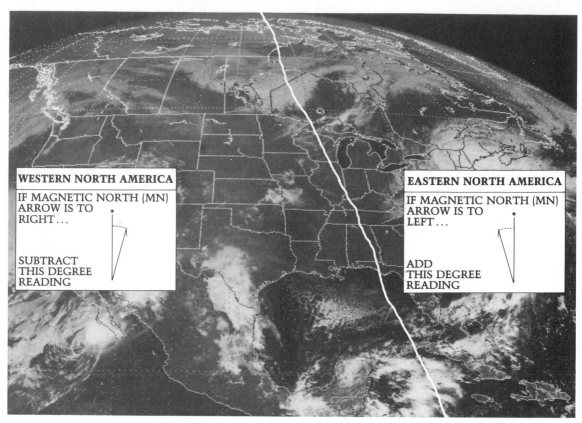

If you are in a region with declination of more than a few degrees and cannot adjust your compass accordingly, remember to add the declination to your compass reading if you are east of the 0° declination line. And subtract the declination from the degree reading if you are west of the 0° declination line. This is described in detail in text on the previous page. (National Oceanic and Atmospheric Administration photo)

Orienting Map, Compass, and Ground

To orient the map and compass with the ground, simply use the magnetic grid lines you have drawn across the map. Set the compass dial on a bearing of 360 degrees (North) and place the compass on your map so that the base plate edges are parallel with the magnetic grid lines you have drawn and the compass points to North on the map. Then rotate the map, with compass still in place on the drawn grid lines, until the north end of the needle points to north on the compass dial. Now map and compass are oriented with the land.

A map can also be oriented by the eyeballing method, if you have a good view of a large tract of terrain. That is, you can turn the map until the symbols for trails, rivers,

OBTAINING YOUR BEARING FROM A MAP

Follow these three basic steps:

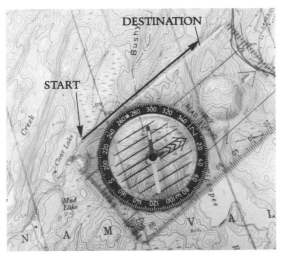

1. Place the compass on the map with edge of the base plate touching (or parallel with) both your starting point and the destination, with the base plate's directional arrow pointing in the direction you want to go.

2. Hold the base plate firmly against the map and turn the dial until the orienting arrow is parallel with the magnetic grid lines you drew and pointing to magnetic north on the map. You can now read your bearing in degrees at the index line.

3. Hold the compass level, with the direction-of-travel arrow pointing away from you, and turn your body until the red end of the compass needle points to north on the dial. The direction-of-travel arrow now indicates the bearing you will be taking to your destination. (Neil Soderstrom photos)

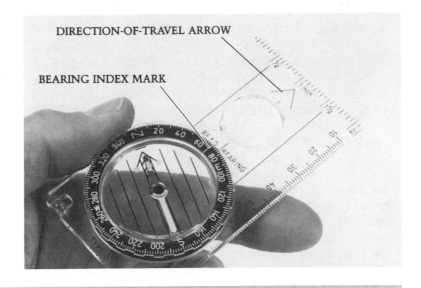

and other landmarks line up with features you can see on the ground.

Taking a Directional Bearing without Map

You can use a procedure similar to that above, without a map, to determine your compass bearing to a distant landmark or object. Simply point the direction-of-travel arrow on the compass base plate at the landmark. Next, keeping the base plate direction-of-travel arrow pointed at the landmark, rotate the compass dial until 0 degrees (N) is aligned with the magnetic needle. Then simply read the compass bearing at the index line on the dial.

Finding Direction by Sun and Stars

What do you do if you get caught in a survival situation without a compass? There are crude methods of using the sun to determine direction, but remember that most of these methods do not give accurate direction. There is no substitute for always carrying a compass, and on wilderness trips, always having a backup compass securely fastened to your person in case the primary compass is lost or destroyed.

Using the sun to find direction. The sun rises in the east and sets in the west. Therefore, when you're facing the morning sun, north is to your left, and when you're facing an afternoon sun, north is to your right. Some people have difficulty with this concept.

Equal-altitude method. The first method of using the sun is commonly known as the "equal-altitude method." Used correctly, this method is reasonably accurate. The theory here is that the height of the sun above the horizon at a given time before noon is the same as it is at the same interval of time after noon. You measure the height by the length of the shadow. This is accomplished

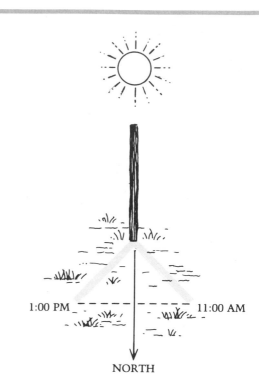

This illustrates the equal altitude method of finding north, as explained in the accompanying text.

by taking a very straight pole, long pencil, or something similar and sticking it exactly vertical on an extremely flat, horizontal plane. This horizontal plane could be a level area of ground, or in winter it could be on an iced-over pond. Remember that the accuracy of this method depends upon how vertical your upright pole is and how flat the horizontal plane is.

In the morning, mark the tip of the shadow that the vertical device casts on the flat surface. Measure the shadow's length from the base of the vertical object to the tip. When the shadow reaches that length again in the afternoon, mark it. The line from the center of the base of the object casting the shadow through the point halfway between your two marks points directly north.

Watch methods. A watch with an hour hand can be used to determine the approximate direction of north. Point the hour hand of your watch toward the sun. An approximate south can be found midway between the hour hand and 12 o'clock. This applies to standard time. During daylight savings time, the north-south line is midway between the hour hand and one o'clock. (This assumes, of course, that your watch shows the correct time.)

Another method can also be used. Place a small stick in the center of the watch and hold it vertically so that the shadow of the stick falls along the hour hand. One-half the distance between the shadow and 12 o'clock is approximately north.

Stick-and-peg method. North can be found

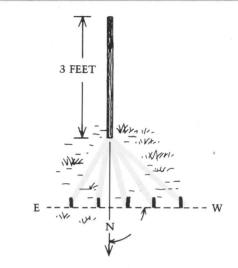

This shows the stick-and-peg method of finding north, as explained in accompanying text.

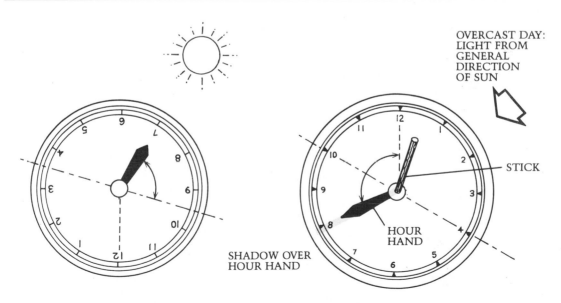

This shows how to use only a watch to find north, as explained in accompanying text.

The watch stick-and-shadow method of finding north, as explained in accompanying text.

FINDING THE NORTH STAR

The North Star remains within 1 degree of north throughout the night. But, owing to the earth's rotation, the dippers appear to rotate around the North Star one complete revolution every 24 hours. Also, through the seasons, at a given hour, the dippers may be in any of the positions shown.

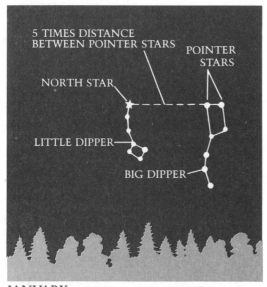

JANUARY

APRIL

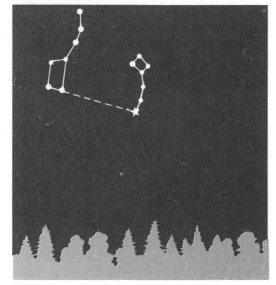

JULY

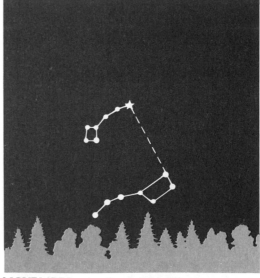

NOVEMBER

by using the stick-and-peg method. Select a straight stick 3 feet long and five small pegs. Place the stick upright in a cleared area. Place a peg into the ground at the end of the stick's shadow line. Wait 15 minutes. Place another peg at the end of the shadow line. Repeat until five pegs are in. Place a straight stick alongside the pegs. This stick points east and west. To find north, place a stick with one end at the base of the upright shadow stick and its length at a right angle to the east-west stick. The stick points north and south.

North Star method. In the Northern Hemisphere, one star, Polaris (the North Star), is never more than 1 degree away from true north. You find this star by locating the Big Dipper, a group of stars which is very close to the North Celestial Pole. The two stars on the outer edge of the Big Dipper are called pointers, as they point almost directly to Polaris. The North Star is the last star in the handle of the Little Dipper.

The Topo Map

Most areas of the United States have been topographically mapped by the U.S. Geological Survey, a bureau of the Department of the Interior. In Canada, the same service is provided by the Surveys and Mapping Branch of the Department of Mines and Technical Surveys. Not only do these maps show the location and shape of mountains, valleys, plains, streams, lakes, and works of man, such as roads, buildings, and utility lines, but they also show the differences in elevation of the terrain.

Each topo map is a quadrangle unit of survey which is outlined by parallels of latitude and meridians of longitude. For outdoorsmen, the most useful maps cover 7½ minutes of latitude and longitude, published at a scale of 1:24,000, or 1 inch to 2,000 feet.

Each map has a name, usually that of a city, town, community, or prominent natural feature located within it. This name appears in bold letters in the upper and lower right-hand corners. In the margins of the map are the names of the eight adjoining maps. Since the 7½-minute maps cover only from 49 to 70 square miles, the area you are interested in may extend over more than one map.

Nearly all 7½-minute maps now come with a woodland overprint, meaning that all woodlands will be shown in green. Man-made features will be shown in black, water areas in blue, and relief features, such as mountains and valleys, in brown contour lines.

To order U.S. topographical maps, write to the U.S. Geological Survey for a state index in map form showing position of maps in the state you are interested in. For areas east of the Mississippi River, including Minnesota, write to Branch of Distribution, U.S. Geological Survey, 1200 South Eads Street, Arlington, VA 22202. For areas west of the Mississippi River, write to Branch of Distribution, U.S. Geological Survey, Box 25276, Federal Center, Denver, CO 80225.

For Canadian maps, write Canada Map Office, 615 Booth Street, Ottawa, CANADA K1A OE9. These maps are now based on the metric system.

When you receive the state or province index map, locate the area you plan to go to. It will have one or more rectangles over it showing map borders, with name of each map printed inside. Then, write to the appropriate U.S. Geological Survey (or Canadian) office requesting the maps you want, identifying them by name, series, and state (or province).

Topo maps are revised periodically. But some are not revised for many years. So be sure to check the date on the map to account for man-made features on the ground that are not shown on the map.

Like any other outdoor tool, the topo map is of little value unless you learn to use it

ADJOINING MAPS AND THE DISTANCE SCALE

U.S. topo maps show the name of the map in the upper right-hand corner and the names of the eight adjoining maps in the margins. The scale of distance is at the bottom, with contour interval.

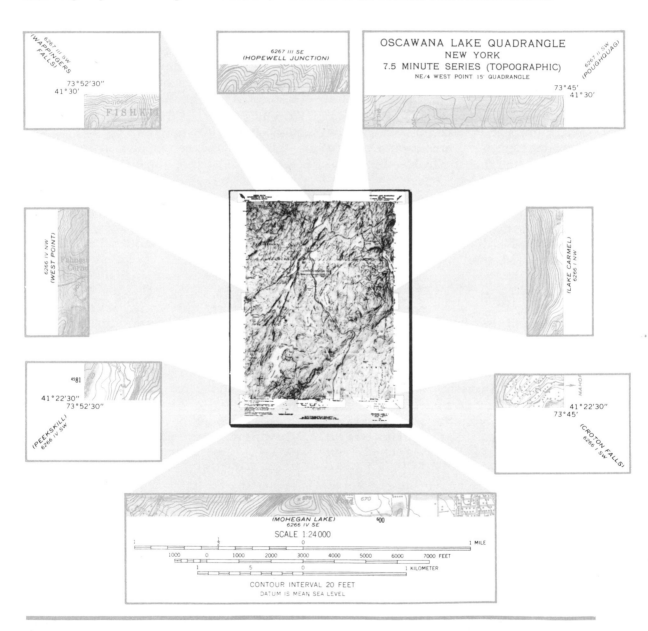

A SELECTED TABLE OF TOPO MAP SYMBOLS

Primary highway, hard surface . . . .

Secondary highway, hard surface . . . .

Light-duty road, hard or improved surface . . . .

Unimproved road . . . .

Trail . . . .

Railroad: single track and multiple track . . . .

Bridge: road and railroad . . . .

Footbridge . . . .

Tunnel: road and railroad . . . .

Small masonry or concrete dam . . . .

Buildings (barn, warehouse, etc.) . . . .

Power transmission line with located metal tower . . . .

Telephone line, pipeline, etc. (labeled as to type) . . . .

Wells other than water (labeled as to type) . . . . oOil . . . . oGas

Open pit, mine, or quarry; prospect x

Shaft and tunnel entrance . . . . Y

Horizontal and vertical control station:

    Tablet, spirit level elevation . . . . BM △ 5653

    Other recoverable mark, spirit level elevation . . . . △ 5455

Horizontal control station: tablet, vertical angle elevation VΛBM △ 9619

    Any recoverable mark, vertical angle or checked elevation △3775

Vertical control station: tablet, spirit level elevation . . . . . BM X957

    Other recoverable mark, spirit level elevation X954

Spot elevation . . . . **X 7369** X 7369

Water elevation 670 670

Index contour . . . . Intermediate contour . .

Supplementary contour Depression contours . .

Fill . . . . Cut . . . .

Levee . . . . Levee with road . . . . . .

Mine dump . . . . Wash . . . .

Tailings . . . . Tailings pond . . . .

Shifting sand or dunes Intricate surface . . . . . .

Sand area . . . . Gravel beach . . . .

Fence or field line . . . .

Perennial streams . . . . . Intermittent streams . .

Elevated aqueduct . . . . . Aqueduct tunnel . . . . . .

Water well and spring . . Glacier . . . .

Small rapids . . . . Small falls . . . .

Large rapids . . . . Large falls . . . .

Intermittent lake . . . . . . Dry lake bed . . . .

Foreshore flat . . . . Rock or coral reef . . . .

Sounding, depth curve . Piling or dolphin . . . . . .

Exposed wreck . . . . Sunken wreck . . . .

Rock, bare or awash; dangerous to navigation . . . .

Marsh (swamp) . . . . Submerged marsh . . . .

Wooded marsh . . . . Mangrove . . . .

Woods or brushwood . . Orchard . . . .

Vineyard . . . . Scrub . . . .

Land subject to
controlled inundation Urban area . . . .

properly. The best way to learn to read a topo map is to begin with a map of an area with which you are familiar. Drive the roads, relating the map's symbols to the man-made and natural features you see. Walk a distance cross-country, up a hill and down into a valley, and relate the contour lines on the map to the rise and fall of the land. Contour lines pass through points of equal elevation. You can think of contour lines as imaginary lines on the ground which take any shape necessary to maintain a constant elevation, like high-water marks along waterways.

Every fourth or fifth contour, depending on the contour interval, will be an "index contour," which is shown by a heavier brown line. The elevation will be given at intervals along this contour. The elevation of any point can be determined by locating an index contour line and interpolating each contour line to your chosen point according to the contour interval of your map. (This is found at

RELATING TOPO FEATURES TO A TOPO MAP

This photo and map allow you to practice relating map symbols to terrain, as you would when navigating. Elevated views such as this let you to determine your own unknown position by taking compass bearings to prominent land features. Or you can use views such as this to take a bearing from your known position to your destination. For practice, you might enjoy relating the four prominent peaks in the photo to camera position. Hint: this northward view is from the peak of Mt. Washington in the White Mountains of New Hampshire. Its elevation of 6,288 feet is the highest in eastern North America. Here winds exceed hurricane force of 75 mph an average of 104 days a year. On Mt. Washington alone, more than 100 people have perished as a result of falls and unforgiving weather. Signs on hiking trails read, "STOP. The area ahead has the worst weather in America. Many have died there from exposure, even in the summer. Turn back now if the weather is bad." (David Lingel and Mount Washington Observatory photo)

HOW TO MOUNT A MAP ONTO MUSLIN

1
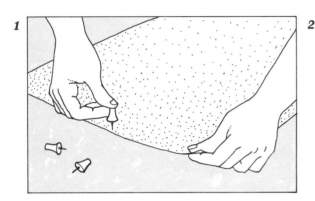

2
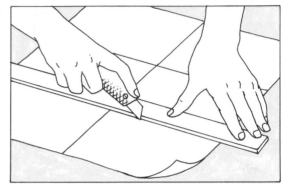

1. Spread a piece of muslin, a bit larger than the map, taut over a smooth, flat surface such as a board or work table, and fasten the map along the edges with tacks about 4 inches apart. 2. To prevent map features from disappearing in the fold lines, cut the map along fold lines and then soak each piece in water before applying paste.

the bottom center of the map under the map's scale.) The closer together the contour lines are, the steeper the slope will be; the farther apart they are, the gentler the terrain.

It is also important to learn to use the map's scale, as this will help you estimate distances and walking time to your destination. For example, on a 7½-minute map, 2⅝ inches equals 1 mile.

Protecting your map. If you plan to take your maps into the field, there are various ways to protect the maps and give them a long life. One method is to use a can of "Storm Proof" spray lacquer on your maps. Storm Proof instantly impregnates and protects paper. It does not make maps brittle and may be marked upon with a pencil or pen. Storm Proof may be ordered from Brigade Quartermasters (See Appendix 3).

A second method of protecting maps is to

SEE-THROUGH MAP POUCH

A homemade clear acetate map pouch allows you to protect several maps at once. It keeps a map dry when you must study it in wet weather and allows the folding of the map so that the map section of prime interest comes immediately to view. No tedious refolding necessary each time you consult the map! (Neil Soderstrom photo)

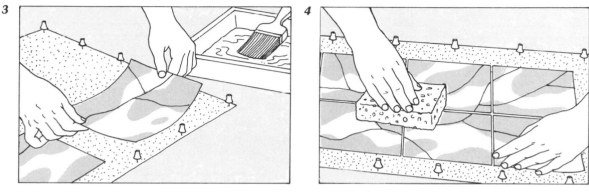

3. *Apply flour and water paste or wallpaper paste onto the backs of the map pieces with a brush. The paste should be the consistency of canned applesauce. If it becomes lumpy, strain it through cheese-cloth. Position the pieces in proper order ⅛ inch apart on the cloth.* **4.** *Carefully wipe the map with a damp cloth or sponge, applying light pressure to smooth out any creases or ripples. Leave the map on the board until it is thoroughly dry. This should take at least a day. Avoid placing it in sunlight while it is drying because the sun will bleach it. When the map is dry, trim off excess muslin.*

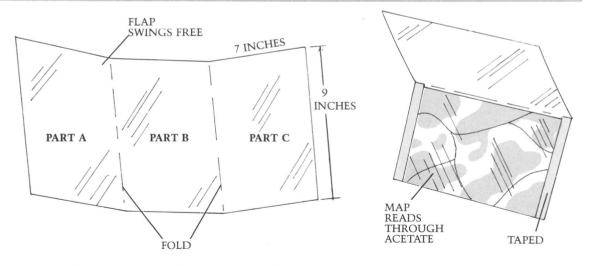

Parts B and C are taped together to form a pocket. Part C becomes a protective flap with hinge that can be cheated outward to protect larger map sections, if needed. The dimensions shown provide a pouch that can be inserted into a pack or tucked conveniently inside your shirt.

mount them on a sheet of thin, unstarched, bleached muslin fabric.

A third method is to create a protective plastic pouch, as shown.

Navigational Techniques

There are two navigational techniques that everyone going into the backcountry should know. If you understand these two basic techniques, you should be able to handle most navigation in North America.

Baseline navigation. Requiring only a compass, baseline navigation helps you find your way and otherwise avoid getting lost. A basic requirement is a straight land feature to use as the baseline. In most cases this will be a road or a river. It may be a power line (which will deflect a compass needle) or other utility right-of-way.

Let's assume that your baseline is a road upon which you have left your car, and you are going to spend the day hunting. You leave the road near your car and hunt inland west-

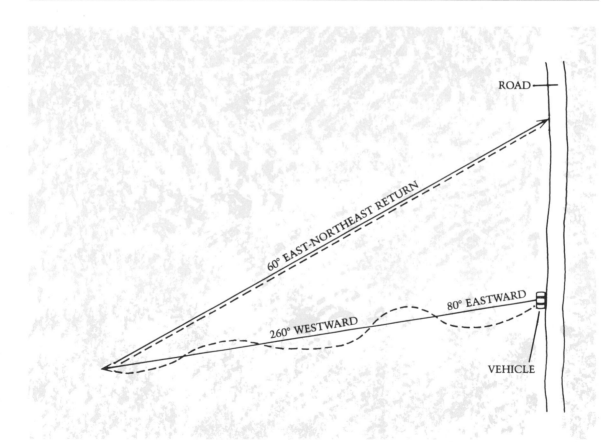

This drawing illustrates the baseline navigation described in accompanying text.

ward to an area that is rich in game, roughly following a bearing of 260 degrees. You take this bearing before you leave your car and head west.

You have walked for 2 miles, wandering to the right and to the left of your intended route, because of logs, trees, and other obstacles. You have not kept track of these slight changes in direction. Then you are ready to return to your car. You know that the road, which is your baseline, is generally to the east. You also know that a back bearing of 80 degrees should put you back on the road near your car. (Here, back bearing is figured by subtracting 180, or half of the 360 degrees that is a complete circle, from the 260-degree bearing you went out on.) However, because of your wanderings, you probably didn't travel exactly 260 degrees westward. So if you return at precisely an 80-degree eastward bearing, there is a good possibility that you will reach the road either north or south of your car. There you might not know whether to go the right or to the left to reach your car. To make certain which side of your car you will be on, you should overcompensate by strongly favoring a target too far uproad or downroad of your theoretical 80-degree return route. For instance, you could return on a 60-degree bearing, putting you north of your car. Then when you come to the road, you will know that you should turn right, heading south. If bearing degree numbers are troublesome for you, you can simply rely on letter abbreviations, such as NW (northwest) and its opposite SE (southeast), and so on.

The one disadvantage of this baseline navigation is that occasionally people use a very faint baseline, such as an abandoned logging road. And when they are returning, perhaps after dark, they do not recognize the road and so pass by it, continuing on their bearing. After they realize that they have walked too far and have not seen the road, they become

Under the supervision of a good instructor, you can practice baseline navigation with a sack over your head. Following the bearings provided by your instructor, navigate through an open field.

confused and get lost. Anytime you are using the baseline method of navigation, you should be especially alert to recognize your baseline.

A good way to appreciate baseline navigation and to gain confidence in your compass skills is to practice in a large, smooth field with a baseline such as a fence or a field road. Standing by the baseline, place a large paper grocery sack over your head so that when you look down you can see only your compass and a few feet in front of you. Mark the starting point on the baseline. Shoot a bearing (walk) into the field. Now, shoot a bearing back so that you will come out on the road to a strongly favored point uproad or downroad of your starting point. After you've done this exercise a few times, you'll better appreciate baseline navigation.

Bearing and distance navigation. The second method of navigating in the backcountry is known as the "bearing and distance" method. The bearing and distance method works well when you are traveling to a point some distance away and where terrain features may be spotted along the way. Using the accompanying drawing, here is how the method works:

Let's say someone has marked a good fishing lake for you on a topo map. In the comfort of your base camp, use your map and compass to line up north. With the edge of the compass base plate, line up the first leg of your trip—say, from where you will park your car on the road to the first well-defined landmark, perhaps the top of a sharp peak. Scale-measure the distance to the landmark and compute the bearing to it and the return bearing from it. Record this information in pencil on your map or on a separate sheet. Do the same thing with each additional leg of the trip. When you finish this, your route should be marked on your map and you should have enough information to travel to and from the lake. Example:

	Distance	Bearing out	−180° Return Bearing
Car to base of mountain peak	1 mile	355 degrees	175 degrees
Mountain peak to rock cliff	1 mile	55 degrees	235 degrees
Rock cliff to fishing lake	½ mile	38 degrees	218 degrees

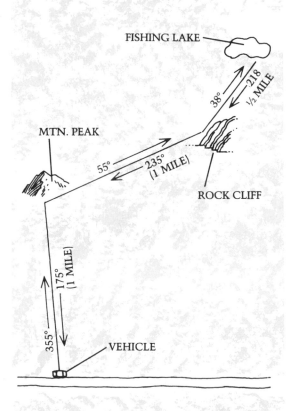

This shows bearing-and-distance navigation as described in accompanying text.

If you carefully follow bearings and watch landmarks, you will find it relatively simple to make a round trip and stay on course. But without landmarks, you will have to attempt to judge distances hiked—a difficult task. As an added help, you might mark your trip out by affixing pieces of white surveyor's tape to tree trunks and collecting them on your return.

Bearing-and-distance navigation is especially useful in lake country, utilizing islands and points of land as points to run your bearings to.

Offset navigation. Often when running a bearing course, you will come to an obstacle, such as a swamp or cliff, which you must go around. In order to do this and stay on course, you must either make a point on the far side to locate after hiking around the obstacle or keep up with four compass angles and three

distances. Let's say you are on a course of 200 degrees and you come to a large swamp, as shown on the accompanying drawing. To go around it, turn a 90-degree angle, which will put you on a bearing of 110 degrees, and count the paces to where you can resume your original bearing, say 1,500 paces. Next, turn 90 degrees back to your 200-degree bearing and walk to where you know you have passed the swamp. Turn another 90 degrees on a bearing of 290 degrees for 1,500 paces. When you reach that point, turn left 90 degrees and continue traveling on your original 200-degree bearing, which should be directly in line with your original line of travel.

Position Finding

If you have a map and compass and don't know your location on the map, you can find that position if you can locate two or three

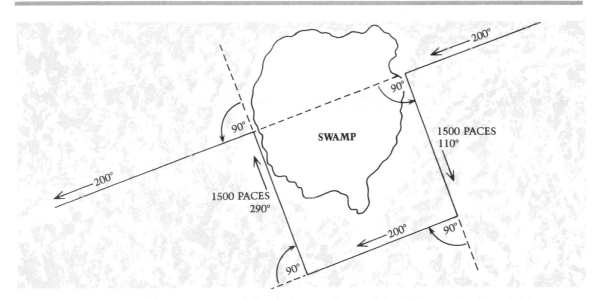

An obstacle such as a lake, stream, or cliff can dictate the need for offset navigation of this type, as described in accompanying text.

This shows how to find your position on a topo map, as you'll find explained in the accompanying text.

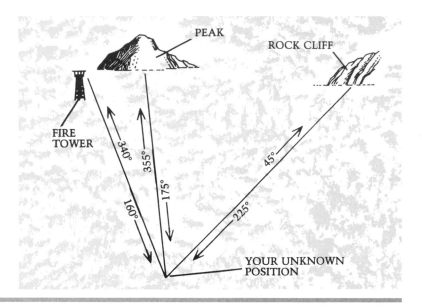

prominent landmarks on the ground that are also on your map. If, for example, you can see a forest fire tower, a tall steep peak, and a rock cliff, take a bearing to each of these points. Next, calculate a back bearing for each by adding 180 degrees, or if the front bearing is greater than 180 degrees, by subtracting 180 degrees. Remember, there are only 360 degrees in a circle. *And you must adjust for declination.* For this adjustment, the rule is

- *West, + East when reading compass to map*
- + *West, − East when reading map to compass*

Then draw lines from each of these landmarks on your map on the back bearing. Your location is where the lines converge.

A similar method may be used for locating an exact point in a large lake. Let's say you are on a lake for the first time and have found a good fishing bed. You want to fish the bed again tomorrow. Choose two prominent land features that you think you can spot again. Each must be identifiable on your map as well. (We'll call them A and B.) With your compass, read the bearing from the fish bed to each of these land features. Then compute their reverse bearings by adding 180 degrees (or if the bearing is greater than 180, by subtracting 180). These will be the bearings from the features to the fish bed. Place the edge of the compass at feature A on your map, and draw a line along its reverse bearing. Do the same from feature B on the map. Your fish bed is where the two lines cross.

Common Sense

This chapter on navigation would be incomplete if I did not stress that the oldest navigational technique known is to pay attention to your surroundings. One of the major reasons why people get lost is that they fail to

Here is how to locate a point in a lake by using back bearings, as described in the accompanying text.

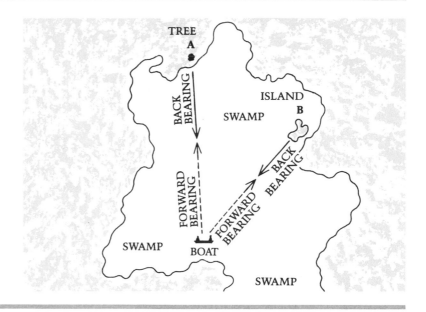

pay attention to their surroundings. As I pointed out at the beginning of this chapter, no one is born with a sense of direction. Accurate backcountry travel is a skill that is learned, and the most important part of the skill is to pay attention to what you see.

In our day-to-day life, around our home regions, we unconsciously use landmarks all the time. But in an unknown area, we must pay conscious attention to landmarks, imagine how they will look from all directions, and implant them in memory. As a small boy I was told by my dad, a master outdoorsman, to look backward periodically so that I would recognize the trail and landmarks on the way out. That teaching is still with me, and I do it almost as second nature now. Many times I would not have found my way out of backcountry had I not been heeding my dad's instruction.

A lost bowhunter I helped find served as a classic example of failing to mentally record landmarks. He had gone from his camp into his hunting area using his compass. Then he had set up his tree stand and gotten comfortable for a day of waiting.

That afternoon he hit a deer. After a few minutes of waiting, the hunter left his tree stand. He also left his coat and daypack behind so that he could trail the wounded deer without overheating and without excess cargo.

The deer was not badly hit. It crossed two beaver swamps. The bowhunter lost the deer's trail in the second swamp and suddenly realized that he had not paid attention to landmarks while following the deer. His compass and map were in his coat, and so were his matches. Dusk was upon him.

We found the hunter the next morning in a state of panic. He was suffering from hypothermia and was scratched and torn from a night of running.

Tracking wounded game usually takes you into unfamiliar places. Be prepared. You will have to come back. So carry your map, com-

BACKUP COMPASSES

Left: *The Dacor skindiver's compass is designed to mount on any watchband.* **Right:** *This pin-on compass mounts and packs compactly.*

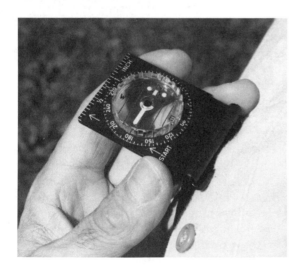 

Left: *The Silva Huntsman pins onto your shirt lapel for convenient reference.* **Right:** *The Huntsman also has a sun dial (bottom flap shown folded on top of compass) for relatively good approximation of time. (Neil Soderstrom photos)*

pass, and survival basics with you. Be observant. Remember landmarks.

Backup Compass

A small second, or backup, compass should be carried by all people in the outdoors. This compass should be easy to glance at as you walk, designed to help keep you generally on the right course. In the event that something happens to your main compass, the backup compass will be available. This backup compass should be attached to you—around your neck, on your wrist, on your shirt.

There are several pin-on compasses designed for backup use. Also, the small skin-diver's compass by Dacor Corporation is an excellent backup. This high-quality compass slips easily onto a watchband and so is always handy. I use one in my guiding business for frequent quick checks of direction.

For Further Information

Anyone serious about backcountry travel should make the effort to take a good course in Orienteering. Many junior colleges and universities offer such courses. Many camping shops, hunting lodges, and city park and recreation departments also offer courses. For more information on Orienteering, write Orienteering Services USA, P.O. Box 1604, Binghamton, NY 13902.

13
SURVIVAL MEDICINE AND SAFETY

One of the major reasons many people get into backcountry survival situations is that they don't take care of themselves. They overexert themselves, they take chances, and they are exposed to weather and other conditions that they aren't accustomed to.

Survival begins at home. No one should venture into the backcountry if he is not in good health and in a reasonably good state of physical conditioning. Your general state of mental and physical health could determine your ability to survive. A well-nourished person in good physical and mental condition can tolerate a lot of stress and deprivation before becoming incapacitated.

This chapter is not intended to make you a backcountry doctor, nor is it designed to take the place of books which cover the details of emergency first aid. Instead this chapter will introduce the situations related to

your well-being that may develop during a survival ordeal and means of preventing and handling such situations. In a survival situation you may be days away from medical help, so you must make every effort to avoid illness or injury.

I further recommend that any backcountry traveler take the Red Cross first aid course and keep the training current. If you are a group leader or if you are planning an exten-

In the outdoors, lightning strikes in many ways. It can strike in the form of lightning itself or in the form of gunshot, broken bones, heatstroke, heart attack, snakebite—to name a few of the ways. This chapter tells how to keep "lightning" from striking, as well as what you can do if it does. (National Center for Atmospheric Research/National Science Foundation photo)

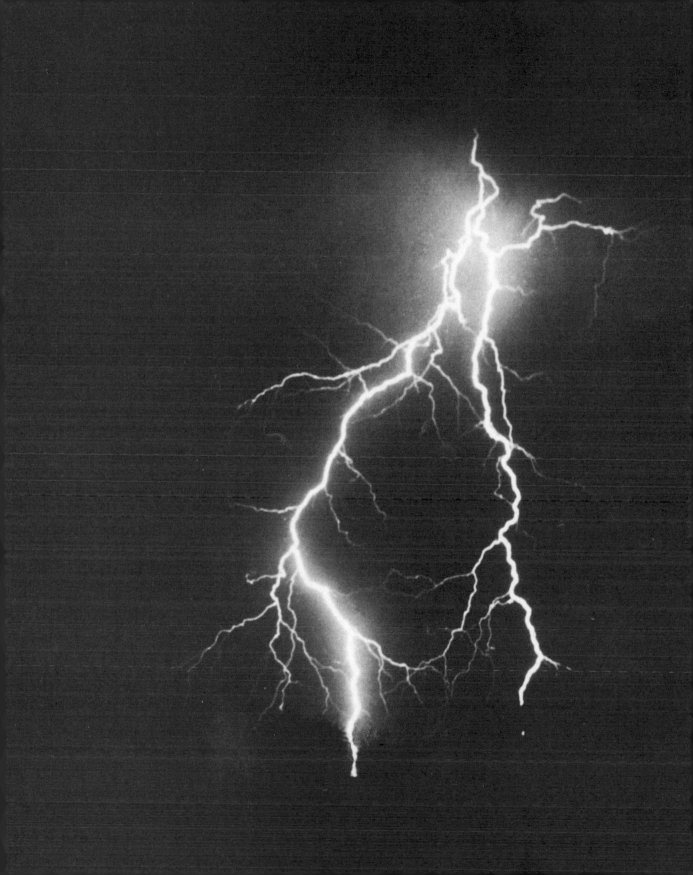

sive backcountry venture, you should take enough training to become a certified emergency medical technician, or EMT.

Mental First Aid

In many of the rescue operations I have participated in, the victims were suffering from significant amounts of psychological duress, negative outlooks, even mental breakdowns. These instances reaffirmed for me that survival can greatly depend on one's state of mind.

I have seen some survivors who had no technical survival knowledge or skills but came through their ordeal with flying colors. Why? Because they had a strong positive mental attitude that largely of itself pulled them through. In fact, I would estimate that survival is almost entirely a mental challenge. It's extremely important to gain control of your mind at the onset of a survival situation and maintain a positive mental attitude throughout the ordeal. Remember that if you take care of your mind first, then your mind will take care of you.

If you are in a group survival situation, chances are good that at least one of you is going to be negative-minded. Stress brings out the worst in many people. In this case, you must help the negative-minded person to become positive. Constructive activity, such as shelter improvement and firewood gathering, can help, but your encouragement and positive attitude will do even more.

Make everyone in the survival group a vital and important part of the total effort. This feeling of importance and comradeship can go a long way toward keeping a weaker individual from wallowing in negative thoughts.

There is an entire chapter in this book on

This wilderness medicine kit contains first aid items to handle practically any emergency the layman should attempt. It was designed by Dr. William Forgey, a well-known specialist in back-country medicine.

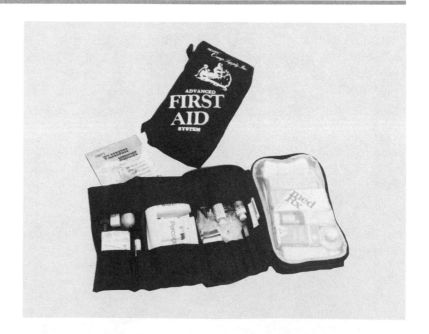

survival psychology (Chapter 2). That information can serve as a mental first aid kit in the event you are actually in a survival situation. Good mental conditioning will also help you carry out physical first aid.

First Aid Kits

Years ago backcountry travelers had to assemble their own first aid kit or use one of the home varieties. Now there are kits designed for the outdoors. Among the best kits are those designed by Dr. William Forgey, one of the best-known physicians in wilderness medicine. His kits are sold by Indiana Camp Supply, Inc. There are kits for the pocket, boat or canoe, vehicle, or remote expeditions or base camps.

The Four Principles of First Aid

Owing to the incidence of and remote locations in which backcountry injuries occur, every backcountry traveler should know and understand the four principles of first aid:

1. Check and clear the airway.
2. Stop the bleeding.
3. Protect the wounds.
4. Treat for shock.

1. Check and clear the airway. A person who is not breathing must be given artificial respiration immediately. When a person stops breathing, he can die within four to six minutes.

If electric shock or poisonous gas has stopped the breathing, the victim must first be removed from the source.

Since it is both simple and effective, the mouth-to-mouth method of artificial respiration is recommended in most instances. If the victim is in water, it is possible to start using this method even before getting him out of the water.

1. Open the victim's mouth and look into it. Check for foreign matter or dentures which may interfere with attempts to start his breathing again. Also, check to see whether the victim may have swallowed his tongue.

2. Placing one hand under the neck and the other on the forehead, tilt the head until the chin juts upward.

3. Pinch the nostrils and form a tight seal with your mouth over the mouth of the victim.

4. Blow and watch for a rise in the chest.

5. Remove your mouth, while watching the victim's chest. The chest should fall and you should hear air escaping.

6. Repeat steps 4 and 5 every five seconds.

If you do not get an exchange of air (that is, if the chest does not rise):

1. Check the victim's head and jaw position. Look for a foreign body and remove it, if necessary.

2. If a foreign body completely blocks the air passage, quickly roll the victim onto his side and deliver several sharp blows between the shoulder blades in an attempt to dislodge the blockage.

3. If the victim still does not ventilate, seek a foreign body that may be deep in the airway by inserting your index and middle fingers inside the victim's cheek and sliding them deeply into the throat to the base of the tongue. Using a sweeping motion, carry them through the back of the throat and along the inside of the other cheek to try to remove the object.

4. If you suspect that a foreign body is blocking the air passage, employ the Heimlich Maneuver, as described and shown later in this chapter.

5. With the air passage clear, roll the victim onto his back, position the head, and continue artificial respiration.

Once the victim begins breathing on his

MOUTH-TO-MOUTH RESPIRATION

These drawings summarize detailed instructions in text beginning on the previous page. **1.** *Tilt the head back to raise the victim's jaw, opening the airway.*

2. *After pinching the victim's nostrils, lift his jaw upward with your other hand to ensure that his tongue doesn't obstruct his air passage. Then by forming a seal with your mouth, blow and watch for the chest to rise.*

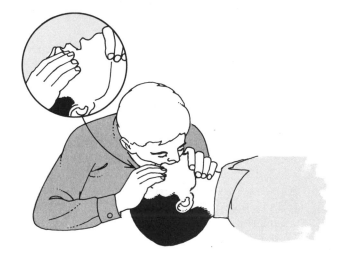

3. *After blowing, remove your mouth and watch for the chest to fall, repeating the cycle every 4 to 5 seconds.*

own, treat for shock and obtain medical attention as soon as possible.

Small children and infants should be treated with an adaptation of the above procedure:

For step 3, place your mouth over the child's mouth and nose, forming a tight seal. When blowing into the child's lungs, use light puffs of air from your cheeks, repeating the ventilation cycle every three seconds.

2. Stop the bleeding. After checking the victim's airway, or reestablishing his breathing, the next most important step is to stop the bleeding.

When blood is spurting or gushing from a wound, it must be controlled *immediately* or death may result within a very short time.

To control severe bleeding, apply direct pressure with the palm of your hand over the entire area of the wound. Also raise the affected part to a level higher than the heart, if there are no fractures and if additional pain or harm will not be inflicted.

If a thick cloth pad is immediately available, hold it between your hand and the wound. While the cloth preferably should be sterile or at least clean, you may have to use whatever cloth is handiest—a handkerchief, piece of clothing. Do not remove this dressing if it becomes blood-soaked. Instead add more layers of cloth and continue direct pressure and elevation.

Do not dab at the wound and do not keep looking to see if the bleeding has stopped. If you release the pressure too soon, the bleeding will start again.

An elastic bandage can replace direct hand pressure on most parts of the body. Apply the elastic bandage by placing the center of the bandage or cloth directly over the pad. Hold the pad in place by circling the bandage ends around the body part. Then tie the ends off

with a knot directly over the pad.

If direct pressure does not control the bleeding, apply pressure at the appropriate pressure point, while maintaining pressure over the wound and elevating the affected limb. As shown in the accompanying drawing, pressure points are located where a major artery is near the skin's surface.

Arm. If the bleeding is from a wound in the lower arm, apply pressure to the brachial artery. This pressure point is located on the inside of the arm in the groove between the biceps and triceps, about midway between the armpit and the elbow. Pressure should be applied by grasping the middle of the victim's upper arm, with your thumb on the outside of his arm and your fingers on the inside. Press or pull your fingers toward your thumb, using the flat inside surface of your fingers, not your fingertips.

Leg. If the bleeding is from the leg, apply pressure to the femoral artery. This pressure point is located on the front center part of the diagonally slanted "hinge" of the leg, in the crease of the groin area and over the pelvic bone. Apply pressure by placing the heel of your hand directly over the femoral artery. Lean forward over the leg with your arm straightened to apply the pressure.

General tips. It is important when using the pressure points (brachial or femoral arteries) that you also maintain pressure over the wound, as well as keep it elevated.

It is also important to remember, especially when more than one person has wounds, that a conscious victim may apply pressure to his own wound to restrict or stop the bleeding, allowing you to assist others.

Tourniquet. The tourniquet should be used only when bleeding is so severe that you cannot stop it with direct pressure and arterial pressure, such that the victim's life is endangered. The tourniquet's reduction of blood flow could result in the loss of the limb.

PRESSURE POINTS THAT REDUCE BLOOD FLOW

Before using these arterial pressure points, attempt to stop bleeding by direct pressure to the wound or, if effective, to nearby flesh on the heart side of the wound.

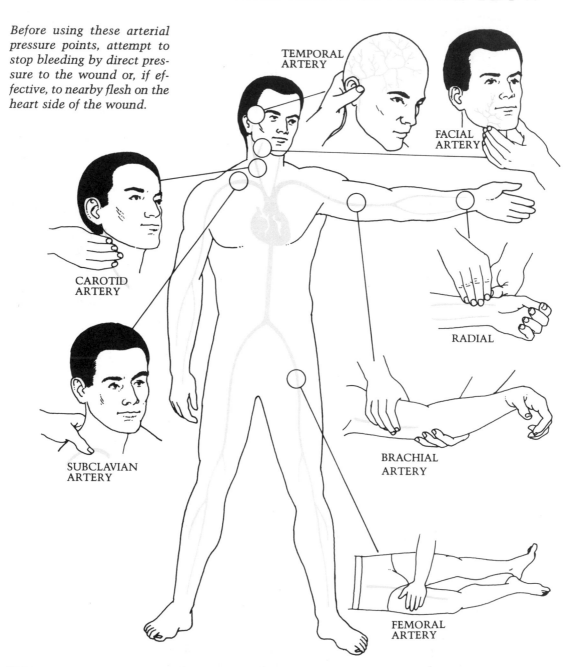

TEMPORAL ARTERY

FACIAL ARTERY

CAROTID ARTERY

RADIAL

SUBCLAVIAN ARTERY

BRACHIAL ARTERY

FEMORAL ARTERY

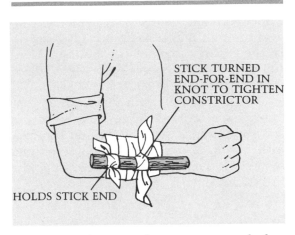

STICK TURNED
END-FOR-END IN
KNOT TO TIGHTEN
CONSTRICTOR

HOLDS STICK END

Since a tourniquet, as shown, can cause the loss of the affected limb, it should be used only when severe bleeding cannot be stopped with other methods. (See accompanying text for details.)

This method is used only on the arm or leg. Use a belt, strips of cloth, or a rolled handkerchief. Never use wire or string. To apply the tourniquet:

1. Place the tourniquet as close to the wound as possible, but not touching the wound edges, and between the wound and the heart. If the wound is in a joint area or just below, place the tourniquet directly above the joint.

2. Wrap the tourniquet band twice around the limb and tie a half knot.

3. Insert a stick in the knot of the cloth or belt and twist to tighten. It should be tight enough to stop the bleeding but not tight enough to cut off all blood circulation.

4. Secure the stick in place.

5. Make note of the time that the tourniquet was applied.

3. Protect the wounds. After the airway has been checked or breathing reestablished and the bleeding has been stopped, the next step is to protect the wounds. Wounds may be classed as open flesh wounds, fractured bones, and burns. Regardless of the class of wound, all must be protected while transporting the victim to a hospital to prevent further injury and to help relieve pain and discomfort.

4. Treat for shock. This fourth and final principle must be considered and followed for each victim, regardless of the nature or extent of his injuries. A victim may go into shock hours after he is rescued and given first aid.

Injury-related shock, commonly referred to as "traumatic shock," is decidedly different from electric shock, insulin shock, and other special forms of shock. Here we'll be considering traumatic shock, which is a condition resulting in a depressed state that affects many vital body functions and could threaten life, even though the injuries themselves would not otherwise be fatal.

To prevent shock or give first aid to it, follow these steps:

1. Keep the victim lying down.

2. Maintain the victim's normal body temperature.

3. Get medical care as soon as possible.

Depending on the injury, the victim's body should be positioned to minimize the danger of shock. Generally, the most desirable position is reclining with the feet raised 6 to 8 inches. If you are uncertain of the type of injury, keep the victim flat on his back.

If weather is cold or damp, put blankets or additional clothing over and under the victim. If conditions are hot, provide shade to protect him from the heat or sun, and do not add heat.

Obtain medical care as soon as possible. If this care will be delayed for an hour or more, water, preferably containing salt and baking soda (½ level teaspoonful of salt and ½ level teaspoonful of baking soda to each quart of water), is recommended. An adult should be given about 4 ounces every 15 minutes, a child approximately 2 ounces, and an infant about 1 ounce.

Do not give fluids if the victim is unconscious, having convulsions, vomiting, or becoming nauseated, or if surgery is likely.

Cuts

Cuts are the most common injuries outdoors, usually resulting from accidents with knives and hatchets.

Once you've stopped the bleeding and treated for shock, any wound should be cleaned. Wash the wound with soap and water that has been boiled for 10 minutes or otherwise disinfected. Be very gentle so as not to cause bleeding to begin again. (Antiseptics and alcohol should not be used to clean wounds. These products do kill germs. But they can also destroy tissue and delay healing.) After cleaning the wound, apply a sterile bandage or gauze compress and hold it in place with adhesive tape.

Anyone planning an outdoor trip should have an up-to-date antitetanus vaccination—as a precaution against serious infection in the event of a cut or puncture wound.

Sprains

A sprain is an injury to ligaments, muscles, and blood vessels around a joint. Sprains almost always occur as a result of excess pull or strain on the supporting ligaments of a joint. If the stress is extreme, ligaments may be torn away from the joint. Sprains cause swelling, tenderness, and pain.

The injured part should rest on a pillow or blanket roll. Rest will permit pulled or torn ligaments to strengthen themselves. Raising the injured limb will help to reduce swelling.

A severe sprain should be treated as a fracture. Splint the injured part and keep it elevated for 24 hours. Apply a cold compress to the sprain to reduce the swelling. Continue using cold compresses for several days, if necessary, until swelling has subsided.

The victim of a sprain must realize that moving sprained joints may tear ligaments and surrounding tissue. However, if movement is a must, the sprain should be splinted securely. If the injury is to the knee or ankle, the victim should improvise a crutch.

Fractures

A fracture is a broken bone. A dislocation, which is the displacement of the end of a bone from its joint, often has the same symptoms as a fracture and should be treated similarly.

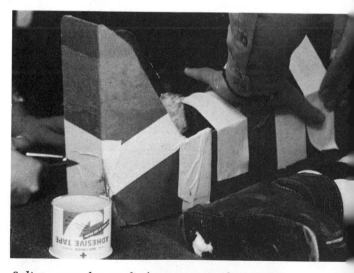

Splints may be made from any rigid material available. This makeshift ankle splint was made from a heavy-duty cardboard box attached by adhesive tape. (National Park Service photo)

ARM FRACTURES

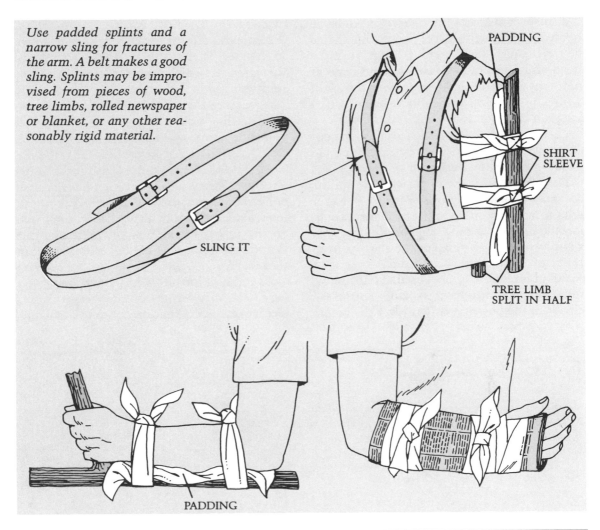

Use padded splints and a narrow sling for fractures of the arm. A belt makes a good sling. Splints may be improvised from pieces of wood, tree limbs, rolled newspaper or blanket, or any other reasonably rigid material.

SLING IT

PADDING

SHIRT SLEEVE

TREE LIMB SPLIT IN HALF

PADDING

Do not attempt to "set" a broken bone. Only a doctor or qualified medical practitioner should do this. Immobilize the fracture or dislocation and guard against further injury. If you are alone, you must decide whether to lie there and hope help comes along or attempt to make the splint yourself.

There are two kinds of fractures: simple and compound. In a simple fracture, also called a closed fracture, the broken bone is under the skin. A dislocation should be treated as a simple fracture.

A compound fracture is also called an open fracture, because the broken bone cuts through the skin and makes an open wound. In treating an open fracture, do not push the bone back inside.

A suspected back or neck fracture must be treated with extreme care. The victim should be moved only on a board, face up, with the head and body moved at the same time as one unit, and should be kept lying very still while he is being transported quickly to a hospital. Do not twist or bend the neck or back; pad each side of the head to prevent excessive movement. With a neck injury, add padding under the neck.

For a fracture of the upper arm, tie splints securely on each side of the break. Put padding in the victim's armpit to make a cushion and prevent chafing. Support the arm with a sling and bind the arm to the chest to keep it still.

When an elbow is fractured, do not move the joint to a different position. Splint the elbow in the position it is in after the break.

Obviously, the injured person should receive professional medical attention as soon as possible, to prevent damage to the forearm or hand.

A forearm fracture often results in two broken bones, because there are two bones in the forearm. The entire forearm should be immobilized by splinting.

A fractured wrist should also be immobilized with splints. Do not attempt to set it yourself. Wait for professional medical attention. Keep the wrist in an elevated position.

An ankle fracture should also be splinted without changing the position of the broken bone. In backcountry, a tight blanket roll makes a good splint. Place the injured foot on the center of the blanket roll and bring the roll up each side of the ankle. Strap or tie securely.

Fractures of the hip, pelvis, thigh, and lower leg can be very serious, so the victim should receive medical attention as soon as possible.

FRACTURED ELBOW

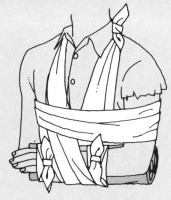

Do not attempt to move or set a fractured elbow. Instead you should splint and immobilize the limb in the position you find it.

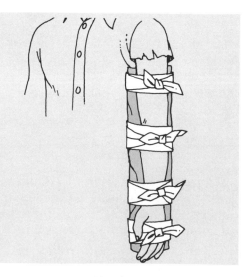

LEG AND ANKLE FRACTURES

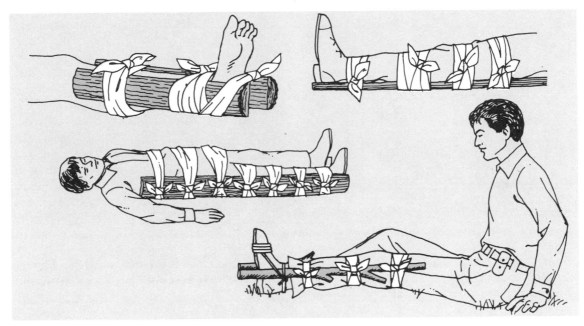

When splinting a fractured ankle or leg, be sure to immobilize foot as well. When possible, use splints on both sides of the fracture.

Keep the broken ends and the joints around them still and in the position in which they were broken. The broken bone should be kept completely immobile and the victim still and quiet.

A fractured rib can be dangerous, because the broken bone could puncture the lung or other internal organs. If the rib has broken through the skin, cover the wound with a thick sterile compress so that air cannot enter the chest cavity. When moving the victim, keep him on his back with head and chest slightly raised. Fractured ribs should be taped over clothing to reduce pain, but must not be taped so tightly that expansion of the lungs is restricted. Broken ribs which

A forked stick with padding tied on becomes a simple crutch for someone with an injured leg.

FRACTURED RIBS

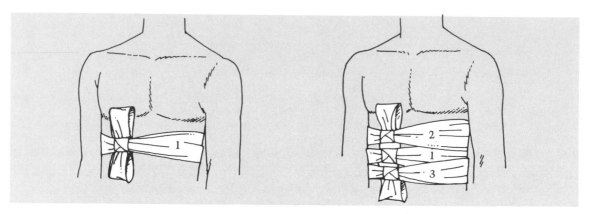

Tie strips of cloth around the victim on, above, and below the break as the victim exhales.

have not damaged internal organs may mend themselves.

When a jaw is fractured, wrap a bandage loosely under the chin and over the top of the head to keep the lower jaw from dropping. Be sure that the bandage does not keep the victim from opening his mouth, preventing breathing and drinking.

Burns

Burns are usually classified by depth or degree of skin damage. Three general classifications are:

First-degree. Redness, mild swelling, and pain

Second-degree. Deeper, with blisters appearing

Third-degree. Very deep burns which may look charred, with complete loss of all layers of skin

Burns also may be described according to the extent of total body surface involved. For

For lower jaw fractures, place your hand below the jaw and raise it gently until the victim's upper and lower teeth meet. Have the victim support his own jaw as you tie the bandage.

BURN CLASSIFICATIONS

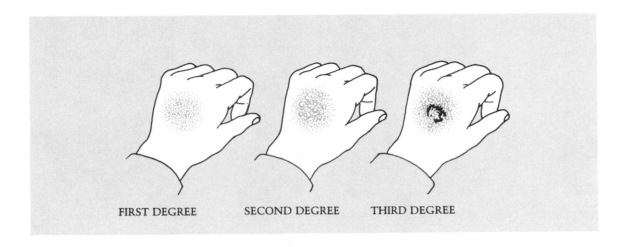

FIRST DEGREE   SECOND DEGREE   THIRD DEGREE

example, a severe sunburn, a first-degree burn, is considered serious and should receive prompt medical attention.

Treatment of burns is determined by these classifications.

First-degree burns. Use running water (preferably cold) or cloths soaked in ice water on the burned area to relieve pain. Dry sterile dressings may be used.

Second-degree burns. Use running water (preferably cold, but not ice water) or clean cloths wrung out in ice water until the pain subsides. Blot dry with sterile or clean cloth, not cotton balls because they stick, and apply sterile gauze or clean cloth as a dressing. Do not break blisters, remove shreds of tissue, or apply additional home medications. Treat for shock and obtain medical attention.

Third-degree (or deep second-degree) burns. Cover the burn to keep out air. This can be done with sterile dressings, freshly laundered clean sheets, or other linens. It is extremely important to treat for shock and to obtain medical attention. Elevate the affected parts. Do not remove charred clothing that sticks to the burn. Do not apply icewater over the burn or apply home medications.

Choking

In any emergency choking situation, use the Heimlich Maneuver. It is carried out by standing behind the choking victim, placing your left fist in the victim's solar plexus, grabbing your fist with your right hand, and pushing sharply upward toward the middle of the choking person's shoulder blades. This forces the diaphragm upward, causing pressure inside the windpipe and forcing the obstruction out. This is a very effective and simple lifesaving technique that everyone should learn.

Diarrhea and Constipation

Diarrhea and other intestinal ailments may be caused by change of water and food, contaminated water or spoiled food, fatigue, fear,

HEIMLICH MANEUVER FOR CHOKING

 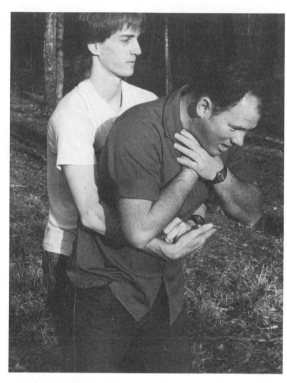

To perform the Heimlich Maneuver, place your fist in the upper abdomen just under the rib cage. Cover your fist with your other hand, and thrust upward and inward sharply. Remember that a choking person cannot speak to ask for help, but the usual reaction is to grab the throat and gasp for air, indicating a need for the Heimlich Maneuver.

overeating in hot weather, or using dirty dishes. Purify all water used for drinking, as explained in the chapter on water. Cook the plants you eat, or wash them carefully with purified water. Use good habits of personal cleanliness. If possible, wash your hands with soap and water before eating.

If one member of your group gets diarrhea, take special care to enforce measures for proper disposal of human waste and to ensure cleanliness in handling food and water.

Make sure feces are buried. Don't let affected members handle food and cooking utensils.

Field treatment of diarrhea is necessarily limited. Rest and fast—except for drinking water—for 24 hours; then take only liquid foods such as soup and tea, and avoid sugars and starches. Keep up a large intake of water to prevent dehydration. Eat several small meals instead of one or two large ones. Overeating of fruit, especially green fruit, may cause temporary diarrhea. Temporarily eliminating fruit from the diet usually relieves this condition.

Don't worry about lack of bowel movement. This will usually take care of itself in a few days, provided you have an adequate daily supply of water.

Under survival conditions, you can eat finely ground black charcoal from your campfire to treat diarrhea, as was done by American Vietnam prisoners of war. The white ashes from the fire may be eaten in small quantity to treat constipation.

Gunshot Wounds

Between my military career and my wildlife management career, I have seen a fair number of gunshot wounds. Some were little more than a cut; others cut the victim almost in half.

The proper care of gunshot wounds involves two parts: taking care of the wound,

and taking care of the rest of the victim's needs, such as shock and fright.

Care of the wound frequently requires the placing of a sterile dressing over the hole. If the wound is in the chest and you hear a sucking noise around it, indicating a punctured lung, make an airtight seal over the wound by covering it with clean plastic or other nonporous material. If nothing else is available, seal the wound with petroleum jelly or shortening applied to a bandage.

The ugliest gunshot wound is the gut shot. This wound will often have several feet of intestines hanging out. Do not try to replace them. Place a moist, clean dressing over the wound. If the wound is to the legs or arms, bandage and splint them.

In many gunshot wounds, especially the larger exit wound, bleeding will be heavy. Apply dressing and control bleeding with direct pressure. Use a tourniquet only if *severe* bleeding cannot be stopped.

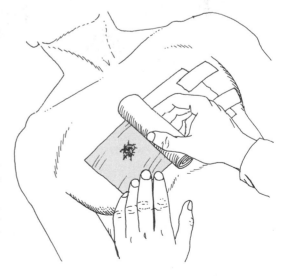

A sucking chest wound indicates a punctured lung. Unless you seal the hole, air may be sucked between the chest cavity and the lung wall, collapsing the lung. To seal the hole, press a folded handkerchief or towel against the hole with the palm of your hand. Such pressure almost always stops excessive bleeding. Taped in place, a sheet of thin plastic sandwich wrap, as shown, would also be effective. If the victim feels comfortable sitting, that position is usually best. If not, turn the lying victim so the injured lung is lower than the other. This helps keep blood from entering the uninjured lung. If symptoms of shock occur (light-headedness, weakness, profuse sweating), temporarily uncover the hole to prevent excessive pressure buildup from blood and air that might themselves collapse the lung. (Caption courtesy of W. Henry Russell, MD)

If the victim is cold, sweaty, and confused and has a rapid, thready pulse, think of shock. Use blankets or a sleeping bag to maintain body heat. Elevate the feet and legs. This maneuver alone can provide a unit of blood pooled in the legs to help maintain vital organs such as the brain, heart, and kidneys.

If proper firearms safety training is received and safety is practiced in the field, you should never have to deal with a gunshot wound. This type of wound is most difficult to deal with under survival conditions. Be extra careful with firearms.

Toothache

Toothache may have ruined more outdoor trips than any other medical problem. Toothache may be a survival problem as well. In the case of a simple toothache, there are two solutions.

The first is to place a small wad of cotton soaked in oil of cloves in the cavity. Take aspirin or other pain reliever.

The second is to dry the tooth and apply toothache gel. This is a nonprescription drug composed of active ingredients that work better than oil of cloves. Take a pain reliever such as aspirin or Percogesic.

There is also a dental care kit available from Indiana Camp Supply. It will help with lost fillings or bleeding gums.

The best measure related to dental problems is prevention. Get a good checkup before you head into the backcountry. Then if you find yourself in a survival situation, your teeth won't add to your troubles.

Heart Attack

Each year more than a million Americans are felled by heart attacks. Of this number, over 670,000 die. Some of these victims are outdoorsmen. While the best "first aid" for heart attacks is prevention—including proper conditioning and medical checkups, there are

Dragging a deer as this man is doing is not only an unaccustomed strain to the heart, but also to muscles and joints. Outdoor activities often require exertion that people are not used to, requiring that they be in good physical condition. While it is a good idea for anyone to have regular physical checkups, it is especially important for outdoorsmen whose activity requires exertion.

EARLY WARNING SIGNS OF HEART ATTACK

Symptoms may begin with a steady pain behind the breastbone that may move to other areas, as shown. Other symptoms may include shortness of breath; sweating; nausea and vomiting; weakness; dizziness; and pale, ashen-gray or bluish skin.

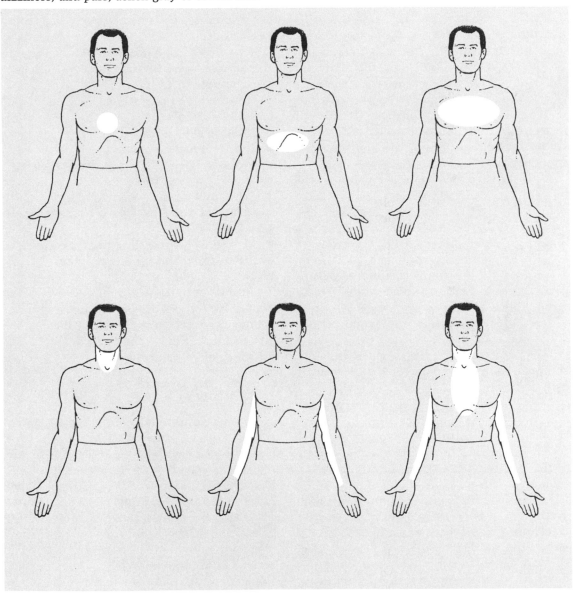

some procedures that everyone should learn to perform on the heart attack victim. The best way to learn these procedures is to take a course that will qualify you to carry out cardiopulmonary resuscitation, commonly known as CPR. CPR is a combination of artificial respiration and manual artificial circulation used in cases of cardiac arrest. Instruction includes practice on a mannequin both individually and as part of a team. Encourage your outdoor companions to take the course with you, because the *first* heart attack is fatal to almost 40 percent of the victims, and 20 percent of these victims die in the first hour. Knowing what to do in a survival situation could save you or your friend's life.

The following treatment is recommended by the American Red Cross for heart attacks:

1. If the victim is unconscious and not breathing, begin artificial respiration, or if a qualified person is there, CPR, at once.

2. If the victim is conscious, place him in a comfortable position, usually sitting up, particularly if there is a shortness of breath, although his comfort is a good guide.

3. Provide ventilation and guard against drafts and cold.

4. Have someone call for an ambulance equipped with oxygen and have the victim's own doctor notified.

5. If the victim has been under medical care, help him take his prescribed medicine. Look for some form of emergency identification if the victim is unconscious. If in doubt, confer with a doctor by telephone as soon as possible.

6. Do not give liquids to an unconscious victim. If he is conscious, do not give him cold liquid, as it passes down the esophagus and chills the back part of the heart. This can cause the blood vessels supplying the heart muscle to contract, thereby reducing the amount of blood flow to the heart, which is already in trouble.

7. Since transportation throws added strain upon the victim, do not attempt to transport him until you get medical advice. Today there are well-trained and well-equipped rescue teams in almost every area of the United States. Call one immediately and keep calm. Do not let panic cause you to take unnecessary chances by trying to carry the victim out unaided.

If you have had a heart problem or go into the backcountry with someone who has, keep these simple rules in mind:

- Never go on a trip alone.
- Avoid alcohol.
- Avoid heavy camp duties.
- Take a nap after lunch.
- Avoid activities in hot, humid weather.
- Move at a slow pace.
- Avoid unnecessary exertion such as pulling a loaded canoe over a log or dragging out a deer.
- Always let your fellow hunters, guide, or outfitter know about your problem.

Outdoor activity is not supposed to be an endurance test, so slow down and enjoy it by following the above rules and your doctor's advice. You can enjoy the outdoors even with a history of a heart problem.

Heat Illness

Heat is a commonly overlooked danger in the summer backcountry. Let's say the temperature is high and there is little or no breeze. Chances are you're not accustomed to such heat or to the hard work of pulling a loaded canoe over logs, winching a jeep out of mud, or paddling a boat through shallow water. These conditions can bring on the deadly condition known as "heatstroke" or the less serious condition known as "heat exhaustion." A person does not have to be in the sun to get either of these conditions. A hot, shaded swamp or creek can be enough.

Heatstroke. Energy production in the human body is accompanied by the production of excess heat. To eliminate this heat, the body increases the flow of blood through the skin and stimulates the production of sweat, the body's air conditioner. Through evaporation, convection, and radiation, the body gets rid of excess heat. If a malfunction occurs in the heat-regulating mechanism, the body temperature can zoom to 110°F. Then the body's vital organs—brain, heart, and kidneys—literally cook in their own juices. The result is death. An average of 4,000 deaths a year in this country are attributed to heatstroke.

While heatstroke can come on with little warning, its symptoms are usually headache; dizziness; lack of sweating; dry, hot, and red skin; fast, strong pulse, constricted pupils; and high temperature.

Treatment for heatstroke is as follows:

1. Move the victim to a cool place and lay him down with his head raised.

2. Open the clothes and cool the body down quickly, using every means possible.

3. Get the victim to a doctor as soon as possible.

Heat exhaustion. While less serious than heatstroke, heat exhaustion is nothing to ignore. If not treated, heat exhaustion will most likely develop into heatstroke.

The symptoms of heat exhaustion are weakness; muscle cramps; headaches; profuse sweating; pale, cool, and clammy skin (as opposed to hot, dry, and red skin with heatstroke); and normal temperature.

Treatment for heat exhaustion is as follows:

1. Move the victim to a cool place and lay him down with his feet slightly raised.

2 Give him slightly salted water to drink.

3. If recovery is not quick, promptly transport the victim to a doctor.

The best way to cope with the dangers of heatstroke and heat exhaustion is to prevent them. Here are the rules you should follow to prevent heat disorders:

1. Before you go on an outing during the summer, spend two weeks getting acclimated to high temperatures and heavy exertion. For an hour each day, exercise in the heat. Start out slowly and rest often. Remember, heavy exertion in hot climates uses up a lot of the body's liquids. Drink large quantities of Gatorade or bouillon, which are relatively balanced salt solutions.

2. Avoid drugs that promote heatstroke or reduce your natural thirst. Check with your doctor if you are taking sedatives, diuretics, tranquilizers, and such. Go easy on all forms of alcoholic drinks. If you're running a fever, stay home.

3. Wear lightweight, loose-fitting clothing that is white or light tan to reflect the sun's rays. Be sure to wear a hat, but make sure that it is ventilated to promote evaporative cooling from the sweat-soaked hair. Be careful when wearing rain gear because it tends to trap body heat.

4. Stop frequently to cool off. Try wetting your hair.

5. Save heavy chores for early morning and late afternoon, when the air is cooler. Relax during the heat of the day.

6. Make sure your liquid intake replaces your sweat output. The body requires 2 quarts of water per day—1 quart to moisten lung air, 1 pint for urine, and 1 pint for perspiration. Dehydration is an important factor in causing heat disorders.

7. Many doctors now tell us to avoid salt pills because they are gastrointestinal irritants. Instead, eat foods such as nuts, chocolate bars with nuts, tomato juice, V-8 juice, bouillon, and dried raisins. The body usually requires 1 to 3 grams of salt daily to replace the salt lost in urine. This lost salt must be replaced, since the body does not make any.

Dehydration

Dehydration is caused by failure to correct the body's "imbalance of liquids" by replacing liquid and salt which have been lost, and also by the failure to allow oneself sufficient rest after being engaged in strenuous activities.

The symptoms of dehydration parallel the symptoms of heatstroke and heat exhaustion. The mouth, tongue, and throat become parched and dry, and swallowing becomes difficult. General nausea may be accompanied by spells of faintness, extreme dizziness, and vomiting. A feeling of tiredness and weakness sets in, accompanied by body aches, especially in the legs.

In addition, the victim may find it difficult to keep his eyes in focus, and fainting or "blacking out" may occur.

Dehydration incapacitates you for a period of from a few hours to several days. It can be prevented during cold weather by following the same general preventive measures applicable to hot, dry areas. Consume salt and sufficient additional liquids to offset excessive body water losses. The amount will vary according to the individual and the type of exertion. Rest is equally important as a preventive measure. Remember that any work you must do while bundled in several layers of clothing is especially exhausting. This is particularly true of any travel by foot, regardless of how short the distance.

A person who has become dehydrated should be kept warm, but his clothes should be loosened sufficiently to allow proper circulation. Liquids and salt should be fed to him gradually, and, most important of all, he must have plenty of rest.

SIGNS AND SYMPTOMS OF DEHYDRATION AT VARIOUS STAGES OF BODY WATER DEFICIENCY

1 to 5 percent of body weight	6 to 10 percent of body weight	11 to 20 percent of body weight
Thirst	Dizziness	Delirium
Vague discomfort	Headache	Spasticity
Economy of movement	Labored breathing	Swollen tongue
No appetite	Tingling in limbs	Inability to swallow
Flushed skin	Decreased blood volume	Deafness
Impatience	Increased blood concentration	Dim vision
Sleepiness	Absence of salivation	Shriveled skin
Increased pulse	Blue colored body	Painful urination
Increased rectal temperature	Indistinct speech	Numb skin
Nausea	Inability to walk	

Hypothermia

Hypothermia is the major killer of people lost or stranded in the backcountry. Many of those found alive are also suffering from hypothermia, a drop in deep body temperature that can be deadly if not detected promptly and treated properly.

The actual number of people killed each year by hypothermia is unknown, in part because many doctors are not familiar with the condition, and because its symptoms are like those of many other illnesses. Even an autopsy will not definitely tell if a person died of hypothermia.

Hypothermia is not selective in its victims. Alberto Salazar, the 1982 winner of the Boston Marathon, had hypothermia as he crossed the finish line, as did many of the runners. Salazar's temperature had dropped to 88°F, and he was in a dazed and trembling state. It took expert medical care to raise his temperature back to normal. According to the chief doctor at the Marathon Emergency Unit, the majority of the runners they see have hypothermia. After the race, it was almost an hour before Salazar finally recognized his parents at his cotside.

Hypothermia affects runners, canoeists, and other outdoorsmen, but also many older people right in their own homes. Let's see how it affects a hiker.

Let's say you are on a fall hiking trip in the foothills near your camp. The day isn't very cold. The temperature has been between 30° and 50°F all day, so you are dressed in a cotton shirt and trousers. You are tired, the wind has started blowing, and a drizzle has started to fall. You start the long walk back to the camp. On the way to the camp you notice the cold. First you begin to shiver, then the shivering becomes uncontrollable. You feel weak and nauseated, so you stop to sit down. Your hiking companion wants to know why you've stopped. You have trouble speaking clearly, and your movements and thinking have become sluggish.

You and your companion have not recognized it, but you have hypothermia—loss of deep body heat. Already your body temperature has dropped to 94°F. While your companion kids you about not being tough enough to take it and looks for material to build a fire, your temperature continues to fall. At 88° the shivering decreases and thinking becomes less clear. Your temperature falls to 85° and you become irrational. Your companion, not knowing what's wrong, starts trying to lead you to the camp. Your temperature continues to slide downward. At 80° you are unconscious. Your companion leaves to find help. Soon after he leaves, your temperature drops to 77° and you are dead.

The cold didn't kill you. You were killed by failure to recognize the signs of hypothermia.

Hypothermia can strike in any season and any climate. All that is needed is a mild air temperature—30° to 50°—and wetness, be it rain, sweat, or a river dunking, a slight wind, and a tired person.

The onset of hypothermia is usually slow, but in the case of boating accidents it can happen quickly. In 1968 nine of the toughest, strongest, and best-trained canoeists in the world—U.S. Marines—were paddling across the Potomac River at Quantico, Virginia, when their canoe capsized. Fifteen minutes later, all of them were dead—victims of hypothermia. This Marine canoe team died so fast because they had been paddling their 25-foot canoe at a racing pace for more than 4 miles when they capsized. Their blood circulation was rapid, they were tired, their cotton sweatsuits were soaked. The day itself was warm and sunny for March, but when they hit the 40° water, their body heat drained away so fast they probably were helpless within two or three minutes. When your body is immersed in cold water, you'll start losing heat fast. In two minutes, your skin temperature will drop to within 3° of the water temperature.

Survival in cold water depends on many factors. The temperature of the water is only one of them. Others include body size, fat, and activity in the water, to name a few. Large people cool slower than small people. Fat people cool slower than thin people. Children, because they are small, cool faster than adults. Anyone swimming or treading water cools faster than those who remain still. An "average" person, wearing light clothing and a personal flotation device (PFD), may survive two and a half to three hours in 50° water by remaining still. Swimming and treading water increase the cooling rate by about 35 percent.

Many people who find themselves in cold water immediately swim for the shore. Some good swimmers have been able to swim about 4,000 feet in 50° water before becoming overcome by hypothermia. Others have not been able to swim 100 yards. Furthermore, distances on the water are very deceptive. Therefore, *do not swim* unless there is absolutely no chance of rescue and you are absolutely certain you can make it. If you do swim, use a flotation device.

The Coast Guard advises that if you are hanging on to your canoe, you should get as much of your body out of the water as possible. Try to climb back into the canoe or cling to a tree or buoy.

If you are caught out in open water alone, go into what is known as the HELP position (Heat Escape Lessening Posture).

The inner sides of the arms are held tightly against the sides of the chest over the "hot" region and the thighs are raised to protect the groin region. This behavior, effective only when wearing a life jacket, results in nearly a 50 percent increase in predicted survival time.

If you are with a group, huddle. Longer survival time is accomplished when several persons huddle together. Studies show that if a huddle is formed so that the sides of the chests of different persons are held close together, a 50 percent increase in predicted survival time is obtained.

Hypothermia attacks a person in two steps. The first is when your body begins to lose heat faster than it produces it. At this point you are aware of feeling cold and the shivering begins.

The second step is when the cold reaches the brain, depriving you of judgment and rea-

HYPOTHERMIA SURVIVAL

Water temperature (Degrees F.)	Exhaustion or unconsciousness	Expected time of survival
32.5	Under 15 min.	Under 15–45 min.
32.5–40.0	15–30 min.	30–90 min.
40–50	30–60 min.	1–3 hr.
50–60	1–2 hr.	1–6 hr.
60–70	2–7 hr.	2–40 hr.
70–80	3–12 hr.	3 Hr.–Indefinite
Over 80	Indefinite	Indefinite

Source: U.S. Coast Guard

HEAT LOSS IN COLD WATER

The HELP (Heat Escape Lessening Posture) increases survival time in cold water by reducing exposed body surface, especially along the sides of the chest.

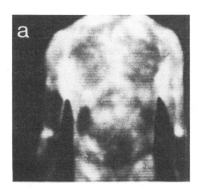 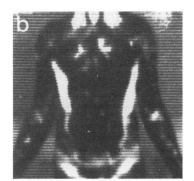 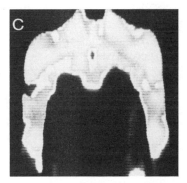

These infrared photos of the upper body of a man show relative heat loss areas under different circumstances. The whiter the image, the higher the temperature of the skin and the greater the heat loss. **Photo A** was taken before immersion and shows fairly uniform surface temperature. **Photos B and C** were taken after immersion in cold water. In **Photo B** the man had remained still in cold water. In **Photo C** the man had been swimming. From the photos, it is obvious that swimming increases the relative amount of skin surface with a higher temperature. This produces a higher rate of heat loss and accounts for the faster cooling rate of the body during swimming. However, cold-water heat loss differs from heat loss in cold air, where heat from exercise is not lost as fast and can slow body cooling. (Photos and caption courtesy of Dr. John S. Hayward, University of Victoria, B.C., Canada)

soning power. This is the reason that almost no one recognizes that he has hypothermia. In this second step your internal temperature is sliding downward. Without treatment, this slide leads to stupor, collapse, and death.

Here are several ways to avoid hypothermia recommended by the Mountain Rescue Association.

1. Stay dry. When clothes get wet, they lose about 90 percent of their insulating value. Wool loses less; cotton, down, any synthetics lose more.

2. Beware of the wind. A slight breeze carries heat away from bare skin much faster than still air. Wind drives cold air under and through clothing. Wind refrigerates wet clothes by evaporating moisture from the surface.

3. Understand the cold. Most hypothermia cases develop in air temperatures between 30° and 50°F. Most outdoorsmen simply can't believe such temperatures can be dangerous. Tragically, sometimes, they underestimate the danger of being wet at such temperatures.

4. Terminate exposure. When you cannot stay dry and warm under existing weather conditions, be smart enough to call it quits and return to camp or home.

5. Never ignore shivering. Persistent or violent shivering is clear warning that you are on the verge of hypothermia.

The symptoms of hypothermia are obvious. Watch for them in yourself and others.

1. Uncontrollable fits of shivering
2. Vague, slow, slurred speech
3. Lapses in memory
4. Immobile, fumbling hands
5. Staggering and stumbling
6. Drowsiness
7. Exhaustion, inability to get up after a rest.

In most cases, the victim will deny he's in trouble, but believe the symptoms, not the victim. Treatment should be immediate.

1. Get the victim out of the weather.
2. Remove his wet clothes.
3. If the victim is only mildly impaired, give him warm drinks and get him into dry clothes and a warm car, room, or sleeping bag.
4. If the victim is semiconscious or worse, he does not have the capability of regaining his body temperature without outside help. Keep him awake. Give warm drinks. Leave him stripped. Put him in a sleeping bag with another person who is also stripped. Skin-to-skin contact is the most effective treatment.

Frostbite

Frostbite is the freezing of some part of the body. It is a constant hazard in subfreezing weather, especially when the wind is strong. As a rule, the first sensation of frostbite is numbness rather than pain. You can see the effect of frostbite as a grayish or yellow-white spot on the skin before you can feel it. Therefore, use the buddy system. Watch your buddy's face to see if any frozen spots show; have him watch yours.

If frostbite occurs, here are some points to remember:
● Get the frostbite casualty into a heated shelter, if possible.
● Warm the frozen part rapidly. Frozen parts should be thawed in water until soft, even though the treatment is painful. This treatment is most effective when the water is between 105° and 110°F. Water in this range will feel lukewarm to a part of the body normally protected from the cold, such as the elbow. At greater than 110°, the water begins to be hotter than can be tolerated without discomfort, but water either slightly cooler or warmer can be used. If warm water is not available, wrap the frozen part in blankets or clothing and apply improvised heat packs.

Severe frostbite kills affected tissues and imposes high danger of infection. Proper treatment is of paramount importance in preventing further tissue damage and life-threatening infection.

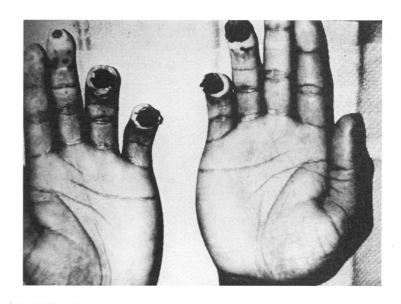

• Use body heat to aid in thawing. Hold a bare, warm palm against frostbitten ears or parts of the face. Grasp a frostbitten wrist with a warm, bare hand. Hold frostbitten hands against the chest, under the armpits, or between the legs at the groin. Hold a frostbitten foot against a companion's stomach or between his thighs.

• When frostbite is accompanied by breaks in the skin, apply sterile dressing. Do not use strong antiseptics such as tincture of iodine. Do not use powdered sulfa in the wound.

• Never forcibly remove frozen shoes and mittens. Place in lukewarm water until soft and then remove gently.

• Never rub frostbite. You may tear frozen tissues and cause further tissue damage. Never apply snow or ice; that just increases the cold injury. For the same reason, never soak frozen limbs in kerosene or oil.

• Do not try to thaw a frozen part by exercising. Exercise of frozen parts increases tissue damage and is likely to break the skin. Do not stand or walk on frozen feet. You will only cause tissue damage.

Snow Blindness

Snow blindness is caused by the exposure of the unprotected eye to glare on snow. Snow blindness can occur even on cloudy days. You can prevent snow blindness by wearing dark glasses whenever you are exposed to the glare. Prevention is the best cure. Don't wait until your eyes hurt before you put your glasses or goggles on. A handy substitute for them is a piece of wood, leather, or other material with narrow eye slits cut in it. This eyeshade is good in a blizzard because you can brush off the slits easily, while glasses may become frosted over.

Symptoms of snow blindness (really a sun-

Simple snow goggles can be made from bark, thin wooden slabs, cardboard, leather, or other material in which narrow slits have been cut. Then tie the goggles loosely around the head.

burn of the surface of the eye) are burning, watering, or inflamed eyes, poor vision, a halo seen when looking at lights, and headaches. Snow blindness may not appear until four to six hours after exposure. For this reason, it is often not suspected because symptoms do not appear until long after sunset.

Treat snow blindness by protecting the eyes from light and relieving the pain. Protect the eyes by staying in a dark shelter or by wearing a lightproof bandage. Relieve the pain by putting cold compresses on the eyes if there is no danger of freezing, and by taking aspirin. Use no eyedrops or ointment. Most cases recover within 18 hours without medical treatment. The first attack of snow

blindness makes the victim more susceptible to later attacks.

Immersion Foot (Trench Foot)

Immersion foot is a cold injury resulting from prolonged exposure to moisture at temperatures from 68°F to freezing. This is a neurovascular injury without ice crystals forming in tissue. In the early stages of immersion foot, your feet and toes are pale and feel cold, numb, and stiff. Walking becomes difficult. If you do not take preventive action at this stage, your feet will swell and become very painful. In extreme cases of immersion foot, the flesh dies and amputation of the foot or the leg may be necessary.

Because the early stages of immersion foot are not very painful, you must be constantly alert to prevent the condition. Here's how:
● Keep your feet dry by wearing waterproof footgear and keeping your shelter dry.
● Clean and dry your socks and shoes at every opportunity.
● Dry your feet as soon as possible after getting them wet.
● Warm them with your hands, apply foot powder, and put on dry socks.
● When you must wear wet socks and shoes, exercise your feet continually by wiggling your toes and bending your ankles. When sleeping in a sitting position, warm your feet, put on dry socks, and elevate your legs as high as possible. Do not wear tight shoes.

Treat immersion foot by keeping the affected part dry and warm. If possible, keep the foot and leg in a horizontal position to increase circulation.

Blisters

Inspect your feet frequently for tender red patches, which are the beginnings of blisters.

Cover these areas with adhesive tape to protect the skin from being rubbed by your footgear and forming a blister.

Once a blister has formed, make a doughnut bandage—a round pad with the center cut out—to protect it.

Do not break blisters because this increases the chance of infection and makes them more painful. Instead, cleanse the area around the edge of the blister and, with a sterilized needle, prick a tiny hole in the side of the swelling. Very gently ease the fluid out through the pinprick. When the blister is empty, cover the area with a sterile dressing or adhesive tape. If tape is applied over the blister, it should remain in place until a new layer of skin has formed.

To relieve pain and inflammation, soak the blistered area in hot water for 20 to 30 minutes, three or four times daily. After each soaking, cover the tender area with a sterile dressing.

The ragged dead skin of a broken blister should be trimmed carefully to prevent damaging new tissue, but should not be completely removed until the new skin has formed and toughened.

Mountain Sickness

Rapid ascent, as by automobile, by persons not accustomed to high altitudes (over 8,000 feet) usually results in what is known as "mountain sickness." You may notice any of the following symptoms: shortness of breath, general malaise (a "run-down" feeling), loss of appetite, nausea, vomiting, dizziness, headache, drowsiness, yawning, weakness, and chilliness. You may notice a whitish pallor of the face and a bluish tinge of the lips and fingernails. Headache is frequent and may be severe. Even slight physical effort can produce troublesome shortness of breath. You may notice pounding or palpitations of the

heartbeat. Sleep can be difficult, and respiration may assume the pattern of several very deep, rapid breaths followed by a period of shallow or even absent breathing, then deep, rapid breaths again. This type of breathing is known as "Cheyne-Stokes" breathing, and is so common at high altitudes that it should not be considered abnormal. Dizziness, ringing in the ears, irritability, and memory defects may appear.

Most of the symptoms of mountain sickness are due to the effect of the lack of oxygen on the body's central nervous system and should disappear when you become better adapted to altitude. Most of them stop within 24 to 48 hours after arrival at altitude, although the shortness of breath, lack of appetite, and headache may persist.

Rest or, at most, very light physical activity during the first 24 hours at altitude is helpful in preventing mountain sickness. More serious symptoms can often be alleviated by descent to a lower elevation for a day or two. Proper diet and fluid intake also are very important. At least 2 quarts of liquid should be drunk daily, and 4 quarts would be better.

High-altitude Pulmonary Edema

Mountain sickness is caused by lack of oxygen and, although extremely disagreeable, is usually not life-threatening unless it complicates some other ailment. High-altitude pulmonary edema (HAPE) is also caused by oxygen deficiency, and although apparently rare, is extremely dangerous. Deaths have resulted within six to ten hours from the onset of symptoms.

The classic symptoms are rapidly increasing shortness of breath and a dry cough which later produces a white, frothy sputum that may be streaked with blood. The victim is usually cyanotic (that is, blueness of the lips and nails is present). Bubbling sounds may be heard, as if the victim is breathing through liquid, as indeed he is. Pulmonary edema means that blood plasma has leaked into the air sacs of the lungs.

Adequate acclimatization seems to be the best protection against HAPE. Above 10,000 feet, at least one day should be allowed for each 1,000 feet of altitude gained. As with mountain sickness, adequate fluid intake is extremely important.

The treatment for HAPE is immediate and rapid descent. Instances have been reported where normal breathing was restored only 2,000 feet lower than the altitude at which symptoms appeared. If oxygen is available, give it at 4 liters per minute while descending.

Carbon Monoxide Poisoning

Carbon monoxide poisoning is a great danger in the Arctic. However, prevention is easy. Maintain good ventilation when a fire is burning. Never fall asleep without turning out a stove or lamp. Don't leave a shelter for long if a stove or lamp is burning and others are immobilized or asleep inside. Always make sure that the entrance is clear of snow and free from all obstacles which might prevent quick exit.

Carbon monoxide is colorless and odorless. It burns with a blue flame and is freely generated by a yellow flame. Therefore, when you see a yellow flame, check your ventilation. If you are cooking, lift your pot from the flame; if the flame turns blue, your stove is operating correctly. If possible, hang your cooking pot over the stove so that the bottom of the pot is approximately 3 inches from the top of the burner. Then the flame will stay blue as long as the stove is operating properly.

Carbon monoxide poisoning can be caused by a fire burning in an unventilated shelter or by incomplete combustion even in a ventilated shelter. Usually there are no symptoms; unconsciousness and death may occur without warning. Sometimes, however, there may be pressure at the temples, burning of the eyes, headache, pounding pulse, drowsiness, or nausea. Treat the condition by getting into fresh air at once; keep warm and at rest. If necessary, apply artificial respiration. Give oxygen, if available.

Snakes and Snakebites

In my survival seminars I can mention that automobile accidents kill some 50,000 Americans each year, and no one becomes troubled. I can tell the students that lightning kills around 200 Americans annually, and no one raises an eyebrow. But the mention of poisonous snakes, which kill only about a dozen Americans annually, sends everyone squirming or climbing up on his chair. For some unknown reason, snakes scare the otherwise most fearless among us. Basically, this is an excessive fear—a phobia.

Poisonous snakes are found in all the states with the exception of Alaska, Hawaii, and Maine. Canada has rattlesnakes only in southern British Columbia, Alberta, Saskatchewan, and Ontario.

North America's poisonous snakes include two species of coral snakes, the copperhead, the cottonmouth, and 15 species of rattlesnakes.

Rattlesnakes are known from elevations up to 11,000 feet in the southern Sierra Nevada of California, to about 8,000 feet on dry, rocky slopes in Montana, and to the tops of the highest mountains in the southern Appalachians. In spite of this, poisonous snakes are rare in high mountains, in northern evergreen forests, and in heavily farmed or urban industrial areas.

POISONOUS SNAKES OF NORTH AMERICA

NO POISONOUS SNAKES

RATTLESNAKES

RATTLESNAKES

RATTLESNAKES

RATTLESNAKES
COPPERHEADS

RATTLESNAKES
COPPERHEADS
COTTONMOUTHS
CORAL SNAKES

RATTLESNAKES
CORAL SNAKES

RATTLESNAKES
COTTONMOUTH
CORAL SNAKES

This shows approximate ranges of the four types of poisonous snakes occurring in North America. (Source: U.S. Air Force Survival Manual*)*

Surprisingly, some species survive well in suburban areas, especially in the southern states. Areas with unusually large populations of poisonous snakes include parts of the Great Plains (rattlesnakes), the lower Mississippi Valley and Gulf Coast (rattle-snakes and cottonmouths), and the southern Appalachians (rattlesnakes and copperheads).

Snakebite is by no means rare in the southern and western United States. Incidence is highest in children from 5 to 15 years old,

WHICH SNAKE IS POISONOUS?

Which one is poisonous? All pit vipers are poisonous and have a heat-sensing pit on each side of the head between the eye and nostril. Pit vipers include rattlers, the cottonmouth, and the copperhead (shown above). Also, pit vipers have a vertical eye pupil as shown. Nonpoisonous snakes lack the heat-sensing pit and have a round pupil, as on the garter snake shown on the next page. (Copperhead photo by Smithsonian Institution; garter snake by Neil Soderstrom)

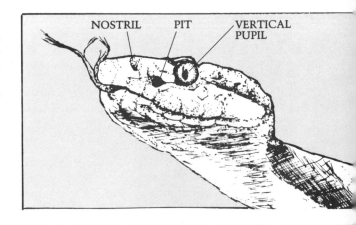

NOSTRIL   PIT   VERTICAL PUPIL

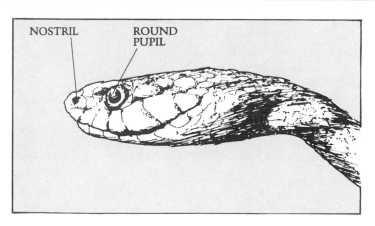

NOSTRIL ROUND PUPIL

WHICH OF THESE IS POISONOUS?

Which of these is poisonous? The snake on the log often measures up to 3½ feet long, with largest specimens going 5 feet. The snake hanging on the branch may exceed 4 feet in length; it is tricolored with black, red (or brown) and white (or yellow), and it eats venomous snakes. Answer: Neither is

poisonous. *The snake on the log is a water snake, sometimes difficult to distinguish from a venomous cottonmouth. The hanging snake is an eastern milk snake. Both of these snakes can bite, as can little garter snakes, but neither injects venom. (Leonard Lee Rue III photos)*

and most bites are sustained close to home whether in rural or suburban areas. Many bites result from deliberate handling of venomous snakes.

Try to learn to identify poisonous snakes and learn where they are found.

Coral snakes. These pretty but deadly snakes are found in the southern United States from the lowlands of North Carolina to the southwestern states. Coral snakes are usually from 20 to 30 inches long. The coral snake has colored rings completely encircling the body. The colors are red, yellow, and black. One sure identification of a coral snake is that the red ring touches the yellow ring.

Coral snakes are usually secretive and hide in leaves, logs, stumps, and debris.

Cottonmouth (Water Moccasin). The color pattern of the cottonmouth, often called water moccasin, is dull and inconspicuous: dark-brown bars on a somewhat lighter background. Many cottonmouths look either dirty brown or uniform black. I have seen some that were difficult to identify because of variance in their color patterns. The most positive identification is the elliptical vertical pupil of the eye, but you don't want to be that close in order to identify it. The cottonmouths get their name from their habit of

Coral snake (Leonard Lee Rue III photo)

Cottonmouth (Florida Game and Fresh Water Fish Commission photo)

threatening an intruder with open mouth, revealing a cotton-white interior.

Although some individual cottonmouths exceed 5 feet in length, most are from 3 to 4 feet long. Occasionally these snakes will grow to 6 feet and weigh up to 12 pounds.

The cottonmouth range is much smaller than most people believe. Generally, their range runs south of a line from south-central Texas up through the Mississippi River Basin in Missouri, down along the Tennessee River Basin, and up the East Coast where the elevation is below 800 feet. More often than not, supposed cottonmouths turn out to be various nonpoisonous water snakes that belong to the Natrix family. These snakes are aggressive, and some do resemble the cottonmouth, but they are not poisonous.

Though the cottonmouth is much scarcer than many believe, when you encounter one, avoid it. It is curious and is no coward. The cottonmouth is slow to retreat. Many times I have seen one hold its ground when escape would have been easy.

The best prevention against a cottonmouth bite is precaution. When you're in cottonmouth territory, keep your eyes open and always watch where you place your feet and hands. When you travel in a boat, watch overhanging limbs, stumps, logs, and the base of trees. Cottonmouths like to sun themselves, as other snakes do. Several times I have almost grabbed a snake by reaching around a tree to tie up a boat. Look before you put your hands anywhere.

Another place you are likely to encounter a cottonmouth is on the end of your fish stringer. There is no more sobering experience than to pull up a stringer of fish and find a big cottonmouth attached, swallowing one of the fish. That hazard is one reason southern fisherman carry an ice chest in which to keep their catches.

Copperhead. The copperhead's back is pinkish-buff, russet, or orange-brown with dark brown to reddish crossbands; the belly is pinkish-white with large dark spots, or mottling; the top of the head is yellowish to coppery red; the sides are paler; and the end of the tail is yellow in young snakes, black to dark greenish or brown in adults. The crossbands are narrow in the center of the back and wide on the sides in eastern specimens, only slightly narrowed in western ones. The pupil of the eye is elliptical. The average length is 2 to 3 feet; maximum, slightly over 4 feet.

The copperhead is found in the eastern

Copperhead (Leonard Lee Rue III photo)

United States (Massachusetts to Kansas and southward exclusive of peninsular Florida), westward into Trans-Pecos, Texas. It frequents wooded, hilly country in the North and West, lowlands in the South, and is sometimes plentiful in well-populated areas. Nocturnal in warm weather, it is diurnal in cool. In rocky country, it frequently hibernates in ledges with rattlesnakes and various nonpoisonous species. The copperhead usually remains coiled and quiet unless closely approached or touched. It vibrates its tail when angry and often seems reluctant to strike, but some individuals are very irritable.

Copperheads account for the great majority of snakebites received in the eastern United States, exclusive of Florida and the Mississippi Delta. However, fatalities from these bites are almost unknown.

Rattlesnakes. Of the poisonous snakes found in North America, the rattlesnake is perhaps the easiest to identify, because of the jointed rattle found at the tip of the tail. However, this is not always the case because the rattle can be broken off. The pupil of the rattlesnake's eye is vertically elliptical, as is that of the copperhead and cottonmouth.

The rattlesnake is found throughout the United States except in Maine, Alaska, and Hawaii. It is also found in southern British Columbia, Alberta, Saskatchewan, and Ontario in Canada.

Here are some don'ts to follow when in snake country.

1. *Don't* put your hands or feet in places you cannot look, and *don't* put them in places without first looking.

2. *Don't* turn or lift a rock or fallen tree with your hands. Move it with a stick, or

Eastern diamondback rattlesnake (Don Pfitzer/U.S. Fish and Wildlife photo)

Canebrake rattlesnake (Don Pfitzer/U.S. Fish and Wildlife Service photo)

with your foot if your ankle and leg are properly protected.

3. *Don't* disturb snakes.

4. *Don't* put your sleeping bag near rock piles or rubbish piles or near the entrance to a cave.

5. *Don't* sit down without first looking around carefully.

6. *Don't* gather firewood after dark.

7. *Don't* step over a log if the other side is not visible. Step on it first.

8. *Don't* enter snake-infested areas without adequate protective clothing.

9. *Don't* handle freshly killed venomous snakes.

10. *Don't* crawl under a fence in high grass or in an uncleared area.

11. *Don't* go out of your way to kill a poisonous snake unless you need the meat to survive. Thousands of people are bitten by snakes each year merely because they try to kill them without knowing anything of their habits or habitats.

12. *Don't* panic!

Snakebite treatment. The proper treatment of a poisonous snakebite has long been one of the most disputed subjects in the medical profession. Two of the best-known doctors in the field of snakebites are Dr. Charles Watt of Thomasville, Georgia, and Dr. Robert Sheppard of Carrollton, Alabama, who is an expert in survival medicine and an experienced outdoorsman. Both of these doctors advocate the following treatment:

1. Get away from the snake. It is not unusual for a snake to bite the victim several times.

2. Try to remain calm.

3. Positively identify the snake, and if possible, have someone kill the snake and take it with you to the doctor so that it can be identified and examined. That knowledge will be helpful in the treatment.

4. Make a constricting band out of a handkerchief, shoestring, shirtsleeve, sock, or belt. Put this band on above the bite (that is, between the bite and the body). It should be so loose that you can easily insert a finger under it. Such a constricting band will not stop the flow of blood through the artery, but it does check the return of blood through the veins and stops the fast spread of venom. Do not loosen this constricting band.

5. If you are within an hour's travel of a doctor, prepare the victim for the trip. Immobilize the bitten limb by putting on a splint. Make sure that the splint's bindings are loose enough not to impair circulation. If possible, keep the limb horizontal. The victim should not walk unless absolutely necessary; other members of the group should carry the victim to the vehicle.

6. If you are more than an hour away from a doctor or in a survival situation, a more complex procedure should be followed if it can be performed within the first five minutes after the bite. If not, forget this step and

Don't put your hands and feet anywhere without first looking. This live, wild cottonmouth is ready to strike the foot of a bowhunter who took a big risk for the sake of this photo.

get to the doctor. Wash the wound with water, soap, alcohol, or whatever you have on hand. Make a short, approximately ½-inch, straight incision (no cross cut) over each fang mark. Cut only parallel with the limb. The two cuts should be no deeper than the fatty tissue under the skin (about ¼ inch). Use an instrument that has been sterilized in the flame of a match and is razor-sharp.

7. If you have no cuts or sores in your mouth, suck the wound vigorously, or have someone else do it for you if he can do so safely. Suction can remove 20 to 50 percent of the venom. A suction cup from a snakebite kit is useful if you are alone and the bite is in an area you cannot reach with your mouth. It is important that you do not delay the trip to the doctor in order to cut and suck. Do this en route. To delay the injection of antivenin is to risk death.

8. Apply a constricting band and a splint as directed earlier and get medical treatment as quickly as possible.

Other points, to remember concerning snakebite:

• *Never* give a snakebite victim alcohol. It speeds up the flow of blood through the system and hastens the effect of the bite.

• Immediately remove rings, bracelets, watches, shoes, or whatever from a bitten limb. The swelling will be fast, and such objects will constrict.

• *Never* use cryotherapy (ice), as this has been shown to be harmful to the snakebite victim.

It may be comforting to know that no venom is injected in 25 percent of all bites by poisonous snakes. However, absence of pain, swelling, or other symptoms does not necessarily mean that no venom has been injected. Bites that at first seem superficial can be fatal.

Most hospitals in snake country have antivenin for the treatment of snakebites. If a hospital doesn't have antivenin, they can call the Oklahoma Poison Information Center at 405-271-5454. The center maintains a computerized inventory of antivenin available across the nation. Keep this phone number taped in the lid of your first aid kit.

The odds are great that you will spend a lifetime outdoors and never be bitten or see a person bitten by a poisonous snake. However, the potential does exist and caution should be taken. If you follow these rules and use a little common sense, you should never get into trouble with snakes.

Spider Bites

Spiders seem to scare almost as many people as snakes do. However, most spiders are harmless to man. Fewer than ten people die from spider bites in North America in any given year. The two North American spiders that can be deadly are the black widow and the brown recluse.

Black widow spider. The female black widow is far more of a toxic hazard than the male. She has a shiny black body, approximately 0.6 inch long, and usually a red hourglass-shaped mark on the underside of her globular abdomen. On some, the hourglass marking is replaced with several triangles or spots or an irregular longitudinal blotch. She has slim black legs with a span of 1.5 inches. The less toxic male is considerably smaller than the female and usually is a patterned brown color.

The black widow is found throughout North America except in northern Canada and in Alaska. Most reported human fatalities have occurred in the southeastern states.

The black widow is generally found in its irregular-shaped web near the ground. Common web sites are under stones, loose bark, or water faucets, or in woodpiles, rodent burrows, garages, storage buildings, outhouses,

BLACK WIDOWS

Black widow spiders: female above left and male above right. The female normally has the red hourglass-shaped marking on her underside, as shown in the photo at right. (USDA photos)

This is the female brown recluse spider. Note the characteristic dark fiddle-shaped marking on the front half of her back. (USDA photo)

and barns. Most human bites occur when the spider is inadvertently trapped against part of the body or when the web is accidentally touched.

Man is seldom bitten by the black widow, but when it happens the bite is serious. The symptoms are severe pain, profuse sweating, nausea, painful cramps of abdominal muscles, and difficult breathing.

Treatment of the bite should be left to a doctor. In transporting the victim, keep him warm and calm. Apply cold compresses to the bite area. If stranded, take pain relievers.

Brown recluse spider. The brown recluse is a medium-size spider with leg span from 0.8 to 1.6 inches and a color range from yellow-tan to dark brown. The most distinguishing characteristics are six eyes (most spiders have eight eyes) arranged in a semicircle of three pairs on top of the head, and a violin-shaped marking extending from the area of the eyes to the abdomen.

Brown recluse spiders occur throughout an area of the south-central states, including Alabama, Arkansas, Georgia, Illinois, Indiana, Iowa, Kansas, Kentucky, Louisiana, Ohio, Oklahoma, Mississippi, Missouri, Tennessee, and Texas. Localized populations of this spider, probably imported from the south-central states, have been reported in Arizona, Wyoming, California, Florida, New Jersey, North Carolina, Pennsylvania and Washington, D.C. Specimens can easily be transported in household goods from the spider's home range in the south-central United States to any other area of the country or Canada. Under favorable conditions, the relocated spiders can survive for an extended time and possibly become established.

Within its range, the brown recluse spider will readily establish populations inside parts of buildings that are generally dry, littered, and undisturbed for long periods. The spider can also be found outside in protected areas (under rocks and loose bark). Members of this species are nonaggressive and normally attempt to escape whenever they are threatened. Thus, most instances of bites occur when the spider is inadvertently trapped, such as when the victim puts on clothing in which the spider is hiding, steps barefoot on a wandering spider at night, or cleans storage areas where the spider resides.

Symptoms of the brown recluse bite include intense local pain, a blister at the bite site, inflammation of the affected area, and an ulcerating sore. Treatment should be the same as for the black widow bite.

Bites from some other spiders can be painful and can lead to infections, but they do not pose the hazards of toxins associated with the brown recluse and the black widow.

Blackflies and Mosquitos

For centuries man has searched for ways to protect himself from mosquitos and blackflies. It has not been too many years since man covered himself with mud or foul-smelling oil, or dusted himself with sulfur, or ate a teaspoon of sulfur, or just didn't bathe for weeks, trying to repel these water-related insects.

Thanks to modern research and much trial and error, modern man is finally learning how to repel the trip-ruining attacks of mosquitos and blackflies. Even with this new information and with effective repellents, many people suffer needlessly from these pesky insects.

Sharing the outdoors with mosquitos and blackflies and enjoying it means that certain rules must be followed. The first is to know something about these biting critters. As a general rule blackflies bite by daylight. Mosquitos tend to become an increasing problem as night approaches.

There are over 1,600 kinds of mosquitos in the world, with at least 120 varieties in North America. Mosquitos mature in standing water. The female mosquito needs a high-protein meal before she is able to lay her eggs. Physiological restrictions make it impossible for her to eat anything which is not in liquid form. The handiest liquid, high-protein meal available to them is blood.

In order to find a meal, the mosquito has sensors which are attracted to warm, moist objects. Since the skin temperature and moisture transpiration of one person can differ markedly from that of another, mosquitos are attracted to some people more than to others.

Sight also plays a big part in the mosquito's location of prey. Mosquitos see best whatever contrasts most strongly with the background. Shiny fabrics and pale colors are easier for them to see than dull-surfaced dark clothing. You may already have noticed that you are not bothered as much by mosquitos when you wear camouflage clothing as when you wear light blue denim. It is also of interest to note that researchers have found that people in motion get bitten more often than those who are still.

Many people swear that the worst bite in the outdoors is that of the blackfly. These small black hump-backed flies will rival mosquitos any day for the most in numbers for a single attack or for the viciousness of the attack. There are over 300 kinds of blackflies in the world, and North America has been cursed with at least 50 varieties.

Unlike the mosquito, the blackfly matures in running water. Rapidly flowing streams are preferred breeding places. Once blackflies are able to fly, the female, which feeds by day, is ready for a meal in order to carry out her reproducing task.

Like the mosquito, the blackfly is found over much of North America, but its largest concentrations are in the woodlands of Canada and in the northern part of the United

States. The blackfly is abundant throughout late spring and summer, with May and June being the worst months in many areas.

The vicious bite of the blackfly is caused by broad blades found in the mouthparts. These blades make large wounds, when compared to the mosquito bite, that continue to bleed after the fly has fed and gone. Often the bite goes unnoticed until a trickle of blood is felt or seen. The blackfly saliva may be toxic, causing pain and itching. Surface irritations are sometimes accompanied by nervous and intestinal disorders.

Not as much is known about the blackfly as about the mosquito. But it is thought that the female blackfly detects the carbon dioxide given off by the skin and then zeroes in by flying up the convection currents of warm, moist air that the host produces.

Now that we know something about the pests, let's see how we can keep them at a distance.

Warding off blackflies and mosquitos. The first rule to enjoying outdoor activities during the warm months in mosquito and

The better insect repellents have high concentrations of DEET.

blackfly environments is to use one of the modern chemical insect repellents. The development of these repellents began during World War II when American troops were suffering from insect-caused diseases in the jungles throughout the world. Many chemicals were tested with only moderate success during the war, and after the war, the search continued. By 1951, the number of chemical insect repellents that had been tested by the Bureau of Entomology and Plant Quarantine in Orlando, Florida, was up to 11,000. In the late 1950s and early 1960s, a repellent compound was developed that started giving the desired results.

With the technical name N,N-diethyl-meta-toluamide and the acronym DEET, this new repellent was found to be effective for up to a week in 100 percent concentration and up to three hours at 50 percent concentration for the volunteers who were tested. How does DEET work? No one is positive, but the theory of many experts is that repellents act as an olfactory (smell) irritant for insects. Other experts think that insects are attracted by carbon dioxide, and the repellents mask the carbon dioxide given off by the skin. To date, DEET is considered to be the best active ingredient to use in chemical insect repellents against mosquitos and is effective against blackflies when aided by other active chemicals. The higher the percentage of DEET, the more oily the repellent is to the touch, but on the other hand, the more effective it is against insects.

Many companies use a mixture of DEET and other chemicals in order to give a wide range of protection. These ingredients, with names like bicycloheptene dicarboximide and tetrahydro-2-furaldehyde, are selective biting-fly repellents. That means that they are used singly or in combination to repel a certain variety of fly.

It is the high concentration of DEET, combined with the selective biting-fly repellents, which gives many repellents their ability to work so effectively and for such long periods of time.

When I am in an area with a limited mosquito/blackfly population, I use a repellent with a lower percentage of active ingredients, including DEET repellent. When I'm in an area with a heavy mosquito/blackfly population, I use the higher-percentage repellent. On trips which take me into areas of heavy mosquito infestation, I use repellents that are at least 95 percent DEET.

When using commercial insect repellents, you should keep them away from fishing fly lines, rod finishes, and monofilament line, because the repellent will dissolve them. Repellents will also take the finish off gunstocks, and some experts say that if you get repellent on fishing flies and lures, the fish can detect an odor and be repelled.

There are two alternative methods of keeping mosquitos and blackflies away which, when coupled with a chemical repellent, could be most effective. The first is to eat one clove of garlic each day. The odor is secreted through the skin and repels insects, as well as your friends.

The second alternative method is one which seems to work well on many people— a dose of vitamin B-1. Those who choose this method of repelling insects suggest that you take one 100-milligram vitamin B-1 tablet every six hours while on an outing in insect country. While there is little research available on this method of insect control, there are many, including some doctors, who swear it works.

Repellents alone will not give you total protection from mosquitos and blackflies in areas of heavy infestations. A headnet may be well worth the bother of wearing at certain times. Always wear a long-sleeved shirt and trousers in bug country. Apply a strong blowing to keep the insects away. Always purchase tents that are insectproof and have fine-mesh screens. When not going in and out of the tent, keep the screen doors fastened tightly. On still, hot nights when mosquitos are inevitable, plan to set up camp early, before dark, and go to bed early. It is amazing how effective a good, tight, but well-ventilated tent can be on a mosquito-infested night.

Anyone going into backcountry in insect seasons should always carry a good supply of chemical insect repellent even if the trip is to be a short one. When using a repellent, the trick is to apply enough to get complete coverage. With the spray-type repellents, it takes approximately five seconds of spray time to spray from the wrist to the elbow. Most people try to do it in less than one second.

Even with effective preventives and precautions, it is hard to be outdoors during the warm months and not be bitten by mosquitos and blackflies. So you should carry bite balms such as Campho-Phenique or calamine lotion in the first aid kit to apply to the irritated region. These will minimize irritation and reduce the itching of lesions.

Another treatment that seems to reduce the swelling and pain of blackfly bites is to place a pinch of meat tenderizer containing papaya on each bite.

By following these suggestions, you can share the outdoors with mosquitos and blackflies and still have a good time.

Ticks

One of the worst pests during warm weather is the tick. There are over 100 species of ticks north of the Mexican border. In fact, there are few dry places on earth where ticks do not exist.

In North America, the three most com-

A headnet can make life outdoors more tolerable when mosquitos and blackflies are thick.

repellent to the clothing, as well as to your exposed skin. Also be sure to take along some short lengths of cord to tie down your shirtsleeves and trouser legs.

When planning a trip, it is well worth a phone call to local authorities to check out the insect situation. Often a few days can make a big difference in the number of insects in an area.

Campers, and especially canoe campers, should learn how to pick a campsite with insect control in mind. Select a campsite away from stagnant water. Pick sites that are on high breezy points or at least in the open where you can take advantage of any breeze

TICKS

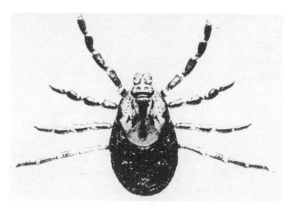

Greatly magnified, this is the minute American dog tick (female shown at right engorged with blood). One of the most common of the several ticks in North America, the dog tick, like others, may carry Rocky Mountain spotted fever. A relatively new tick-related hazard in the East is Lyme disease. It can have serious and varied health effects. (USDA photos)

mon ticks are the Lone Star tick, the American dog tick, and the Rocky Mountain wood tick. Many sportsmen believe that there is a fourth type called a "seed" tick, about the size of a pinhead or smaller and found in large numbers. This is actually the larval stage of any of the above-named ticks.

Ticks, like many insects, have four stages of development: egg, larva (or seed tick), nymph (or yearling tick), and adult. Ticks are in no hurry to complete their life cycle. After the eggs hatch, the larvae start feeding as soon as they can find flesh. They feed four or five days, then drop off to molt into the nymph stage and find a new host to feed upon, this time feeding longer. In many types, the nymphal stage hibernates over the winter before continuing the developmental stage. The nymphs can go as long as a year without feeding, and an adult tick may survive as long as two years without a meal. The life cycle does not end until after the eggs are laid.

Many of the ticks found in the United States can transmit germs of several diseases, including Rocky Mountain spotted fever (RMSF), a disease that occurs in the eastern United States as well as in the West. RMSF

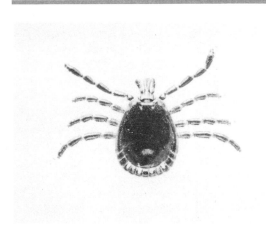

The lone star tick (USDA photo)

symptoms, which may appear from 2 to 12 days after a bite by an infected tick, include sudden chills, high fever, severe headaches, and other aches and pains. A distinct spotted rash, which may be mistaken for measles, usually appears on about the third day. The rash begins on the wrists, ankles, and back. This tick-transmitted illness can be very effectively treated with antibiotics, if it is detected early. The treatment is neither painful nor complicated.

A person may be bitten by a tick without knowing it and later be infected with RMSF. At the first symptoms, a doctor should be called. Make sure he knows the patient was in a tick-infested area. Not all ticks are carriers of RMSF. Even in heavily infested areas, in fact, only about 5 percent of the ticks are able to transmit the disease.

Since ticks are found in grass and on bushes, you should routinely check yourself thoroughly for ticks at least once each day. A methodical check should be made on the hairy parts of the body, especially the head.

When in tick-infested woods, use a heavy coat of commercial insect repellent which has DEET as its active ingredient. Products with at least 95 percent DEET seem to work best. The insect repellent should be rubbed on legs, hands, arms, and neck, around the hairline, and around the waist.

Also wear long-sleeved shirts and long pants when in areas where ticks are common. Keep the pant legs tucked into the boots, or use rubber bands to keep pant legs tight around boots. Keep shirtsleeves buttoned tight at wrists, and wear a hat to protect the head.

No matter what you do, though, if you frequent the woods, from time to time a tick will try to draw a meal from you. Early detection of ticks by a thorough examination of your body and proper removal can keep you from getting a disease from a tick. The longer a tick imbibes, the greater your chances of infection.

The recommended way to remove a tick is to make it loosen its grip by coating it thoroughly with petroleum jelly, baby oil, or a vaporizing salve, such as Vicks VapoRub; or by putting a drop of gasoline, kerosene, benzine, alcohol, or ether on the general region of the tick's head; or by touching it with a lighted match or the tip of a burning cigarette. However, the tick will take its own time releasing its grip, and the host must be patient. It may be ten minutes or so before the tick drops off, but when it does, it will take its mouthparts with it. A tick can also be killed by covering it with a drop of paraffin or fingernail polish, for these substances will close the two tiny breathing openings on its sides and suffocate it. Under no circumstances should an attached tick be squeezed. This will only force more toxin into the bite.

After removing the tick, wash the bite area with soap and water and apply iodine or another antiseptic. If a growth or granuloma appears at the site, consult your physician once you have returned to civilization. Do this also if signs of infection appear in the bite area.

Stinging Insects

A sting from the Hymenoptera order of insects—bees and yellow jackets, hornets, and other wasps—can be dangerous. Some 50 deaths a year from these stings are recorded in the United States, and many doctors believe the real figure is far higher. There are far more fatalities from stings than from snakebite.

Among the greatest dangers are the large nests of paper wasps, which reach the size of a man's hat and are built in bushes that hang over the water. The careless fisherman can get into trouble fast if he accidentally

TYPES OF HIVES

The nests of hornets are often in the open like this one. (L.L. Perkins photo)

The nests of yellow jackets are usually inconspicuous— in the ground as shown here or at ground level in stumps. Females of the species attack viciously if you blunder over their door. Nest holes are most readily located by noting the constant flight of yellow jackets in and out. Here one yellow jacket is shown at the door threshold about to take flight. (Neil Soderstrom photo)

disturbs one. If you're keeping your eyes open for cottonmouths, you'll spot these nests.

Also be especially careful in selecting a campsite. Scout the area carefully, and be observant for yellow jacket nests. Yellow jackets build their nests in the ground and are particularly fond of old stumps. The nest opening is often one small hole that is difficult to see.

Insects of the Hymenoptera order inject venom under the skin when they sting. Under normal conditions, the venom produces a few minutes of burning followed by itching and reddening at the sting site. Ice, calamine lotion, or a product named "After-Bite" will normally remedy the trauma.

To the person who is venom-sensitive, however, the situation is extremely serious. Such a person may experience labored breathing, difficulty in swallowing, chest constriction, abdominal pain, nausea, weakness, and unconsciousness. This person is in serious trouble and needs help fast. It is estimated that eight out of every 1,000 people are venom-sensitive.

People who are allergic to insect venom may receive desensitizing treatments from a physician. Desensitizing is a procedure which employs injections of freeze-dried, purified insect venom.

There are also emergency sting kits containing a pre-loaded syringe of epinephrine.

Allergic people should always wear medical identification bracelets so that proper treatment can be given should they be unable to speak for themselves.

The best prevention is to follow these simple rules:

1. Watch for nests of bees, wasps, hornets, and yellow jackets. If you find such a nest, leave the area quickly and quietly.

2. Wear shoes and socks when walking around outdoors.

3. Avoid use of scented soaps, lotions, perfumes, and the like. These attract stinging insects.

4. Avoid bright-colored clothes.

5. Keep a clean camp and do not leave food uncovered. Keep your garbage tightly sealed.

6. Don't swat at stinging insects.

7. Use insect repellent.

Chiggers

Chiggers, or red bugs, as they are commonly called, are a common pest around summer campsites. These tiny red pests burrow into the skin to feed, and they create an intense itching. Usually their bites are only a small discomfort, but the bites become much more uncomfortable when there are many of them. Medical attention is occasionally required.

Chiggers can be avoided by treating your clothing with sulfur dust. It also helps to apply commercial insect repellent to clothing and exposed skin. Once a chigger bite is discovered, an application of clear fingernail polish or the product called "After-Bite" will usually be a quick remedy.

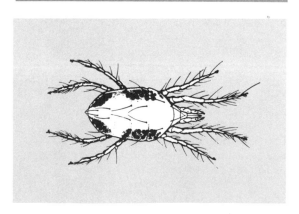

"Chiggers" is the common name for several species of mites whose bite causes severe itching. (USDA drawing)

Contact Poisonous Plants

Three poisonous plants commonly present hazards upon contact. These are poison sumac, common poison ivy, and oakleaf poison ivy. Everyone should learn how to identify these plants and avoid them because the body's reaction to urushiol is unpredictable. You may suffer a bad reaction sometimes, always, or never. Some people are extremely sensitive and react strongly any time they come into contact with the poisonous plants. Others may have an adverse reaction suddenly, after having been relatively immune for years.

Poison sumac. Poison sumac is usually found eastward to the Atlantic Coast from a line along eastern Minnesota, Illinois, Indiana, Kentucky, and Tennessee down to southeastern Texas. This tree-like shrub is usually found in swamps and bogs. The plants range in height from 5 or 6 feet, even to small trees that may reach a height of 25 feet. The leaves

of the poison sumac are divided into 7 to 13 leaflets, arranged in pairs with a single leaflet at the end of the mid-rib.

Many nonpoisonous sumacs are found along rivers and are easily distinguished from the poisonous variety. The nonpoisonous sumacs have red fruits and seed clusters that always grow upward from the tip of the branches. The poisonous variety has white fruits and seeds that grow upward at first but then hang down in late summer and in autumn.

Common poison ivy. Common poison ivy, in some form, may be found in almost every part of the United States, with the exception of the dry southwest. It is also found along the southern fringes of Canada. Common poison ivy is most often found as a vine growing in woods and river bottoms where it depends on trees for support. Quite often, especially in a river bottom, its vines will grow for many years, becoming several inches in diameter and quite woody.

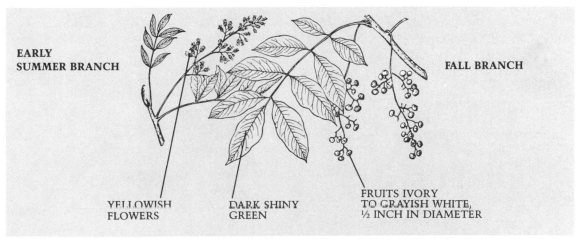

EARLY SUMMER BRANCH

FALL BRANCH

YELLOWISH FLOWERS

DARK SHINY GREEN

FRUITS IVORY TO GRAYISH WHITE, ½ INCH IN DIAMETER

Poison sumac (From Charles Sprague Sargent's Manual of the Trees of North America*)*

Poison ivy is always three leaved. See also other photos of this troublesome plant on page 170. (USDA photo)

The most distinctive identifying characteristic of poison ivy is its leaves, which always consist of three glossy leaflets. Most of the vines or shrubs of poison ivy produce some flowers that are always in clusters on the side of the stem immediately above a leaf. When fruits do develop, they serve as a positive way of identifying the plant. The berries are not easily confused with the fruits of other plants. They are white and waxy and have distinct lines marking the outer surface, similar to the way the segments appear in a peeled orange. The fruit is especially helpful in identifying plants in late fall, winter, and early spring when the leaves are not present.

Oakleaf poison ivy. The oakleaf form of poison ivy that occurs in the eastern and south-

ern states usually does not climb as a vine, but occurs as a low-growing shrub, usually with rather slender branches. The leaflets occur in threes and are lobed, somewhat like the leaves of some kinds of oak. The middle leaflet is usually lobed somewhat symmetrically and very much resembles a small oak leaf, while the two lateral leaflets are often irregularly lobed.

The fruit of oakleaf poison ivy has the same general appearance as the fruit of common poison ivy, although the individual fruits and stems are often covered with a soft down, while most of the other forms have a waxy, smooth, cream-colored fruit.

Contact with poisonous plants. The skin irritant of poison ivy, poison oak, and poison

Oakleaf poison ivy, often called poison oak (Leonard Lee Rue III photo)

sumac is the same toxic agent. It is a non-volatile, phenolic substance called *urushiol* that is found in all parts of the plant, including the roots and fruit. It occurs in great abundance in the plant sap. The danger of poisoning is greatest in spring and summer, when the sap is abundant, and least in late fall or winter.

Poisoning is usually caused by contact with some part of the plant. A very small quantity of the poisonous substance is capable of producing severe inflammation of the skin and can easily be transferred from one surface to another. Clothing may become contaminated and is often a source of prolonged infection. Dogs frequently touch the plants and transmit the poison to unsuspecting owners. The poison may remain on the fur of animals for a considerable period after they have walked or run through the poisonous plants. Smoke from burning plants will carry the toxin and can cause severe reactions on skin and in eyes, nose, throat, and lungs. No part of the plant should ever be taken internally because it is a violent irritant and poisonous to man.

The time between contamination of the skin and the first symptoms varies greatly among individuals and conditions. The first symptoms of itching or burning sensation may develop in a few hours, or after five days or more. The itching sensation and subsequent inflammation, which usually develops into water blisters under the skin, may continue for several days, even from a single contamination. Persistence of symptoms over a long period is likely to be caused by new contacts with plants or with previously contaminated clothing or animals. Severe infection may produce more serious symptoms, such as abscesses, enlarged glands, fever, or complicated constitutional malfunction, which cause intense pain. Secondary infections are always a possibility in any break in

the skin, such as that produced by the breaking of the blisters.

Treatment. Once you have been exposed to a poisonous plant, wash thoroughly with a strong, non-oily soap. Brown laundry soap works best. After washing, swab the contacted skin with rubbing alcohol. If irritation appears on the skin, it can be reduced by using calamine lotion or Solarcaine. Avoid scratching the irritated skin because it can cause infection. If the rash becomes painful, get medical attention at once.

Of course, if you are lost or stranded when symptoms occur, these treatments will not be available. In that case, wash the affected area if possible and, above all, do not scratch. You will be in for some discomfort, but probably in no danger as long as the skin is kept clean and is not irritated.

STAYING OUT OF TROUBLE

This chapter covers many common hazards and how to cope with them. But important as it is to know what to do when you're in trouble, it's even more important to know how to stay out of trouble. I conclude this chapter on survival medicine with prescriptions that are basically preventive medicine. These cover three additional hazards that common sense and a bit of knowledge should enable you to avoid. The hazards are bears, rabies, and lightning.

Bear Problems

From time to time people are attacked by bears, both black and grizzly. In most cases, this is the fault of the people and not the bears because bears don't normally hunt people. The most dangerous bears are those that have become accustomed to people—especially in parks, campgrounds, and garbage

BLACK BEARS

Black bears can become pests if you don't keep a clean camp—free of smelly food and food scraps. Even a fish smell on your clothing can attract bears from great distances. For practice in bear track distinctions, compare the characteristic short-clawed forepaw track of the black bear below with that of the grizzlies on page 308. (Leonard Lee Rue III photo)

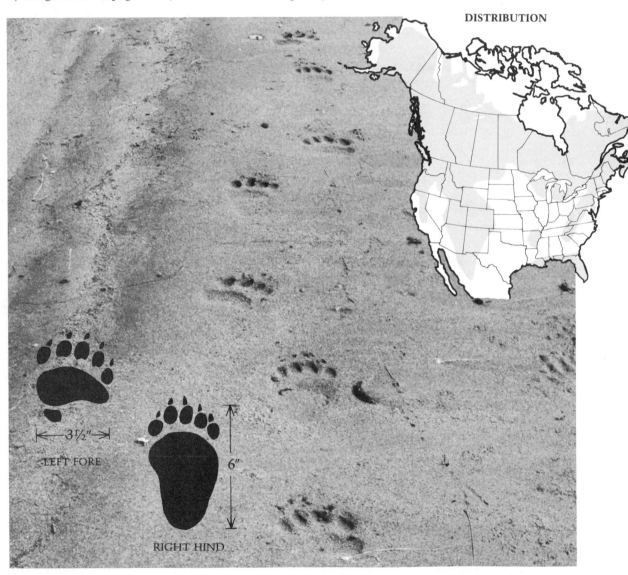

DISTRIBUTION

3½"

LEFT FORE

6"

RIGHT HIND

In the West, many black bears have brown or even cinnamon-colored fur, with the result that some people mistake them for the generally more-aggressive grizzlies. Black bears lack the distinctive shoulder hump of grizzlies, shown on upcoming pages. (Young-bear photo by author; older bear by U.S. Forest Service)

GRIZZLY BEARS

This photo shows a path that Alaskan coastal grizzlies (popularly called "brown bears") use when moving forth and back between resting and salmon fishing sites. These bears have killed people who unwittingly camped too near such trails. Tracks of large grizzlies (browns) can be distinguished from those of the generally less-aggressive black bear by their larger size. But the tracks of a large black and a small-to-medium-size grizzly may be hard to distinguish except for the far longer forepaw claws of grizzlies. See black-bear tracks on page 306. (Photo by Leonard Lee Rue III)

DISTRIBUTION

□ GRIZZLY
□ BROWN

6½"
LEFT FORE
GRIZZLY BEAR
12"
RIGHT HIND

8"
LEFT FORE
15"
BROWN BEAR
RIGHT HIND

In profile, grizzlies have a pronounced shoulder hump and a dished, rather than straight, line from ear to nose tip. Otherwise large blacks that have brown fur and small- to medium-size grizzlies might look quite similar. Note the longer claws of the grizzly and resultant track on the previous page. (National Park Service photo)

This grizzly is often called an Alaskan coastal brown bear. Although it tends to grow larger than the inland grizzly, probably owing its evolution to a fish-rich diet, it is still a grizzly. If you are caught in a survival situation along the Alaskan coast, especially during the salmon spawning season, you may have fierce competition for the best fishing spots. The salmon shown here measured 28 inches. (Leonard Lee Rue III photo)

dumps. These bears have lost their fear of man and can be highly unpredictable.

Basically, wild bears like to keep their distance from man, but when man and bear are suddenly thrown together, the result can be grim for man. A man who has come between an old grizzly sow and her cubs is not a pretty sight.

Bears shouldn't keep you from enjoying the outdoors, but when you are going into bear country, you should know what to do and what not to do in order to live in harmony with these powerful animals.

Here are mistakes Alaska game biologists suggest you avoid:

1. Feeding bears. It is unwise and in many areas illegal to feed bears. Feeding of bears almost invariably leads to either human injury or the destruction of the bears once they become accustomed to mooching food from humans.

2. Keeping a dirty camp. When people leave food in places accessible to bears or fail to dispose of garbage properly, bears are likely to be attracted. Most bear/human problems stem from keeping a dirty camp. It is now illegal in Alaska to leave food or garbage in such a manner that it attracts bears, foxes, wolves, or wolverines. In other words, leaving food out where bears can get to it is just as illegal as feeding them. Suspend your food in a tree out of reach of bears.

3. Camping on bear trails. Bear trails are likely to be found along salmon streams, near berry patches, and in saddles on ridgetops. Use common sense and pick a campsite downwind from and not on any recognizable bear trail. Such trails are often characterized by staggered oval depressions in the trail because bears commonly step in the same tracks they have made on previous outings.

In bear country, keep food that might emit odor inside sealed plastic bags and suspended high enough from a tree limb to be beyond the reach of bears. This is part of "bear-proofing" a camp.

4. Encountering a sow (female bear) with cubs. Sow bears are very protective mothers, and nothing can prompt a full-blown charge any quicker than a startled squall from a cub. Even if a cub doesn't utter a sound, a sow may feel that you are a threat and initiate a charge. Avoid these family groups. Curious cubs have been the cause of more than one mauling.

5. Approaching a bear's food cache. If you detect the foul odor of decomposing meat while on the trail, stop. It's a cinch that a bear has already smelled it, and is probably on or near the carcass, be it moose, caribou, sheep, or some other animal. Try to avoid the area entirely, if possible. Brown and grizzly bears can be particularly short-tempered where food is concerned. If you approach a food cache from upwind and don't smell it, you're sure to recognize it when you see it. Bears often cover their food with branches and forest litter and bed nearby after they've eaten their fill. If you stumble onto

It's wise to avoid sow bears with cubs, especially grizzlies. Mother bears protect their cubs from all potential threats, notably other bears that will kill and devour cubs if the chance arises. Evolution has granted life to cubs of the most ferociously protective mothers. Thus, if you blunder close to a sow with cubs, your other survival worries may lose importance. (National Park Service photo)

such a semiconcealed cache, leave as quietly and quickly as possible. (Even if you feel you are starving and would risk a bear attack in order to steal some meat from the cache, the meat would probably be too decomposed for you to digest it.)

6. Blundering onto a bear at close range. All bears have a certain "critical space." If you surprise a bear at close range (a few feet to 50 yards), almost anything can happen. It is often possible to approach within this "critical space" unnoticed if a bear is busy picking berries, ripping open a log, or fishing. When hiking in densely vegetated bear country, it is good insurance to make noise as you travel. You may wish to tie a bell or a can of rocks on your pack or to whistle or sing while you walk. If possible, walk with your back to the wind. These precautions will warn bears of your approach and give them time to move away. A startled bear is a dangerous bear; don't surprise one, or you may be surprised too.

In a confrontation with a black or a grizzly when sufficient firearm is not immediately available, your first defense can be to climb a nearby tree. If there are no climbable trees, you have no alternative but to play dead. I have never met a man who could outrun an angry bear.

If a bear should ever attack, play dead by rolling up into a ball, keeping your arms, legs, and head tucked into your body. Lie still and don't move. As difficult as this may sound, it has saved many people. Once the bear thinks you are dead, it may lose interest.

By using some common sense and following the rules, you will probably never need to play dead.

Killing a bear. If you need to kill a bear, you must have enough firearm to do it because bears, especially grizzlies, are among the most difficult North American animals to kill. You must also have plenty of ammunition because it may take several shots to kill a bear. Wounding a bear makes it even more dangerous. And you must be calm and skilled enough to place several killing shots in the animal. I would advise any survivor to avoid any confrontation with bears and to use a firearm only in self-defense.

Rabies

Everyone, whether a trapper, hunter, fisherman, picnicker, hiker, or casual outdoor visitor, should be aware of the ever-present killer rabies.

The instance of rabies in wildlife is much higher than many people believe. According to information from the Centers for Disease Control, Rabies Surveillance, doctors reported 6,212 confirmed cases of rabies in animals in the United States in a recent year. Of these, 729 were in domestic animals, while 5,483 were in wild animals.

Rabies is an infection that affects dogs, cats, and other carnivores—including man. All warm-blooded animals are susceptible to the deadly virus.

The wildlife most susceptible to rabies are foxes, skunks, bobcats, raccoons, and bats. In domestic animals, cattle, horses, dogs, and cats are most susceptible. Opossums have occasionally been known to have rabies, but they appear to be quite resistant to the disease. Rodents such as chipmunks, rats, mice, and squirrels only rarely acquire rabies.

You run the risk of contracting rabies when handling wild animals. Some 30,000 people each year are required to undergo postexposure rabies treatments. Many of these treatments could be prevented if people would be more cautious of wildlife.

But you do not have to be bitten by a rabid

wild animal to be endangered by the deadly virus. Let's assume that a dog has been bitten by a rabid skunk. The virus in the skunk's saliva goes into the dog's body at the point of the wound. The virus multiplies and penetrates the nerve cells, and slowly moves to the spinal cord, and ultimately to the brain. From the brain the virus moves to the saliva glands. It is at this point that the dog becomes dangerous. If it bites now, it can transmit rabies through its infected saliva. The normal time for the virus to move from the bite to the saliva glands is 15 to 25 days.

Recognizing a rabid domestic animal is relatively easy. According to veterinarians, here are some indications that a dog may be rabid: He may become restless, aggressive, lethargic; there may be a change in his vocal quality; he may persistently howl; you may notice a paralyzed lower jaw; he may go into convulsions and eventually paralysis. Dogs usually die in ten days or less after the virus reaches the saliva glands. It is for this reason that technicians watch dogs closely after a bite for up to ten days.

Wild animals may show only one or two of the symptoms common in domestic animals, or none at all. It is important to know that wild animals do not die in as short a period as affected domestic animals. The most reliable indicator in wildlife with rabies is either a show of aggressiveness or a lack of the usual fear of humans.

Several years ago when I was working as a wildlife manager in southern Georgia, my son and I were checking a number of fishing ponds. As we came upon the dam of one pond, a raccoon started walking toward us as though it were someone's escaped pet. The raccoon had no fear of us at all and walked with a slight stagger. As the raccoon approached, I became suspicious of rabies. So I killed the raccoon and sent the head off to be examined. Sure enough, the animal was rabid.

In all cases, avoid sick or strange-acting animals as survival food. The risk in killing and eating them is greater than the likelihood of your starving.

Bites from wild animals, as well as domestic animals, are nothing to take lightly. Any bite from any animal should be treated with suspicion until it is proved that the animal does not have rabies. The first thing to do when bitten by an animal is to make the animal available to health authorities. Domestic animals can be captured and caged. Wild animals should be killed. If the animal is captured and killed, notify local health authorities immediately so that the head may be sent to a laboratory to be checked for rabies.

Second, as soon as possible, scrub out the wound with soap and warm water. Authorities recommend at least 20 minutes of scrubbing to clean the wound properly.

Third, seek medical attention as soon as possible. The treatment will depend upon the circumstances involved. If the animal is killed, then the laboratory will be able to examine the brain of the animal for the rabies virus. If it is a domestic animal and it is captured, the animal should be quarantined and observed for ten days. If the animal dies or shows signs of rabies within that time, the brain is sent to a laboratory for examination. If the examination indicates the presence of rabies, the inoculation series should begin at once.

Rabies is known throughout most of the world. All of Latin America, most of Asia with the exception of Japan and Taiwan, and Africa are risk areas for rabies exposure. Australia, New Zealand, and most of the Pacific Islands are rabies-free.

Any traveler abroad who is bitten by an animal in a country that is known to have rabies should check with medical authorities immediately to receive post-exposure treatment. The only time that this would not be advisable is when the animal can be caught and is available for quarantine or laboratory examination. Two recent human cases in the United States arose from bites abroad by pet dogs that supposedly had been adequately immunized.

There are several controls that help stem the expansion of rabies virus. First, it is extremely important that domestic pets be vaccinated against rabies. Also, there should be strict control of feral or stray dogs and cats.

Education programs are helpful also. Strong leash laws help prevent pets from running loose where they can be bitten by rabid wildlife.

Another control measure should be tight restrictions on the movement of wild animals from one area into a new area. This is especially true in areas where rabies carriers are known to exist in fairly high numbers.

Control should also be placed upon the ownership of wild animals as pets. Wildlife, as the word "wild" implies, belongs in the free outdoors and not penned up in someone's house or apartment. However, anyone who does have a wild animal as a pet should be especially cautious of the signs of rabies. There is no rabies vaccine for pet wildlife. Vaccines that protect dogs and cats do not necessarily protect wild animals. In fact, vaccines that immunize domestic animals may even prolong or cover up existing rabies infections in wild animals. Some rabies vaccines developed and proved to protect domestic animals for as long as three years have actually been known to cause rabies in wild pets. Thus, a cute pet skunk can become a hazard after his trip to the vet.

Lightning

Each year, lightning kills over 125 people in the United States, and a large number of these

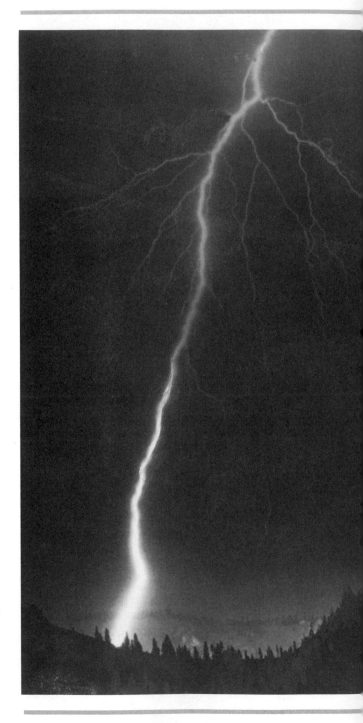

Lightning is a greater threat than most people realize. The effect of lightning on this tree, points up the inadvisability of camping under a tall tree in a lightning storm. (National Oceanic and Atmospheric Administration photos)

people are killed while fishing, camping, hunting, or participating in other outdoor activities.

The most lightning-prone places on earth are Kampala in Uganda and the island of Java. Authorities suggest that lightning strikes on Java as many as 300 days a year.

Running a close third in lightning hazard, and considered by many experts in the weather service to be the "lightning capital of the world," are the Gulf Coast states of the United States. Other areas of the United States with a higher-than-average incidence of lightning fatalities and property damage are along the Mississippi, Ohio, and Hudson rivers and their drainage basins. The Rocky Mountains, especially in Colorado, are also hard hit by lightning.

During thunderstorms, lightning kills people in many situations. But two situations have proven especially hazardous: (1) the bases of tall trees and (2) open water—situations that many outdoorsmen find themselves in.

What can you do to protect yourself from lightning?

The first rule is to get the latest weather forecast from the television or radio before setting out for the outdoors. If severe thunderstorms are forecast for the area you are going to, consider postponing your trip. Remember, the more severe the thunderstorm, the greater the intensity and frequency of lightning.

Develop a habit of keeping an eye on the weather. You don't need an official warning to see a thunderstorm coming. In most cases, especially on large lakes, you can see the towering clouds called thunderheads and occasional flashes of lightning at least a half hour in advance. This is usually ample time to find shelter.

When a thunderstorm threatens, all lightning experts agree, the most important thing you can do is to get inside a house or large building, or inside an all-metal vehicle.

Outdoorsmen frequently overlook the fact that their all-metal automobile is an excellent lightning shelter. This is so because the metal of the car conducts the lightning current around the people safely tucked inside. Many believe the rubber tires insulate the car from a lightning strike. Some people believe they are safe in the bed of a pickup or the seat of a tractor because of the tires. They are wrong. Lightning, after traveling through miles of insulating air, has no trouble flashing across the tires. A car struck by lightning will almost always be found with the occupants unhurt but the tires blown or aflame.

But what about situations when people outside really don't have time to reach a safe building or an automobile, as when hunting, hiking, canoeing, horseback riding, or camping in remote areas far from civilization?

Under these circumstances, say the experts:
• Do not stand underneath a natural lightning rod such as a large tree in an open area.
• Avoid allowing yourself to project above the surrounding landscape. Thus, avoid standing on a hilltop, in an open field, on a beach, or fishing from a boat.
• Get out of and away from open water. If you're swimming, lightning current from a nearby stroke can travel through the water to you.
• Get off and away from motorcycles, three-wheelers, bicycles, and other open metal vehicles or objects.
• Stay away from wire fences, clotheslines, metal pipes, rails, and other metallic paths that could carry lightning to you from a distance.
• Avoid standing in small isolated sheds or other small structures in open areas.
• In a forest, seek shelter in a low area under a thick growth of small trees. In open areas,

go to a low place such as a ravine or valley.
• If you're hopelessly isolated in a level field or prairie and you feel your hair stand on end—indicating that lightning is about to strike—drop to your knees and bend forward, putting your hands on your knees. In this position, if lightning strikes near you, the chances of its using your body as a conductor are minimized.
• Groups of persons in exposed situations should spread out so that if lightning strikes nearby, the smallest number will be affected.

Many people apparently "killed" by lightning can be revived if quick action is taken. When a group is affected, the apparently dead should be treated first. Those unconscious but breathing will probably recover spontaneously.

According to the American Red Cross, first aid should be given to those not breathing within four to six minutes or less to prevent irreversible brain damage. Mouth-to-mouth resuscitation should be administered. If the victim is not breathing and has no pulse, cardiopulmonary resuscitation is necessary.

Medical attention should also be given to victims who seem only temporarily stunned or otherwise unhurt, since there may be hidden effects.

Avoiding Falls

Falls while hunting, mountain climbing, cross-country skiing, wade fishing, and so on leave people stranded in a survival crisis more frequently than most people would believe. Searchers can also become fall victims. I was once involved in an extensive search for a youngster. Several of the searchers were looking along the edge of a high cliff when one lost his footing and fell to his death.

Hunting accident reports are showing more accidents caused by the use of portable and

Old tree stands should never be trusted, owing to wood rot. (Chris Fears photo)

permanent tree stands. Anytime you climb into an elevated tree stand, there's potential for falling. As an avid bowhunter and frequent user of portable commercial tree stands, I have taken a few falls over the years. As I assessed each fall, I found that they were my fault and not the manufacturer's. I simply didn't use the stand correctly, or I took foolish chances. You should take the time to learn to use your portable tree stand correctly, and take all safety precautions seriously. For many stands, an approved safety belt is essential.

It is not unusual for hunters to find old tree stands built into trees and left by former hunters in that area. Never trust a tree stand you find in the woods. Many are poorly constructed in the beginning, and others are made of wood that deteriorates rapidly. If you didn't construct the stand and don't know it to be safe, you had best avoid it.

Another hazard is abandoned wells at old homesites. Some are covered with rotted boards. Always be cautious of where you step around former homesites.

Also old mines and caves are often tempting. Few can resist the lure to look inside. The result can be a serious fall. Also, don't try to look over cliffs or bluffs, because edges may be ready to collapse.

14

ARCTIC SURVIVAL

The Arctic is a forbidding wasteland to many people. To others, it is home or a fascinating place to visit for the excellent hunting and fishing it offers. I am among those who find the Arctic fascinating and visit this part of the world as often as possible.

The Arctic is a vast wilderness for the most part. And because of Arctic weather extremes, planning is a must for backcountry travel. Cold, isolation, and seasonal extremes of daylight and darkness are dominant characteristics of the Arctic environment. These conditions prevail far south into subarctic areas. In fact, temperatures there range lower than in the true Arctic. To draw a hard and fast line between a northern woods outing and an Arctic survival experience is difficult. In Arctic country, survival extremes are part of everyday life.

Since much of the travel in the Arctic is

done by aircraft, much of the information in this chapter is based on the U.S. Air Force survival training program. Theirs is one of the best programs on Arctic survival.

The feeling of isolation is pronounced in the Arctic. Members of Arctic expeditions often grow depressed because of it. This vast land and accompanying sense of isolation quickly tell the visitor that chances of rescue are slim unless proper planning was done be-

---

The Arctic is home to many people, and others visit this fascinating place for its recreational opportunities. The equipment these cross-country skiers have would indicate that they are prepared for the weather extremes. Arctic travel requires extensive planning. (Coleman Company photo)

fore venturing away from settlements or a base camp.

During an Arctic emergency survival experience, life may swing between fear and discomfort on the one hand and self-assurance and relative comfort on the other. Self-assurance is often a matter of temperament, but it may be strengthened by knowledge and experience. Comfort and a sense of capability result from intelligence, ingenuity, good training, and common sense.

Seasonal extremes of daylight and darkness result from the tilt of the earth's axis. Arctic nights are long, even continuous in winter. Conversely, north of the Arctic Circle the sun is visible at midnight in summer.

Darkness presents a number of problems to the Arctic survivor. No heat is received directly from the sun in midwinter; thus the cold reaches extremes. Outside activities are curtailed of necessity, although the light from the moon, stars, and auroras shining on a light ground surface, is of some help. Confinement to cramped quarters adds boredom to discomfort, and depression often becomes the dominant mood as time drags on.

Just as the bitter cold is the dominant characteristic of the long arctic winter, rain and clouds of insects are dominant during the short summer. Heavy rains can keep the survival camp constantly wet. Often swarms of insects, biting and nonbiting, can make life miserable. They are sometimes so thick that one has to cover the mouth and nose to keep from inhaling them. Summer travel can be extremely tiring because of the boggy conditions.

Since most of the Arctic year is locked in cold, this chapter will deal with this aspect of survival for the most part.

The equipment shown, including a cold-weather tent, lantern, frame backpacks, snowshoes, and saw, demonstrates that a great deal of planning went into this Arctic camping trip. Even when winter camping in areas far south of the Arctic, arctic-like weather extremes can occur, requiring that you be prepared for the worst. (Coleman Company photo)

Clothing

Clothing is the first line of defense against the cold.

In order to prevent hypothermia and frostbite, one must understand his source of heat and the ways in which this valuable warmth is lost. Humans, like all other mammals, are homoiotherms, that is, warm blooded, which means we must maintain a stable body temperature. If we are away from external sources of heat, our only heat is that which is produced internally, primarily from the burning of food. Carbohydrates, which include sugars and starches, are our major source of this warmth. They are easily digested and provide fast energy for muscles, nerves, and the brain. The body does not store them for future use because they are burned within a short time and must be replenished often if we are to stay warm. Some of our sources of carbohydrates are raisins, chocolate, candy, sugar, and fruits.

In cold weather, warmth is lost in five ways: conduction, radiation, convection, evaporation, and respiration. While we have very little control over *respiration*, as the air we breath enters cold and leaves warm, we can have some control over the other four heat robbers.

Let's say that while on an Arctic hunt you are sitting on a rock outcropping. Your body is transferring heat from you to the rock you are sitting on. This heat loss is by *conduction*. If your clothing is damp from sweating, you are losing more heat by conduction; the cold, wet clothing touching your flesh conducts away your heat.

If you are not wearing a hat, your head is a major source of heat loss through *radiation*. The head is the only part of the body where blood vessels do not constrict to conserve heat, since they must supply the brain continuously to maintain its proper func-

tioning. A substantial amount of the body's total heat loss may be through an unprotected head.

If your clothing is made of poorly insulating materials, you will lose more body heat through *convection*. The horizontal motion of air creates a windchill factor that can move body surface warmth away and replace it with cold air faster than the body can rewarm it.

If you have done much walking, climbing, or other activity and are not dressed properly, chances are that your clothing is damp with sweat. The resultant heat loss is known as *evaporation*. While evaporation is the natural way the body cools itself, sweating is very dangerous during cold weather. If you're improperly dressed, your clothing absorbs the moisture, which moves through layers of clothing until it reaches a layer that is below dew-point temperature. Here it condenses and wets the layer. Then the moisture "wicks" back to the skin. Sweat-soaked clothing causes rapid chilling of the skin. There is a big difference between the healthy sweating of a hot day of fishing and the sweat of the Arctic, which can lead to chills, frostbite, and hypothermia.

The best way to dress for the Arctic outdoors is to wear clothing that retains your body heat, or *insulates*, while allowing body moisture to evaporate freely, or *ventilate*.

Insulation. Any material that resists the flow of heat is known as an insulating material. Dry air is an excellent insulator. Materials which hold pockets of motionless air are the best insulators. Woolen cloth contains thousands of tiny pockets within its fibers. These air pockets trap the air warmed by the body and hold it close to the skin. The principle of trapping air within the fibers of clothing provides the most efficient method of insulating the body against heat loss. Fur provides warmth in the same way; warm, still air is trapped in the hair and is kept close to the body.

Ventilation. To combat the effects of evaporation, proper cold-weather clothing is designed so that the neck, waist, hip, sleeve, and ankle fastenings can be opened or closed to provide ventilation. Fabrics are also available which "breathe," allowing moisture to escape. Cool air enters and insulates the body against heat loss, but moisture is wicked away from the skin rather than to it. Fishnet underwear has been worn for many years for this purpose. Scandinavian fishermen first used it after discovering that they could stay warm by covering themselves with their nets.

Arctic dress must begin with a layer such as fishnet underwear which can effectively trap insulating air while allowing moisture to escape. The next layer should be wool, with a third layer being an insulated parka.

The idea has been developed down through the years, and today's fishnet underwear, having ⅜-inch-square mesh, will effectively allow moisture to escape rather than soak your clothing.

A newer fabric which is being used for underwear, hat and glove liners, and various other types of clothing is called polypropylene. This synthetic long-chain polymer fiber will not absorb moisture and provides surprising warmth even under the coldest, dampest conditions.

Another means of achieving proper ventilation, as well as better circulation, is by wearing suspenders rather than a tight belt around the waist. Outdoorsmen in cold climates have been doing this for centuries. Wear suspenders to keep your pants loose around the waist.

Layering. Multiple layers of clothing which provide adequate insulation and ventilation will be more effective in keeping your body temperature at a constant level than one or two very thick layers, even if the single heavy garment is as thick as the combined layers. The secret lies in the layers of air trapped between the layers of clothing. These air layers, as well as the minute air pockets within the fibers, are warmed by the body heat.

An added benefit of layering is that you can add or remove layers as you warm or cool off, keeping you from dampening the layers from sweat caused by wearing too much clothing for the activity.

The layers of clothing are most effective if they are of different design. For instance, begin with underwear that provides for proper ventilation, keeping moisture away from the body, such as fishnet or polypropylene.

Following should be layers of insulating materials such as wool, as it insulates better than any other fabric, even when wet, and even fur.

Layering is a must in cold climates when you are active. This cross-country skier is wearing snowsuit, sweaters, vest, scarf, wool cap, gloves, and polypropylene underwear so that layers can be peeled off as his body heats and then replaced as his body cools. The ability to peel layers prevents excessive dampening of clothing. (Coleman Company photo)

In subzero weather, the outer coat should be of skin or fur. Otherwise, the outer garments may be of wool or water-repellent material filled with Thinsulate, Quallofil, down, Dacron II, or PolarGuard. Each of these fillers has its strengths and weaknesses. You should buy a well-known brand-name coat or parka intended for the type of terrain and weather conditions you will be wearing it in. This is important in selecting the filler material. For instance, down collapses when wet and loses its insulating value.

The best way to find out what insulating materials to wear in the Arctic is to check with local experts in the area you will be going into to see what insulation works best for that area.

One of the most important items of clothing is a head and neck covering. At 5°F as much as 75 percent of your body heat loss can be from your head. Since it is a principal point of heat loss, a proper covering for the head can help keep other parts of the body warm. The mountain men had a saying— "When your feet are cold, put on your hat." There's a lot of merit in that. A wool balaclava or ski mask which covers the entire head, with a fur hood over it, is best for the Arctic.

The best way to keep your hands warm is to wear wool mittens with outer shells of skin and fur. Be sure your mittens have a string attached to keep them from getting lost.

The part of us that seems to get the coldest the fastest is the feet. This is not without good reason. Our body is programmed to automatically regulate its warmth requirements for survival. In cold conditions, your body adjusts heat production and circulation to maintain life, with the brain and central nervous system receiving highest priority. Circulation to the extremities is curtailed if necessary to keep those vital areas warm.

SPECIAL ARCTIC CLOTHING

Mittens, socks, and head protection are considered by many Arctic explorers to be the secret of body heat conservation. It has been said that 75 percent of the body's heat that is lost is lost through an unprotected head. (Jim Elder photo)

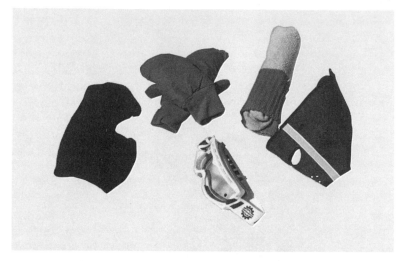

The white Mickey Mouse boot, named for the bulbous toes resembling those of the Walt Disney character, has a layer of felt sealed between layers of rubber. The air valve on the outer calf can be opened and closed to equalize air pressure in nonpressurized aircraft. The Mickey Mouse boot is conservatively rated to −40° F at a standstill, but perspiration buildup from walking can leave your feet cold and clammy after you stop. Also, a leak in the rubber inside or out can allow moisture to saturate the felt and greatly reduce insulation. You can check for leaks by immersing each boot in water and watching for bubbles. The Sorel shoe pac, shown at right with its felt-sock liner removed, can be bought large enough for extreme cold to allow insertion of an extra felt sole pad and the wearing of extra wool socks, making the shoe pacs as effective as the Mickey Mouse boots in most respects. An advantage of shoe pacs is that their liners can be removed and dried or rotated with a second pair. Both boots shown are available by mail from Okun Brothers Shoes. (Neil Soderstrom photo)

Since the feet are farthest from the body core, they are the first to feel the reduced circulation. This is why a hat can help keep your feet warm.

Start by wearing two pairs of wool socks. Since the feet are notable sweat producers, wool is required, because it still insulates when wet. If wool next to your skin bothers you, wear a thin pair of silk, nylon, or polypropylene inside the wool. In selecting boots, be sure to choose a pair that not only insulate well, but keep your feet dry. Some choices which work well include the white Mickey Mouse boots made for the U.S. Army, L. L. Bean's Maine Hunting Shoe, and a similar boot made by Sorel, all of which have felt liners. When determining the size boots to buy, keep in mind that you will be wearing two pairs of socks.

When you put on your socks and boots, be sure to eliminate all wrinkles. Wrinkles slow down the blood circulation to the feet and toes, causing them to get cold. Also, for the same reason, be careful not to lace your boots too tightly.

Use and care of clothing. The acrostic COLDER can help you remember how to use and care for your clothing:

Keep it	Clean
Avoid	Overheating
Wear	Loosely layered
Keep it	Dry
	Examine often
	Repair at once

Keeping clothing clean is always important from a standpoint of sanitation and comfort. In winter, in addition to these considerations, it is necessary for maximum warmth. If clothes are dirty, much of their insulation property is destroyed; the air pockets in the clothes are crushed or filled up and the heat can escape from the body more readily. Underwear requires the closest attention because it will be the dirtiest.

In cold climates, overheating should be avoided whenever possible to prevent perspiration. When indoors, a minimum of clothing should be worn and the shelter should not be overheated. Outdoors, if the temperature rises suddenly or if you are involved in vigorous activity, you should adjust your clothing accordingly. Assuming you are dressed properly in layers, remove layers as necessary or ventilate by partially opening your parka or jacket. In cold temperatures, it is better to be slightly chilly than too warm.

Loosely layered clothing is also important. Clothing and footgear that are too tight restrict blood circulation and invite cold injury. Be sure that boots, parkas and other clothing are bought large enough to loosely accommodate the layers beneath. Layering loses its effect when there is no air space between the layers.

Under winter conditions, moisture will soak into clothing from two directions—inside and outside. Dry snow and frost that collect on the outer clothing will be melted by the heat radiated by the body. While water-repellent outer clothing will shed most of the water collected from melting snow and frost, the surest way to keep dry is to prevent snow from collecting. Before entering a heated shelter, snow should be whisked or shaken from parka, pants, and boots. It should not be rubbed off because this will drive snow into the fabric.

Whenever possible, footgear should be removed and the frost cleaned from the boots. Your leather boots should be kept water-repellent with a wax-type surface compound such as Sno-Seal. (Greases and oils soak into the leather and reduce its natural insulating properties.) When Sno-Seal, composed of beeswax and silicone, is applied to leather, it is rubbed on with a cloth, then heated with a hair dryer to melt the wax. It soaks in like grease or oil, but unlike these lubricants, it seals the pores, creating dead air space in leather. This affords insulation. Sno-Seal helps prevent drying or cracking.

In spite of all precautions, there will be times when you cannot help getting wet. Then the drying of clothing may become a major problem. On the move, damp mittens and socks should be hung on the pack; even in below-freezing temperatures, wind and sun will help dry this clothing. Damp socks or mittens may be placed under the parka, close to the body; body heat will dry them out. In camp, damp clothing may be hung inside the tent, near the top. It may even be necessary to dry each item piece by piece by holding it before an open fire. Clothing and shoes should not be dried too close to a fire; they might burn or scorch. Leather articles, especially boots, must be dried slowly.

Be sure to examine your clothing often. Watch for tears, worn spots, ripped seams, or zippers that don't work. If the examination reveals any damage, repair it at once. Take good care of your clothing and it will take good care of you.

Keep in mind that wind increases the loss of body heat and the danger of frostbite. A moderate temperature combined with a high wind can be more chilling than a lower temperature on a calm day. When traveling by snowmobile, remember that snowmobile speeds increase the chill factor. Dress to give proper protection.

Wear as few clothes in a sleeping bag as the situation permits. Remove your underwear at night and air it or let it get cold and beat the frost out with a stick. To sleep in your underwear in a sleeping bag is to have damp underwear to wear the next day.

On any Arctic trip, always take sunglasses or goggles to wear even on an overcast day.

Snow blindness is a dangerous reality. During an emergency, snow goggles may be made from strips of bark, wood, leather, or other material in which narrow slits can be cut to see through. As an alternative on sunny days, lampblacking on nose and cheeks helps cut down glare from the sun.

Equipment

Always prepare yourself for a possible stranding or disaster before leaving a settlement or base camp, even if you are going to be gone for only a short time. I learned this the hard way on my first trip into the Arctic. I got into a plane one afternoon for a short ride to look at a future campsite. At that site, we were weathered in for two days, me without any emergency gear. Never again have I left camp without my pack containing emergency gear. This gear has come in handy numerous times.

Whenever leaving to go into the Arctic backcountry, carry the following in a pack:

1. Survival kit
2. Waterproof matches and fire starter
3. Knife strong enough to cut firewood
4. Lightweight liquid-fueled stove (for regions where wood is scarce)
5. Sleeping bag
6. Emergency rations for five days
7. Flashlight with fresh batteries
8. Map of the area and compass
9. Clothing to match the weather

The University of Alaska Cooperative Extension Service has a list of emergency rations that have been tested. The following food and energy pack would be easy to carry and provides nourishment for one man for five days. Put each item in a small plastic bag and seal. Put all of this into a small metal can that can double as a cooking pot. Seal with another plastic bag and tape. When you're cold and tired, nothing tastes better

than a cup of hot bouillon, coffee, or tea.
- 2 or 3 cans of Sego, Nutriment, Metrecal, or similar product for liquid and energy
- 30 sugar cubes, wrapped
- 25 crackers
- 10 packets of salt, restaurant-style
- 3 tea bags
- 12 pieces rock candy
- 5 sticks gum
- 10 bouillon cubes

- 20 protein wafers (if available)
- 1 small jar instant coffee
- 1 small packet powdered cream

File a Trip Plan

Whenever you depart from camp or a settlement, leave the following information with a responsible person who would be in a po-

Anyone venturing into the unforgiving Arctic should carry basic elements for survival: snowshoes, extra wool socks and gloves, high-energy food, flashlight, map and compass, signal kit, knife, cook kit, backpack stove, and matches in waterproof container. Except for snowshoes, the items should be carried in a daypack.

sition to start search-and-rescue procedures should you be overdue:

1. Name
2. Purpose of trip
3. Departure date and time
4. Mode of transportation
5. Route
6. Destination
7. Estimated time of arrival
8. If round trip, expected time of return
9. Any alternative destinations

Survival Camps

During the winter, you will need shelter against the cold. Don't live in an aircraft—it will be too cold. Try to improvise a better-insulated shelter outdoors.

Look for cabins and shelter houses. They are likely to be located along bigger streams, at river junctions, and along blazed trails in thick, tall timber leeward of hills. Some may even have emergency food stocks.

Camp in timber, if possible, to be near fuel. If you can't find timber, choose a spot protected from wind and drifting snow. Don't camp at the bases of slopes or cliffs where snow may drift heavily or come down in avalanches.

In wooded country, make a tree-pit shelter if snow is deep enough. Enlarge the natural pit around a tree trunk and roof it with any available covering.

In country without timber, make a simple snow cave or burrow by digging into the side of a snowdrift and lining the hole with grass,

If possible, camp in timber to be near fuel, but near openings for signal purposes.

In timberless country, a snow cave may be made into a survival shelter. But snow-cave construction expends a tremendous amount of energy. Front openings should be tunnel-like and, if possible cross wind.

brush, or tarpaulin. Snow caves must be ventilated.

Keep the front openings of all shelters crosswind. A windbreak of snow or ice blocks set close to the shelter is helpful.

In making shelters, remember that snow is a good insulator. Caves in the snow are usually rather satisfactory.

With little between you and the ice, your sleeping bag and preferably also an insulating undergarment can be pretty valuable. Keep the bag dry.

To keep frost from your breath from wetting the sleeping bag, improvise a frost cloth from a piece of clothing, a towel, or some parachute fabric. Wrap this around your head in such a way that the breath is exhaled through a sort of tunnel opening in the fabric, which goes to the outside of the bag. A piece of fabric dries easier than the sleeping bag. If you should get cold during the night, exercise by fluttering your feet up and down, fluff out the down in your sleeping bag by beating against the inside of it with your hands, try eating something, or make yourself a hot drink. Remember, a sleeping bag doesn't warm you. It simply retards the escape of heat generated by your body. Thus, food and hot drinks are needed to help you continue generating heat.

In a snow cave, getting up is a slightly slower process than going to bed. Take your time. Begin dressing inside the bag.

In the cramped quarters of any small emergency shelter, pots of food or drink can easily be kicked over accidentally. In a survival situation, this may seriously affect your chances of coming through safely. The cooking area, even if it is for only a Sterno stove, should be located out of the way, possibly in a cooking alcove.

Generally, it is safer to fill gasoline stoves outdoors or in a separate room in a snow shelter. A period of good weather should be chosen for this task. At this time, any needed maintenance work may be done. Proper maintenance will make it less likely that the stove will burn out or clog up while you are using it.

Standard practice in snow shelters is to relieve yourself indoors whenever possible. This practice conserves body heat. If the snowdrift is sufficiently large to dig connecting snow caves, one may be used as a toilet room. If not, tin cans may be used for urinals, which may be emptied in a remote corner opposite the side from which snow is taken for cooking. Try to have your bowel movement just before leaving the shelter in the morning and remove the fecal matter with the trash.

Discipline should be exercised so that "there is a place for everything and everything is in its place." A tent or snow cave can be buried so deep by drifting snow that you may have difficulty finding it, if it isn't marked with a long pole. Therefore, you can't expect to leave small objects lying out on the snow and find them again. A little organization should minimize the chances of losing equipment.

In the Arctic in winter you have the problem of warm storage, not cold storage. A game carcass frozen rock-hard at $-50°F$ is extremely hard to cut unless you have a saw. The alternative is either to cut it into small pieces while it is warm or to insulate it from freezing. A caribou carcass may be kept from freezing for several days by placing the skinned carcass between an envelope of two skins, which will seal quickly by freezing along the edges. Then bury this fur bundle in the snow during the night.

A small stove such as this white-gas Coleman is efficient for melting ice and snow. Whenever possible, melt ice rather than snow for water because it contains more water per equal volume and can be melted down faster.

Thawed canned rations may be kept from freezing overnight by stowing them in the foot of your sleeping bag.

Water. In the winter, ice and snow provide water, but fuel is needed to melt them. Never waste fuel melting snow or ice when drinkable water from other sources is available. In the summer, there is plenty of water in lakes, streams, and ponds. Surface water on the tundra may have a brownish color, but it is drinkable.

Whenever possible, melt ice for water rather than snow—you get more water for the volume with less heat and time. If you melt snow by heating, put in a little snow at a time and compress it, or the pot will burn. If water is available, put a little in the bottom of the pot and add snow gradually.

If the sun is shining, you can melt snow on a dark tarpaulin, signal panel, flat rock, or any surface that will absorb the sun's heat.

Arrange the surface so that meltwater will drain into a hollow or container.

Use old sea ice for drinking water; it is bluish, has rounded corners when broken, and is free from salt. New sea ice is gray, milky, hard, and salty; don't drink it. Water in pools at the edges of ice floes is probably too salty to drink. Icebergs are good sources of fresh water and should be used if they can be approached safely.

If fuel is plentiful, try to drink at least 2 quarts of hot beverage or water daily instead of cold water or snow.

Be sure to study Chapter 8 for information on how to purify your drinking water.

Food. In the Arctic winter, food is of added importance for survival. The colder the weather, the more rapidly heat is dissipated. Our source of body heat is the food we eat. Food is needed to compensate for the accelerated heat loss in the Arctic winter.

Food sources, such as the caribou in the photo, are available in limited areas of the Arctic. However, there are vast areas where such food does not exist. And during the winter, hunting can be extremely difficult even in areas with lots of game. Therefore, the arctic traveler should take at least a few days' stock of food with him.

In this book, I suggest that you always carry extra food with you in the Arctic, because living off the land in this region is especially difficult. In no part of the Arctic are native animals and plants a reliable source of food. Chances for survival are best along the coastlines, because seafood is more common there.

Depending on the time of year and the place, your chances for obtaining animal food vary considerably. Arctic shores are normally scraped clean of all animals and plants by winter ice. Inland animals are migratory. Watch for tracks, trails, or droppings.

Be sure to read Chapter 11 in this book on edible wild animals.

Signaling. Tramp out ground-to-air signals in snow. Fill them in with boughs, sod, moss, or fluorescent dye powder. In brush country, cut conspicuous patterns in vegetation. In tundra, dig trenches and turn sod upside down at the side of the trench to widen the signal and cast a shadow.

Keep snow and frost off aircraft surfaces to make a sharp contrast with the surroundings. Build your fire on a platform so that it will not sink into snow. A standing spruce tree near the timberline burns readily, even when green. Build a "birdnest" of quickly flammable material in the branches to ensure a quick start.

For more details on these and other signals, read Chapter 5.

Glacier Travel

On several occasions I have had to use glaciers as a route of travel over mountains, and I was shocked at the potential dangers that exist in this environment. One year I was hunting in Alaska and learned of an experienced outfitter who was hunting near us and landed his ski-equipped plane on a glacier. The plane started sliding backward when it came to a stop. Both the plane and the outfitter disappeared into a crevasse. Glaciers are killers, but if travel is necessary, they may offer travel routes.

Here is what the U.S. Air Force Survival School suggests you know about glaciers.

To cope with the problems that can arise in using glaciers as avenues of travel, it is important that you understand something of the nature and composition of glaciers.

A "valley glacier" is essentially a river of ice. The valley glacier flows at a rate of speed that depends largely on its mass and the slope of its bed.

A glacier consists of two parts: the lower glacier, which has an ice surface that is devoid of snow during the summer; and the upper glacier, where the ice is covered, even in summer, with layers of accumulated snow that grade down into glacier ice.

To these two integral parts of a glacier may be added two others which, although not a part of the glacier proper, generally are adjacent to it and are similar in composition. These adjacent features, the ice and snow slopes, are immobile, since they are anchored to underlying rock slopes. A large crevasse separates such slopes from the glacier proper and defines the boundary between moving and anchored ice.

Ice is plastic near the surface, but not enough to prevent cracking as the ice moves forward over irregularities in its bed. Fractures in a glacier surface, called crevasses, vary in width and depth from only a few inches to many feet.

Crevasses form at right angles to the direction of greatest tension, and since within a limited area tension usually is in the same direction, crevasses in any given area tend to be roughly parallel to one another.

Generally, crevasses develop across a slope. Therefore, when traveling up the middle of a glacier, you usually encounter only trans-

PARTS OF A GLACIER

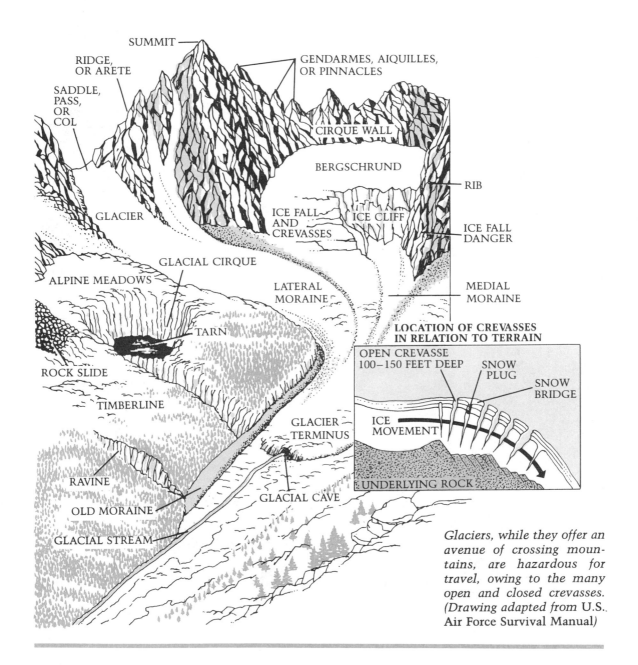

Glaciers, while they offer an avenue of crossing mountains, are hazardous for travel, owing to the many open and closed crevasses. (Drawing adapted from U.S. Air Force Survival Manual)

A glacier can be as beautiful as it can be treacherous.

verse crevasses (crossing at right angles to the main direction of the glacier).

Near the margins or edges of a glacier, the ice moves more slowly than it does in midstream. This speed differential causes the formation of crevasses which trend diagonally upstream away from the margins or sides.

While crevasses are almost certain to be encountered along the margins of a glacier and in areas where a steepening in gradient occurs, the gentlest slopes may also contain crevasses.

As a glacier moves forward, debris from the valley slopes on either side is deposited on its surface. Shrinkage of the glacier from subsequent melting causes this debris to be deposited along the receding margins of the glacier. Such ridges are called "lateral moraines."

Where two glaciers join and flow as a single river of ice, the debris on the adjoining lateral margins of the glaciers also unites and, flowing with the major ice stream, forms a "medial moraine."

Where the snout of the glacier has pushed forward as far as it can go—that is, to the point at which the rate of melting equals the speed of advance of the ice mass—a "terminal moraine" is usually found. This moraine may be formed of debris pushed forward by the advancing snout or it may be formed by a combination of this and other processes.

Lateral and medial moraines may provide excellent avenues of travel. When the glacier is heavily crevassed, moraines may be the only practicable routes.

Ease of progress along moraines depends upon the stability of the debris that composes them. If the material consists of small rocks, pebbles, and earth, the moraine usually is loose and unstable and the crust may break away at each footstep. If larger blocks compose the moraine, they have probably settled into a compact mass and progress may be easy.

In moraine travel, it is best either to proceed along the crest or, in the case of a lateral moraine, to follow the trough which separates it from the mountainside. Since the slopes of moraines are usually unstable, there is great risk of spraining an ankle on them.

Medial moraines usually are less pronounced than lateral moraines, because a large part of their material is transported within the ice. Travel on them usually is easy, but do not rely upon them as a route for long distance, since they may disappear beneath the glacier's surface.

Only rarely is it necessary for a party traveling along or across moraines to be roped together.

On those portions of a glacier where melting occurs, runoff water cuts deep channels in the ice surface and forms surface streams. Many such channels exceed ten feet in depth and width. They usually have smooth sides, and their banks are usually undercut. Many of these streams terminate at the margins of the glacier, where in summer they contribute to the torrent that constantly flows between the ice and the lateral moraine. You must exercise the greatest caution in crossing a glacial surface stream, since the bed and undercut banks are usually of hard, smooth ice which offers no secure footing.

Northern glaciers may be vast in size, and the heat of the summer sun can release enormous amounts of water from them.

Glacial ice is extremely unpredictable. An ice field may look innocent enough from above, but countless subglacial streams and water reservoirs may be under its smooth surface. These reservoirs are either draining or are temporarily blocked or dammed. Mile-long lakes may lie under the upper snowfields, waiting only for a slight movement in the glacier to liberate them and to send their

This crevasse is typical of those found along the margins of a glacier.

Glacier streams such as this one near Juneau, Alaska, fluctuate frequently and are often dangerous to cross. Lacking debris for support, it can be wise to use a walking staff.

millions of gallons of water flooding into the valleys below.

Because of variations in the amounts of water released by the sun's heat, all glacial rivers fluctuate in water level. The peak of the floodwater usually occurs in the afternoon as a result of the noonday heat of the sun on the ice. For some time after the peak has passed, rivers which drain glaciers may be unfordable or even unnavigable; however, by midnight or the following morning, the water may recede so that fording is both safe and easy.

When following a glacial river that is broken up into many shifting channels, choose routes next to the bank rather than taking a chance on getting caught between channels.

Glacial crossing demands special knowledge and techniques, such as the use of a lifeline and poles for locating crevasses. There are, however, numerous places in the north where mountain ranges can be negotiated on foot in a single day by following glaciers.

Be especially careful on glaciers. Watch out for crevasses that may be covered by snow. Travel in groups of not fewer than three men, roped together at intervals of 30 to 40 feet. Probe before every step.

Always cross a snow-bridged crevasse at a right angle to its course. Find the strongest part of the bridge by poking with a pole or ice ax. When crossing a bridged crevasse, distribute your weight by crawling or by wearing snowshoes or skis.

Snowmobile Travel

Snowmobiles have become a common means of travel in the Arctic as well as other snow-covered regions of North America.

Snowmobile manufacturers work overtime to build reliable sleds that take you into the backcountry and bring you home again without a hitch. Unfortunately, not everyone takes proper care of his snowmobile, operates it wisely, or uses good judgment on the trail. Such people not only get themselves into trouble, but also can involve others in an emergency. Not all emergencies are caused by negligence, however.

Always travel with another snowmobiler. Actually, a group of four is better than two. If someone is hurt, one person can stay with him and the other two can go for help.

Keep your snowmobile in good repair and make recommended maintenance checks before and throughout the season. Check your fuel supply before you leave and fill the tank, if necessary.

Take an extra set of spark plugs, an extra drive belt, basic tools, and a tow rope. If you have a sled with oil injection, carry an extra can of oil in the storage box.

Be sure that in studying your trail map, you orient yourself in all directions.

On the trail, drive defensively to avoid unnecessary risks. Observe posted warnings and trail markers. Avoid avalanche areas, thin ice, deep powdery snow, and excessively steep slopes. Don't snowmobile in areas or conditions beyond your skill.

Know the round-trip fuel range of your sled and be conservative. Turn around and head back *before* half your fuel is gone. Don't stay far away too late and risk a breakdown or accident in unfamiliar territory at night.

Don't overtire yourself; keep a reserve of energy.

In watching for landmarks or rock formations to help guide you back to the main trail or lodge, use permanent features rather than snow or ice formations that could melt or fall away.

Never travel alone when snowmobiling in the arctic. There is safety in numbers.

Always take extra parts and tools as a part of your snowmobile survival kit. (Jim Elder photo)

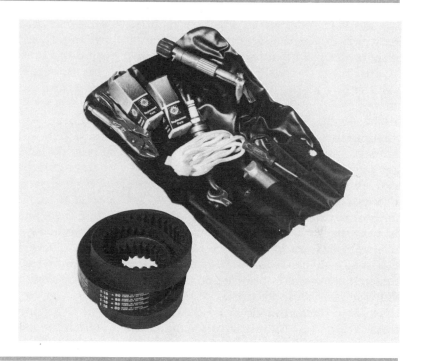

Be sure everyone in your group agrees on hand signals before leaving. The leader should look over his shoulder periodically and stop for anyone who signals for a rest.

In extremely cold weather, stop frequently to check for frost-nip, a mild form of frostbite that can be treated on the trail. Frost-nip shows up as a sudden blanching or whiteness of the skin, usually on the nose, cheeks, fingers, or chin. Cover the affected area with a warm hand and apply firm, steady warming pressure. Don't rub the area, because rubbing can cause tissue damage.

If a snowmobile has broken down, fix it, tow it, or ride with someone else to get help. If you are alone, determine whether or not you can make the repair yourself and estimate how long it should take. If you can make the repair and start for home before dark, do so. If not, use the remaining daylight

hours to prepare for an overnight survival experience. Only you can judge whether to stay overnight or try to walk out.

Do not leave your snowmobile unless absolutely necessary. Rescuers will be looking for a snowmobile.

The fuel in your snowmobile tank is an aid to consider when building a fire. However, be careful how you transport the fuel from the tank to the firewood. Don't slop it around. Lower a handkerchief, shop cloth, or rag into the tank, perhaps tied to one end of a tow rope. Place the fuel-soaked cloth under the kindling to provide a controlled fire starter. Be sure to recap the fuel tank to prevent flashback to the tank. Keep gasoline off your skin, because evaporation lowers surface temperatures and can lead to frostbite. Wipe away any fuel that spills on your gloves or snowmobile suit to prevent your clothing from catching fire. Light the fire from the upwind side. Remember, gasoline vapor is heavier than air. And, of course, do not build a fire too near your snowmobile's fuel tank.

Understand Windchill

In the Arctic, as well as other areas, windchill can be a killer. For this reason, all backcountry travelers should understand what windchill is and its effect on the individual.

Windchill can rob your body of vital heat at a rapid rate. Windchill can best be described as the combined effect of wind and temperature. It is expressed as an equivalent chill temperature as it relates to danger to exposed flesh. For instance, if it is 10°F outside and the wind is blowing 35 mph, then the windchill temperature is 35° below zero to exposed flesh, and the exposed area may freeze within one minute. A windchill chart gives you a quick way of knowing what the windchill temperature is outside.

On still days, windchill can become crit-ical when snowmobiling, skiing, riding in the back of a truck or open vehicle, or motorcycling. The outside temperature and the wind you create by these activities result in an equivalent chill temperature that can be dangerous.

What to Do

If you do have an emergency in the Arctic, here is what the Alaska Division of Public Health suggests you do.

1. If you have crash-landed, stay away from the plane until the engines have cooled and spilled gas has evaporated.

2. Check injuries. Give first aid. Make the injured comfortable. Be careful moving victims with injured backs and fractures.

3. Get out of the wind and rain. Throw up a temporary shelter. If you need a fire, start it at once. In cold weather, make hot drinks.

4. If you have an emergency radio, get it operating on schedule. But you should also

Windchill can be increased by activities which take you out into the open where the wind can rob you of body heat. Activities that involve motion can greatly increase the windchill effect, as illustrated in table on next page.

		WINDCHILL																			
WIND SPEED		**TEMPERATURE (°F)**																			
CALM	*CALM*	*40*	*35*	*30*	*25*	*20*	*15*	*10*	*5*	*0*	*−5*	*−10*	*−15*	*−20*	*−25*	*−30*	*−35*	*−40*	*−45*	*−50*	*−55*	*−60*
KNOTS	MPH	EQUIVALENT CHILL TEMPERATURE																			
3–6	5	35	30	25	20	15	10	5	0	−5	−10	−15	−20	−25	−30	−35	−40	−45	−50	−55	−65	−70
7–10	10	30	20	15	10	5	0	−10	−15	−20	−25	−35	−40	−45	−50	−60	−65	−70	−75	−80	−90	−95
11–15	15	25	15	10	0	−5	−10	−20	−25	−30	−40	−45	−50	−60	−65	−70	−80	−85	−90	−100	−105	−110
16–19	20	20	10	5	0	−10	−15	−25	−30	−35	−45	−50	−60	−65	−75	−80	−85	−95	−100	−110	−115	−120
20–23	25	15	10	0	−5	−15	−20	−30	−35	−45	−50	−60	−65	−75	−80	−90	−95	−105	−110	−120	−125	−135
24–28	30	10	5	0	−10	−20	−25	−30	−40	−50	−55	−65	−70	−80	−85	−95	−100	−110	−115	−125	−130	−140
29–32	35	10	5	−5	−10	−20	−30	−35	−40	−50	−60	−65	−75	−80	−90	−100	−105	−115	−120	−130	−135	−145
33–36	40	10	0	−5	−15	−20	−30	−35	−45	−55	−60	−70	−75	−85	−95	−100	−110	−115	−125	−130	−140	−150
WINDS ABOVE 40 MPH HAVE LITTLE ADDITIONAL EFFECT.		LITTLE DANGER					INCREASING DANGER (Flesh may freeze within 1 minute)						GREAT DANGER (Flesh may freeze within 30 seconds)									
		DANGER OF FREEZING EXPOSED FLESH FOR PROPERLY CLOTHED PERSONS																			

keep other signaling equipment handy.

5. Determine your location by the best means available. Include this information in radio messages.

6. Now relax. Take stock of everything around you and in your possession.

7. After you have organized your thinking, organize the camp. Put one man in charge of all food and equipment. Prepare shelter. Collect all possible fuel, including oil from the downed aircraft or other vehicle. In cold weather, drain oil before it congeals. Look for a water supply.

8. Prepare signals so that you will be recognized from the air.

9. Stay with the airplane or vehicle unless you know where to go. If you travel, leave a note with your planned route. Stick to your plan so rescuers can locate you.

10. *Keep calm.* As soon as it is known you are overdue, search-and-rescue organizations will begin looking for you.

15
DESERT SURVIVAL

Each year the deserts of North America give us many true survival stories. Take, for instance, the story of the vacationing Phillips couple from Iowa.

Marshall and Doris Phillips had driven to Phoenix, Arizona, to visit relatives and enjoy a summer vacation in a part of the country they had never seen. When they departed Phoenix, they decided to take a side road into the desert to take some pictures. At mid-morning they selected a dirt road that left the main highway and led across the desert.

Undecided as to how far to go, they continued driving their station wagon farther out into the desert. Two hours later, they decided to turn around because the road was becoming increasingly rutted. As Marshall backed the station wagon off the road, they felt a hard jolt and heard metal striking rock. He

had backed into a rocky wash, smashing the oil pan and leaving the rear wheels suspended. Suddenly they were in the hot desert with no way to travel.

Since they had told no one of their side trip, Marshall knew he must walk back to the highway for help. Before departing, he made sure that Doris had all the windows in the vehicle down and dug two cans of soft drink out of their luggage. Taking one of the cans of drink, he started walking. The walking was rough and unbearably hot. Several

---

The desert of the American Southwest, such as that looking out from under this Joshua tree, can be unforgiving to those unprepared.

times, he was unsure of which way he should go.

When he finally staggered out onto the paved highway, it was nearing midnight and he was practically delirious. It was almost an hour more before a truck stopped to give him a ride. Arriving at a nearby town, he was unable to give accurate information of where he had left his wife.

It was 10 A.M. the next day when searchers finally found his station wagon. Doris was not there. A ground and air search spread out from that point. At 1:30 P.M., a ground search team found Doris unconscious and in serious condition. Having had no survival training, she had panicked and left the car, running across the desert. It was only luck that she was found. An innocent side trip into the desert had turned into a nightmare.

The southwestern corner of the United States is primarily a desert environment and requires some special cautions and skills. The

Most desert travelers mistakenly assume that heat and dryness are the only dangers in a desert. Little do they know that deserts, such as this one, are extremely rugged and hazardous to travel in, even in colder seasons, especially in survival predicaments. (Robert Godfrey/Outward Bound USA photo)

area is characterized generally by brilliant sunshine, a wide temperature range, sparse vegetation, a scarcity of water, a high rate of evaporation, and low annual rainfall—in other words, a desert. Some areas are flat and sandy, some mountainous and rocky, and others may be salt marsh or dunes. As opposed to the summer conditions of extreme heat and severely parched character that are normally thought of, the rest of the year usually enjoys moderate temperatures and, especially in the spring, a surprising amount of life and color. A large variety of animal and plant life can be found there, although it is generally small in size or different than the rest of the United States due to evolutionary adaptation to the environment.

Rules for Desert Survival

By following a few basic rules, you can assure yourself of a safer trip into the desert.

1. Never go into the desert without first informing someone of your destination, your route, and when you will return. *Stick to your plan.*

2. Carry at least one gallon of water per person per day of your trip. (Plastic gallon jugs are handy and portable.)

3. Keep an eye on the sky. Flash floods may occur any time "thunderheads" are in sight, even though rain may not fall where you are.

4. If you have water, drink it. Do not ration it.

5. If water is limited, keep your mouth shut. Do not talk, do not eat, do not smoke, do not drink alcohol, do not take salt.

6. Do not sit or lie directly on the ground, which may be 30°F or more hotter than the air.

7. A roadway is a sign of civilization. If you find a road, stay on it. For there's a good chance that help will happen along.

Desert Travel

Travel in the desert can be an interesting and enjoyable experience to those who are adequately prepared and educated to its possible hazards. To the foolhardy, though, it can be a fatal or near fatal nightmare.

Walking. When in the desert, even travelers in good physical condition should walk slowly and rest about 10 minutes per hour. At this rate, a man in good physical condition can initially cover about 12 to 18 miles per day. After he becomes fatigued or if he lacks sufficient water or food, this distance becomes less.

Walking at night may be a good idea, because it is cooler then, and if lack of water is a problem, you will dehydrate less. You can navigate by the stars. However, the disadvantages are that you may not be able to see the ground well enough and may stumble or overlook water and food sources and signs of habitation. It is always best to travel in the desert in early morning or late evening, spending midday in whatever shade may be available. Also, the position of the sun early and late in the day will give you a better sense of direction.

Pick the easiest and safest way to walk. Go around obstacles instead of over them. Rather than going up or down steep slopes, zigzag to prevent undue exertion. Go around gullies and canyons instead of through them. Watch for snakes because the desert is home to many rattlesnakes. When walking in sand, lean well forward, keeping your knees bent. When walking with companions, adjust the rate to the slowest man.

During breaks, try to sit down in the shade and prop your feet up high, remove your shoes and change socks, or straighten the ones you are wearing. If the ground is too hot to sit on, no shade is available, and you cannot raise your feet, do not remove your shoes because you may not be able to get them back onto swollen feet. However, you can unlace boots or shoes, adjust socks, and re-lace.

Aircraft. Be sure to file a flight plan before flying across a desert. When flying in this type country, be sure that you have a survival kit, extra water, and clothing suitable for ground conditions. Land before you are completely out of fuel because dead-stick landings in desert terrain are dangerous. Also, if you land before being out of fuel you will have gasoline with which to start signal fires. Fires should be built well away from the plane because gusty desert winds could endanger your survival camp. It is usually best to remain at the plane instead of trying to walk

out. You can survive longer without water in the shade of the plane's wing than you can by exhausting yourself walking. Walk only if you are sure you can reach help easily and are absolutely sure that you have enough water to make it.

Driving. On little-used desert roads, driving can be hazardous. But if a few simple suggestions are followed, desert driving can be done safely.

Have a map of the area you are going into. Obtain current information from the highway patrol, game warden, or forest ranger as to the conditions of the roads in that area.

Drive slowly. If in doubt about the terrain, stop and check it out first on foot. Do not attempt to drive on questionable roads without first checking the footing and clearances.

The desert sand can render even a four-wheel drive useless unless caution and driving skill are exercised.

Items that should be in any vehicle traveling in a desert include extra gasoline, tool kit with spare parts, air compressor, extra water, survival kit, shovel, axe, pick, rope, and tow chain.

High centers or rocks may rupture the oil pan. Washes may cause the powered wheels to become suspended above the ground.

In sand, the wheels may sink, resulting in a high center and loss of traction. Avoid spinning wheels to gain motion because this will only cause the wheels to dig in further. Instead, apply power very slowly.

Under emergency conditions when driving in sand, traction can be increased by partially deflating tires. Be careful not to remove so much air that the tire may slip on the rim. Then, drive slowly. Start, stop, and turn grad-

ually because sudden motions cause wheels to dig in.

Be sure to take these tools and equipment if you intend to drive off the main roads: one or more shovels, a pick, a tow chain or cable, at least 50 feet of strong nylon tow rope, portable compressor, ax, full water containers, at least two full gas cans, extra fan belts, and your regular spare parts and auto tools. Be sure that your car is in sound condition and that your fuel tank is full, and that you have a filled clean radiator, a filled battery, and new fan belts. If you become stuck or your car breaks down, raise the hood and *stay with the car.* The raised hood is an indication to other desert travelers that you need help. If you are positive of the route to help and must leave your vehicle, leave a note for rescuers saying when you left and the direction you were taking.

Desert Survival Shelter

One of the first rules in desert survival is that once you realize you are lost or stranded, you should find shelter from the direct rays of the sun as fast as you can.

Shade and shadows. If nothing else is available, try to find some natural shade. The shadows of a large rock, sand dune, rock cliff, pole, or brush can give you some relief. Don't lie down; squat or stand instead. It may be uncomfortable, but it will minimize your body contact with hot ground. An airplane wing can also provide shade.

Space blanket. If you have a space blanket in your survival kit, then you have an excellent source of shade since this space-age gold·or silver-colored blanket reflects 90 percent of the heat. With some string and sticks, build a high lean-to using the blanket. At night, use the blanket as a sleeping bag if you get cold. You would do well to carry several of these small space blankets in your vehicle, plane, or trail bike survival kit. Be sure you have at least one per person.

Vehicle shelter. One of the best shelters you can utilize, if you are stranded, is your vehicle. First of all, don't get into the vehicle because it will be an oven. What you want is a double layer of insulation between the sun and you, and your car or truck can provide this. Here's how to construct a shelter.

1. Open all of the vehicle doors and windows for ventilation. Disconnect interior car lights which come on when doors are open. This will conserve the battery for other uses.

2. Using a shovel, board, or hubcap, scoop out the dirt from under the vehicle. Dig away the top 15 inches or so.

3. Be sure to dig under the side or end of the vehicle where the shade is. Avoid the motor, muffler, or tailpipe because they will still be hot.

4. Take your time and avoid getting too hot.

5. Once you have the trench dug, crawl in and enjoy the shade. The ground temperature down 15 inches deep should not be more than the mid-80s.

6. Be sure you have your ground-to-air signals out, and stay alert for rescue aircraft. If you decide to work on your vehicle or enlarge your shelter, wait until the cool of the evening.

Since the roof of the vehicle takes much of the sun's heat and the floor of the vehicle takes the secondary heat, the space under the vehicle can be one of the best in the desert.

Parachute shelter. The U.S. Air Force teaches students to construct a desert shelter from parachute material. This shelter could be made from two tarps or other cloth material. The principle is similar to the vehicle shelter in that it depends upon two layers of insulation between the sun and you. Here is how it is built:

1. Dig a pit in the dirt approximately 24 inches deep and wide and long enough for you to crawl into.

2. Using rocks as the four corner posts, stretch a piece of parachute or other material (about 5 feet × 8 feet) over the pit some 3 feet above ground level.

3. Build up the rocks 2 more feet and stretch another piece of material. Use brush

Owing to the ovenlike effect inside a vehicle in the desert, if you are stranded, dig a shelter trench under the end of the vehicle opposite the engine. (Chris Fears photo)

to keep the two pieces of material separated.

4. If available, four strong sticks or poles could be used in the place of rocks.

5. Crawl into the shady pit.

If the ground is too hard to dig, you can build up a platform of rocks and dirt 24 inches above the ground and erect the same type double insulation as above. The point is to dig below the hot surface or to get above it.

Whatever shelter you decide upon, stay with it and await rescue. This is especially true if you are with a vehicle of some type. Desert search-and-rescue units report that many desert deaths occur within two hours after the victim left his shelter.

Edible Desert Plants

The main desert edibles are the fruits of cacti and legumes. All cactus fruits are safe to eat. In the summer the fleshy and thin-walled ripe fruits can be singed over fire to remove spines. Then they can be peeled and eaten. Old cactus fruits contain seeds which can be pounded between two stones into a powder and eaten, or mixed with water into a gruel called *pinole*. New, young pads of the prickly pear can be singed, peeled, and boiled.

The legumes are the bean-bearing plants. The main ones are the honey and screwbean mesquites, the palo verde, the tesota (ironwood) and the catclaw acacia. All are small trees with fernlike leaves. The palo verde is recognized by its open growth, greenish bark, and feathery leaves. Ironwood has rough, dense growth and will grow into a large tree under favorable conditions. Catclaw is a small grayish tree with numerous short, curved thorns. All have bean pods which can be boiled and eaten when green and tender. Dry, mature beans, like cactus seeds, are too hard to chew and must be cracked to be digested.

The night-blooming cereus looks like a cluster of weather-beaten sticks and is found close to trees and bushes; it has a large, edible, beetlike root. Slice the root and fry it. This root has a very high moisture content and may be used as a water source.

Also consult earlier chapters in this book on edible wild animals and plants.

DESERT FOOD PLANTS

These drawings are reproduced from Charles Sprague Sargent's Manual of the Trees of North America.

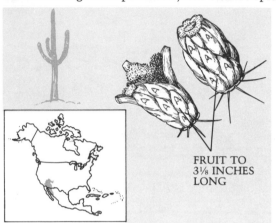

FRUIT TO
3⅛ INCHES
LONG

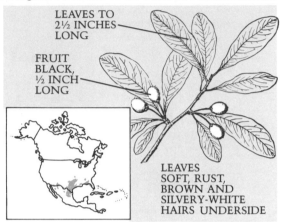

LEAVES TO
2½ INCHES
LONG

FRUIT
BLACK,
½ INCH
LONG

LEAVES
SOFT, RUST,
BROWN AND
SILVERY-WHITE
HAIRS UNDERSIDE

Left: *The saguaro (pronounced* sa-WAH-ro), *also called giant cactus, is the largest native cactus. It sometimes grows 50 feet tall. Its fruits offer sweet food and drink when consumed fresh and can also be dried. Birds, as sources of eggs and meat, often nest in holes near the top.* **Right:** *The ironwood, or gum bumelia, is a small tree or a shrub. It has shiny-black berrylike fruits that are edible, although they can cause dizziness and stomach upset if eaten in large doses.*

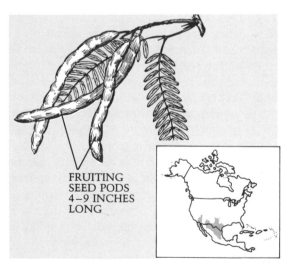

FRUITING
SEED PODS
4–9 INCHES
LONG

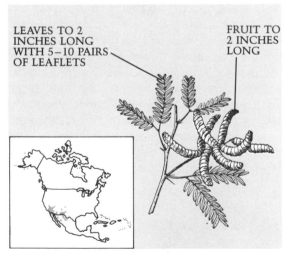

LEAVES TO 2
INCHES LONG
WITH 5–10 PAIRS
OF LEAFLETS

FRUIT TO
2 INCHES
LONG

Left: *The honey mesquite is a low tree. Indians have long made meal from its pods. And as the plant's name implies, the flowers are important sources of nectar for bees.* **Right:** *The screwbean mesquite is a small, thorny tree. Its coiled pods are tender, sweet, and nutritious, whether raw or cooked. Indians have made meal, cakes, and syrup from the pods.*

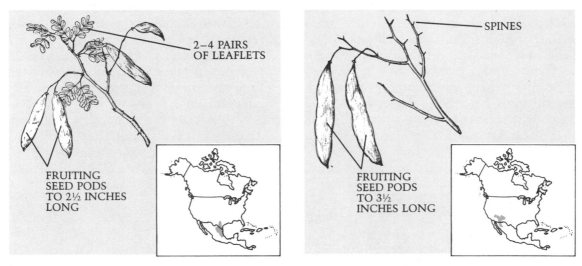

2–4 PAIRS
OF LEAFLETS

FRUITING
SEED PODS
TO 2½ INCHES
LONG

SPINES

FRUITING
SEED PODS
TO 3½
INCHES LONG

In Spanish, palo verde *means "tree green or pole green." Indians have cooked the young pods and seeds like lima beans and have ground the seeds into meal.* **Left:** *Border palo verde has zigzaggy branches.* **Right:** *Blue palo verde is named for its blue-green branches and leaves.*

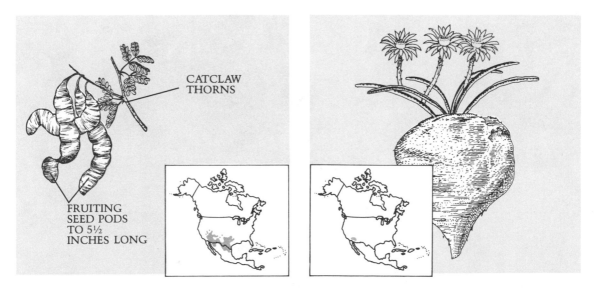

CATCLAW
THORNS

FRUITING
SEED PODS
TO 5½
INCHES LONG

Left: *The catclaw acacia is a shrub or tree to 20 feet high that often grows in thickets. Its catclaw-like spines can tear clothes and flesh. From the pods, Indians ground a meal, called* pinole. **Right:** *Night-blooming cereus has an enormous edible beetlike root. (Lloyd Birmingham drawing)*

Water for Desert Survival

During the warm months in the desert, you need about a gallon of water a day. If you walk at night, you may walk about 20 miles with that gallon, but if you walk in the daytime heat, you will get less than 10 miles with the gallon.

Be sure to keep your clothing on, including shirt and hat. In the desert you should wear light-colored clothing to reflect some of the heat of the sun. Clothing helps ration your sweat by slowing the evaporation rate and prolonging the cooling effect. It also keeps out the hot desert air. Stay in the shade during the day. Sit on something 12 or more inches off the ground, if possible. If you must travel, do so slowly and steadily.

Rationing water at high temperatures is only inviting trouble. Small amounts of water will not prevent dehydration, and loss of efficiency and collapse always follow dehydration. It is the water in the body that maintains life, not the water in a canteen.

Rain comes seldom in a desert, but when it does, travel can be more dangerous than usual. After a rain, a dry canyon or, as here, a gentle stream can become a murderous, roaring torrent in a matter of minutes. (Outward Bound USA photo)

Keep your mouth shut and breathe through your nose to reduce water loss and drying of mucous membranes. Avoid talking for the same reason. If possible, cover your lips with grease or oil.

Alcohol will accelerate dehydration. Consider alcohol as food and not as water, since additional water is required to assimilate the alcohol. For the same reason, food intake should be kept to a minimum if sufficient water is not available.

Carrying water. When planning your trip, give your water supply extra thought. Carry enough water, at least one gallon per person per day, in unbreakable, lightweight containers. The best containers for desert use are gallon or half-gallon plastic containers similar to those containing bleach or milk. Carrying several of these, rather than one large one, assures a water supply if one container is punctured.

Finding water in the desert. If you are near water, it is best to remain there and prepare signals for your rescuers. If no water is immediately available, consider the following:

Flocks of birds will circle over water holes. Listen for their chirping in the morning and evening, and you may be able to locate their watering hole. Quail fly toward water in the late afternoon and away in the morning. Doves flock toward watering holes morning and evening. Also, look for the diggings and browsings of wild animals because animals tend to feed near water.

Water may be found at the base of rock cliffs for some time after a rain. It may be found in the waste rock at the base of cliffs or in the gravel-wash from mountain valleys that get regular seasonal rains. Limestone and lava have more and larger springs than any other type rocks. Springs of cold water are safest. Limestone caverns often have springs,

Commonly called Spanish bayonet or datil, this is Yucca baccata. *Its fruiting stalk may grow up to 5 feet tall. The flowers, stalks, and leaves provide moisture, and the reddish-brown fleshy fruit shown can be eaten raw, roasted, or boiled. The seeds can be separated and roasted for eating. There are no poisonous lookalikes. (U.S. Forest Service photo)*

but do not venture deeper than sight of the entrance because you may get lost. Look for springs along walls of valleys that cross the lava flow. Springs may be found along valley floors or down along their sloping sides. See if there is seepage where the dry canyon cuts through a layer of porous sandstone.

Toxic water is always a possibility in mineral springs, but there are some signs you can

Left: Commonly called soapweed, this is Yucca glauca. *In spring the white-flowering stalk may grow over 3 feet tall. The unripe fruits that develop are bitter but become palatable after baking. There are no poisonous lookalikes. (U.S. Forest Service photo)* **Right:** *This is* Yucca whipplei *in flower in California. (U.S. Forest Service photo)*

look for that may help you know not to drink. Observe whether or not insects are thriving. If not, the spring may be toxic. Also, skeletal remains of animals may be in the area, and if so, may indicate contamination.

Dry stream beds may have water just below the surface. Look at the lowest point on the outside of a bend in the stream channel. Dig until you hit wet sand. Water will seep out of the sand into the hole.

Damp surface sand marks a place to dig a shallow well. Dig at the lowest point and go down 3 to 6 feet. If the sand stays wet/damp, keep digging. Look at hillsides to see where the grass is lush and green. Dig at the base of the green zone and wait for water to seep into the hole.

Water is more abundant and easier to find in loose sediment than in rocks. Look for a wet spot on the surface of a clay bluff or at the foot of the bluff and try digging it out.

Look for the "indicator" plants that grow only where there is water: cottonwoods, sycamores, willows, hackberry, cattails, and arrowhead. You may have to dig to find this water. Also keep on the lookout for windmills and water tanks built by ranchers. If cactus fruits are ripe, eat a lot of them to

Left: This is fairly typical of several barrel cactus species. As the long sharp spines warn, attempting access to the moist inner parts with only a pocketknife can be more work than the moisture would be worth. *Right:* This agave is about 2 feet tall, but its moist flower stalks (not shown) can grow over 10 feet high. (Thomas S. Elias photos)

help prevent dehydration.

The immature flower stalks of agave, yucca, and sotol contain moisture, or if no flower stalks are present, the main stalks may be split open and the pith chewed to fight dehydration. The barrel cactus contains a high amount of moisture. But pressing out water is myth because the mucilaginous, acrid juice thickens rapidly. To obtain moisture, chew on the pith, but do not swallow it. Carry chunks of the pith with you to suck on to alleviate thirst. Young plants 6 to 18 inches in height and with a soft green color will have the highest moisture content. The root of the night-blooming cereus is also high in moisture.

A pebble carried in the mouth will alleviate the sensation of thirst, but is not a substitute for water and will not aid in keeping your body temperature normal.

Avoid smoking because it encourages oral breathing, exposing large areas of mucous membrane to drying influences, thereby increasing the rate of dehydration and need for water. Salt will do you definite harm unless plenty of water is available. So, don't worry about obtaining enough salt, but you should try to keep up your water intake.

16
BIG WATER SURVIVAL

We frequently read of people who are boating in big water and suddenly get into big trouble. Let's look at a few instances.

It was supposed to have been a two-hour, 23-mile pleasure cruise on a 20-foot cabin cruiser for 21 residents of the sparsely populated, South Pacific island nation of Kiribati, formerly known as the Gilbert Islands. They left Abaiang Island the morning of March 26 for Tarawa, the capital island of Kiribati.

Two months and 1,300 miles later, nine were dead and the other 12 had survived only by drinking rainwater and eating fish—including a shark that they had caught with their bare hands. The islanders had drifted helplessly in the Pacific Ocean for 60 days until they were spotted by the helicopter of a San Diego based tuna boat about 700 miles southeast of Guam.

"A good term to describe the boat would be 'overcrowded,'" said a Coast Guard spokesman on Guam. Most of the people on board had been headed to Tarawa for a vacation. The rest were bringing food to a market there.

At one point the ship's only engine failed and the boat began drifting to the west. As prevailing currents carried the boat through an area of few landfalls, the islanders lived on the goods that were being taken to the market. The supply of fresh water lasted about four days, the food about two weeks. Once the initial supplies ran out, those on

Each year many recreational boaters find themselves in survival situations. Radio contact with the Coast Guard will result in prompt rescue action, such as this removal of an accident victim by means of an aircraft hoist.

the ship survived by catching rainwater and fish with their bare hands, said a Coast Guard spokesman. Their last fish—the shark—was caught two weeks before their rescue.

"Each rainfall would provide enough water for about three or four days," according to the Coast Guard spokesman. Officials said the bodies of the dead were buried at sea one by one.

When the helicopter for the U.S. tuna vessel *Tifaimona* spotted the cabin cruiser, the survivors were using several bedsheets as a makeshift sail.

In another instance, a short fishing trip resulted in a near tragedy.

On a quiet day of fishing, Allen Zovar and Susan Shepherd were blown out to sea to spend four days in a rubber raft surrounded by sharks, overwhelmed by waves, and without food or water.

"It's the happiest Thanksgiving of our lives," Zovar said when they were picked up after rowing to an island. "We just kept our faith up, kept our willpower up, and prayed a lot."

Both were reported in good condition and were not hospitalized. The couple had been fishing ¼ mile off the coast on a Sunday when their raft was blown out to sea. "The Santa Ana wind came up in about one minute and we ripped loose from the kelp," said Zovar. "We yelled and screamed but nobody heard us. I had a pair of fins and I jumped overboard and kicked while my girlfriend rowed, but it did nothing."

Their first encounter with sharks came shortly after they were blown into the Santa Barbara Channel between the southern California coast and offshore islands. "We had two or three fish floating next to us on a stringer, and the sharks came up and grabbed them," said Zovar. "We cut the stringer loose and just prayed.

"The third night out, two or three sharks started circling and sliding underneath the raft. We could feel them bumping the bottom of the boat. They did that for about an hour. What we did was remain silent and keep our feet off the floor so the sharks wouldn't sense there was anything alive. We figured if we were silent they might go away, and that's what they did."

The winds blew them an estimated 40 miles offshore and kicked up large waves, Zovar said, adding that they stayed awake all the night, just bailing and fighting the waves."

On Tuesday morning the couple saw Anacapa Island about 6 miles away, but were blown away from the island. On Wednesday, Zovar said, "We woke up in front of Santa Cruz Island and we tried again. We hadn't seen any rescue craft and we were being dehydrated pretty rapidly, so we started out rowing Wednesday morning." They reached the island at sundown and landed in a cove. Zovar said, "In the morning we woke up and saw a mast and immediately waved everything we could."

He and Miss Shepherd were taken aboard a boat anchored in the cove.

These are but two examples of how fast people can get into trouble with boats. While researching this chapter, I spent a good deal of time talking to a U.S. Coast Guard boating education officer who opened my eyes to how deadly boating can be to those who don't take proper precautions.

In one year, 1980, there were 1,360 boating fatalities in the United States. The annual average of boating deaths is about 1,200. According to the Coast Guard, 85 percent of these deaths are from drowning. A vast majority of these victims didn't wear personal flotation devices.

Why do so many people die in boating accidents? The reasons are many. Many accidents occur when boats break down and those on board are trying to repair them. Another major reason is drinking alcohol. Fatigue causes accidents, as does dehydration and carelessness with the weather.

Keep Your Boat in Good Working Order

According to the Coast Guard, one of your primary responsibilities is to keep your boat in good working order. Many boating accidents occur during breakdowns, and they are usually minor breakdowns. Keep your boat in good working order and know how to make minor repairs. If you don't have the skills necessary to do minor repairs, learn them.

A few basic hand tools and spare parts are a must for every boat. This list will give you some idea of what to have, but many more tools and parts, especially tools of special nature for your engine, should be carried aboard.

Hand tools. Insulated adjustable tools are best for the average small job. Some of them are:
- Adjustable wrench
- Slip-joint pliers
- Pipe wrench
- Vise-grip pliers
- Screwdrivers (various sizes)
- Box-end wrench set
- Hammer
- Plug wrench

Spare parts. This is a list of basic spare parts:
- Points for distributor
- Condenser
- Coil
- Spark plugs
- Fuel pump
- Fuel filter for diesel engines
- Shear pin for propeller

Following manufacturer's recommendations and keeping your boat and engine in

Always carry tools with you when boating so that you can make repairs necessary to return. (Evinrude photo)

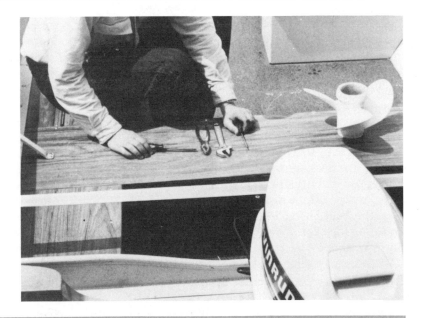

good repair will help to make your boating trouble-free. To find out if your boat meets the highest standards of safety and has all the legally required equipment, ask a qualified member of the Coast Guard Auxiliary for a Courtesy Motorboat Examination.

This examination is free and there is no obligation. If your boat passes, it will receive the CME "Seal of Safety" decal, which indicates that at the time of the examination your boat met the safety-related equipment requirements of the state in which the examination was conducted, and it not only met but exceeded federal regulations. If it does not pass, *no* report is made to any law enforcement authority. The examiner will advise you of deficiencies so that you can correct them.

A toll-free telephone number has been established by the Coast Guard in the Boating Technical Division of the Office of Boating, Public and Consumer Affairs, to assist boaters with technical questions. That number is (800)368-5647. It is intended primarily for the transmission of information and inquiries which are not usually handled by local Coast Guard district offices.

Get a Marine Communications System

If you plan to operate a boat in large lakes or in the ocean, then you should consider getting a marine communications system. In selecting radiotelephone equipment for a boat, many things must be considered. How will the boat be used—for business, for pleasure, or for both? Will it be operated on inland waters or lakes? Will it be operated in U.S. coastal waters? If so, how far offshore? Regardless of the area, what coastal stations exist, or are planned, and how far apart are they? What frequencies do they monitor? Lots

of questions, but better to consider them now than later when your life may be in jeopardy.

Types of marine communications systems. The boating public has three communications systems, or bands, from which to choose: the 2–3 megahertz (MHz) radio-telephone band, the Very High Frequency–Frequency Modulated (VHF-FM) maritime mobile band, and citizens band (CB). CB is *not* strictly a marine communications band and may be operated from ships, boats, cars, trucks, and fixed land stations.

In making your decision you should know that the 2–3 MHz and the VHF-FM bands have been officially designated and internationally recognized as marine communications bands. For this reason, the Coast Guard and maritime rescue organizations throughout the world continuously monitor the distress frequencies of these bands.

The Coast Guard also monitors the emergency channel for citizens band radio, but it is on a "not-to-interfere" basis, with its primary responsibility for monitoring distress frequencies on the recognized marine bands. In other words, if the Coast Guard receives a distress call over the 2–3 MHz or VHF-FM bands, it may cease monitoring CB in order to devote its entire efforts to respond to the emergency. However, if the Coast Guard receives a distress call over the CB emergency channel, it will respond immediately, but it will not cease monitoring the distress frequencies of the designated marine communications bands.

Marine weather forecasts are available from the National Weather Service on VHF-FM. Also, in some areas the Coast Guard will broadcast weather information on both 2–3 MHz and VHF-FM. You should contact the National Weather Service, your marina, or your boating equipment store for information on which channel serves the area you will be boating in.

How to use a marine radiotelephone. With the number of radio-equipped boats continuing to increase, it is important that each boater observe a few basic procedures when using the radio. These procedures are:

1. Prior to sailing, make sure your equipment is operating properly. Obtain a radio check. To do this you must call a specific station on a working frequency and, after establishing contact, ask, "How do you hear me?" Radio checks on 2182 kHz are prohibited by law, and on VHF-FM channel 16 are strongly discouraged. The Coast Guard will not respond to a radio check on CB channel 9.

2. Be courteous. Always listen to see if the channel is clear before transmitting. Try not to cut into someone else's conversation.

3. When transmitting, always identify your boat by name and call sign.

4. Distress frequencies can be used to establish contact with another station, but after establishing contact, you must shift to a working frequency unless you are in distress or have knowledge of a distress.

5. Complete all conversations as soon as practical. Don't tie up a frequency with chit-chat.

6. Federal Communications Commission regulations require that boats equipped with 2–3 MHz and VHF-FM radiotelephone maintain a listening watch on 2182 kHz or channel 16, respectively, if the radio is turned on.

Distress communications procedures.
    1. Make sure your radio is turned on.
    2. Turn to the distress frequency: channel 16 for VHF-FM, 2182 KHz for 2 MHz radiotelephone, or channel 9 for citizens band.

3. Speak slowly and clearly.
4. Press microphone button and transmit, "Mayday, Mayday, Mayday."
5. Identify yourself by saying, "This is (your boat's name), (your boat's name), (your boat's name), (your call sign)."
6. Give your position. Give as much information on your location as possible—nearby landmarks, longitude and latitude, etc.
7. Tell what is wrong.
8. Tell what kind of assistance you need.
9. Give the number of people who are aboard your boat and, if any are injured, their condition.
10. Give the estimated seaworthiness of your boat.
11. Give a description of your boat—such as length, type, color, number of masts.
12. Tell which channel or frequency you will be listening to.
13. End your message with: "This is (your boat's name and call sign). Over."
14. Wait for a response. If no answer, repeat your call. If still no answer, try another channel or frequency.

Survival Gear to Have on Board

The Coast Guard has regulations concerning the minimum amount and type of equipment a boat must have. Each boat owner should comply with these regulations. All boats operating at sea, on large lakes and rivers, or in big swamps should have the following survival gear:

1. A Type I personal flotation device for each person on board
2. A Type IV personal flotation device for rescue work
3. Fire extinguisher as per Coast Guard requirement
4. Horn that is audible at least ½ mile
5. Boat survival kit (see Chapter 4)

*Always have a fire extinguisher on board.
(Mercury Motors photo)*

6. First aid kit
7. Spare engine
8. Protective clothing for each person (rain and sun)
9. At least 1 gallon of drinking water per person
10. A three-day supply of food per person
11. Day and night signal devices
12. Survival suits if your boat is in cold waters. A survival suit is a bulky suit designed to protect shipwreck victims from hypothermia. It is *not* a wet suit. The suits are often supplied on boats, ships, and other watercraft that frequent frigid waters.
13. A 10-by-17-foot orange emergency tarp

Signaling

Chapter 5 in this book deals with signaling in the wilderness, but since signaling is a vital survival tool in big water, I will address boat signaling in detail in this chapter.

Coast Guard requirement for visual distress signals. Boats less than 16 feet in length are required to carry only visual distress signals suitable for use at night when operating after sunset. Boats 16 feet or more in length must carry on board the required number of signals suitable for night use, or signals suitable for both day and night use. In addition, boats for hire carrying six or fewer passengers must also carry the required number of signals on board.

Devices suitable for day use, night use, or both must be carried depending upon when the boat is to be used. Select the device that will best meet your needs, read the directions as to their use, storage, and safety, and promptly store them on board your vessel in a readily accessible place. Each signal must be in a serviceable condition and have a current service life, so indicated by a date marked on the signal.

Principles of visual signaling. Even with precautions, knowledgeable boat operators can encounter problems beyond their control that require the use of visual signals. The following is intended to provide you with a better understanding of the principles involved with visual signaling so that you can be properly prepared and react accordingly should you ever find yourself in a signaling situation.

Basically, there are four factors that must be considered when selecting visual signals. These are:

- Alert/locate
- Distance
- Opportunities to signal
- Use

The principle involved in alert/locate is simple—attract attention and then provide a homing signal for the responding party.

Remember, nothing can happen until someone's attention is attracted. The most effective alert signals are meteors and parachute flares, since they move, go into the air, are more spectacular, and cover more sighting area.

Once attention is secured, locate signals help pinpoint the specific location of the distress. Hand-held flares, smoke signals, SOS lights, and flags fall into this category.

In equipping your boat with signals, the following should be considered:

1. Alerter signals.

2. Meteor flares. Because of their relatively short burn times, these should be fired in a sequence of two. Fire the first and, when it extinguishes, immediately fire the second. This permits the potential rescuers to confirm the sighting and/or direction. (The Canadian law requires tandem meteor firing for this reason.)

3. Parachute flares. These do not need to be fired in tandem, since they have adequate burn times—25 to 30 seconds—to allow sighting and/or direction confirmation.

4. Locator signals. These are intended as homing devices. The key here is distance. The surface-to-surface sighting range is approximately 3 to 5 miles, depending on boat elevation. If a rescuer is 5 miles away and is doing 20 miles per hour, he will need 15 minutes to reach you. As a result, you should have at least 12 minutes of locator time available.

5. Distance. In structuring a signal package for your boat, distance is an important consideration. Because of the earth's curvature, sighting distances are limited. The type of signal selected will also depend on your boating practices. Basically, if your boat is within 10 miles of shore, meteors would be adequate for an alert signal. At 10 miles, a meteor flare would appear at approximately 125

BOATING SIGNALS

Description	Accepted use	Required
Red aerial flare	Day/night	3
Red hand-held flare	Day/night	3
Distress flag	Day only	1
Orange smoke (either hand-held or floating)	Day only	3
Distress signal light S.O.S.	Night only	1
Red parachute flares	Day/night	3

MARINE SIGNAL KITS

This deluxe U.S. Coast Guard-approved Olin Alert/ Locate Kit includes a 25mm launcher, a 12-gauge insert for the launcher barrel, two 25mm meteors, three 12- gauge meteors, and three hand-held red flares. The hand-held flares last 2 minutes to allow searchers to pinpoint the distress area. Both the meteors and flares are suitable for day or night use. The kit is provided with two storage canisters, joined by a bracket for wall mounting, which will float even if fully loaded. One of the canisters is empty to permit storage of extra signal devices.

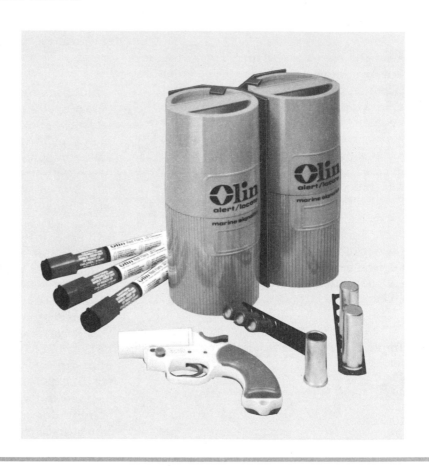

feet over the surface. The 10 miles allows a margin of sighting safety.

Beyond 10 miles, one should consider the 1,000-foot parachute flare. A 250-foot meteor at the maximum distance of 21 miles would appear as a brief surface signal. At 41 miles the signal will appear as a brief signal. At 20 miles it would appear as a 500-foot signal. Weather can also affect sighting visibility and must be kept in mind. The brighter the day, the more difficult the signal is to see; the darker the day or night, the easier it is to see.

DISTANCES SOME SIGNALS MAY BE SEEN

Method	Distance
Signal mirror	20–100 miles
Dye marker on water	8,000 feet
Smoke that is constant	7 miles
Night flare	30 miles
Tracer ammunition at night	3 miles
Strobe light	2–20 miles

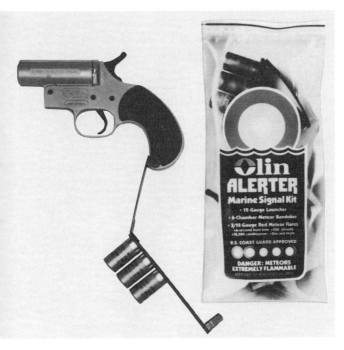

The U.S. Coast Guard-approved Olin Alerter Marine Signal Kit consists of a 12-gauge launcher gun, bandolier that holds up to six meteor flares, and three 12-gauge red meteor flares, all contained in a waterproof bag. Each meteor burns at 10,000 candlepower for 6 seconds at an altitude of 250 feet and can be used both day and night.

For the boater who prefers nonpyrotechnic signals, this Olin S.O.S. Light/Flag Kit includes a 2500 candlepower S.O.S. light for night use and a 3 × 3-foot orange flag designed to Coast Guard requirements for day use. The light automatically flashes the S.O.S. sequence for up to 12 hours in a 360-degree arc as well as in a straight beam.

6. Opportunities. Due to random travel patterns and distance on water, a signal could go unnoticed; therefore, it is important to have maximum signals available for use when a signaling opportunity presents itself. This allows you the best chance of attracting the attention and securing assistance of someone over the horizon or on shore.

7. Use. If you are in a signaling situation:
• Conserve your signals until you are reasonably sure of being detected.
• Wait until you see or hear a vessel or aircraft before using "one-time" signals or locate signals.
• Stay with the boat if it is safe to do so. A boat is easier to spot than a swimmer.
• Familiarize yourself with your signals prior to having to use them. Time is important in an emergency and shouldn't have to be spent reading instructions.

8. Emergency position indicating radio beacon. Boat owners who go out into the ocean should consider the Emergency Position Indicating Radio Beacon (EPIRB), made by ACR Electronics, Inc. This device is a self-contained transmitter in a sealed cylinder about the size of a thermos bottle. It transmits a coded "help" signal over VHF channels 15 and 16. This device can be homed in on by rescuers.

SIGHTING DISTANCES FOR SIGNALS USE OVER WATER

Signal height in feet	Max. sighting distance in all directions (miles)	Sighting area (square miles)
6	3	28
250	21	1,385
1,000	41	5,275

There are three classes of EPIRB, including one which starts transmitting as soon as it makes contact with water. These devices float and are a great signal device for offshore boats.

Watch the Weather

Nothing, save his boat and motor, is more important to the pleasure boater than the weather. Be it big or small, power or sail, a boat is at the mercy of Mother Nature. It's a wise skipper indeed who heeds weather signs.

Pay attention to weather forecasts. A network of marine weather stations across the country broadcast continuous marine weather reports over VHF radio bands.

But if there isn't such a facility within your radio range, or if you don't have the proper receiver, a standard battery-operated AM or FM portable radio will let you listen to the commercial broadcast station's weather reports.

Many harbors, particularly those on large bodies of water, fly weather advisory flags. Heed them. They're up there to tell about approaching weather.

Smart skippers also take along a barometer. A sudden rise or fall of the indicator predicts unsettled weather ahead and dictates the need for extra caution.

Beware of sudden calms. They often signal that a major weather change is coming—quickly.

Watch clouds. Buildups of massive cumulonimbus clouds indicate heavy weather ahead. Squall lines move quickly, so don't stray far from a safe harbor or anchorage.

Be in Shape for Boating

Contrary to what many people think, boating can cause fatigue. Get plenty of rest before a day of boating. Do not plan a schedule that is too strenuous. Keep alcoholic beverages to a minimum and drink plenty of water, not colas, tea, or coffee, as they are diuretics and can speed up dehydration. Remember that dehydration is a common boating condition which can lead to poor reflexes, poor judgment, and trouble. Be in good shape to go boating or postpone the trip.

Have Enough Fuel

The Coast Guard states that many boaters get into trouble simply because they run out of fuel. Be sure your tanks are full before leaving the dock. Don't take a trip so long that you can't reach your destination on a third of a tank. Use a third going out and a third returning, and have a third in reserve for emergencies.

Safe Boating Tips

Here are the Coast Guard's safe boating tips:

1. Know the various distress signals. On boats over 16 feet long, you are required to carry signals that are recognizable both day and night.

2. Gasoline vapors are explosive. Close all doors, hatches, and ports while fueling. Extinguish galley fires and pilot lights. Smoking is strictly prohibited. Keep the filling nozzle in contact with the tank to prevent sparks. Portable tanks should be fueled out of the boat. Do not use gasoline stoves, heaters, or lights on board.

3. Do not operate electronic gear, such as radios, while fueling.

4. Know your fuel capacity.

5. After fueling, ventilate all compartments and check the machinery and fuel tank spaces for fumes before starting the motor. Remember, the electrical ignition system could provide the spark to an accumulation of gasoline vapors. Keep fuel lines tight and bilges clean.

6. Always have children and adult non-swimmers wear personal flotation devices. Make sure everyone on board knows how to put them on.

7. Keep an alert lookout for obstructions. Serious accidents have resulted from failure to do so.

8. Do not operate in the vicinity of a diver's flag—a red flag with a white diagonal slash which marks the approximate center of the diver's activities.

9. Watch your wake. You are responsible for any damage and injury caused by it.

10. Know and obey the "Rules of the Road."

11. If you capsize and the boat continues to float, stay with it.

12. Good housekeeping is even more important afloat than ashore. Cleanliness di-minishes the possibility of fire and tripping hazards.

13. Have an anchor and sufficient line to assure a good hold in a blow. Anchor by the bow of the boat, not the stern.

14. Carry a secondary means of propulsion on small boats—a second small engine, oars, or paddles.

15. Make sure your boat is equipped with a bailer. It's a good idea to carry a hand bailer or scoop even if you have an electric bilge pump.

16. Carry a compass if you normally operate on large bodies of water.

17. Learn the weather warning signals.

18. Water ski only when you are clear of other persons. There should always be two

Every boat should be equipped with a marine compass that the operator has learned to use properly. Marine compasses come in a wide range of prices. Buy the very best you can afford. This compass is made by Silva, one of the most reliable names in compasses.

FLOAT PLAN

1. Name and phone of person reporting_____

2. Description of boat: Type _____ Color _____

    Trim_____Registration no._____

    Length _____ Name _____Make _____

    Other info_____

3. Names, ages, addresses of persons on board

    _____   ___   _____

    _____   ___   _____

    _____   ___   _____

4. Engine type_____ HP_____

    No. of engines_____ Fuel capacity_____

5. Survival equipment (check as appropriate)

    PFDs_____ Flares _____ Mirror _____ Smoke signals _____

    Flashlights _____ Food _____ Paddles _____ Water _____

    Others _____ Anchor _____ Raft or dinghy _____ EPIRB _____

6. Radio: (yes/no) Type _____ Frequency _____

7. Trip expectations: Leave at (time) _____

    From _____ Going to _____

    Expect to return by (time)_____

    And in no event later than _____

8. Any other pertinent info._____

9. Auto license_____Color/Make _____

    Where parked_____

10. If not returned by (time)_____, call Coast Guard or

    _____ Phone:_____

    _____ Phone:_____

    _____ Phone:_____

Know where you are going, and use up-to-date charts. Also fill out a float plan like that shown on the previous page and leave it with an office that will make note of your failure to confirm your arrival on schedule.

people in the tow boat—one to watch the skier, the other to operate the boat.

19. Be extremely careful of your footing. Falls are one of the chief causes of accidents. Stay seated in small boats.

20. Always instruct at least one other person on board in handling your boat in case you become disabled or fall overboard.

21. Before departing on any boat trip, leave a float plan with a responsible person ashore. Advise the person you left your plan with of your arrival or return.

22. Properly maintain and stow safety equipment carried on your boat or vessel. Teach your passengers to locate and use it before an emergency occurs. In an emergency, the equipment will do you little good if it is unserviceable or stowed in an unreachable location, or if you are unfamiliar with its operation or use.

23. Carry sufficient tools for minor repairs.

24. Enroll in a safe boating course.

Survival at Sea

At the very first sign of trouble with your boat, be it mechanical or weather, make sure everyone on board puts on a personal flotation device (PFD). If you are in cold water, get out the survival suits and have them ready to put on.

If your trouble is anything more than minor, radio your situation and position to some responsible party.

Assuming you are in radio contact with the Coast Guard or have filed a float plan and the weather is not too bad, time spent on a boat until rescue arrives is usually short. But what if for some reason you must spend

Alert Coast Guard by radio as soon as possible if you are having trouble on big water. (U.S. Coast Guard photo)

days on your boat awaiting rescue? Here are some tips to remember.

1. If you can anchor or tie up to a buoy safely, do so. It is much easier to be found if you stay in one location.

2. If you are in stormy weather, put out a sea anchor, which reduces drifting and keeps the boat headed into the wind.

3. Protect everyone on board from the sun, wind, and chill and from getting wet, which can result in hypothermia. If your boat does not have a cabin, rig up a shelter using an emergency tarp.

4. Keep your signal devices handy and be prepared to put them to use at a moment's notice.

5. Keep an alert person awake and on duty at all times. Rotate shifts.

6. Drinking water is nonexistent in salt water except for old sea ice and snow. Avoid drinking salt water. If it rains, use buckets, cups, tin cans, boat cover, tarp, or whatever you have to catch the fresh water. Wash salt off this gear with the first of the rain so that your drinking water will not be salty. If dew forms, use a windshield wiper or sponge to collect it in a cup. Always carry plenty of drinking water on your boat. Your stomach is the best container for water, so drink your fill of water when you can. There is no substitute for water. Do not try these misconceived substitutes: fish juice, salt water, blood, or urine. Remember that with only 1 pint of water per day, you can live from 14 to 24 days. On 1 quart of water per day you can expect extended life.

7. If you have fishing tackle on board or in a survival kit, the first rule in gathering food is that *if you have no water you should not eat.* If you do have water, fish may be caught for food. Often baited hooks, with the line tied to the boat, can be used to catch seagulls. Turtles, crabs, and shrimp may be netted to eat. Seaweed is edible, but very salty, and like all foods with salt should be avoided unless there is an abundance of water.

Fish. Eat only healthy-looking fish; avoid fish with a bad smell or indented skin. Bleed, gut, and skin the fish immediately, and either consume raw, cook and eat, or preserve them within two hours. If you eat fish raw, eat saltwater varieties only. To preserve fish, cut them into thin strips and sun dry. Keep cool and dry in a ventilated container.

Remember to first smell, taste, and visually inspect raw (or preserved) fish for spoilage.

Shore seabirds. Cut, clean, and skin the bird; don't eat the skin because it has an oily taste. The meat should be eaten raw only if you are unable to cook it, and you should use only the meaty portions.

The meat may either be cooked or smoked, or you can cut it into thin strips and sun dry to preserve it.

When eating pelicans and other birds which swallow fish whole, you can also cut open the gullet and eat the partially digested food there. It requires less water to digest.

Crustaceans. Saltwater varieties of crustaceans, such as crabs, shrimp, and lobsters, may be eaten raw. If possible, though, you should boil them for about 20 minutes to kill parasites. They can be stored in a saltwater pool to ensure freshness.

Shellfish and mollusks. Oysters, clams, and other bivalves can be eaten raw, or you can cook or smoke them. Keep them alive in a container of water until you are ready to use them.

Several precautions should be taken when using mollusks and shellfish as a food source:

1. Don't collect during a red tide, that is, when the water is red due to infestation of red algae.

2. Don't take from colonies where some are dead or dying.

3. Don't select from areas where they are not covered by water 75 percent of the time.

4. Avoid conical shell life.

Seaweeds and algae. Wash seaweeds and algae and eat raw, sun dry to preserve, or boil. Eat in moderation until you are accustomed to these plants. Seaweeds and algae provide vitamins and minerals for the diet that cannot be gained from fish sources.

Turtles. Cut the bottom shell away from the top shell. Cut all the lean meat from the body of the turtle. Save the top shell for use such as a bowl or shovel. You can then either eat the meat raw, cook, smoke, or sun dry. Turtle liver, fat, and eggs are also edible.

Seals. Skin and gut the seal immediately. If possible, freeze the flesh. Either cook or sun dry the meat.

The best method of preparing any food source when a landfall has been made is to boil the food thoroughly. You may drink the broth, and boiling kills internal parasites.

Conserve your energy. Sleep regularly. Maintain a positive mental attitude. Maintain the will to live.

If you must abandon the boat, stay with it or its larger parts if they float. This will help you stay afloat and be easier to spot. Keep the members of your group together if possible.

If you take all the precautions advised earlier in this chapter by the Coast Guard, chances are you will never have to practice survival at sea.

17

SWAMP SURVIVAL

During my many years of search-and-rescue work, I have probably looked for more lost people in swamps than in any other North American environment. The word "swamp" means many things to many people. To some, it is a forbidding, wet environment that humans should avoid at all costs. To others, it is an adventurous place rich in game and fish, where peace of mind comes easy.

Webster's defines swamp as "wet spongy land saturated and sometimes partially or intermittently covered with water." The U.S. Department of the Interior's Fish and Wildlife Service has an official definition: "Swamp is all wetlands with greater than 50 percent of its area in cover of woody plants, that is, trees, brush, vines, etc."

Many people confuse marshlands with swamps. Marshes are almost totally devoid of any bushes or trees. Most marshes are cre-

ated by tidal activity, and they are usually in areas with high saline or alkaline content in the soil. Marshes are usually covered in grasslike plants and are usually associated with the ocean.

Other people mistake bogs for swamps. Bogs are usually the remains of ancient lakes. While swamps have a covering of trees and

---

Backpacking in swamps is difficult at best, and a thorough knowledge of trails and terrains is necessary. Since swamps are basically a watery environment, backpacking is usually secondary to travel by boat. Highly specialized equipment, including hip boots or jungle boots, a supply of dry clothes in the pack, and (during warm months) mosquito-proof tent are needed.

TV and movies have done much to create fear of swamps in the minds of outdoorsmen. Being able to distinguish fact from myth on this mysterious setting can turn an otherwise frightening wetland into a fascinating wonderland.

woody plants, bogs are covered with mosses, ferns, and lichens. Until you step in a bog, you usually don't see the water. Then the bog acts like a wet sponge.

There are swamps in almost every region of North America. This comes as a surprise to many people who normally think of swamps as something found only in the Deep South.

The origins of swamps are varied. Many are the result of centuries of change in river flows. Swamps along the Mississippi River and the Ohio River were formed this way. Some swamps are the result of glacial activities. Swamps in Canada, around the Great Lakes, and in New England are of this type. Still other swamps were created by falling meteorites, such as the Carolina Bays; by receding ocean, such as the Okefenokee Swamp; or by an earthquake, such as Reelfoot Swamp. Today new swamps are being created at a rapid rate by the activity of beavers. There seem to be almost as many ways that swamps are created as there are swamps.

When you begin to consider exploring, hunting, fishing, camping, canoeing, or trapping in the swamps, you may be surprised at how much negative talk you will hear about swamps in general. For centuries, Americans have been kept out of game-rich swamps by horror tales and negative folklore. Quicksand...black panthers...snakes...spiders ...alligators...*lost.* These associations and others have been too often connected with swamps. Television and movies have capitalized on these fears in misleading movies filmed in so-called swamp settings.

Historians tell us that this fear of swamps came about during the early exploration of North America. Since there are few swamps in Europe, the European explorers avoided swamps. Lack of experience with this new swamp environment made them mysterious to explorers. The Indians were quick to rec-ognize white men's fear of swamps and told them frightening stories to keep the swamps to themselves. With the passing of each generation, these swamp stories grew and were handed down as fact. We still have many swamp phobias with us today that are the result of centuries-old tales.

Swamps are among our last wilderness areas, and many of them offer a backcountry setting near urban areas. Because of the fear and ignorance so many people have of swamps, there are still a good number of swamps scattered over North America that remain totally wild. These swamps serve many beneficial purposes, and we are fortunate that we have them. These swamps are the last preserves for many of our endangered plants and animals. They are also great water storage areas and are constantly recharging underground water supplies. The trees and lush plant life in swamps help keep us in oxygen. Many of the swamp streams purify water as it slowly meanders through.

Of equal importance is the swamp's role in providing recreation and adventure. Swamps are excellent game and fish habitats; nowhere will you find better hunting and fishing. Because swamps are rich in suitable wildlife habitat and have suffered less from the pressures of progress than any other part of the American landscape, they constitute the last outdoorsman's paradise. At the same time, swamps may suddenly require survival skills.

Why Are Swamps Difficult?

Because swamps are a wet environment in which there are few roads and thick vegetation, they can put you in a survival predicament quickly. Basically, there are three swamp predicaments that are dangerous.

1. With the debris typical in swamp water, it is easy to foul an outboard motor or to

Swamp terrain is flat, often interlaced with changing waterways, and vegetation, such as cypress, Spanish moss, water lilies, and low-growing bushes. Usually terrain looks confusingly similar throughout a swamp. Therefore, landmarks are difficult to identify and directions are hard to decipher even with a map. It's best to arrange for a local guide when going into a large unfamiliar swamp.

puncture a canoe, or for a four-wheel-drive vehicle to become hopelessly stuck in the always unpredictable mud.

2. It is easy to get lost. Since swamp terrain is generally flat, everything tends to look alike on an overcast day. Much of the vegetation in the swamp looks the same, and landmarks are often impossible to establish or recognize.

3. You or a partner could become sick or injured and not be able to get help. Strandings in swamps are often difficult to avoid, but a top priority when you go into a swamp should always be to let someone know where you are going and when you plan to return. Always keep your equipment in good repair and have a backup system or at least a repair kit that you know how to use. Avoid weather that could get you into trouble, and avoid areas from which your return may be impossible. In other words, anytime you are venturing into a swamp, use common sense.

No one should ever go into a swamp alone. Be sure to let your partner know generally where you plan to hunt, fish, or hike, and when you plan to return. Also always let

Swamp waterways are often clogged with water weeds just under the surface, requiring a great amount of energy to paddle or pole through. So it is best to travel with a companion who can supply needed horsepower, whether you set out by paddle or with a motor that could break down.

someone at your home, motel, or lodge know where you are going and when you plan to return. An extra precaution is to leave a note on the windshield of your car stating your name, the direction you are going in, and when you plan to return. While these basic rules, which I emphasize many times in this book, can't prevent you from having an immobilizing accident, they can cut down on the number of hours your ordcal lasts.

Swamps are difficult also because they are watery environments, and travel in a straight line is usually impossible for any great dis-

tance. Following the known water course across the swamp often defies most navigational principles. In most cases, a local guide who is familiar with the swamp is a must if you are to go from one point to another in a reasonable amount of time.

Swamp Dangers

As I stated at the beginning of this chapter, there are many stories about swamp dangers. While some are false, some are true. Let's take a look at some of the myths and facts about swamp dangers.

Quicksand. One of the most often-repeated myths about swamps has to do with quicksand. The pulsating beds of quicksand we have all seen on the movies and on TV have misled many would-be swamp visitors into thinking they will be swallowed up in a bubbling pool of sand and water if they make a wrong step. Throughout most of my life I have traveled in swamps all over North America, and I have never seen a bed of quicksand. I am told by engineers that quicksand is more myth than fact, particularly in swamps.

Quicksand is a condition and not a soil type. Gravels, sand, and silt become "quick" when an upward flow of groundwater takes place to such an extent that the particles are lifted. When the uplift pressure and the total stress are in balance, the mass may look deceptively stable. However, a machine or a structure on the soil surface will sink slowly if it is heavier than the saturated soil. This condition would normally occur in areas around a spring, for instance, that has been silted in, or perhaps in an old oxbow lake that has silted in. But the danger would be in only the immediate area and would present little danger to man. Quicksand as depicted in TV dramas and the movies is generally considered by soil scientists and engineers to be an exaggeration of an unlikely situation in North American swamps.

I don't mean to imply that there aren't some bogs and mud deposits in which you can sink. I have seen bogs in the Rocky Mountains above timberline in which a horse could sink up to its belly. I have also seen mud, especially in overused, wet logging roads, where you could sink up to your knees. Also, I have seen oxbow lakes where someone who tried to walk across what appeared to be mud could sink out of sight. With proper precautions, however, none of these situations presents a problem to the swamp traveler. The best precaution whenever you are approaching an area that appears to be muddy is to proceed carefully. This is particularly true in any low depression which may have once been a streambed or lake. Test the mud before you venture very far into it. If you begin to bog down, ease out and go around. The few situations I have seen where one could get into trouble could usually be avoided by walking around.

In short, in swamps there are no bubbling pools of quicksand waiting to swallow you up.

Black panthers. Another popular myth about swamps is that people are apt to be attacked by black panthers. First of all, since there are no black panthers in the wild of North America, there is little reason for anyone to believe stories about black panthers. Most swamps do have bobcats, but they don't want anything to do with man. In the Deep South there remain a few eastern mountain lions, but again, there are no documented cases of their attacking humans, and you'll probably never see one. Like bobcats, these few big cats stay away from people.

Bears. There are a lot of swamp stories about bears. Black bears and swamps go together hand in glove. In many areas of North America, swamps are the last holdouts for black bears. But I have never known anyone traveling in a swamp to have a dangerous encounter with a black bear. On a few occasions I have had my camp torn apart by a bear, and I have known of others who have had their food stolen by bears and an occasional tent knocked down. If we had kept our food and garbage stored out of reach, the bears probably would never have bothered the camp.

Other than looking for food to steal, black bears stay away from people. If a bear does come into your swamp camp, snap on a light, bang on a pan, or do something to let it know you are there. Generally, it will run away. Unless it is cornered or its cubs seem to be threatened, a bear wants little to do with humans.

Alligators. Alligators are associated with swamps; however, remember that alligators are found only in the swamps of the Deep South. The only time I have seen alligators appear to be dangerous is when they are threatened—when someone gets too close to a nest or to the little alligators or tries to get too close to half-wild alligators to feed them. I have spent days in the Okefenokee Swamp in which I was around alligators both day and night and had no problem at all. When I am in swamps that contain alligators, I take a few extra precautions, such as not hanging

American alligators usually tend to stay out of your way and represent little threat. But, like bears, those that are fed often or antagonized by people are generally the ones that injure people. If you spot an alligator, ignore it. An injured alligator can be very dangerous with both its mouth and tail, so never attempt to kill an alligator unless you are properly armed and know what you are doing.

fish over the side of the boat and making sure that the alligators hear me coming so that I don't surprise them.

In short, the alligator, black panther, and bear stories we hear grow more from folklore than from reality. Even the person who is lost in the swamp with only a survival kit will have very little, if any, problem with critters of this type. Fear of bears, black panthers, and alligators should be your least concern when surviving in a swamp.

Snakebite. This is another highly overrated danger in swamps. This is especially true in the northern half of North America. While snakes do inhabit swamps in the warmer part of North America, they are rarely the danger that many weavers of tall tales would have us believe. The best prevention against snakes when you are in a swamp that may have a poisonous snake population is to keep your eyes open and always watch where you place your feet, hands, and bottom. When you travel by boat or canoe, watch overhanging limbs, stumps, logs, and the bases of trees.

Cottonmouths, as well as other snakes, like to sun themselves, and the cottonmouth will generally hold his ground, whereas the more common water snakes will drop into the water. By keeping your eyes open, you can avoid problems with cottonmouths.

Another place you are likely to encounter cottonmouths is at the end of your fish stringer. Anytime you put fish in the water, there is the remote possibility that a cottonmouth may attempt to swallow the fish on your stringer. Again, it is not likely to happen, but does on occasion. By being cautious, you can avoid pulling up a stringer with a cottonmouth attached.

In swamps known to contain poisonous snakes, your survival camp should be chosen with care, and it should be kept clean so that you can always see where you are placing your hands and feet. Rarely does a snake come into a camp, but by keeping a clean camp, you can see what's going on and avoid any encounter with a snake if one should venture in.

It is a common practice in swamp travel to turn a boat or canoe over at the end of a

The venomous cottonmouth can easily be mistaken for a nonvenomous water snake. One difference is that a cottonmouth is more likely to hold its ground when disturbed. Other differences are discussed and illustrated beginning on page 280. (Luther C. Goldman photo)

day. An overturned boat or canoe is an attractive resting site for water snakes, including the cottonmouth. So turn boats upright cautiously and make sure you don't have a stowaway coiled under a boat seat or deck. Once you have shoved off into a swamp is a poor time to realize that you have a snake for a passenger. If you use common sense and your eyes in any survival situation in a swamp, you should be able to avoid most of the problems that are associated with snakes. In fact, if you do encounter a snake, remember that you are looking at a potential meal; a visit from a snake doesn't have to be all bad.

The real dangers of swamps. The real dangers associated with swamps are those you may encounter in many outdoor environments. Since swamps are a watery environment, there is always the risk of drowning. Also, there is a risk of hypothermia as in any damp situation. During the summer, lightning can be a problem. On several occasions I have been caught in electrical storms in which trees nearby were struck by lightning. And since swamps contain thick tangles of fallen trees, limbs, vines, etc., anyone who panics and tries running through a swamp risks falling and breaking or spraining a limb.

I've been involved in many search-and-rescue operations in swamps, and I have never brought anyone out who was hurt by snakes, bears, alligators, quicksand, or any of those exaggerated dangers. I have brought people out who were in serious trouble because of numerous mosquito bites and others who had broken a limb because they panicked and tried to run through the thick, entangled vegetation. I have also brought out victims who panicked and drowned or had heart attacks. Perhaps the most common dangerous condition I have found in those rescued from swamps is hypothermia.

Most of the dangers we have in swamps are myth. The true dangers that one faces in a survival situation in a swamp are those which may be encountered in any backcountry situation. If swamp visitors would let people know where they are going, when they are going, and when they expect to return, seek the services or advice of a qualified guide, and take survival gear with them, chances are that very few search-and-rescue operations would be necessary in the swamp environment.

Preparing to Go into Swamps

One of the most important steps in any trip into the backcountry is the planning, and it is especially important when going into a swamp, particularly if it is a large swamp and you plan to stay for several days. The first step should always be to obtain a U.S. Geological Survey topographical map. Also, since many North American swamps are owned by government agencies (state wildlife management areas, federal wildlife refuges, state parks, national forests, national parks, and timber management areas) there will be special maps that will be extremely helpful in trip planning.

When you have a good map or set of maps, you can begin to phone officials to learn details of the swamp you are going into, keeping notes right on the maps. Be sure to mark such things as good campsites, fishing and hunting hotspots, sources of safe drinking water, safe places to leave your car, and so on. It is easy to forget this valuable information, but if you write it on your map it will be available not only for this trip, but for future trips.

When planning your trip, be sure to plan to take a survival kit. (Kits are discussed in detail in Chapter 4 of this book.) For whatever type travel you plan, be it canoe, four-

This guide gained his wealth of experience in swamp navigation by trapping throughout the Alabama swamp in which he works. I know him well. He's my dad—George Fears. Here Dad is collecting his traps at the end of trapping season while making mental notes of the swamp's constantly changing features. Since navigation is so difficult in the swamp, a local guide is often a wise investment.

wheel-drive vehicle, or backpacking, you should have an appropriate survival kit.

Until you know a swamp well enough yourself, you'd be wise to hire a reputable local guide. Good swamp guides can rarely be booked on short notice. Those who can be may not be of the quality you want, so make arrangements for your guide or outfitter well in advance. Take the trouble to check out references. Two days into the heart of a remote swamp is no time to learn that your guide is a drunk who brought only beans and whiskey to feed you. Also arrange well in advance for any rental gear that you may need, such as boat, canoe, or outboard motor, and secure them with a deposit.

If you are taking a float trip down a swamp river, you'll want to arrange well in advance to have someone meet you downriver at a designated pickup point. I have found that for a small fee, the proprietors of reputable service stations in nearby towns will usually drop you off at your starting point, safeguard your car, and pick you up at the end of your trip. This arrangement is much better than leaving cars along the river at the edge of a swamp where they could be vandalized or stolen. Another advantage of this arrangement is that if you do not show up at the designated time, you have a local person who can notify the proper authorities.

Before going into a swamp, select the right equipment and know how to use it. If you are going in by canoe or boat, be sure to take a repair kit. Once I was unloading my canoe at a public access area on a stream when I saw a weary-looking lady walking toward me. She tearfully said that she had been walking all day. She and her companion had knocked a hole in their canoe while running some rapids, and with their load of camping gear, they could not bail the water out as fast as it came in. She had left her companion with the damaged canoe while she walked for help.

Since good swamp guides are in demand, it is wise to begin research for booking a guide well in advance of your planned trip. Be sure to check out references because there are many inept or otherwise unlikable guides available.

Duct tape is a valuable aid in repairing canoes and boats. Dry the canoe shell first, then place tape on both sides of the puncture with at least an inch margin of tape around the gash. While I recommend duct tape as only a temporary repair, I have used a canoe repaired in such a fashion for several days without its leaking.

When we arrived at the damaged canoe, the hole was easy to repair temporarily, and the canoeists were soon on their way down the river. Had they known anything about repairing a canoe in the field and had a repair kit, they would have lost only an hour, not an entire day.

No matter how hard we try to avoid it, canoes and boats take a beating in a swamp. When a canoe or boat is damaged on a trip, there is only one thing to do to avoid a stranding: patch it up well enough to complete the trip. There are many ways to plug tears and holes in canoes and boats, including bubble gum, wooden pegs, tape, glue, and patches made from plastic bags, pitch from trees, and drippings from a burning nylon rope. However, you will not have to resort to such primitive repair methods if you learn something about your boat or canoe and carry a repair kit with you.

The first step in knowing how to repair

your canoe or boat begins when you purchase it. Have the salesperson show you how to make repairs. Know what material your boat or canoe is made of and understand how it is constructed. Have the salesperson help you put together a repair kit. Many boats and canoes come with repair kits for a small additional cost. If you purchase a used craft, ask if the previous owner has a repair kit. If not, write the manufacturer or go to a canoe or boat shop for help in putting one together.

Repairing a tear or hole in a canoe or boat can be done quickly and easily with 2-inch duct tape. Simply place overlapping strips of tape over the tear or hole until it is com-pletely covered. I would never consider going into a swamp with any type of water craft without taking plenty of duct tape with me. While duct tape does not provide a permanent repair, many times it has brought me out when otherwise I would have been stranded.

When planning a trip into a swamp, find out the local conditions of significance. Is this the worst summer in history for mosquitos there? If so, you will want to take along an extra supply of repellent. Check the netting of your tent for rips, and perhaps pack a mosquito headnet. If the water level of the swamp is lower than usual and wading is a

Before going swamp camping, be sure to check the netting on your tent for rips and tears because mosquitos can be a major problem.

must, then an extra pair of waders or jungle boots, pants, and socks may be necessary.

Weather should have a strong influence on your choice of equipment. Check recent weather conditions. During hunting season, snow may be deeper than you are prepared for, or maybe you are preparing for snow when it is unseasonably warm. Perhaps heavier-than-usual rains have made getting to the swamp a job for a four-wheel-drive vehicle and you'll have to give up your plan to use your family car. Maybe you are planning to float a swamp river and camp on sandbars, but because of the rains the river is rising, the sandbars will be underwater, and the river will be dangerous. See what the weather conditions have been, and by all means see what the weather forecast is for the time of your trip. Weather surprises can be dangerous, especially if you take the wrong equipment. Plan your gear around sound weather advice, then remember to keep an eye on the sky and use common sense.

One of the greatest dangers in a swamp is from mosquitos. If you are properly prepared, you can live with these pests under most circumstances and with little discomfort. But if you go unprepared into the swamp you can literally be putting your life on the line.

Several years ago I was asked to lead a search for two canoeists who were overdue from a one-day trip into an Alabama river swamp. The pair hadn't taken along any survival gear or camping gear, and they had chosen a swamp that was impossible to cross in one day during a period of low water. We

Jungle boots are excellent swamp footwear because they have drain holes just above the sole and canvas uppers that dry fairly quickly. Also these boots are relatively lightweight.

Left: Hip boots are ideal for swamp use, provided the water is not deep. *Right: Waders are recommended for wading swamps in colder months, especially when hunting waterfowl.*

found the overdue canoeists early the next morning. They had spent the night without the aid of fire, shelter, or insect repellent. They were swollen so badly from the hundreds of mosquito bites that we had to take them to a hospital.

Every swamp visitor should know that during the warm months, any swamp is going to have mosquitos. Plan accordingly. Not only are these flying pests a nuisance, but their bites can be dangerous. The best way to live in mosquito-infested areas is to go prepared to keep mosquitos away from you. There are several good repellents available that will keep these flying pests at a comfortable distance. Insect repellents that are from 95 to 100 percent DEET do an excellent job of keeping mosquitos away. There is a great deal more on this subject in Chapter 13 of this book.

Another method of keeping mosquitos from becoming too dangerous is to dress with them in mind. Long sleeves, hat, long trousers, socks to protect the ankles, and even a mosquito net will go a long way toward ensuring comfort in the swamp. If you are camping, be sure that your tent is mosquito-proof and has mosquito netting on the doors and windows and that the netting is in a good state of repair. I once had to spend the night unexpectedly in a mosquito-infested Michigan swamp. The guide built two smoky fires and we spent the night between them. We were bitten, though not nearly as badly as we would have been without the fires. Many times during that long night I wished for a high-quality mosquito repellent.

Swamp Navigation

Navigation is a necessary skill in all swamp travels. But the difficulty of using conventional navigational techniques in swamps is the chief reason that our swamps are among the last truly wild areas left to explore. In swamps, more so than in other types of backcountry, a guide may be crucial. The first step in learning to navigate in a swamp on your own, though, is to have a good lesson in the use of topographical maps and a compass. This is covered in detail in Chapter 12 of this book.

The map and compass are basic for all swamp navigation, but you should also be aware that various types of swamps require special navigational techniques appropriate to the swamp's character. Let's look at a few of these techniques.

The river-bottom swamp, or floodplain, as it is often called, can be traveled by boat, or during dry periods, by walking. If it is to be traveled by boat or canoe, the river should be the main route of travel. If the river-bottom is flooded, you can make side trips from the river.

The first step in a trip of this type is to sit down with someone familiar with the swamp river and have him show you the best course on a topo map. Many times a swamp river will meander, offering several channels from which the boat user must choose. If he chooses the wrong one, it can mean a return trip upstream for another selection or a stranding. (Caution: In swamps, channels can change, and they may not always be accurately represented on the map.)

Most local people know the best channel. Find out how long it takes to float a stretch of river and what obstacles, such as fallen trees, can be expected. In a slow-moving, log-choked swamp river, a lot of time may be needed to float just a mile. Many swamp travelers have stayed in the swamp several days longer than they had planned because they miscalculated their speed of travel.

Also find out good campsite locations before making your trip. Campsites that are good during periods of low water may be underwater during periods of high water. On the other hand, good campsites during high water may be inaccessible during low water. Mark these campsites on your topo map. Also mark any known sources of drinking water. In many swamps, clean drinking water is extremely difficult to find.

Navigating down a river is relatively easy, if you know the proper channels to follow. The more difficult navigating starts when you want to boat or canoe into the flooded river swamps adjacent to the main river. Here the approach most often used is what is known as "baseline navigation," using the river as the baseline. See Chapter 12 in this book for details on baseline navigation.

If you are backpacking or walking into a river swamp during a dry period of the year, baseline navigation will work, provided you are using a logging road or some other straight feature as your baseline. There is no doubt that some of the best hunting in North America is in riverbottom swamps, but such places are among the easiest in which to get lost. Because the terrain is so flat, a topo map is often of little use.

In this situation, your compass becomes very important. Your understanding of baseline navigation can make travel reasonably direct and proficient. Incidentally, the ice in many northern swamps can be traveled upon during the winter, and the baseline method works well under these conditons also. (But falling through ice can spell big trouble.)

The vast wet swamps of the Southeast such as the Great Dismals, Okefenokee, and Everglades make baseline navigation impractical. Here navigation is reduced to following existing canals and trails cut through the swamp. You can try it on your own if you are capable and if the trails and canals are well marked, or you can go with a guide. To venture off these marked waterways is asking for serious trouble. Getting from one point to another without using existing trails is generally impossible because of the thick growth on the swamp floor. Sticking to existing trails is not an admission of inferior woodsmanship, but a wise policy that will assure your enjoyment of your trip.

Other vast swamps such as the Big Thicket of Texas and the Atchafalaya Swamp of Louisiana require the services of a local guide for newcomers. It has been said that the best navigational wisdom is to know when you need a guide. These and other large swamps that do not have a trail or marked waterway system are no place for you to practice amateur navigational skills. After all, you are in the swamp to enjoy camping, hunting, and fishing, not to practice survival. It is not like being lost on dry land—if you get lost in a swamp, chances are you can't walk out and you can't paddle in a straight line. Use a local guide and concentrate on your outdoors interests.

An additional method for swamp navigation is called the bearing and distance method. You can learn this method in Chapter 12 of this book. The bearing and distance

method works well in swamps that are not too thickly vegetated and where terrain features can be spotted at a distance.

Navigating across swamps is complicated, even for well-trained navigators. Swamp maps generally lack detail. The swamps themselves lack prominent terrain features, and you run into problems such as dense undergrowth, a sudden shallowness or lack of water for the boat, or a sudden wetness for the hiker.

The best navigational skill in any swamp is the familiarity that comes with many days and nights of experience in that swamp.

Swamp Survival Techniques

Techniques for surviving in a swamp are very similar to techniques discussed throughout this book. However, there are a few points peculiar to swamp survival that should be emphasized.

Making it easier to be found. Once you realize that you are lost in a swamp, the very first thing you need to do is to *stop*. A swamp is no place to be wandering about. The same thing applies if you are stranded, as by a hole in your boat or canoe, or an outboard motor which has stopped. Don't attempt to walk out. Stay where you are, or move only a short distance to get into a more open area where you may be spotted easily from the air.

The importance of an opening cannot be overemphasized in the case of a swamp. Many times I have been looking in a swamp for someone who was lost and had a canoe or boat with him. Because of the lush overhead vegetation, I have flown over such people many times without ever seeing them.

If you have a boat or canoe, try to secure it where it can be seen from overhead. Once you have an opening in which to await rescue, use some sort of signal so that you will be more easily spotted. Review Chapter 5 in this book on signaling. Also use your imagination. However, many times in the case of a boat or canoe, once it is in the opening, it is easily spotted from the air, especially if those who are searching for you know that you were traveling by boat or canoe.

Protection from the elements. Once you have established an opening in which to await rescue, the first thing to consider is what protections are necessary. During cool or cold weather in a swamp, hypothermia is one of the first concerns. Being in a wet environment, being tired, being scared—all go together to bring on hypothermia. As quickly as possible, get a fire going. Even in this wet environment, a fire can be started by following the techniques discussed in Chapter 6. Obviously, if you have to await rescue in a boat because getting on dry land is impossible or not practical, bundle up as much as you can to prevent hypothermia. Consider putting on raingear to cut the chilling effect of the wind.

If you are caught in a swamp during warm weather, your immediate attention may be directed to protection from mosquitos and blackflies. These biting insects are just as dangerous as, if not more dangerous than, any snakes or other critters you are likely to run into in the swamps. Fortunately, the blackflies stop biting at dark. Unfortunately, that's when the mosquito activity increases.

Lightning is another danger during warm weather. As an example of how terrifying lightning can be, several years ago I was guiding an Ohio fisherman in a swamp in East Texas when a sudden and fierce thunderstorm hit. We were caught out in some tall timber. I asked my client to lie down in the boat and prepared to crank the motor and move into a stand of thick, low-growing brush. He was shocked that I would even think of putting the boat into that "cotton-mouth-infested brush." As he was preaching to me the dangers of snakes, a bolt of lightning clobbered a nearby cypress with an ear-splitting crack. Pieces of bark flew in all directions. My client dived into the bottom of the boat and begged me to get into the low-growing bushes. The storm lasted two long hours, with the severity of a mortar attack. On the way back to camp, my pale client told me that snakes were now only his second-biggest fear in the swamp—lightning was first!

There is more information on lightning in the Chapter 13 on survival medicine.

Drinking water. You'd think that the last problem you'd have in a swamp survival situation would be that of finding water. Granted, there is usually plenty of water available in most swamps, but many times the water is not safe to drink. In fact, most swamps offer few, if any, sources of safe drinking water. Many of today's swamps are fed by waters that originate upstream, and these streams may be polluted by waste from cities, industries, agricultural areas, and even rural septic tanks. Regardless of how clear the swamp water may look, don't trust it. Some swamps that are made up primarily of standing water contain stagnant water that is subject to bacteriological contamination from animals. Other swamps, such as the rapidly growing number of beaver swamps, contain populations of animals that carry disease. It is interesting to note that beavers are quite often infected with tularemia, which can be transmitted to man through water.

Beavers are a common carrier of tularemia, a bacterium which can bring on a high fever, headache, and often chills. Man may get the disease from beavers by drinking water which beavers have contaminated by urine or feces. Water in which beavers are known to live should always be boiled or filtered through one of the systems discussed in Chapter 8, on water, beginning on page 116.

The National Park Service states "We know of no swamp waters that have met a safe drinking water test." It is only good judgment to purify the water regardless of how pure it may look. I can testify that this is true. Several years ago two of my fishing partners and I went deep into a swamp in southern Mississippi on a week-long search for bull bluegills. The running water next to our camp looked so clean that we didn't bother to treat it. That was a mistake that cut our trip short. We were weeks getting our digestive systems back into proper working order.

In my years of swamp living and travel, I have found only two natural sources of safe drinking water. The first source is the artesian wells found in many of the swamps in the South. Most of these ever-running fountains of fresh water are indicated on USGS topographical maps. In my home state of Alabama, many of these wells are located along the Sipsey and Tombigbee river swamps and continuously flow through large pipes that stick 3 to 4 feet above the ground. These wells were discovered and piped by early settlers and plantation owners who had hoped to convert swamps into agricultural lands. Artesian wells are also found along other southern river swamps and coastal swamps and marshes.

The second natural source of safe water I have used is the water found in the interior of the Okefenokee Swamp. The Okefenokee is a natural-depression swamp, but it is higher than its border lands. Because of this unusual feature, the Okefenokee has no pollutants or contaminants washing in from outside. The swamp is fed by rainwater, and to a great extent by clear, bubbling springs. Since the swamp is 130 feet above sea level, the water

Finding edible wild food such as cattails in most swamps is relatively easy.

is in constant circulation. It drains away from a series of ridges in the center of the swamp into two distinct watersheds. As in most cypress swamps, the water of the Okefenokee is dark brown. This color is the effect of tannic acid from decaying vegetation, primarily cypress, and does not hurt the water quality. I have spent many days in this great swamp using the tea-colored water for drinking and cooking. I was always amused at the looks on the faces of the city-dwellers I was guiding when I dipped a cup of the water and asked them if they wanted a drink. But the Okefenokee, like many of our other back-country areas, is changing rapidly because of increased visits by man. Now the manager of the Okefenokee Swamp suggests that the swamp water be treated by boiling.

Needless to say, if you're dying of thirst, the long-range effect of drinking contaminated water is something you will have to worry about later. However, if it is at all possible to treat the water you are going to drink, you should do so. Chapter 8 in this book concerning drinking water is very important. With the modern methods of treating water, there is no excuse for not having good water to drink while you are in the swamp, even in a survival situation. Think ahead. If your swamp trip takes you far from treated water, go prepared. Either take enough water with you or take along a method of treating the water.

Other survival considerations. Finding edible wild food in most swamps is relatively easy. Most swamps in North America are rich in plant and animal life, and if you study the chapters in this book concerning edible wild plants and animals you should have little problem finding survival food while awaiting rescue in a swamp. Still, it behooves anyone

The machete is one of the best survival knives for use in the swamp or jungle. It can handle heavy-duty jobs such as trail clearing, cutting firewood, and shelter building.

going into a swamp environment to take additional food in case a stranding or survival situation occurs. If I had to sum up the best means of finding edible wild food in the swamp, in most cases, with the exception of northern swamps and during the winter, fishing would be my choice.

Gear for swamp survival is very similar to survival gear for other areas. Many times in southern swamps, I have used the same survival kit that I use in the Arctic. However, also be sure to have insect repellent, a good supply of waterproof matches, and, if possible, a machete. The machete is one of the best survival knives in a swamp environment. It can do much to make your stay more comfortable. It can be used for everything from simple camp chores to opening up a clearing where you may be spotted from overhead.

The person who finds himself stranded or lost in the swamps of North America has very little to fear, provided he has let someone know where he was going and when he expected to return. Many of the fears associated with swamps are unfounded. In fact, if I had my choice of places to have to survive, I think a swamp would be number one, because most swamps are filled with edible plants and materials to make a comfortable survival camp. If you study this chapter and the other chapters in this book I refer to, you should be prepared for survival in a swamp, awaiting rescues, while creating means of staying relatively comfortable.

18

MOUNTAIN SURVIVAL

The mountain environment, whether it be in the southern Appalachians of Georgia or the Brooks Range of Alaska, can be one of sudden weather changes. In the Cassiar Mountains of British Columbia, within one hour I have seen warm sunshine, rain, sleet, and heavy snow. In the Snowbird Mountains of North Carolina, I have seen weather go from a bright, bluebird day to a fierce electrical storm with little advance warning.

Mountain Dangers

The basic rule of mountain survival is to understand the dangers of the mountains, put a lot of planning into any trip into the mountains, and go prepared. If a survival crisis should occur in the mountains, travel should be halted as soon as practical. Rarely can you improve your lot by trying to struggle out of the mountains. It is usually wiser to estab-

lish a position where you can be easily seen and then await rescue.

Falls. Falls and the survival situations resulting from falls probably account for more search-and-rescue efforts in the mountain environment than any other hazard. These mishaps can occur not only to those involved in the seemingly more dangerous mountain sports, such as mountain climbing, rappelling, and other rock-climbing activities, but to anyone hiking, fishing, or hunting in a mountainous terrain.

A fall in the mountains is a life-threaten-

These alpine travelers are roped together as a safety precaution when walking across a glacier. (Outward Bound USA photo)

ing occurrence. You cannot be too careful to avoid this very real and ever-present danger.

Lightning. The fiercest electrical storm I have ever witnessed occurred the first year that I guided in Colorado. I had a pack string of animals above timberline one afternoon when without warning an electrical storm hit. Lightning was popping the rocks along the mountaintop on which we were riding. The horses were going crazy, and there was little for us riders to do but get off, ease down the side of the mountain, spread out, and lie flat on the ground. The storm lasted for almost an hour. It was one of the most frightening hours I have ever spent.

Electrical storms are to be expected in mountains during the warm months. You must keep a constant eye on the weather, and make an effort to drop below timberline when an electrical storm is approaching.

Although thunderstorms are local in nature and usually short in duration, they can be a real threat. For more on lightning precautions, see page 314.

Wind. In high mountains, the ridges and passes are seldom calm. But in protected alleys, strong winds are rare. Normally, wind velocity increases with altitude, since the earth's frictional drag is strongest near the ground, and this effect is accentuated by mountainous terrain. Winds are accelerated when they are forced over ridges and peaks or when they converge through mountain passes and canyons. Because of these fun-

Camping in the mountain environment above the timberline requires that campers take several special precautions. Note that the climbers in this photo are air-drying their bedrolls to keep the danger of hypothermia to a minimum. Avalanches, wind storms, and blizzards are just a few of the special hazards this environment presents. Planning for a winter high-country trip requires attention to equipment and details.

Falls, such as the fall that required emergency treatment and evacuation of this climber, account for a large share of mountain mishaps. (Boulder Daily Camera photo)

neling effects, the winds may blast with greater force on an exposed mountainside or summit. In most cases, the local wind direction is controlled by topography.

The force exerted by wind quadruples each time the wind speed doubles; that is, wind blowing at 40 miles per hour pushes four times harder than does wind blowing 20 miles per hour. At increasing wind strengths, gusts become more important and may be 50 percent higher than the average wind velocity.

Dehydration. High mountain air is dry, especially in winter when the humidity in the air condenses into ice. This dryness increases with the altitude. The amount of vapor in the air decreases in geometric proportion as the altitude increases. Consequently, dehy-

This avalanche sequence followed detonation of an artillery round near an ominously accruing cornice high on the slope. Although this slope appears relatively modest, the avalanche's momentum carried snow beyond the foot of the slope onto the road near the photographer. (Jerry Cleveland photos)

This downward view onto the pile-up after a slab avalanche conveys the high magnitude of weights and forces that come into play. (U.S. Forest Service photo)

dration is a common problem with people in the mountains. Drink water, even you aren't thirsty, to avoid this condition.

During my years as a hunting guide, especially when sheep or elk hunting, many times I have had hunters who complained of a constant headache. Most of the time this was because they were dehydrated.

Flash floods. Since many mountains receive heavy rainfall, particularly near the top, flash flooding is common. It is not unusual for a pleasant mountain brook to suddenly become a rushing wall of water. When camping, keep flash floods in mind. Especially when you are under the stress of a survival situation, avoid siting your camps along a creek. Otherwise, you may be placing yourself in danger of a flash flood.

Snow. Snow can cause many problems for winter mountain travelers, including hampered travel. Many times each fall, news reports from Rocky Mountain states announce that hunters are snowed in and that rescue efforts are under way.

Associated with snow slopes is the avalanche. Even small avalanches can have tremendous force and are a serious threat. Snow avalanches are complex natural phenomena. Since experts do not fully understand all the causes, it is difficult to predict avalanche conditions with certainty.

The more time you spend in high country skiing, snowshoeing, snowmobiling, and engaged in other winter activities, the greater are your chances of being caught by an avalanche. Understanding the basic types of avalanches and the contributing terrain and weather factors, as well as carefully selecting a safe route, can help you avoid being caught. It also pays to know the best means of surviving should you be buried in an avalanche.

There are two principal types of snow avalanches: *loose snow* and *slab*. Loose snow avalanches start at a point or over a small area. They grow in size, and the volume of snow involved increases as they descend. Loose snow moves as a formless mass with little internal cohesion.

Slab avalanches, on the other hand, start when a large snow mass begins to slide at once. There is a well-defined fracture line where the moving snow breaks away from the stable snow. In slab avalanches snow crystals tend to stick together. The slab will break into angular blocks or chunks of snow as the avalanche slides.

Practically all injuries and fatalities are caused by slab avalanches. Many times the victims have triggered the avalanche themselves. Their weight may stress the snow slab enough to break the fragile bonds that hold it to the slope.

Avalanche terrain factors. Four terrain factors affect snow avalanches: slope steepness, slope profile, slope aspect, and ground cover.

Slope Steepness. Avalanches are most common on slopes of 30 to 45 degrees (60 to 100 percent), but large avalanches can occur on slopes ranging from 25 to 60 degrees.

Slope Profile. Dangerous slab avalanches are more likely to occur on convex slopes, but may also occur on concave slopes. Short slopes may be as dangerous as long slopes.

Slope Aspect. Snow on north-facing slopes is more likely to slide in midwinter. South-facing slopes are dangerous in the spring and on sunny days. Leeward slopes are dangerous because wind-deposited snow adds depth and creates hard, hollow-sounding wind slabs. Windward slopes generally have less snow and the snow is compacted, but usually strong enough to resist movement.

This slab avalanche in British Columbia shows the well-defined fracture line where the moving snow broke away from the stable snow.

A fracture line in the snow indicates a possible avalanche, and the area below the line and as far as possible above it should be avoided. The safest route for you to take on a dangerous slope is along the ridgetop.

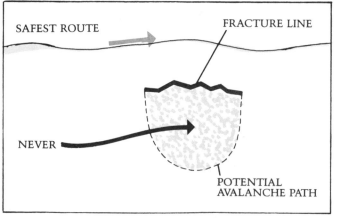

This dry-slab avalanche was intentionally released by exploding a 77mm artillery shell near a once dangerous wind slab area. Such wind packed slabs commonly form on the lee sides of slopes. (U.S. Forest Service photo)

Cornices, deposits of snow left by the wind near the mountaintop on the leeward side, present a danger of avalanche. So you should avoid disturbing them from above or below. The best route is a detour around the cornice area on the windward side.

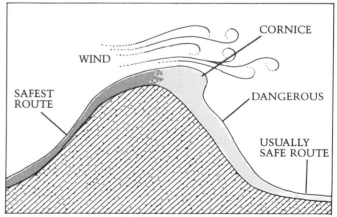

Below: Slab avalanches are most likely to occur on convex slopes. Right: Slope steepness is a good indicator of avalanche likelihood. Avalanches are most common on slopes of 30 to 45 degrees, but large avalanches can occur on slopes of 25 to 60 degrees. Avalanches are less frequent on steeper slopes because snow sluffs off.

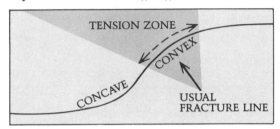

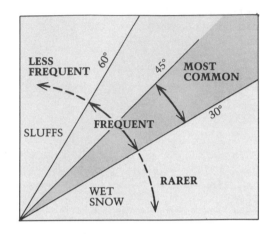

Ground Cover. Large rocks, trees, and heavy brush help anchor the snow, but avalanches can start even among trees. Smooth, grassy slopes are more dangerous.

Avalanche weather factors. Many weather factors affect the chances that a snow avalanche will occur: temperature, wind, storms, rate of snowfall, and types of snow.

Temperature. Snow persists in an unstable condition under cold temperatures. It will settle and stabilize rapidly when temperatures are near freezing.

Storms starting with low temperatures and dry snow, followed by rising temperatures, are more likely to cause avalanches. The dry snow at the start forms a poor bond and has insufficient strength to support the heavier snow deposited late in the storm.

Rapid changes in weather conditions (wind, temperature, snowfall) cause snowpack adjustments. Such adjustments may affect snowpack stability and cause an avalanche. Therefore, be alert to weather changes.

Wind. Sustained winds upwards of 15 miles per hour rapidly increase the danger that an avalanche will occur. Snow plumes (loose snow lifted by wind) from ridges and peaks indicate that snow is being moved onto leeward slopes. This can create dangerous conditions.

Storms. About 80 percent of all avalanches occur during or shortly after storms. Be extra cautious during these periods. Loose, dry snow slides easily. Moist, dense snow tends to settle more rapidly. Thawing snow or rain on snow can be extremely dangerous.

Rate of snowfall. Snow falling at the rate of 1 inch per hour or more rapidly increases avalanche danger.

Crystal types. Observe general snow-crystal types by letting them fall on a dark ski mitt or parka sleeve. Small crystals—needles and pellets—result in more dangerous conditions than the larger ones do.

Other avalanche signs. Look for signs of recent avalanche activity and old slide paths; listen for sounds and look for cracks; be alert to snow conditions.

Recent avalanche activity. If you see new avalanches, suspect dangerous conditions. Beware when snowballs or "cartwheels" roll down the slope.

Ground cover is beneficial because it can anchor snow to help prevent avalanches.

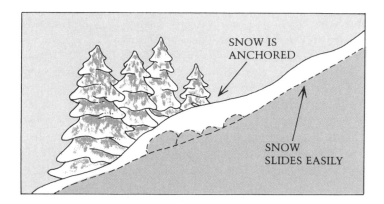

SNOW IS ANCHORED

SNOW SLIDES EASILY

Old slide paths. Generally, avalanches occur repeatedly in the same areas. Watch for avalanche paths. Look for pushed-over small trees and trees with limbs broken off the uphill side. Avoid steep, open gullies and slopes.

Sounds and cracks. If the snow sounds hollow, particularly on a leeward slope, conditions are probably dangerous. If the snow cracks and the cracks move away from you, slab avalanche danger is high.

New snow. Be alert to dangerous conditions with 1 foot or more of new snow.

Old snow. When the old snow depth is sufficient to cover natural anchors, such as rocks and brush, additional snow layers will slide more readily. The nature of the old snow surface is important. Rough surfaces favor stability; smooth surfaces, such as sun crusts, are less stable. A loose, underlying snow layer is more dangerous than a compacted one. Check the underlying snow layer with a ski pole, ski, or rod.

Wet snow. Rainstorms or spring weather with warm winds and cloudy nights can warm the snow cover. The resulting free and percolating water may cause wet snow avalanches. Wet snow avalanches are more likely on south slopes and under exposed rock.

While winter travelers expect avalanches during times of heavy snowfall, avalanches are also a serious threat during spring thaw. Here, I cross the base of a large spring snow slide while on a bear hunt in May. (Sherry K. Fears photo)

Travel and survival in avalanche areas. The safest routes are on ridgetops and slightly on the windward side, away from cornices, as shown in the drawings on pages 402 and 403. Windward slopes are usually safer than leeward slopes. If you cannot travel on ridges, the next safest route is out in the valley, far from the bottom of slopes subject to descent of avalanches.

Avoid disturbing cornices from below or above. Gain ridgetops by detouring around cornice areas.

An avalanche cord tied around your waist and trailed behind you might in part remain on the surface if you were buried. Rescuers could then follow the cord to extricate you. (Bill Hotchkiss/ National Ski Patrol photo)

If you must cross dangerous slopes, stay high and near the top. If you see avalanche fracture lines in the snow, avoid them and similar snow areas.

If you must ascend or descend a dangerous slope, go straight up or down; do not make traverses back and forth across the slope.

Take advantage of areas of dense timber, ridges, or rocky outcrops as islands of safety. Use them for lunch and rest stops. Spend as little time as possible on open slopes.

Snowmobiles should not cross the lower part of the slopes. Do not drive a snowmobile across especially long open slopes or known avalanche paths.

Obey signs authorities post closing slopes because of danger. If you must cross a dangerous slope, only one person at a time should cross. All others should watch. To cross a dangerous slope, remove ski pole straps and ski safety straps, loosen all equipment, put on mitts and cap, and fasten clothing before you travel.

Authorities now recommend that all members of a party in avalanche country carry transceivers, which are pocket size devices that can transmit and receive signals. When crossing avalanche-prone terrain, all members of the party switch into the transmit mode. Then if one or more members are caught and buried, other members switch into the receive mode and home-in on the victims. Also probe poles that can be assembled in sections are highly useful in probing for victims.

If you are caught in an avalanche:
- Discard all equipment.
- Get away from your snowmobile.
- Make swimming motions. Try to stay on top; work your way to the side of the avalanche.
- Before coming to a stop, get your hands in

This ski patroller demonstrates the use of an avalanche transceiver in receive mode to locate a buried victim whose transceiver would have been switched into transmit mode when he left his car or the trailhead. The ski pole/probe in the background would then be used to locate the victim precisely and create holes that would improve air flow to the victim. (Bill Hotchkiss/National Ski Patrol photo)

member, you must consider not only the time required for you to get help, but the time required for help to return. After 30 minutes, the buried victim has only a 50 percent chance of surviving.

If there is more than one survivor:
• Send one for help while the others search for the victim. Have the one who goes for help switch his transeiver to transmit mode, in case he gets buried by another avalanche. He should also mark the route effectively so a rescue party can follow back.
• Contact the ski patrol, local sheriff, or Forest Service.
• Administer first aid.
• Treat for suffocation and shock.

For information on the existence of possible avalanche conditions in an area, check the local weather forecasts and contact the Forest Service snow ranger or the nearest winter sports area ski patrol.

With ski pole handles and baskets removed and draped around her neck, this ski patroller converts her two ski poles into avalanche probe poles by screw-mounting them together. The probes are used both for rescue and for testing the snow depths for instability when assessing avalanche danger. (Bill Hotchkiss/National Ski Patrol photo).

front of your face and try to make an air space in the snow as you are coming to a stop.
• Try to remain calm.

If you are the survivor:
• Mark the place where you last saw victims.
• Search for victims directly downslope below the last-seen point. If they are not on the surface, scuff or probe the snow with a pole or stick.
• Do not desert victims and go for help, unless help is only a few minutes away. Re-

Here ski patrollers practice close-order coarse avalanche probing. Thirty inches apart, the rescuers probe once just 1 foot in front of themselves before moving forward together 28 inches. The guide-on cord held by rescuers at the ends of the line ensures that the crucial incremental advances are exact. (Photos courtesy of Bill Hotchkiss/ National Ski Patrol)

In open-order coarse probing, each rescuer probes 15 inches to the left and the right of his body's centerline before moving 28 inches forward on command. This open-order probing is used when relatively few rescuers are available to probe a large area or when deep snow makes uphill movement by probers difficult.

Trip Planning

Anytime you are going into the mountains, the trip should be planned carefully. The route taken, the condition of the roads to and from the mountains, the short-range and long-range weather forecasts, and all other aspects of the trip should be carefully researched.

Allow plenty of time for your trip. Often people think that they can accomplish many goals in the mountains in a day or two and return, not realizing that the steepness of the terrain, the elevation, and sudden changes in weather can all cause the trip to take much longer than expected.

Remember to set your limit and to know when to turn back when any member of your party cannot safely continue. The mountain will still be there another day.

Are you in shape for the trip? The majority of the people I have guided on mountain hunts have not been in shape for the rigors of the hunt. Also, you must be acclimated to the higher elevation. Coming from a city located near sea level and trying to climb a mountain that is over 10,000 feet high within a day or two is almost impossible and downright dangerous. Mountain illnesses are discussed in Chapter 13. In addition, fatigue causes bad judgment and carelessness, both of which have killed many people in the mountains.

In planning your trip, be sure that you have the proper equipment for the terrain and for the weather conditions that you can expect. Early in my career, I learned a hard lesson about wearing the right equipment in the Rocky Mountains. For quite some time I resisted buying a cowboy hat. I didn't want to look like a character from a Zane Grey novel on the high mountain trails. The local guides I was working with kept telling me that the day would come when I would wish I had a cowboy hat. I realized just how right they

were one afternoon when a violent hailstorm hit our packstring. There was nowhere to go, and my bare head took a tremendous beating, as golfball-sized hail pounded us for 15 minutes. Needless to say, as soon as I arrived

Since many mountain accidents result in broken bones, special equipment such as this basket-type stretcher enables rescuers to immobilize limbs and secure victims for lowering through rocky terrain. (Robert N. McIntyre/National Park Service photo)

Headgear of guides is often good authority on the most practical headgear in any region. The traditional cowboy hat wards off sun, wind, rain, and hail. (Erwin A. Bauer photo)

back in civilization, I bought a cowboy hat.

Choose all mountain equipment carefully. If you doubt your ability to select the right equipment, get advice from someone in the outfitting business. The following story illustrates the need for good equipment.

In 1983, two men were hunting deer on the Idaho-Oregon border at the 7,000-foot range. They had shot a deer, but left it because it was too heavy to carry out, and returned with horses to recover it. It took them much of the day to ride the few miles from their parked truck to the deer, which they sliced in half and packed onto the horses. They then started back up the steep, slippery trail.

By late afternoon, they realized they were in trouble. Rain and sleet were being whipped by a 50-mile-an-hour wind. Both hunters were soaked to the skin. They decided to camp overnight, but high winds kept them from lighting a fire, and both men started suffering from hypothermia. Eventually the wind reached 80 miles an hour. During the night one man cut meat from the deer, and the two men ate it. But the food did little to restore their energy. Recognizing that they were in serious trouble, the men shot their pack animals at approximately 9:00 P.M., gutted the carcasses, and crawled into the body cavities for shelter and warmth from the body mass.

By 2:00 A.M., the carcasses had lost their heat, and by 5:30, the men were again shivering uncontrollably. They crawled out and decided they would walk. Promptly they became lost and walked 6 miles before finding their truck and driving it to safety. Meanwhile, friends and relatives looking for the missing hunters recovered their saddles, gear, and deer. Not having proper camping gear almost cost these men their lives. According to them, they owe their survival to those few hours of warmth they received from the car-

Mountain climbers are generally well-equipped. Here the danger of falling rocks and falls themselves is so high that impact-resistant helmets get the nod. (Karl Zeise/Outward Bound USA

casses of their horses and to the encouragement they gave each other.

Survival Techniques in the Mountains

The basic survival techniques that also apply to the mountain environment are covered in many of the other chapters in this book. However, there are a few techniques which are especially important in the mountains.

Shelter. Many shelters can be used for mountain survival. Lean-to, tube tent, hole in the snow, snow trench, and fallen tree are among the many possibilities. However, most mountains contain a lot of rocks and rock overhangs; these can provide excellent natural shelters. Locate near boulders or a cliff that may offer pockets large enough for you to fit into. If you are sitting out an electrical storm, be sure to try to locate shelter that is low on the mountainside. Rock overhangs and caves on high ridges or summits can be very dangerous in lightning storms. Also, when selecting a rock shelter, watch out for bees, snakes, scorpions, or other troublesome critters. My son and I were once using a rock shelter in the mountains of South Carolina when we suddenly realized that we were sharing the shelter with an extremely active yellow jacket nest.

In a rock shelter a fire 5 to 6 feet away from the rock wall is an excellent means of staying warm. Then build a reflector wall on the far side of the fire and sit between the fire and the rock wall so that heat is reflected from both sides. I once spent several nights in New Mexico in a makeshift camp beside a cliff and stayed reasonably warm this way.

Signaling. Be sure you get out where you can be seen, or have your signals out there. On numerous occasions I have participated in mountain searches for lost hunters. In many cases, the hunters had made their survival camp down in the bottom of a canyon or far back in a hollow or cove. Searchers could not see the ground-to-air signals the hunters had laid out because of the hidden location.

Also consider using fire and smoke signals. Since many of our mountains are located within the boundaries of national forests, fire tower rangers and aircraft spotters look for fires. Many times alert Forest Service personnel have spotted signal smoke early in survival situations.

Food and water. Never venture into the mountains, even in less remote areas, without taking an ample supply of food and water. Sudden changes in the weather, a fall, or many other adverse situations can suddenly force you to survive on what is immediately avail-

able. When going into the mountains, even on a one-day hiking trip, I take three to four days' supply of freeze-dried food and two canteens of water. In many of our mountain regions, water is readily available. But much of it is not to be trusted. So boil it or have some other water treatment system in the daypack.

The person going into the mountains should also take a survival kit, which, in my opinion, should contain a tube tent. A hunter-orange tube tent made from plastic serves many purposes. It is useful as a signal, it is an excellent windbreak, and it provides adequate shelter for survival. Even in the Appalachian Mountains of Georgia I have seen summertime temperatures dip after an intense rain to an uncomfortably cool level, even to the point that hypothermia could occur.

In spite of the brevity of this chapter, do

Mountain rescue is a very specialized skill, as demonstrated by this team of rescuers bringing an injured climber down a straight rock cliff. Rescue in such treacherous places should be left to professionals. (National Park Service photo)

Falls are one of the leading causes of rescue missions in the mountains. Here a rescue team prepares a helicopter with ropes to extract a fall victim below.

not consider mountain environments less dangerous than others. The mountains are a great place to visit, but they can be extremely dangerous. For the survival tips that also apply in mountains, read the other chapters in this book on shelter, signaling, fire building, edible wild plants and animals, and survival medicine.

Again, plan your mountain trip carefully. Let someone know where you are going and when you will return. Take along the items necessary for survival, especially items that may possibly be needed, such as raingear, sleeping bag, and extra food and water. And don't take chances. Once you realize you are in a bad situation, pick a survival campsite where you can be easily spotted from the air, build a comfortable survival camp, and await rescue. Wandering around in the mountains is dangerous and hampers rescue efforts.

19
STRANDINGS CAN HAPPEN

People usually think of survival crises as occurring only when a natural disaster hits their home or when they get lost in backcountry. Few people consider that a survival crisis can occur when they go for a walk or ride. Yet many people find themselves suddenly unable to continue their trip for a variety of reasons. They fall into an abandoned well while on a hunting trip, their car breaks down on a lonely stretch of road, their plane goes down in a snowstorm, or their snowmobile stops running miles from anyone. These stranded people find themselves in a survival crisis and need survival skills.

Strandings usually occur when you least expect them. Here is an example of a stranding that occurred in Tennessee in 1981.

Jeff Hogue, a biologist, was trapped for eight days in an 18-foot-deep sinkhole. Finally, two teenage squirrel hunters heard his cries from the hole and alerted rescuers.

"All I wanted to do was get out of there," Hogue said before leaving University of Tennessee Hospital, where he was treated for hypothermia, trench foot, and dehydration. "That's what I thought about most of the time when I wasn't sleeping. I tried to make

I shot this photo of my departing outfitter's plane after I was dropped at a little lake in northern British Columbia, eager to begin a 150-mile float trip down the Stikine River. As I recount later in this chapter, this photo kicked off a week-long ordeal in which I was stranded here with inadequate gear, an impossible route to negotiate, and camp visits from a grizzly.

a ladder out of some sticks and my long underwear, but every time I made some progress the earth just cracked under the weight. It was hell," he said.

While on a walk Hogue had lost his footing and slipped into the sinkhole. When he failed to return, Mrs. Hogue reported her husband missing and notified the Knox County Sheriff's Department.

Hogue said he calmed himself about ten minutes after his fall. "I never lost sanity while I was in that hole," he said. "The entire time I was in the hole I just followed what I knew and it worked out." He had managed to make mud pockets to catch dripping ice for drinking water.

Another true example of just how fast a stranding can become a survival situation happened to a Connecticut magazine reporter who traveled to Nevada on a story assignment. This reporter arrived in Elko, rented a car, and got directions to the ranch 50 miles away where he was supposed to go for the story. The reporter was dressed in business clothes and had no survival gear.

Some 40 miles out of town, he made a wrong turn and got lost. Trying to find his way back on the rocky roads, he hit a rock and ruptured the car's oil pan. The car stopped, in the middle of nowhere. The reporter started walking in what he thought was the ranch's direction.

During the next four hours as he walked, the temperature dropped from 90° to 50°. After four hours of walking, the cold, footsore reporter decided to make a survival camp in a grassy meadow. He had only six matches for a fire. He used them all, but did not get a fire started.

Being too cold to sleep, he started walking back to the car at 11:30 P.M. Walking was painful with his sore feet, and his knees began to stiffen. He was in big trouble, and he knew it. He continued to walk slowly. And

imagination was fevered.

At 4:00 A.M., he saw headlights and up drove a cowboy in an old pickup truck. The reporter was saved from further torture. He learned that his stranding could have been much worse because it was 40 miles to the next person and a vehicle used that road only once every three days or so.

The first thing to learn about strandings is that they can happen to anyone, near home or on a trip, usually at the worst possible time.

So plan your trips with survival in mind, whether you are going for a walk in the woods at the end of the street where you live or flying a light plane across the Rockies. Let some responsible person know your plans — where you are going, how long you will be gone, your method of transportation, and all other pertinent data. If you walked out of your backyard for a short late-evening stroll in a city park and fell, breaking a leg, no one would know where to look for you if you had neglected to leave the pertinent information with a responsible family member.

How often do you file a trip plan when you are going to a nearby town? One lady took her two children with her for a few hours of shopping at a shopping mall only 20 miles from her home. Since she expected to be back before her husband returned home from work, she didn't tell anyone where she was going. Her car broke down on a busy interstate highway. She had no survival gear, no CB radio, and nothing to use for a distress signal. She waved all afternoon to passing cars and trucks. No one stopped. She and the children spent the night in the car, terrified. The husband didn't know where to start looking for them. He and the police expected the worst when the wife and children couldn't be located with family or friends. At daylight the next morning, a highway patrolman stopped to check the stalled car. That family now

This fisherman unexpectedly found himself wading a creek, pulling his boat back to its launching point after the motor developed a minor problem. If he had taken a repair kit along, he might have repaired the motor and continued his fishing trip.

files trip plans and carries survival gear.

I stress the need to carry simple survival gear over and over in this book. Every vehicle, boat, snowmobile, trail bike, or plane that you have or travel in should have a survival kit suitable for the weather and terrain in which you will be traveling. For cross-country ski trips, hikes, and fishing or hunting trips, you should carry a compact personal survival kit or a daypack with the necessities to sustain life. Even for a stroll in a woodland adjoining your community, it's a good idea to carry a pocketknife,

matches in a waterproof container, and a cigarette-pack-size space blanket. Chances are if you tell someone where you are going you won't need the survival items, but if you do, they are worth your comfort or maybe your life.

Keep Your Transportation in Good Working Order

The vast majority of the people who get stranded do so because they leave on a trip with equipment that is something less than ready for a trip. A worn fan belt on a four-wheel-drive vehicle can leave you miles back in a desert. A weak battery in a boat can leave you paddling miles out in the Gulf of Mexico.

In order to avoid such strandings, follow these rules:

1. Keep your maintenance and inspection schedules up-to-date on all mechanized equipment.

2. Before departing on any trip, do a spot check. If you are in a hurry, leave your vehicle with a service center for a spot check. The extra cost could save your life.

3. Carry spare parts and tools. Know how to make simple repairs.

4. Always leave with plenty of fuel. If you are going out where there are no refueling stations, use the "one-third" rule—one-third tank out, one-third tank back, and one-third tank in reserve.

Operate with Caution

The second major reason for most strandings is that the operator drives carelessly and isn't observant. A rock in a backcountry road stopped the magazine reporter I discussed earlier in this chapter. Running a snowmobile off into a creek will do the same thing. A boat that hits a submerged log can leave you floating in big water.

Anytime you travel by machine, you have the responsibility to operate it with care and common sense. Here you must keep your eyes open and not take chances. Several times I have been stranded in four-wheel-drive vehicles simply because the driver tried to take them where they weren't intended to go.

Drinking alcohol and operating a vehicle is asking for trouble. Have those drinks after the trip, not during.

Know Your Guide and Outfitter

Sometimes you can be stranded because you depend upon someone else for your well-being while on a backcountry trip. Let me give you an example of what happened to me.

In planning to float the remote headwaters of the Stikine River in British Columbia, I spent a lot of time gathering gear and weather

Foolhardy operation of vehicles is a common cause of strandings, which are often accompanied by injuries.

Here I am studying a map when I first realized that my outfitter had stranded me in British Columbia, where survival skills saved me. This story is recounted in accompanying text.

information. Since I needed to have someone fly me in and out as well as furnish a canoe, food, and camping gear, I looked for an outfitter. A friend told me of an outfitter he used on the Stikine, and a call to the outfitter assured me that he was as good and reliable as I had been told. I checked no further. This outfitter agreed to completely outfit me with the best, including a new canoe specially designed for running far-north rivers. He also told me that he knew the waterway well and I didn't need to bother studying river conditions and portages. He would have every-

thing set up when I arrived. I believed him.

The outfitter's plane dropped me off on a small lake that fed the stream that was to be the start of my float trip. From the time I arrived at the outfitter's base camp the previous night until the outfitter shoved me out the plane door the next morning, 300 miles from anywhere, he didn't have time to discuss my trip in detail. He had too many guests to bother with me. As he was closing the plane door, he told me he would meet me a week later at a point on the Stikine River some 150 miles from where I was.

With a strong feeling that this trip had gotten out of control, and at my expense, I assessed the gear my outfitter had supplied. The wrong kind of canoe, an alcohol stove that didn't work, a three-day supply of dehydrated eggs, a few matches, and a tent. He had not supplied a means of cutting wood. Nor had he provided a spare paddle or many other things that a responsible outfitter should. I was glad I had brought my own camping and survival equipment.

But I got a big surprise when I opened my bag I'd marked "Camping Gear." Customs officials had switched the contents of my two bags. Instead of camping gear, I had a bag of extra clothing.

With the feeling I'd been had, I shoved off on what was becoming a survival trip. I canoed down the lake and found the stream I was to go down to the Stikine River. About a mile below the lake, the stream became a series of Class VI rapids, with powerful flow, standing waves, and boiling eddies. A 2-mile portage down the side of a mountain was in order, according to my topo map. I decided to hike down to where the stream leveled off again to scout my portage route before I made what I figured would be four round trips.

A Canadian rescue 'copter here practices for a real stranding.

There was no portage trail, and I needed two hours without a load to descend over the rocks and through hundreds of windfalls to reach the valley floor. There I found the stream went from a Class VI raging creek to a wide, slow, 6-inch nothing of a stream that couldn't possibly be floated.

I climbed back to where I had left my canoe, put on my waders, and plunged into the icy water to pull the canoe back up the swift stream to the lake. There I found an old camp where someone had left a good supply of wood, set up camp of sorts, and hoped someone would find me before I ran out of firewood. For several days, I spent much of my time cussing the outfitter, catching fish to eat, watching the sky for a plane, and shooing off a grizzly bear that kept hanging around. About a week later, I managed to flag a plane in with my red shirt, and my float trip was over.

Not checking several of the outfitter's references cost me a float trip, plus time and money.

Always check out guides and outfitters carefully. Ask for a list of references and call each one of them yourself. Also, don't depend on anyone else for route information; take the time to get it yourself. Had I done this, I would have known beforehand that the route the outfitter had planned for me was impossible.

If you plan to use equipment that is furnished by an outfitter, demand that you review the equipment before you depart, and don't go if it isn't the proper equipment, doesn't work, or isn't packed properly. An outfitter who checks out well with several references usually has good equipment or else you would hear about it.

I have known of hunters and fishermen who used an outfitter to drop them off in the backcountry and failed to pick them up on the prearranged date. In some of these instances, the weather caused a delay of several days. But in a few cases, the outfitter just forgot to pick them up. In either case, they were stranded. Thus, always let local authorities know your trip plans so that if something happens to your outfitter, someone will know where you are and come looking for you.

Strandings are common, and many become serious. Of all survival crises, getting stranded is probably the easiest to avoid simply by following a few simple rules.

20

DOWNED AIRCRAFT SURVIVAL

"Mayday, Mayday, Mayday." This emergency code comes in from many airplanes in trouble. In fact, the Civil Air Patrol participates in an average of 1,000 search missions each year, most of which are for downed aircraft. Most of the people in these aircraft never thought it would happen to them. One minute they were comfortably flying over rough, remote terrain; the next minute they were on the ground in a survival situation. Here is an account of a downing that occurred in December 1978.

On a 55-minute flight across the Continental Divide from Steamboat Springs to Denver, a Rocky Mountain Airways plane went down with 19 passengers and two crewmen. Searchers on snowmobiles followed a high-voltage line knocked out by the crash to reach the 21 occupants 10,000 feet up in the mountains. One woman died in the crash.

Temperatures dipped into the teens and winds swept the mountain at 35 mph while the survivors waited 11 hours for rescue. The commander of the Colorado Civil Air Patrol said the windchill index during the night reached −50°F. "If you'd been up there and

This single-engine, five-seat plane crashed during a snowstorm on the Yukon-British Columbia border on February 4, 1963. The crash tore off both of the plane's wings and broke the engine loose. The pilot, Ralph Flores, and his passenger, Helen Klaben, survived crash injury, frostbite, and starvation for seven weeks and were finally spotted and rescued on March 25th, weeks after search efforts had been called off. Their amazing story of deprivation and perseverance was featured that year in Life *magazine and in* The Saturday Evening Post. *That story is further illustrated and described later in this chapter. (Photo courtesy of Ralph Flores)*

422

seen the weather we had, you'd be amazed that they survived," said the Grand County sheriff, one of the rescuers.

Except for an eight-month-old boy who escaped unscratched and a 20-year-old man who was treated and released, all the survivors were hospitalized, five in critical condition.

According to the Civil Air Patrol, of every 100 persons involved in air crashes, only 35 will survive initially, only 18 will survive for 24 hours and less than ten will live more than 72 hours.

Some of the after-crash deaths can be avoided. With the proper survival gear, survival training, and a will to live, many of these people could live for days or weeks.

What to Do Before You Fly

Before anyone, either passenger or pilot, takes off on a private plane trip he should make sure that a few basic rules are followed.

File a flight plan. Be sure a flight plan is filed, and stay with the plan. If you change your plans en route, notify the Federal Aviation Administration (FAA) of this change at once. Upon arrival at your destination, file an arrival report. Remember that a search normally starts after you fail to report in and enough time has passed that your fuel is exhausted—usually three hours. Don't delay your arrival report.

When no flight plan is filed, the rescue attempt can be delayed for a long time or may never be made. Here is what can happen:

"It was the longest night. It was an eternity," said one of six persons who survived a subzero night after their plane crashed near the Continental Divide.

The six were Iowa residents on a vacation trip to Las Vegas. Their single-engine plane slammed into a steep mountainside about

1,000 feet from the summit of 13,000-foot Tin Cup Pass in the Rockies of south-central Colorado.

No flight plan had been filed and no search was under way when a father and his two sons, stopping to cool the engines of their snowmobiles, heard the cries for help about 18 hours later.

Another six hours passed before all six sur-

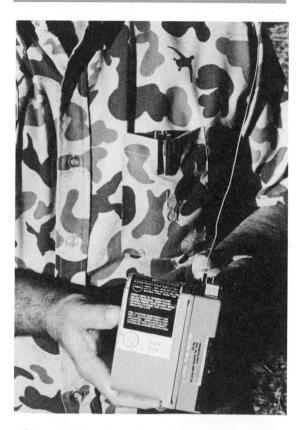

This small box is an Emergency Locator Transmitter (ELT). After a crash, it lets searchers zero-in on the crash site. Pilots should frequently check the ELTs in their planes to be sure they are working properly and that batteries are fully charged so the ELT will automatically activate upon crash.

vivors could be brought from the rugged mountain to a hospital.

Check the Emergency Locator Transmitter. The Emergency Locator Transmitter (ELT), usually located in the tail of the aircraft, has proved to be the best aid to searchers and the best hope for timely rescue of survivors of air crashes. The ELT is a small electronic box which can beam out a strong signal when activated. This signal can be picked up by commercial and military aircraft. It can also be picked up by satellites owned by the United States and the Soviet Union that are carrying a SARSAT (Search and Rescue Satellite Aided Tracking) package. With the aid of the SARSAT satellites, the science of finding aircraft and oceangoing vessels in distress has taken a giant step.

During the first few months the first SARSAT became operational aboard the Soviet Union's COSPAS satellite, the system paid off. Here are some examples.

● A Cessna 172, boxed in by lowering ceiling and a rising terrain, crashed 50 miles off course in the wilderness of northern British Columbia. The three persons aboard suffered a variety of injuries, including leg, arm, and rib fractures. The ELT antenna got lost during the crash, but the survivors found a wire, jammed it into the antenna socket, and carried the unit to a nearby hill. During the evening, the COSPAS satellite passed over; the signals led rescuers to within about 14 miles of the wreckage.

● A private plane crashed in heavy terrain 160 miles north of Montreal, with one person surviving. Rescuers reached the scene

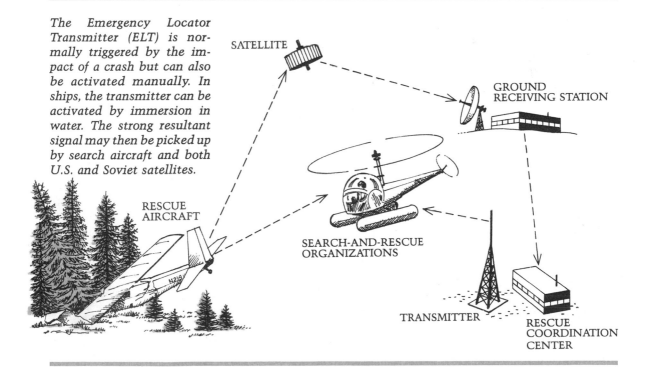

The Emergency Locator Transmitter (ELT) is normally triggered by the impact of a crash but can also be activated manually. In ships, the transmitter can be activated by immersion in water. The strong resultant signal may then be picked up by search aircraft and both U.S. and Soviet satellites.

SATELLITE

GROUND RECEIVING STATION

RESCUE AIRCRAFT

SEARCH-AND-RESCUE ORGANIZATIONS

TRANSMITTER

RESCUE COORDINATION CENTER

two and a half hours after signals were picked up by SARSAT.

● The pilot of an oil company's Jet Ranger helicopter in Canada was saved when SARSAT picked up ELT signals after two passes of the COSPAS satellite.

Statistics show that when a downed aircraft is equipped with a functioning ELT, the average elapsed time in getting aid to survivors is 23 hours. But in crashes with no ELT, the average time to get help to the crash site is nearly five days. Also, the average flying time for the search effort is only 19 hours on ELT missions and 130 hours on non-ELT missions.

In summary, the ELT greatly increases survival chances of crash victims and reduces both operating costs of search aircraft and exposure to danger of search personnel. Therefore, even with all the false alarms caused by inadvertent activation of ELTs, the ELT is still an excellent search aid.

However, like any other survival gear, the ELT is of no use to survivors if it is not in proper working order. In 1976, Lauren Elder and two friends crashed in a small plane in the Sierra Nevadas. No search-and-rescue planes came. Lauren was forced to climb from 12,360 feet down to 4,000 feet over some 10 miles of rugged mountains. Then she walked another 10 miles across the desert in order to reach help. The ELT in her friend's plane had never been activated; its batteries were dead and the connection was too corroded to make electrical contact.

Make sure the ELT in your plane is working!

Carry survival gear. Be sure your plane has a survival kit and survival gear as suggested for aircraft in Chapter 4. This survival gear should be stored in a daypack so that it will be kept together in the plane, making it easy to retrieve after a crash and easy to carry if you must change locations. Don't forget to include food and water in your survival gear. You could be in for a long wait.

Dress and equip yourself according to ground weather. It is important for you to dress according to the ground weather you will be flying over. You may be going from warm airport to warm airport and therefore dress in light clothing. Then, if you're forced down in cold mountains, you don't have much of a chance of survival. If you don't want to wear the clothing, at least take it with you. A sleeping bag per person should be taken during cold weather. Raingear should be taken during wet weather.

Watch the weather along your entire route and cancel or postpone the trip if there is any question as to the weather or changes in weather.

If your route takes you over large bodies of water, take along a self-inflatable life raft, and know how to use it.

When You Go Down

Here are steps to take if your aircraft goes down:

1. Get survival gear and exit aircraft immediately.

2. If possible, move everyone a safe distance from the aircraft to avoid dangers from fire and explosions. Wait until the engines have cooled and spilled aircraft fuel has evaporated before you return to the aircraft.

3. Check everyone for injuries and administer first aid to those with injuries.

4. While awaiting your return to the aircraft, make temporary shelter to protect everyone from inclement weather.

5. Get signals ready for use in the event rescue units arrive at the scene quickly.

6. Reassure everyone, including yourself, and remain calm.

7. If the aircraft radios are still serviceable, they should momentarily be turned to the distress frequency to ensure that the ELT is operating. Once the ELT is activated, it must be left on since turning it off can result in a search aircraft being thwarted in its attempt to home in on the transmission.

8. If the aircraft radios are operational, try to make contact with the FAA on a local frequency.

9. Search the aircraft for items that you may have to use in survival—maps, clothing, tools.

At this point, a major decision must be reached, and that is whether to stay with the aircraft or leave the crash site. The basic rule is to stay with the aircraft if at all possible, since searchers will be looking for it soon and because it has an ELT working for you. You will also avoid the possible hazards of travel. Your chances will be good if you have made radio contact; if you have come down on course or near a traveled air route; or if weather and air observation conditions are good.

The aircraft is generally easier to spot from the air than are men traveling. Someone may even have seen your plane come down and may be along to investigate. The aircraft or parts from it can provide you with shelter, signaling aids, and other equipment. If the temperature is neither too cold nor too hot, the cabin of the plane can be used as a shelter. However, in temperature extremes, the cabin can be an oven or refrigerator. If the weather is cold, the plane's insulation and upholstery can be used to make many items, such as sleeping bags, caps, or mattresses. Wings, rudder, or doors may be used to make a shelter. The battery can provide a spark for fire-starting, and the aircraft fuel and oil can be used for fuel. Such items as maps, curtains, and newspapers can be used to improve the shelter and to provide warmth. Use cowling for reflector signals, tubing for shelter framework, and the generator for radio power.

However, there are rare occasions when you may need to move some distance from the aircraft, such as if it is down under trees and cannot be seen from the air, as in the classic case of Helen Klaben and Ralph Flores in 1963. The pair left Whitehorse, Yukon, heading for San Francisco in a small private airplane. Neither had survival training. Over the Yukon-British Columbia border, they ran into a blinding snowstorm which caused them to crash.

For over a month search-and-rescue aircraft flew over the area looking for the downed plane, but the thick trees in which Helen and Ralph had crashed hid the plane from view.

Both Helen and Ralph were injured in the crash, but they managed to set up a survival camp at the aircraft. They had very little survival gear on the plane: matches, a little food, some vitamin pills, two tubes of toothpaste, hammer, cold chisel, hunting knife, books, canvas motor cover, and extra clothing. For a blanket, they tore the carpet from the plane floor and insulation from the walls and ceiling. Seat and back cushions were used for beds. Firewood was cut with the chisel and hammer. During their ordeal, temperatures dropped to 40°F. below zero.

Their food ran out the first week. From then on it was only water, which they got by melting snow in a can. Their drinking cup was made from a light reflector from the plane. They made several attempts to kill rabbits that came near their camp, but nothing worked.

For 33 days they stayed with the aircraft, but after hearing 40 to 50 aircraft pass nearby, they decided they must move if they were to be found. On snowshoes made from

This SOS stomped in the snow of a burned-over Yukon mountainside in March 1963 brought rescue to crash victims Ralph Flores and Helen Klaben. They had suffered without food or adequate shelter for seven weeks. The temperature at one point plummeted to 48 degrees below zero. The arrow in the photo points to the site of the lean-to that sheltered Klaben, while Flores struck out overland in search of help. The SOS letters, which Flores stomped using makeshift snowshoes, measured 75 feet high. During the night after rescue, a snowstorm obliterated the SOS. (AP/Wide World Photos)

After rescue, crash survivor Ralph Flores is shown at Watson Lake, Yukon, being helped to a plane that would carry him to the hospital at Whitehorse. During the crash of his plane, shown on page 423, Flores suffered a broken jaw, broken ribs, and facial lacerations. Except for meager soups and snacks of canned fish during the first of seven weeks, Flores had no food. Instead he daily drew energy for strenuous signal efforts from his faith and his body's fat reserves. As the baggy pants and cinched belt attest in this photo, Flores lost 58 pounds during the ordeal. (Photo courtesy of Ralph Flores)

This is Helen Klaben the day she was found at the lean-to shelter she and Ralph Flores fashioned in a clearing away from their plane to improve chances they would be spotted. Klaben suffered a broken arm in the crash, lost 40 pounds during the seven-week ordeal, and—after rescue—lost the toes of her frostbitten right foot. (UPI/Bettmann Archive photo)

Pilot Chuck Hamilton, who spotted Ralph Flores's SOS and then Helen Klaben the day before, is shown on snowshoes carrying frozen-footed Klaben to his plane—a 3-hour trek away. Meanwhile Flores was being rescued by Indian trappers and dogsled sent by pilot Hamilton the day before. Reunited at the cabin of the trappers, Flores and Klaben partook of moose meat, tea, and crackers before Hamilton flew them out. Klaben describes the ordeal in her book Hey, I'm Alive! (UPI/Bettman Archive photo)

branches and a toboggan made from aircraft parts, they moved their meager supplies through deep snow to an opening in the forest. Since they were very weak, this ¾-mile journey was quite tough. Here they used the engine cover tarpaulin to make a tent. Ralph then moved to another clearing about two miles distant and tramped SOS in the snow as well as an arrow aimed in Helen's direction. Also, they placed in the snow a fragment of their plane which showed the plane's identification number.

This new camp and signals resulted in their being found. A bush pilot flying supplies to trappers spotted the SOS and the arrow, and then Helen, and 49 days after crashing into the frozen wilderness, they were rescued.

If your aircraft is hidden, the first thing to do is try to cut trees and brush so as to make it visible from the air. If this is impossible, move only a short distance to the first clearing you can find and set up your ground-to-air signals.

Organize for Rescue

If you are with a group of survivors, organize them and your camp so that everyone that is able will stay busy and the camp organized for rescue.

The first step in organization of the party is to appoint individual members to specific jobs, based on their abilities and their physical and mental capacities to handle them. Pool all food and equipment with one person in charge. Prepare a shelter to protect everyone from rain, sand, snow, wind, cold, or insects. Collect all possible fuel, the variety of which will be determined by your geographical location. Always try to have at least one day's supply of fuel on hand. Then look for water and for animal and plant food. Make

sure your signals are always in good shape and ready for instant use.

Reassure everyone and try to keep the will to live alive even if rescue is several days in coming. As we saw in the beginning of this chapter, many survivors of aircraft crashes die while waiting for rescue. This is an unnecessary loss of life. By carrying the necessary survival gear, taking precautions such as filing flight plans and learning survival techniques, and using survival skills when the aircraft is down, you could make it through aircraft survival situations.

At no time should you attempt to move unless you know exactly where you are and where you are going. To wander aimlessly uses up vital energy that is very difficult to replace under survival conditions. If you are leaving a crash site, even for a short distance, leave a message for rescuers indicating the date and direction of your travel. Regardless of your reason for moving, consider the weather. Stay put if adverse weather would further endanger you. If travel for help is indicated, send the best fit people—two, if possible. To travel alone is dangerous.

Make a definite plan to follow. Determine the nearest rescue point, the distance to it, the possible difficulties and hazards of travel, and the facilities and supplies at the destination. Travel is extremely risky unless you have the necessities of survival to support you during travel. You should have sufficient water to reach the next possible source of water as indicated on your map or chart, enough food to last until you are able to procure additional food, and a means of shelter.

While this chapter has given some pointers on traveling away from the crash site, such travel is not usually recommended. The most important rule of downed aircraft survival is to stay with the aircraft.

21

DISABLED VEHICLE SURVIVAL

Automobiles, trucks, and four-wheel-drives are responsible for some of the most common stranding situations we have. We see these vehicles alongside our roads and interstate highways every day. For highway drivers, the stranding is usually nothing more than a nuisance because help is usually nearby. However, for those who travel into little-traveled areas and suddenly find themselves stranded, the situation can become serious quickly.

In March one year, I drove to northern Georgia to give a speech. The day following the speech, I decided to take the long way home and drive my station wagon into a remote section of the Chattahoochee National Forest to look at a camping area. From the map, the drive seemed simple enough and not too far out of the way. In spite of a hard rain, I took off, dressed in a business suit. I

didn't bother to let anyone know my plans. Since my station wagon was new, I had all the confidence in the world that nothing could go wrong.

By midmorning I had left the paved road and was climbing high into the mountains on a one-lane Forest Service road. The rain was pouring down. I noticed my car kept pulling to the right, but I thought the rocks and pitch of the road were causing it. Suddenly a red light came on, warning me that the car was overheating. I stopped just as a

---

The traction of four-wheel-drive vehicles sometimes encourages risks that often result in strandings. Although four-wheel drives can tackle rugged terrain indeed, they are not meant to substitute for boats. (Chuck Adams photo)

cloud of steam poured from under the hood.

Upon inspection, I found that I had been driving on a flat right front tire. The new station wagon came with two-ply tires, definitely not tires for a one-lane mountain road. Driving on the flat had caused the car to overheat, and the radiator hose had split. I changed the tire, used some tape to patch the radiator hose, used a hubcap to partially refill the radiator, and got back into the vehicle to drive the short distance to the campground.

I was soaked, and by this time all I wanted to do was to fill the radiator and get back to civilization. I drove only 100 yards or so before I heard the loud hiss that told me another two-ply tire had lost its battle with the rocky road. This time, there was no spare. As I pulled off the road, the red light came on again. My tape had not held the leak in the radiator. I was stranded. I had no survival gear. I wasn't properly dressed. I hadn't seen a person since I left the paved road miles below, and no one knew where I was.

I decided that in spite of the weather there might be someone camping in the campground. So I walked in the rain the mile or so to the campground. It was closed and a sign indicated the campground would remain closed until the following month, April! I walked back to the car to think. As I sat in my wet suit thinking, I decided that I should walk back down to the paved road. There had been some houses there. I was in good shape, so I figured the hike wouldn't take me all afternoon.

After walking down the steep, rocky road for two hours in street shoes that were full of water, it was apparent that I was in for a long hike. Then I heard a car coming. I stood in the center of the road and waved. I must have looked like something from a horror movie, because the old mountaineer driving the car cleaned out a ditch to avoid stopping for me. I walked on through the night with

the air temperature of 45° to 50°F, stopping for an hour or two to rest and build a fire to avoid hypothermia. By morning I reached a house. Three dogs came out to assault me, tearing my wet trousers and snapping at my heels. They saw to it that I sought another house. The people in the second house proved to be most helpful after I spent a few minutes convincing them through a window that, in spite of my looks, I was a decent person.

This story could have had a sad ending. It just illustrates how quickly we can get into trouble with vehicles.

Anyone going anywhere with a vehicle should let someone know his plans. This is especially true if the trip, long or short, takes the vehicle off the beaten path. File a trip plan—where you are going, when you plan to arrive at your destination, when you plan to return. If you should fail to show up at your destination, the authorities would have something to go on. Had I not walked out of the Georgia mountains, no one would have known where to start looking for me. Everyone I knew thought I was in Atlanta.

Keep your vehicle in good working order. Have it checked before trips. The two-ply tires that caused my problems were not designed for remote mountain roads, and I should have known better than to leave them on my station wagon.

Fan belts account for many strandings, as does running out of fuel. Make sure your belts are in good shape and carry a spare. Plan the fuel for your trips on the one-third tank rule—one-third of a tank going, one-third of a tank returning, and one-third of a tank in reserve. If it is doubtful that your vehicle can make a trip, don't take it.

Watch the weather. Each winter we read of people who get caught in snow and ice storms and are found dead by rescue squads. Our need to travel in storms gets many of us in trouble every winter.

There was a story in the papers in 1973 of a young couple and their infant daughter who ignored weather reports of an approaching winter storm. They took a drive into an Oregon national forest. Suddenly a snowstorm struck, and then they took a wrong turn and wound up stuck some 20 miles off on a logging road. After spending the night in their car, the couple with their baby decided to walk out. It was a tragic mistake. While the baby survived and was okay, the mother died and the father suffered frostbitten toes.

Listen to a weather radio before you depart on a trip. If there are storm warnings, stay home. If, as this couple did, you get caught in a snowstorm, stay with your vehicle. If possible, keep the top of the vehicle free of snow so that it can be seen from the air, and rest up for rescue. Carry survival gear with you and, if your car color blends in with the snow, a bright orange panel.

Vehicle Survival Gear

Every vehicle should carry basic survival gear that is upgraded periodically to match the season and the terrain in which you will be traveling. A fully equipped survival kit should be carried. See Chapter 4 in this book on survival kits for vehicle travel.

Every vehicle should have a CB radio. I like to carry the GE "HELP" portable CB radio. It packs well, can be moved from vehicle to vehicle without installation, and can simply be plugged into the cigarette lighter socket in the vehicle. This small CB can be stored under a seat or in the trunk. A CB radio can be a great general travel aid, and I highly recommended that it be part of your survival gear.

Another vital survival item that all vehicles should carry is a portable air compressor. The one that I have tested is the Coleman

A CB radio can be a valuable piece of survival equipment for any vehicle. There are very few areas in North America where you cannot reach help when using CB radio.

The Coleman Inflate-All can have a slow-leak flat tire ready to drive on within a few minutes. (Coleman Company photo)

Inflate-All. The multipurpose Inflate-All takes care of low tires on passenger vehicles, four-wheel-drives, pickups, RVs, motorcycles, and bicycles on the spot. One advantage is that it can re-inflate tires without your needing to jack up the vehicle. It plugs into a vehicle's cigarette lighter socket to operate the 12-volt motor and positive displacement compressor. Included are a 13½-foot power cord and 3-foot air hose, along with two air chuck adapters to inflate footballs, basketballs, and other sports equipment. There is a positive-latching tire valve connector with pressure-check stem to allow pressure checking without removing the connector from the tire. The compact air compressor fits into a high-impact plastic case and weighs less than 5 pounds.

Additional survival items that you should keep in your vehicle include a first aid kit, a gallon of water (much more if you are traveling in desert country), emergency food, matches in a waterproof container, basic tools for repairs, spare parts, tow rope, raingear, shovel, ax, and during cold weather a sleeping bag per person and tire chains.

During cool or cold weather, your vehicle makes an excellent shelter and is easy to spot, so there is no need to leave it. Since most cars are very tightly built, keep a window slightly open to allow fresh air to enter. This is especially true if you are burning anything in the car or running the motor to keep warm.

In extremely hot weather, the vehicle can become an oven. In this case, seek shelter in the shade beside or under the vehicle. See Chapter 15 on desert survival.

Four-wheel-drive Vehicles

My work in wildlife management brings me into contact with hundreds of outdoorsmen each year who use four-wheel-drive vehicles to get into the backcountry. Most of these people are experienced outdoorsmen but are obviously somewhat inexperienced in driving through the mud and sand. I see scores of these vehicles stuck, and most could have avoided the problem.

A lot of new owners of four-wheelers think that because they paid double what they would pay for a standard car and because their four-wheeler has big tires, plus a winch, it can swim through the deepest mudhole. This attitude can only lead to trouble.

Let's start from the beginning and see how the driver of a four-wheel-drive vehicle should approach backcountry driving.

Get your vehicle ready for the trip. Proper tires should have round shoulders and a moderately aggressive tread such as the standard mud-grip tread. You should have a power winch installed if your budget can stand the cost. You should also have a tool chest that includes snow chains (even though you don't expect snow), shovel, ax, hand-operated tire pump, two jacks, 50-foot nylon rope for towing (10,000-pound-test), two planks 2 inches thick, 1 foot wide, and 2 feet long, and a set of wrenches.

If you don't have a winch, be sure to add what's known as a "come-along" to your tool chest. The come-along is simply a hand-powered winch. It is best described as a hand-cranked, cable-filled wheel and ratchet. You attach one end of the cable to a tree and the come-along to the vehicle frame. Each time you pump the handle, the wheel takes up the cable, winching you out of the mudhole.

Once you leave maintained roads, the trick is to travel slowly and study the road carefully. If there is any doubt about the conditions of the road ahead, stop, get out of your vehicle, and do a little walking. How deep is the mud, or how deep is the hole under the water? Use a stick and test each situation. Common sense should tell you when to turn around and find a new route.

If the going looks as though it's going to

Even four-wheel drive can get stuck. Notice that this vehicle has street tires that have not been deflated enough to provide optimum traction in deep sand. The key is to know when to detour and when to stop and walk.

WINCHES

A come-along is a simple hand-powered winch that can take the place of an electric winch. When the ratchet handle is pumped, the cable-filled wheel takes up the cable that is attached to the vehicle, winching your vehicle to solid ground.

get rough, put on your tire chains. They work as well in slick mud as they do in snow. Another trick, especially useful in deep sand, is to decrease your tire pressure to approximately 12 pounds. This allows your tires to "float." Don't forget to re-inflate them when you get out of trouble.

Learn to use your electric winch (or come-along) before you actually need it. Numerous times I have come upon a stuck shiny new four-wheel-drive vehicle and found that the owner did not know how to use his winch.

When you buy your winch, make sure the salesman gives you a good lesson in its proper use.

The most frustrating situation, and one of the most common, that four-wheelers find themselves in is to have all four wheels stuck, unable to move forward or backward. If you have an electric winch, the solution is to hook the cable to a tree and throw the switch. If you don't have a winch, then hook up your come-along and be prepared to sweat a little. Use your shovel to clear the way for each tire

Learn to use a winch properly before you go into areas where it may be needed. A flooded creek such as this is certainly not the place to try a winch for the first time.

Even a winch is of no use to a stuck vehicle when there is no tree or other firm structure to attach it to. In such a predicament, a second vehicle is needed.

GETTING UNSTUCK

The following tips are adapted from What to Do When Your Car Gets Stuck, *a Popular Science Book by Herbert R. Pfister.*

Left: *On soft ground or in snow, avoid sharp turns, as shown, that cause the back tires to leave the compacted track of the front tires, thereby creating undesirable resistance to forward travel.* **Right:** *A downed tree or large tree limb can often be cleared away more easily with rope and vehicle than it can be with ax or saw.*

Left: *Stuck in deep ruts, it's sometimes possible to jack up front and back ends in turn and push each end of the vehicle onto firmer ground. Note that the spare tire is used to increase the base size of the jack.* **Right:** *A spare tire, as shown, or rocks can be used to plug a pothole and allow escape.*

A second person flexing a taut rope can help shift a vehicle out of hopelessly deep ruts while moving the car slightly in the desired direction. This technique can also be used on either end of the vehicle to swing it if it has slid sideways and lodged against a tree or other obstruction.

Left: *Sticks and branches jammed under the drive wheels on both sides can be drawn under the spinning tires to provide needed traction. It may be necessary to place sticks and branches both in front and in back of each drive wheel and then shift gears from low to reverse several times to create a rocking motion of the vehicle that ultimately gives it enough momentum to allow a hard rev in the desired direction.* **Right:** *When assisting a driver by pushing his vehicle, avoid standing in the path of potential flying debris.*

TRACTION SAVVY

 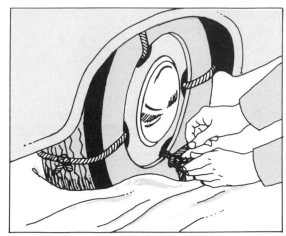

Left: *Rather than endlessly spinning your wheels on ice, chip away the ice in front of each drive tire for a distance that will allow the car to gain momentum before the tires hit sheer ice again.* ***Right:*** *Rope tied around tires can work as modest substitutes for tire chains.*

Left: *As a substitute for the more tedious job of mounting tire chains, you can spread the chains like mats in front of the drive wheels. For added stability of the chain mats, attach them to a post or tree in the desired direction of travel.* ***Right:*** *Rope looped through wheel slots can move the vehicle a foot or more before you must retie it.*

to move. If you don't have either of these devices, a third possibility is to get an accompanying vehicle to pull you out.

If you have none of these options, you are in for some work. You must shovel away all the mud underneath that's supporting the chassis and keeping weight off the tires, thereby causing the tires to lose traction.

Once you have the vehicle's underside free of mud, get out a jack and plank. Using the plank as a platform for the jack, raise the wheel that is deepest in the mud. Dig out the mud beneath the wheel down to a firm base. Then fill up the hole with rocks, logs, brush, and such. Now lower the wheel slowly down onto the firm platform you've constructed. Do the same thing to each of the other wheels. Then extend the solid platforms for several feet in front of each wheel. If you don't, you'll be able to move forward only a few feet and then will be back into the same predicament.

Sandy areas should be driven over with caution. The important thing to remember in sand or soft dirt is to keep moving steadily and not too fast. Don't apply an excess of power that would cause the wheels to dig in. Try to avoid abrupt changes in speed or direction, and aim as straight as possible across the area. Avoid sharp turns. Sharp turns cause the front tires to scrub sideways, turning them into plows that can raise impassable sand pileups.

A booklet entitled *A Close Look at 4-Wheel Driving* covers most stuck situations and is available free by writing to Ford Motor Company, P.O. Box 1978, Dearborn, MI 48121.

It would take a book-length text to list all the ways people get stuck with vehicles in backcountry and the various ways to get them out. If drivers would learn the capabilities and limits of their vehicles and know how to read backcountry roads, most of these strandings would be avoided. Usually, una-

voidable mirings can be remedied in a short time if you know how to use your emergency equipment and add to that a little common sense.

The Vehicle as a Survival Tool

The vehicle can aid your survival in many ways. The mirrors can be used for signaling. The battery can produce sparks for fire starting. The cigarette lighter can start materials burning for fire starting. Hubcaps can be used for shovels or buckets or cooking vessels. Floor mats can be used to give wheels traction to get unstuck. The spare tire can be

I became stranded in a remote area of North Carolina when this one-lane dirt road was swept away by a landslide, causing the vehicle's front wheels to become wedged in the cracked earth.

If you try to drive out after a blizzard, you may need to set up a winch often for short pulls. Be mindful of overexertion and also of carbon monoxide working its way into the passenger compartment as a result of a snow-blocked exhaust pipe. (Chuck Adams photo)

used as a seat to elevate you off hot sand, or it can be burned for a smoke signal. Car wiring can be used for animal snares. The list could go on and on.

The vehicle can provide you with a vast variety of survival tools, but if you carry the proper survival gear, this will not be necessary.

If a Blizzard Traps You in Your Car

• Stay in the vehicle. Do not attempt to walk in a blizzard. Disorientation comes quickly in blowing and drifting snow. Being lost in open country during a blizzard is extremely dangerous. You are more likely to be found in your car and will at least be sheltered there.
• Avoid overexertion and exposure. Exertions from attempting to push your car, shoveling heavy drifts, and performing other difficult chores during strong winds, blind-

ing snow, and bitter cold of a blizzard may cause a heart attack, even for someone in apparently good physical condition.
• Keep a downwind window slightly open for fresh air. Freezing rain, wet snow, and wind-driven snow can completely seal the passenger compartment, making it difficult if not impossible to open doors or even windows.
• Beware of carbon monoxide. Run the engine, heater, or catalytic heater sparingly, and only with a downwind window open for ventilation. Make sure that snow has not blocked the exhaust pipe, backing exhaust fumes underneath and into the vehicle.
• Exercise by clapping your hands and moving your arms and legs vigorously from time to time. Do not stay in one position for long. But don't overdo it. Exercise warms you, but it also increases body heat loss.
• Take turns keeping watch. If more than one person is in the car, don't all sleep at the

same time. If you're alone, stay awake as long as possible.

● If you hear snow-clearing crews at night, turn on the dome light to make your vehicle more visible.

● Don't panic. Stay with the car.

Stay Calm

The major danger in a vehicle stranding is not from going unrescued, dying from the elements, or being attacked by a wild animal. It is from panic. People who have suddenly become stranded are under stress. They jack up cars unsafely, they decide to walk out rather than stay put, they spill valuable drinking water, they overlook simple solutions to their problems.

Stay calm and keep those with you calm. Think through your situation. Use your CB radio. Use signals or set up signals to use when potential help comes near. Make your shelter comfortable, whether it is inside or outside your vehicle. Don't take chances—stay put and prepare for rescue.

22

KEEPING TRACK OF CHILDREN IN BACKCOUNTRY

Today families are visiting national parks and other outdoor recreation and rural areas in unprecedented numbers. The lure of the great out-of-doors has encouraged many young families to take up backpacking, cross-country skiing, canoeing, rock hunting, snowshoeing, and other outdoor activities. Along with these adventure activities, thousands of families are enjoying picnicking, nature walks, scenic drives, and other more leisurely forms of outdoor recreation. In many cases, children, from infants to teenagers, are brought along into areas where, without proper guidance and parental awareness, a short walk can turn into a family emergency.

A National Park Service official said, when questioned about the number of children reported lost in national parks each year: "These cases are so numerous that they are not sent in for a national total. Would you include a three-year-old missing half an hour or one of our lost victims whom we have never found? We experience many lost-child reports each day. Fortunately, most children are found within a short time."

The backcountry is full of places where

The potential hazard for a lost child here gains weight, owing to the apparently cold temperature and clothing on these kids that would blend with terrain, making spotting by searchers difficult. (Neil Soderstrom photo)

children can get lost. There are ways you can prevent your child from getting lost in the first place, or at least make it a short-term ordeal. But first, let's look at what can happen when an adventurous youngster strikes out on his own.

A woman ran up to the park ranger's car. Terrified, she screamed, "My child! My Bobby is lost!"

Getting out of his car, the park ranger tried to calm the woman and then asked a series of typical questions: What is your name and your child's name? How old is he and what does he look like? What was he wearing and what color was his clothing? How long has he been missing? Where did you last see him?

The woman was understandably scared. But it was also clear she had no idea a picnic at a state park might turn into such a nightmare. As she attempted to answer the ranger's questions, it became obvious she was completely unprepared for this turn of events. She was not sure how long the boy had been missing and couldn't even remember the color of clothing her boy was wearing. And because everyone had been having so much fun walking and wading up a nearby stream, no one remembered where they last saw Bobby.

Walking over to the stream, the ranger found the boy's father questioning other picnickers about the missing boy. The ranger asked Bobby's father the same questions he had asked before, but again the answers were vague. The father wasn't even sure which branch of the stream they had followed.

The ranger realized this family was totally unprepared for an outing in the backcountry. Neither parent had ever considered just how easy it is for a child to get lost in a recreation area. Now their lack of preparedness was jeopardizing their son's life.

The ranger was faced with the task of organizing a search for a little boy without knowing where he had been seen last or how long he had been lost. Out there somewhere was a terrified youngster. Fortunately for all concerned, Bobby was eventually found. But his parents, had they been properly prepared for the unexpected, might have prevented his getting lost, or at least made it easier to find him.

Children do get lost, but this should not make you afraid to enjoy outdoor activities with your children. By following a few simple rules and getting a little training, any family can go into the outdoors with confidence.

The first step to take is to teach your children how to avoid getting lost. Granted, this instruction will vary from toddlers to teenagers. Stress the importance of staying with the group. The best way to assure this is to have a buddy system within the family. Assign each younger child a parent or older brother or sister as a buddy. Each buddy should always know the whereabouts of the other.

Require that your child let you know when he wants to leave the group for any reason. A short roadside stop to take a picture of a rushing mountain stream is long enough for a venturesome youngster to become lost on an unscheduled side trip into the woods. Remember, in many areas the wilderness is just a few steps off the road.

Purchase bright clothing for your child to wear on outings. A blaze-orange windbreaker can be seen from great distances, especially from the air, if air search is required. Bright shirts, pants, and caps make children much easier for you to see as well.

Each family member should have a plastic police whistle. Since a whistle can be heard much farther away than the human voice and will last much longer, it is a terrific signaling device. Children should wear their whistles on a cord around their neck. Fasten

Bright-colored windbreakers on children make them easier to spot. And a whistle is an excellent signal device that all children should carry on outings and know when and how to use it.

the cord with a safety pin, or attach it in some other secure fashion. You will have to check small children often to make sure they haven't taken it off. An excellent blaze-orange whistle, complete with neck cord, is made by the P. S. Olt Co., well-known maker of game and bird calls.

The next step is completely up to you as the parent. Remember, your child is only a child. Do not expect a child to act as an adult while on an outing. Always be aware of what your children are doing and where they are. Have fun on your outdoor trip, but don't get so engrossed in the beauty of a waterfall or the climb to a mountaintop that you forget your children. Art Graham, a National Park Service authority on search and rescue for lost children, put it this way:

"The people who put their families in greatest jeopardy are those who take off into 'Mother Nature's domain' for a short, unplanned scenic jaunt. Parents simply cannot relax fully when their children are in a potentially hostile environment. A nap at a scenic turn-out could give your child enough time to wander deep into a forest, where he may not be found alive."

On hikes also remember that tired children tend to lag behind, and it is generally the straggler who takes the wrong trail or tries a cross-country short cut. Travel at the pace of the slowest member of your family. Don't plan a trip too strenuous for your children. Fatigue causes children to get lost. Also, don't let your child run ahead of the group. Stay together!

Perhaps the most important step is to teach your child what to do when he first realizes he is lost—an extremely frightening moment.

The child should be taught to remain where he is—to stop and wait for help. Unfortunately, many children, as well as adults, forget this rule, but you should try to get your child to understand its importance. Any additional walking will probably take him farther away from searchers. Also, a frightened child may run blindly, increasing the likelihood of running over a cliff, into a stream, or into branches or thorny underbrush. Children must understand that stopping as soon as they realize they are lost is the first step toward being found.

Explain to your child that should he become lost, he should try to be brave and not panic. If he stays where he is and starts blowing his whistle, people will soon be looking for him. When he hears his parents' whistle, he should return the signal on his own whistle. Also tell your child that if he is on a trail or road when lost he should stay on it. Lost people are easier to spot from the air when they are in open areas, such as trails, roads, and clearings.

When my son Steve was five years old, he strayed from the campsite while we were camping near the Cohutta Wilderness Area in Georgia. I had spent much time trying to teach him what to do if he got lost. But when Steve realized he was lost, he forgot everything I had taught him, except for one thing. He knew he was supposed to stay on the logging road on which he had become lost. Because he remembered this one lesson, he was found relatively quickly. Had he tried to find camp by wandering off the road, the story would perhaps have had a much different ending.

Park rangers have found that many lost children will try to hide from searchers even though they may be very near them. There is still considerable mystery about the psychological impact of being lost. In order to reduce the likelihood of this odd behavior, tell your child that getting lost is no reason for embarrassment or punishment and that he shouldn't hide. Tell him to listen for the searchers and whistle as loudly as he can

This boy has built his own shelter during a survival training course. Such courses should also teach youngsters to stop when they realize they are lost and to stay put until found.

when he hears them. Also, if you have taught your child to beware of strangers, make sure he understands that when he is lost that rule does not apply. Searchers are usually strangers.

In July 1983, an eight-year-old boy was lost for a week in the rugged mountains along the Tennessee–North Carolina border. Tourists reported seeing the little boy during this time, but said he hid from them as they approached. A six-man search team finally found the youngster in a blackberry thicket 1½ miles from where he was first lost. When found, the boy was hallucinating because of hypothermia, his feet were swollen, and he suffered from scratches and insect bites. During the week the lost boy had eaten only three apples and a few berries.

An excellent program to help children with the psychological problem of being lost is called "Hug-A-Tree" and is being used in California. This program is offered in schools

Ab Taylor, former U.S. Bor-der Patrolman and nation-ally known tracker, co-founded the Hug-A-Tree Program, which is widely publicized in elementary schools. Says Taylor, "The whole concept is to get kids to stay in one place when they get lost and not run in blind panic. We want kids to feel that a tree can be the friend they're looking for in that wilderness. It's alive, it can provide shelter and shade, and it serves as a marker for searchers." (Keith Griffiths and Response *Magazine photo)*

and teaches children aged 5 to 12 what to do if they are suddenly lost. The program includes a slide presentation showing the children what actions to take when lost. One action is for the child to hug a tree. Hugging a tree and even talking to it calm the child down and prevent panic. If the child stays in one place, he will be found far more quickly and cannot be injured in a fall.

It can be fun as well as educational to play at being lost with your child at home in your yard. Get him to show you what he would do if lost, and explain what you will do to find him. He may not remember it all when he is actually lost, but almost without exception, children with proper training are found within an hour or so.

The last series of steps in "lost prevention" includes what *you* should do if your child is suddenly missing.

1. Don't panic! The next few minutes may be the most important.

2. Try blowing your whistle and listening. You may hear a response immediately.

3. Mark the last spot where you saw the child. Use a handkerchief, jacket, or anything bright that is easy to spot.

4. Leave one person at that spot to blow his whistle. Another person should seek out a ranger, sheriff, or forester as soon as possible.

5. Be able to give the searchers a detailed description of your child and his clothing.

6. Remember how to take the searchers back to the last known location of the child.

These basics should be taught to all family members who plan any type of outdoor activity. Many youth groups take outdoor trips with little or no preparation to prevent a member from getting lost. We normally think of lost children as toddlers, but just as many teenagers, not to mention adults, are lost each year. The shock effect of being lost knows no age limit.

If you have taken the time to teach your children how to conduct themselves on outings, if you use the buddy system, if you use the whistle, if you dress your child in bright-colored clothing, and if you exercise parental awareness, chances are you will never need to seek a ranger to find your child. Those are a lot of ifs, but if you put them together you and your family will enjoy many outings together without undue stress.

23
SURVIVAL TRAINING COURSES

I've recommended survival training throughout this book. Without training, survival can be a nightmare. With training, it can be an interesting adventure. The strange thing is that in all my years of search-and-rescue work I don't recall that many people who had training in survival ever needed it. Their training often kept them out of trouble. Here are descriptions of some courses available.

Water Survival Training

There are several sources of training for survival on or in the water. Check with your local Red Cross concerning its Small Craft School or survival swimming classes. Many universities offer courses in survival swimming. Often your local YMCA or YWCA will teach a course in survival swimming. If your professional or recreational activities take you, your family, or your passengers on or over the water, then consider taking the sea survival course offered by NOVA University. The one-day sea survival training course is a combination of classroom instruction, water training routines, and emergency simulations. It provides essential information and "hands-on" training.

Medrick Northrop, an instructor of outdoor skills around the U.S., teaches students at the Stagshead Lodge Survival School in Alabama the pros and cons of the solar still as a means of collecting water. For more on solar stills, see page 120.

Here is the course outline:

Part I: Classroom

1. Introduction. An overview of what you will experience during the day and background information showing how training can increase your chances of survival

2. Pre-Abandonment/Abandonment. Precautions to take prior to an emergency and essential actions you must take during and following a disaster at sea

3. Survival in Water and Rafts. All physiological and psychological aspects of staying alive for an extended period of time while you are in or on the water

4. Detection. How you can increase your chances of being located following an accident at sea

5. Retrieval. Familiarization with a variety of rescue techniques you could encounter at sea

Part II: Field

1. Rafts and Equipment. Demonstration of marine and aviation rafts, inflation systems, repair, and basic accessories

2. Non-Pyrotechnic Signals. Demonstration of and use of signal mirrors, dye markers, and "improvised" detection signals

3. Solar Still. A demonstration of how you can easily set up and operate a functional drinking device at sea

Part III: Water

1. Survival Swimming/Flotation. How you can stay afloat without equipment

2. Night Vest Donning. Simulated practice in life vest donning at night in the water

3. Height Entry. Procedures for safe water entry from above

4. Helicopter Pickup. Practice of simulated rescue devices used by helicopters in emergency situations

5. Hypothermia. Training and practice in controlling your body heat loss in water

6. Evacuation Slide. The use of an airline evacuation slide for emergency flotation

7. Marine Life Raft. Simulated emergency abandonment, assisting panic-stricken and unconscious victims; raft survival

8. Aviation Raft. Boarding from water, discussion of equipment, erection of canopy, and the actual operation of pyrotechnics

9. Review and Critique. Wrap-up session with questions and answers

For more information write NOVA University, 3301 College Ave., Ft. Lauderdale, FL 33314.

Desert Survival Training

For those who want to get a professional course in desert survival, the Arizona Outdoor Survival Institute offers weekend courses, five-day courses, and a 21-day course. Here is an example of the five-day course:

● *MONDAY:* 8:00 A.M. until evening— Classroom learning covering geography of the desert regions and plant and animal life; environmental physiology, or how your body reacts to the extremes of heat and cold stress; water sources on the desert; map reading; surviving the unexpected desert survival situation

● *TUESDAY:* 8:00 A.M. until afternoon— Hands-on demonstration and practice of survival skills: building solar stills, primitive fire building, signaling for help, shelter building, compass course, survival kits, and edible plant identification

● *TUESDAY NIGHT TO FRIDAY:* The next three days and nights will be spent on a cross-country "worst case" survival trek carrying nothing more than a knife and a blanket and survival kit—no food, no water, no sleeping bags. The third night and day will be a solo experience, separated from everyone else.

The three-day trek is fairly strenuous, so you will need to be in good physical condition. You will probably lose at least 5 pounds on the trek, covering about 15 miles across the desert and up over a 1,000-foot mountain pass. You will travel both day and night in some instances experiencing 120° heat and cool nights.

For more information write: Arizona Outdoor Survival Institute, 6737 N. 18th Place, Phoenix, AZ 85016.

Wilderness Survival

Anyone who goes into fairly remote areas to work or play should attend a wilderness survival course. There are many wilderness survival courses offered throughout North America in conjunction with universities, hunter education programs, and outdoor education programs. If there is no wilderness survival course offered in your area, it is relatively easy to persuade a college continuing education department to find an instructor and offer a course.

Air Force instruction. If you and your group are willing to pay the expenses of getting a survival instructor to your training site, the U.S. Air Force will provide you with expert instruction. Write the USAF Survival School, Public Affairs Office, 3636th CCTW, Fairchild Air Force Base, WA 99011 and request that a survival instructor come to give a training course.

Stagshead Survival School. At my Stagshead Lodge in Alabama, I teach three-day week-

One of the missions of the U.S. Air Force Survival School is to help civilians in conducting survival schools and programs. These military pilots are practicing the use of signal mirrors.

end wilderness survival courses. The curriculum includes:

● *FRIDAY*: Why Survival Training; Survival Psychology; Signaling Techniques; Firemanship; Shelter Construction; Edible Wild Plants; Survival Medicine.

● *SATURDAY*: Backcountry Navigation; Making and Using the Survival Kit; Briefing on Solo. At about 2:00 P.M., students will be placed in designated areas where each will be on his own to build a survival camp and live throughout the night under survival conditions, using only the basic materials he has in his survival kit.

● *SUNDAY*: Evaluation of Solo Camps on Site; Evaluation of Solo Camps at Training Site with Class; What to Do When a Member of Your Party Is Missing

For more information, write Stagshead Lodge, PO Box 2565, Tuscaloosa, AL 35403.

Outward Bound USA. Since its inception in the early 1960s, Outward Bound has grown from a small program for youth to a giant organization offering over 500 courses annually, and in many U.S. states, to people of all ages and physical abilities. (You may have noticed that a goodly number of photos in this book show Outward Bound students and instructors.)

Though the courses are not essentially backcountry survival, they are weighted heavily to strenuous wilderness activities, knowledge, and camp crafts that are basic to survival and to avoiding survival predicaments. Course focus may be on one or more of the following: mountaineering, backpacking, ski trekking, canoeing, sailing, whitewater rafting, kayaking, dogsledding, caving. Most courses run about a week, but many run several weeks, and the special high school

Teamwork and group planning play a large role in Outward Bound. (Outward Bound USA photo)

The solo remains an important part of most of the Outward Bound courses, and may last from one to three days. (Outward Bound USA photo)

and college-credit courses run two to three months. The courses are designed to help you discover your abilities under challenging conditions and thereby also tend to build self-confidence and improve team and leadership skills. No tobacco, alcohol, or other drugs are allowed. Courses include the following:

Phase 1: Training and physical conditioning. You receive instruction in safety, first aid, search and rescue, shelter construction, wilderness cooking, environmental awareness and conservation, map and compass reading, knot-tying, rope handling, rock climbing, rappelling, and more.

Phase 2: An extended journey. You apply the skills just learned and get to know your instructor and the other 8 to 12 people in your group.

Phase 3: The solo. You have an uninterrupted period of contemplation of one to three days away from people, cares, and distractions.

Phase 4: The final expedition. You plan and execute an expedition with your group with a minimum of supervision.

Phase 5: Reflection. After a final event usually involving running, paddling, or skiing, you and your group reflect on the course, your experiences, feelings, and personal discoveries.

For more information, write Outward Bound USA, 384 Field Point Road, Greenwich, CT 06830.

Boulder Outdoor Survival School. If you want to attend an in-depth wilderness survival school, consider the Boulder Outdoor Survival School (BOSS). This school was incorporated in 1978 with the assignment of inheriting the survival programs traditionally housed at Brigham Young University. BOSS encourages men and women to survive on their own initiative without any commercially made survival equipment. Courses offered by Boulder Outdoor Survival School are patterned to:

● Develop skills and proficiency in the out-of-doors
● Increase self-confidence and awareness
● Enhance interpersonal relationships
● Increase spiritual awareness
● Contribute to positive behavioral changes

The BOSS 30-day course is designed for the student who wants the challenge of testing his or her endurance and stamina. It teaches a great number of primitive survival skills and demands the participant to be physically conditioned and committed to completing the course.

The first two days of the course are spent in classroom preparation in Provo, Utah. The actual in-field experience is 28 days and divided into five main phases.

1. *Impact.* Each student experiences an adjustment to the environment through two and a half days of rigorous hiking.

2. *Group Expedition.* Men and women are placed in separate expedition groups; each group, with instructor support, follows a planned route to a common destination.

3. *Survival Week.* Primitive outdoor survival skills are emphasized.

4. *Student Expedition.* Students are organized into small groups and assigned routes to follow to a common base camp.

5. *Solo.* Each student spends from four to five days alone in a supervised area.

The BOSS 14-day course is patterned after the 30-day program and is designed for those who aren't able to spend 30 days. It provides challenge and skills, and like the 30-day program, requires the participant to be physically fit and committed.

The first day of the course is classroom preparation in Provo, Utah. The actual in-field experience is 13 days and divided into four main phases.

1. *Impact.* Each student experiences an adjustment to the environment through two and a half days of rigorous hiking.

2. *Survival Week.* Primitive outdoor survival skills are emphasized.

3. *Group Expedition.* Students are assigned a route to follow to a common base camp.

4. *Solo.* Each student spends from two to three days alone in a supervised area.

For more information, write Boulder Outdoor Survival School Inc., PO Box 7215, Provo, UT 84602.

American Mountain Men. For excellent training in primitive survival skills as were practiced in the 1700s and early 1800s, consider a group known as the American Mountain Men. These men are dedicated to preserving and practicing the skills used by the early explorers. Members of the American Mountain Men conduct classes in how

A member of the American Mountain Men organization, Medrick Northrop here teaches primitive survival skills to a class sponsored by the University of Alabama.

to live in the wilderness utilizing only the tools and materials nature provides. For more information write the American Mountain Men, P.O. Box 259, Lakeside, CA 92040.

Search and Rescue. Anyone wanting to form a search-and-rescue team or to be trained as a search boss should contact the National Association for Search and Rescue. Search bosses get detailed training in a search management course devised by the National Park Service and the National Association for Search and Rescue. Write the association at P.O. Box 50178, Washington, DC 20004.

Survival Consultants. There are several well-known survival consultants who can help you put together almost any type of training program in survival. Write the following:
● Survival Consultants Group, P.O. Box 2565, Tuscaloosa, AL 35403
● Survival Education Association, 9035 Golden Given Rd., Tacoma, WA 98445

● Highland Survival School, P.O. Box 4754, Colorado Springs, CO 80930

Survival Training for Youth

Survival training is available for youth through the YMCA, Scout programs and Outward Bound. This type of training is good because it not only teaches youngsters what to do in emergencies, but also teaches them discipline and how to maintain control under stress. Here is an example of a survival program held in Birmingham, Alabama.

Selected youths learn how to survive almost anything, including fire, famine, and flood. The young men and women, many of whom are from programs such as Big Brother, take part in the YMCA Youth Survival Adventure Program. The adventure is a pilot for other possible nationwide survival instruction programs.

The first week of the course is devoted to jungle survival, as members of Birmingham's

This Boy Scout group learns trapping skills. (Boy Scouts of America photo)

20th Special Forces National Guard Unit give the young people lessons in mountain climbing, rappelling, and building rope bridges, animal traps, and jungle shelters.

Jungle survival week is topped off by a four-day raft trip down the Tallapoosa River. The youngsters camp out along the way, living solely off edible plants for the last 36 hours of the trip.

Upon completion, the survival students

receive Green Beret certificates from the Special Forces and prepare for the second phase of their training—fire survival. The participants travel to the Birmingham Fire Academy to begin a period of fire safety training. The exercises include running 1½ miles in less than 12 minutes, learning mouth-to-mouth resuscitation, and operating a pump and ladder truck.

From the Fire Academy the troop goes to

the Gulf of Mexico, where marine biologists give a week's instruction in sea survival techniques, stressing defenses against sharks. The last week of the program is spent studying survival during a nuclear attack. The young people take a three-day Civil Defense course which includes spending the night in a bomb shelter and experiencing a simulated nuclear attack.

Upon completion of the Civil Defense phase the participants receive another certificate—that of a bomb shelter manager.

APPENDIX 1: SURVIVAL ORGANIZATIONS

You can write any of the following organizations to obtain further information about specific survival-related topics and activities.

Air Force Rescue Coordination Center, Scott Air Force Base, IL 62225

Air Force Survival School, 3636th Combat Crew Training Wing, Fairchild Air Force Base, WA 99011

American Rescue Dog Association, 10714 Royal Springs Dr., Dallas, TX 75229

Canadian Coast Guard, Tower "A," Place de Ville, Ottawa, Ont., CANADA K1A CK2

Civil Air Patrol, Maxwell Air Force Base, AL 36112

Explorer Search and Rescue, 790 Lucerne Dr., Sunnyvale, CA 94086

International Association of Dive Rescue Specialists, 2619 Canton Court, Ft. Collins, CO 80525

Mountain Rescue Association, P.O. Box 396, Altadena, CA 91001

National Cave Rescue Commission, c/o National Speleological Society, Cave Ave., Huntsville, AL 35810

National Association for Search and Rescue, P.O. Box 50178, Washington, DC 20004

NOAA Weather Radio, National Weather Service, 8060 13th St., Silver Spring, MD 20910

Outward Bound USA, 384 Field Point Road, Greenwich, CT 06830.

Royal Canadian Mounted Police, 1200 Alta Vista Dr., Ottawa, Ont., CANADA K1A OR2

Survival Consultants Group, P.O. Box 2565, Tuscaloosa, AL 35403

Survival Education Association, 9035 Golden Given Rd., Tacoma, WA 98445

U.S. Coast Guard, 2100 2nd St., N.W., Washington, DC 20590

Weatheradio Canada, Atmospheric Environment Service, Room 1000, 266 Graham Ave., Winnipeg, Man., CANADA R3C 3V4

In this actual rescue of an injured climber, skilled alpine crews create a traverse by means of rope and pulleys. (Boulder Daily Camera photo)

APPENDIX 2: RECOMMENDED READING

The following publications can provide a wealth of survival information. Magazines appear at the end of this listing. Many of the books may be obtained at bookstores or ordered through bookstores by consulting *Books in Print.* Or, for books still in print, you could write the publisher direct. For out-of-print books, your options include libraries, used-book stores, and dealers that specialize in used and rare books. Dealers are listed in telephone directory yellow pages, often with indication of their subject specialties. If a dealer should not have the books you want in stock, there's still hope. Some dealers will conduct searches—for a fee.

Aircraft Survival

Search and Rescue Survival Training, Air Force Regulation 64–4, Superintendent of Documents, U.S. Government Printing Office, Washington, DC 20402. This 1985 survival manual teaches U.S. Air Force pilots how to survive under most conditions in the Arctic, tropics, and desert. This is one of the best survival manuals available. It is loaded with survival techniques, including a guide to edible wild plants.

Hey, I'm Alive!, by Helen Klaben, McGraw-Hill Book Company (hardcover with photos), Scho-

---

In addition to the books listed in this section, many others hold survival lessons even though the books aren't focused on outdoor survival as such. Many offer time-proven advice on animal behaviors. For example, it's important to know how to avoid surprising a sow grizzly with cubs. That knowledge can help prevent violent survival ordeals of very short duration. (Bear photo by Erwin A Bauer; books by Neil Soderstrom)

lastic Book Services (softcover without photos). This is a compelling autobiographical account of the seven-week survival ordeal of the author and Ralph Flores, following the crash of Flores's plane on the Yukon-British Columbia border in February 1963. Painfully injured and with meager supplies and clothing, the two endured minus-40° temperatures, nourished almost exclusively with heated water. Flores felled trees for firewood, using only a hammer and chisel. This classic tale of deprivation, teamwork, and perseverance was featured in *Life* and *The Saturday Evening Post*, as well as in a national TV docu-drama.

Down But Not Out, Canadian Government Publishing Centre, Supply and Services Canada, Hull, Quebec, CANADA K1A 0S9. This survival manual used by the Canadian Armed Forces is excellent for pilots, commercial and private. It is well illustrated and is a practical guide for all climates.

Survival Guns

Survival Guns, by Mel Tappan, Caroline House Publishers, 920 W. Industrial Drive, Aurora, IL 60506. This is a comprehensive guide to the selection, modification, and use of firearms for defense, food gathering, and pest control. Paperback, 400 pages.

Wilderness Navigation

Be Expert with Map and Compass, by Bjorn Kjellstrom, Charles Scribner's Sons, 597 Fifth Ave., New York, NY 10017. This is a 200-page complete course in navigation using a map and compass. Easy to read, it should be a basic reference for anyone going into remote areas.

Land Navigation Handbook, by W. S. Kals, Sierra Club Books, 530 Bush St., San Francisco, CA 94108. An easy-to-read, 230-page book that covers all aspects of land navigation, including choosing and using a compass, reading topographical maps, altimeter navigation, celestial navigation, and much more.

Snowmobile Survival

The Snowmobiler's Handbook, edited by Robert L. Tracinski, Deere & Company, John Deere Rd., Moline, IL 61265. This well-written, 160-page paperback is a complete guide to snowmobiling. It includes an excellent chapter on cold-weather survival.

Primitive Cooking Skills

Backcountry Cooking, by J. Wayne Fears, Backcountry Press, PO Box 2844, Tuscaloosa, AL 35401. How to cook on an open fire in the wilderness. Includes chapters on cooking without utensils, Dutch oven cooking, use of the reflector oven, smoking food, much more, plus over 100 recipes.

Trail Foods You Can Make at Home, by J. Wayne Fears, Backcountry Press, PO Box 2844 Tuscaloosa, AL 35401. This 12-page booklet contains hard-to-find recipes for trail foods that are easy to make in your own home, including pemmican, bannock, jerky, gorp, hardtack, and others.

Search and Rescue

Wilderness Search and Rescue, by Tim Setnicka, Eastern Mountain Sports, Two Vose Farm Rd., Peterborough, NH 03458. Written by the former head of search and rescue at Yosemite National Park, this 656-page handbook is authoritative and up-to-date. It includes chapters on rescue techniques for whitewater, snow, ice, avalanche, and caves. Also included are many case studies, drawings, and photos. Excellent!

Tracking: A Blueprint for Learning How, by Jack Kearney, Pathways Press, 525 Jeffree Street, El Cajon, CA 92020. Supervisory Border Patrol Agent Jack Kearney of the El Cajon, California, Border Patrol Station has specialized in tracking people for more than 17 years. The officers of the El Cajon station are renowned throughout the Border Patrol for their tracking expertise and have, in the last eight years, found over 60 lost persons with their tracking skill. During this period they have had no failures on searches that involved small children. This book is an outgrowth of Jack's many years of tracking, teaching, and writing, and is the most comprehensive work available on tracking people.

Edible Wild Foods

Field Guide to Edible Wild Plants of Eastern and Central North America, by Lee Peterson, Houghton Mifflin Company, Boston, MA 02107. A complete guide to identifying, harvesting, and preparing nearly 400 species of edible wild plants in eastern North America. Basic recipes and cooking times are provided for every species. In addition, common poisonous plants that resemble edible ones and thus might be confused with them are discussed and shown. An excellent book.

Western Edible Wild Plants, by H. D. Harrington, University of New Mexico Press, Albuquerque, NM 87131. A well-written guide to edible wild plants found in the western part of North America. The text is thorough, but nontechnical. Includes recipes.

Field Guide to Edible Wild Plants, by Bradford Angier, Stackpole Books, Box 1831, Cameron & Kelker Sts., Harrisburg, PA 17105. This is an excellent field guide to 100 of the more common edible wild plants in the U.S. and Canada. Full-page full-color paintings face each plant text. Plants are arranged alphabetically by most-common *common* name. Also includes preparations for eating.

Edible Wild Plants, by T. S. Elias and P. A. Dykeman, Outdoor Life Books, Times Mirror Magazines, Inc., 380 Madison Ave., New York, NY 10017. This is one of the best books on the subject. A season-by-season guide to identification, harvesting, and preparation of over 200 wild plants.

Trapping

Deadfalls and Snares, by A. R. Harding, Fur-Fish-Game, 2878 E. Main St., Columbus, OH 43209. This valuable little 218-page book was written by a well-known trapper in 1935. The information is still valid and a must for those who want to learn to trap in survival situations.

Snares and Snaring, by Raymond Thompson, Thompson Snare Co., 15815 Second Place West, Lynnwood, WA 98036. A thorough training manual on the art of using snares, this is written by the maker of the well-known Thompson Snares.

Trapping Handbook, by Tom Krause, National Trappers Association, Box 3667, Bloomington, IL 61701. A good book on the basics of trapping wild animals, this includes a great deal of information on the habits of wild animals and how to locate them.

Trapping and Tracking, by George Clawson, Winchester Press, 220 Old New Brunswick Rd., Piscataway, NJ 08854. This covers the basics of trapping and tracking as well as detailed information on a wide variety of wild animals.

Cleaning Wild Animals

Dress 'em Out, by Captain J. A. Smith, Stoeger Publishing Co., South Hackensack, NJ 07606. A good guide for learning how to prepare big game, upland birds, and waterfowl for eating. Well-illustrated, 255-pages.

Hunting Skills

Basic Hunter's Guide, by NRA staff, National Rifle Association, 1600 Rhode Island Ave., Washington, DC 20036. This excellent 300-page guide on the skills for successful hunting includes color photos of game and much information on survival.

Desert Survival

Alive in the Desert, by Joe Kraus, Paladin Press, Box 1307, Boulder, CO 80306. This 113-page book covers all aspects of desert survival.

General Survival

Live off the Land in the City and Country, by Ragnar Benson, Paladin Press, Box 1307, Boulder, CO 80306. A complete how-to book on survival techniques for long-term survival. It includes advice on medicine, firearms, fuel storage, diesel generators, and food gathering.

Wilderness Survival

Surviving the Unexpected Wilderness Emergency, by Gene Fear, Survival Education Association, 9035 Golden Given Rd., Tacoma, WA 98445. An excellent book on topics such as coping with psychological stress, problem analysis, surviving cold and heat, leadership, survival experiments, and how to assemble various survival kits.

Wilderness Survival, by Bernard Shanks, ICS Books, Inc., P.O. Box 344, Pittsboro, IN 46167. A 200-page handbook covering all phases of wilderness survival. Written by an experienced survival educator.

Mountain Wilderness Survival, by Craig E. Patterson, And/Or Press, Inc., P.O. Box 2246, Berkeley, CA 94702. Written by a Yosemite National Park ranger, this is straightforward information on how to stay out of trouble in the mountains.

Swamp Camping, by J. Wayne Fears, Backcountry Press, PO Box 2844, Tuscaloosa, AL 35401. A 270-page handbook covering all aspects of swamp survival, travel, and how to live in swamps. The only book devoted to swamp survival.

Hip Pocket Survival Handbook, by Robert E. Brown, American Outdoor Safety League, 13256 Northrup Way, Suite 8, Bellevue, WA 98005. An excellent guide that should be in every survival kit. It covers basic first aid, shelter, signaling, and many other survival skills. The center pages are signal mirrors and the cover is wax-impregnated to serve as a fire starter. And the staples can be bent into fishhooks.

Outdoor Survival Skills, by Larry Dean Olsen, Brigham Young University Press, Provo, UT 84602. This guide stresses survival by the most primitive means. It covers shelter construction, fire making, finding water, making primitive weapons, trapping, and edible wild plants and animals.

Modern Survival, by Dwight Schuh, Arco Publishing, 215 Park Ave. So., New York, NY 10003. A well-written wilderness survival book for modern times. It covers all basic survival skills and is well illustrated.

Survival, FM 21–76, by U.S. Army Staff, Superintendent of Documents, Washington, DC 20402. A detailed survival manual that teaches soldiers how to survive in all climates. An excellent reference.

Outdoor Safety and Survival, by Paul H. Risk, John Wiley & Sons, 605 Third Ave., New York, NY 10158. A good basic guide on handling a wide variety of survival situations. 340-pages.

Survival Medicine

The Ship's Medicine Chest and Medical Aid at Sea, Early Winters, Ltd., 110 Prefontaine Place S., Seattle, WA 98104. This book is published for the Merchant Marine by the U.S. Public Health Service and is a complete guide to recognizing and treating many illnesses and injuries. It is well illustrated and written so laymen can understand it.

The Merck Manual, by Robert Berkow, M.D., Merck & Co., P.O. Box 2000, Rahway, NJ 07065. This medical reference book intended for doctors and pharmacists covers the treatment of every kind of human disease or disorder that can be influenced by drugs or medicines.

Medicine for Mountaineering, edited by James A. Wilkerson, M.D., The Mountaineers, 719 Pike St., Seattle, WA 98101. An excellent, thorough handbook on diagnosis and treatment of injuries and diseases that occur in wilderness.

Wilderness Medicine, by William W. Forgey, M.D., ICS Books, P.O. Box 344, Pittsboro, IN 46167. An excellent manual on assembling medical kits for wilderness trips. The book includes much useful information on medications for and prevention, diagnosis, and treatment of wilderness diseases and injuries.

Where There Is No Doctor, by David Werner, The Hesperian Foundation, P.O. Box 1692, Palo Alto, CA 94302. This detailed handbook was written for use in villages where there is no doctor and is probably the best book available for long-term survival situations. It gives information on how to examine and care for sick people, first aid, sanitation, nutrition, childbirth, and much more.

Insects and Allergy and What to Do About Them, by Claude A. Frazier, M.D., and F. K. Brown, University of Oklahoma Press, 1005 Asp Ave., Norman, OK 73019. A thorough and easy-to-read book on all aspects of insect bites and allergies. It is illustrated in color and contains a wealth of information that anyone going into the outdoors should have access to.

The Red Cross Standard First Aid Manual. Available from your local Red Cross chapter. A must for all medical kits, it covers all types of medical emergencies and tells how to give first aid.

Special Forces Medical Handbook, by U.S. Army staff, Paladin Press, Box 1307, Boulder CO 80306. A detailed field medical handbook that covers a wide range of medical emergencies.

Management of Wilderness and Environmental Emergencies, by P. S. Auerbach, M. D., and E. C. Geehr, M.D., Macmillan Publishing Co., 866 Third Ave., New York, NY 10022. While this book is not written for the layman, it is a must for the serious survival student, because it covers, in detail, all known wilderness medical emergencies. 656 pages, 200 illustrations.

Primitive Survival Skills

The Book of Buckskinning I and II, edited by William H. Scurlock, Rebel Publishing Company, Texarkana, TX 75501. Two excellent how-to books written by survival experts covering a wide range of long-term survival skills. Included are making clothing from animal skins, fire starting, making camp gear, and more.

Extreme Weather Skills

Harsh-Weather Camping, by Sam Curtis, David McKay Co., 2 Park Ave., New York, NY 10016. Excellent information on living in the rain, heat, cold, and mixed weather.

Winter Camping, by Bob Cary, Stephen Greene Press, Fessenden Rd., Brattleboro, VT 05301. A complete book on how to live in the outdoors during the winter.

Survival Magazines

Woodsmoke, Highland Publishing Co., Box 474, Centerville, UT 84014. Covers survival, aboriginal lifestyles, and primitive living for people with an outdoor interest.

Response, P.O. Box 2123, La Jolla, CA 92038. While written for professionals in the search-and-rescue and emergency management fields, each issue contains a lot of worthwhile information for the serious survival student.

The Backwoodsman. Rt. 8, Box 579, Livingston, TX 77351. Primarily teaches primitive survival skills, many of which are unique methods of surviving in the backcountry with a minimum of survival aids.

The Trapper and Predator Caller, Box 550, Sutton, NB 68979. Written primarily for trappers. Gives a wealth of backcountry living information that would be a great aid to anyone interested in learning more about survival.

APPENDIX 3: SURVIVAL EQUIPMENT SUPPLIERS

Mail Order

Finding survival items and equipment can sometimes be a difficult task. If your sporting goods store, backpack shop, army-navy surplus store, or hardware store comes up short, consider requesting catalogs from these mail-order sources.

The Alpine Map Co., P.O. Box 1979, Boulder, CO 80306. Survival kits.

Atlanta Cutlery, 911 Center St., Conyers, GA 30207. Military, hunting, and survival knives and knife-making supplies.

Eddie Bauer, P.O. Box 3700, Seattle, WA 98124. Full line of outdoor gear, including survival equipment.

L.L. Bean, Inc., Freeport, ME 04033. Complete line of outdoor clothing and gear, including survival equipment.

Brigade Quartermasters, Ltd., 266 Roswell St., Marietta, GA 30060. Military equipment, camping gear, survival kits, and general outdoor accessories.

Cabela's, 812 13th Ave., Sidney, NB 69162. Products for outdoorsmen, including survival equipment.

Country Ways, Inc., 15235 Minnetonka Blvd., Minnetonka, MN 55343. Arctic survival gear.

Dixie Gun Works, P.O. Box 684, Union City, TN 38261. Accessories for muzzleloading hunters and primitive skills enthusiasts.

Early Winters, Ltd., 110 Prefontaine Pl. S., Seattle, WA 98104. Outdoor equipment, survival needs, camping gear.

Eastern Mountain Sports, Two Vose Farm Rd., Peterborough, NH 03458. Full line of survival and other outdoors equipment.

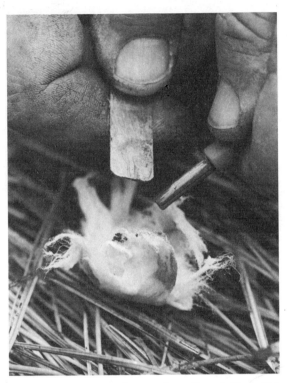

Equipment such as flint and steel with Heat Tab fire starter and pine needles can do the job of matches if you've practiced beforehand. (Dwight Schuh photo)

Indiana Camp Supply, P.O. Box 344, Pittsboro, IN 46167. Expedition equipment, medical supplies.

Lifeknife, Inc., Box 771, Santa Monica, CA 90406. Survival knives and survival kits.

Okun Brothers Shoes, 356 East South St., Kalamazoo, MI 49007. Cold-weather boots.

Parallex Corporation, P.O. Box F, Chicago Ridge, IL 60415. Full line of military and survival items.

Thompson Snares, 15815 2nd Place W., Alderwood Manor, WA 98036. Maker of wire animal snares.

Tru-Turn, Inc., Box 7504, Montgomery, AL 36107. Survival fishhooks.

Wallet Survival Guides, P.O. Box 2947, Everett, WA 98203. Survival guides small enough to be carried afield.

Z Ztove Corporation, 10806 Kaylor St., Los Alamitos, CA 90720. Lightweight survival stoves.

Manufacturers

You might also consider writing to these manufacturers of survival equipment for information on purchasing their products.

Benchmark Knives, P.O. Box 2089, Gastonia, NC 28053–2089. Manufacturer of hunting and survival knives.

Camillus Cutlery Co., P.O. Box 38, Camillus, NY 13031–0038. Manufacturer of hunting and survival knives.

Charter Arms Corp., 430 Sniffens Lane, Stratford, CT 06497. Manufacturer of handguns, Skachet, and AR-7 survival rifle.

Diamond Machining Technology, Inc., 85 Hayes Memorial Dr., Marlborough, MA 01752. Maker of knife and tool sharpeners.

Four Seasons Survival, 1857 Park Forest Ave., State College, PA 16803. Manufacturer of Spark-Lite Fire Starter and related supplies.

Michaels of Oregon, P.O. Box 13010, Portland, OR 97213. Manufacturer of gun accessories.

Northern Cross Survival Co. Ltd., P.O. Box 4527, Topeka, KS 66604. Supplier of survival kits.

Philip S. Olt Co., P.O. Box 550, Pekin, IL 61554. Maker of game calls and survival whistles.

Precise International, 3 Chestnut Street, Suffern, NY 10901. Manufacturer of compasses and sporting and survival knives.

Sigma Scientific, Inc., 1830 S. Baker Ave., Ontario, CA 91761. Manufacture a line of survival kits.

INDEX